WOLFISH

Erica Berry is a writer based in her hometown of Portland, Oregon. She has an MFA from the University of Minnesota, where she was a College of Liberal Arts Fellow. Her writing has appeared in the *Guardian*, *The New York Times*, *Yale Review*, *Orion*, *Atlantic*, *Outside Magazine* and elsewhere. Winner of the Steinberg Essay Prize and the Kurt Brown Prize in non-fiction, she has received fellowships and funding from the Bread Loaf Writers Conference, the Wurlitzer Foundation, the Ucross Foundation, the Minnesota State Arts Board and the Institute for Journalism and Natural Resources. She is currently an Associate Fellow at the Attic Institute for Arts and Letters and a writing instructor with Literary Arts in Portland.

@ericajberry | ericaberry.com

'Explores the contours of human relationships – and what it means to be a woman – through this most familiar yet mysterious of creatures'
Financial Times

'Startling in its scope, covering everything from fairy tales to domestic violence. This book should be required reading'
LA Times

'Singular . . . a book entirely its own'
TIME

'Terror propels Erica Berry's exhilarating book . . . No matter where Berry weaves, she sniffs out fascinating insights. And she writes about it in clear, beautiful language'
Washington Post

'I devoured every startling, lyrical, haunting, yet all-too-familiar page of *Wolfish*. Such a stunning achievement, it left me feeling like one of the pack'
ELIZABETH RUSH

'An exhilarating book – intricate, thoughtful, and thick with connections'
MEGHA MAJUMDAR

'Berry's braided approach renders *Wolfish* both a vulnerable self-investigation and a wide-ranging exploration of fear – and, ultimately, an antidote to it. She makes a stirring case for walking alongside the symbolic wolf'
Atlantic

'Erica Berry's *Wolfish* is a marvel: a beautiful piece of work as wide-ranging as it is precise. Berry's keen eye and fresh, startling prose are not only an excellent guide to nature and the world around us, but also to what our reactions to the landscape tell us about ourselves, what we fear and who we might become. You won't want to miss this'
V. V. GANESHANANTHAN

'*Wolfish*'s explorations of predators and prey in the natural world and in the man-made world defies easy categorisation. The way Berry weaves an ecological adventure story about OR-7, a wolf that makes a record-breaking journey away from its Oregon pack, with tales from her own coming-of-age, asks readers to reconsider their relationships with fear and the creatures who cause it'
Harper's Bazaar

'Powerful . . . delivered with an unflinching and vulnerable honesty. Berry is just as adept conveying the pangs of heartache and homesickness as she is the tightening walls of anxiety and the shadows of surveillance. As she slowly unravels humans' misplaced fear of wolves, she makes a compelling argument for coexistence between species, creating a necessary environmental memoir: that which acknowledges fear in its ongoing pursuit of hope'
Vulture

'Kaleidoscopic . . . [A] lyrical inquiry, Erica simultaneously details her own coming-of-age as she moves away from home and wrestles with inherited beliefs about fear, danger, femininity and the body'
Rumpus

'Elegant and elegiac, *Wolfish* asks how we live alongside, and honour, both the wilds we do such harm to and the fears that run wild within us. Erica Berry beautifully weaves literature, science, philosophy, history and her own memories to deconstruct millenia of myth-making around wolves, urging a return to something even more powerful than the tales we've spun: untangling the creature from our fear, to better understand both it and ourselves'
ALEX MARZANO-LESNEVICH

'The space between humans and wolves is filled with stories, from fairy tales to family histories to our own fears and desires. With courage and insight, Erica Berry illuminates this tangled territory, inviting us to explore it for ourselves'
MICHELLE NIJHUIS

'*Wolfish* starts with a single wolf and spirals through nuanced investigations of fear, gender, violence and story. A gorgeous achievement'
BLAIR BRAVERMAN

'Insightful and gorgeously written, *Wolfish* shows us that stories we tell about predators and prey are always about more than they seem. This exploration of violence and vulnerability never stopped surprising me'
RACHEL MONROE

'I can't stop talking about Erica Berry's debut *Wolfish* – it is a passionate and personal portrayal of the wildness in the world and in ourselves. This is a fierce book and an important one. *Wolfish* is a triumph of a debut – cementing Berry as an important new voice'
LYZ LENZ

'Part nature essays, part cultural symbolism analysis, *Wolfish* is captivating all the way through, exploring fear, myth, meaning, and our relationship to nature'
Bustle

'Enticing . . . There's a lot to unpack here, but the deft storytelling makes for a sensitive, satisfying read'
Reader's Digest

'Throughout *Wolfish*, Berry intersperses critical explorations of wolf, fear, and nation with passages of self-writing, from joyful narratives of communion with natural places to accounts of sexual harassment and assault. Her book is an invitation to similarly "rekindle" connections with a broader "collective" of creatures – even those who feature in scary stories with big teeth'
Stinging Fly

'Subtle and erudite'
The Week

'Berry's path of inquiry is a deeply personal one. This unorthodox approach allows for the complexity of both Berry's personal journey and the wolf's status as a rich cultural avatar ... [she] is a skilful guide, highlighting the wolf's influence on everything from creation myths to viral memes and from government policies to proverbs'
Scientific American

'Berry writes with a strong sense of assurance, suspense and wit, balancing her personal experiences, the peregrinations of OR-7 and the history of humankind's fraught relationships with wolves'
High Country News

'A book unlike any other ... A surprising and powerful read'
Debutiful

'Ferocious and beautiful ... The most powerful theme that runs through *Wolfish* is human fear, and here Berry's vulnerability and strength is displayed in poignant detail'
Minneapolis Star Tribune

'Comparisons to Helen Macdonald's *H is for Hawk* are a fine starting point, but *Wolfish* leans wilder and more primal'
Philadelphia Inquirer

WOLFISH

The stories we tell about fear,
ferocity and freedom

Erica Berry

CANONGATE

*Author's note: I researched and wrote this book over almost a decade,
but some of the memories recounted here are much older. I have done my
best to represent them exactly as they occurred, which is to say, as they
appeared to me. In some cases, I have changed character details to protect
the identity of those who appear in these pages.*

This paperback edition published in 2024 by Canongate Books

First published in Great Britain in 2023 by Canongate Books Ltd,
14 High Street, Edinburgh EH1 1TE

canongate.co.uk

First published in the USA in 2023 by Flatiron Books

1

Designed by Donna Sinisgalli Noetzel

Map copyright © 2022 by David Lindroth Inc.

Grateful acknowledgement is made for permission to reproduce from the following:
Natalie Diaz, 'Wolf OR-7' from *Postcolonial Love Poem*.
Copyright © 2020 by Natalie Diaz.
Reprinted with permission of Faber and Faber Ltd
Robert Hass, 'Winged and Acid Dark' from *Time and Materials*.
Copyright © 2007 by Robert Hass.
Reprinted with the permission of HarperCollins Publishers.
Linda Hogan, 'The Fallen' from *The Book of Medicines*.
Copyright © 1993 by Linda Hogan.
Reprinted with the permission of Coffee House Press, coffeehousepress.org.
Catherine Pierce, 'True Story' from *The Tornado is the World*.
Copyright © 2016 by Catherine Pierce.
Reprinted with the permission of Saturnalia Books.

British Library Cataloguing-in-Publication Data
A catalogue record for this book is available on
request from the British Library

ISBN 978 1 83885 463 8

Printed and bound in Great Britain by Clays Ltd, Elcograf S.p.A.

To all who have been trapped by someone else's fear

On a digital map, OR-7's trek is charted—by a GPS . . .
In the tourmaline dusk I go a same wilding path.

—NATALIE DIAZ, "WOLF OR-7," *POSTCOLONIAL LOVE POEM*

But think!—a woman after all,
Contending with a wolf!

—ROBERT BROWNING, "IVAN IVANOVITCH"

Contents

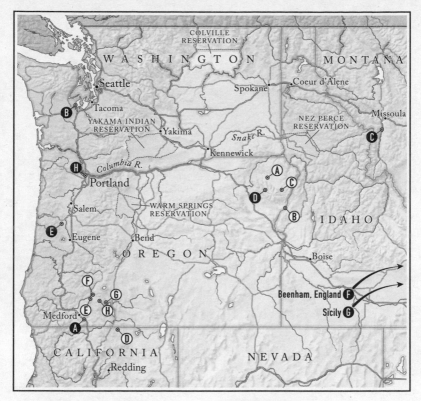

Introduction

Ⓐ OR-106 is found shot by the roadside in January 2022.

Ⓐ Curious about poachings, Erica calls the U.S. Fish and Wildlife Forensics Lab in Ashland, Oregon.

1. Adventure v. Wolf

Ⓑ B-300, mother of OR-7, may have first crossed the Snake River into Oregon here, in Hell's Canyon.

Ⓑ Erica begins a writing residency alone in a cabin in the woods on the Olympic Peninsula.

2. Girl v. Wolf

Ⓒ OR-7 is fitted with a satellite collar.

Ⓒ Erica's grandparents' house in Montana, some 170 miles to the northeast.

3. Town v. Wolf

Ⓓ OR-7 crosses into California, becoming the first known wolf in the state in more than 85 years.

Ⓓ Erica goes camping near the territory of OR-7's home pack.

4. Truth v. Wolf

Ⓔ OR-7 meets a mate who has also dispersed from her family and traveled solo to the southern Cascades.

Ⓔ Erica's grandfather's sheep farm outside Corvallis, Oregon.

5. Land v. Wolf

Ⓕ OR-7's mate has pups, making them the first breeding pack in western Oregon since the early twentieth century.

Ⓕ Erica visits the UK Wolf Conservation Trust in Beenham, England, roughly 5,000 miles away.

6. Self v. Wolf

Ⓖ OR-7's collar shows he ate from a cow carcass on a ranch in the Wood River Valley.

Ⓖ In Sicily, nearly 6,000 miles away, Erica accidentally eats mandrake.

7. Mother v. Wolf

Ⓗ OR-7's satellite collar dies more than 4,000 miles after he was first tagged.

Ⓗ Erica moves back home during the pandemic.

Introduction

This is one of those stories that begins with a female body. Hers was crumpled, roadside, in the ash-colored slush between asphalt and snowbank. Eyes open and facing the road, a gaze that seemed to demand reciprocity. *See me.* Or at least that was what I told myself when I could not look away from the photograph, unable to close the tab on my computer. Unable to blink away the wolf.

She was two years old, a lone wolf, the Oregon State Police (OSP) report said. OR-106, the 106th wolf biologists collared in Oregon. She would have left her nearby pack for the normal reasons, looking for a mate or new territory. How could she have known her journey would end so soon, on a road six miles outside Wallowa, a town of about eight hundred people in northeastern Oregon? A "concerned citizen" notified authorities of her presence at 10:36 a.m. on the cool, clear morning of January 8, 2022. In the photograph OSP circulated on Twitter with a "Seeking #PublicAssistance" hashtag, she looks small, her legs slim. The fur on her belly is the color of cream, her tail a brush dipped in ink, a ridge of black painting her spine to her ears. Her body is the same palette as the snow beneath her, but her winter coat is plush and glossy. No signs of trauma or blood. The GPS collar a golden ring around her neck. Nearly ten days after her death, I would think of her while watching the swelling glow of a yellow moonrise. The full moon is often called a "wolf moon" in January because it's the time of year wolves are thought to be hungriest. Hunger, said that old French proverb, drives the wolf from the wood. I hoped OR-106 had not died with a gnaw in her belly.

But how had she died? By the placement of her body, you would think her death was by car, and I wonder if that's what the passerby thought when they raised the flag of alert that Saturday morning. A wolf being killed by a car could mean bad luck. Maybe someone leaving the bar too late, blood already toxic as they wove through the forest. I can almost imagine, in such a situation, how a driver could panic. Swearing in a frozen cloud of whiskey breath as they stepped onto the road to investigate the bump, unable to stand sentry as the wolf's breath slowed, or maybe just unable to pick up the phone and call the collision in. I play this out in my head as if it will help me understand her death, but it doesn't matter. OR-106 wasn't killed by a car, the subsequent investigation found. She was killed by a gun: a human with a gun. Poached.

The root of the Greek word for forgetting, *lethe,* suggests an act of hiding. "[W]e could extend the image and say that to forget is to bury," writes Lewis Hyde in *A Primer for Forgetting.* In this case, there would be two sorts of burials: one in which something is covered up and forgotten because "we can't stand to look at it," and another because something has been "revealed and examined, and . . . may be covered up . . . for good." In the second form of forgetting, rites have been observed. Maybe that was why I could not close the tab on my computer; I wanted to make sure OR-106 could have the right kind of burial, if only in my mind. I wanted to bring her body rest.

The previous year I had tried to visit the U.S. Fish and Wildlife Forensics Lab, located in Ashland, Oregon, a few hundred miles from my home in Portland. I wanted to see a necropsy of a wolf because I'd heard scientists there worked to "build the story around the animal's death," and I thought I might have the same goal. Every medical student knows you learn a body by cutting it apart, and I was committed to learning the body of a wolf. It seemed like good luck that the lab near my house was also the hub where wolves from all over the country came after dying in mysterious ways, arriving frozen and "preserved so they don't stink up the FedEx truck," as a veterinary forensic pathologist told me. I did not like to think about wolves in those terms, but I have a taxidermist uncle in Montana who stuffs zebras shipped to him from Africa. I am used to side-eyeing the trucks that blaze by me on the highway, saying a prayer for whatever life their invisible cargo may have once held. I did not have to worry about seeing a frozen wolf at the lab, though, because my desire to visit did not prevail over the plague sweeping the world. Instead, I spoke with pathologist Tabitha Viner over the phone. She told me the key to doing a job like hers was to be intentional in her mindset. It was hard to roll up her sleeves and face so many creatures who had died, often defenseless, often at human hands. "My mindset is that every animal I get, it's more or less an inanimate object," she told me. "And it always has been." She said she had worked on "a lot" of wolves over the years. If each one was "an inanimate object with a story to tell," her goal was to untangle the "what" of their story, not the "who." Definitely not the "why."

A few months after I spoke with Tabitha, the Oregon Department of Fish and Wildlife (ODFW) notified OSP Fish and Wildlife Division troopers that they were getting mortality signals from a wolf collar. When troopers hiked into the woods to verify, they found a body. And then, nearby, another. Then another, and another, and another. Three males, two females. It was February 2021, and suddenly the whole Catherine Pack was dead, veins tunneled with poison in the same corner of northeastern Oregon where, almost a year later, OR-106 would be found too. In the months between, the carcasses of three more wolves would turn up, as well as a skunk and a couple of magpies. Tests at the forensics lab would reveal poison in each body.

Though hunting wolves is, as I write this, legal in Wyoming, Montana, Idaho, and Wisconsin, it is still illegal to kill a wolf in the western two-thirds of Oregon, period, and in far eastern Oregon—where these wolves had been found—unless the wolf is "in the act of biting, wounding, killing or chasing livestock or working dogs." In a state with around 170 wolves, the mass poisoning of eight is significant, and has attracted coverage from national media. In the last twenty-one years, over thirty wolves are known to have been illegally killed in Oregon, while two additional wolves have died under mysterious circumstances; arrests and convictions have been made for only three of those thirty-two. In March 2022, the Oregon Department of Justice hired a special prosecutor committed solely to enforcing anti-poaching laws and investigating and prosecuting poaching crimes.

As I write this, the reward for information leading to a citation or arrest of the Catherine Pack poisoner is near $50,000, "a level that can make significant changes in a person's life," ODFW Stop Poaching Campaign coordinator Yvonne Shaw said in a press release. Nonprofit groups have pledged the bulk of that sum—enough for, as Shaw said, a down payment on property, or a college degree, or "a new truck. Or a new start." In her words I hear the suggestion that, in leaking the identity of whoever would kill so many wolves, someone might actually need to hit the road. Find safety. Start over.

———

I wrote this book because I, like Tabitha, felt autopsying a wolf could help me figure out the story. The story I was trying to figure out was not "what" or "who," but "why" and "how." Why, in a time and place where wolves present no tangible threat to human safety, does a human kill a wolf—or eight—in the middle of a forest? In other words: What, when the shooter looked down the barrel of the gun, did he see? And when I imagined encountering a wolf in the forest, what did I see? There is always the creature in front of you and the creature in your mind. I think of the moment in the Disney movie of J. M. Barrie's *Peter Pan,* when Peter loses his shadow in Wendy's room. While he dives for it, peering under furniture as he tries to pin it down, his shadow rebels, leaping high against the wall, impishly eluding him until he wrestles it to submission and Wendy can sew it back on. The wolf in the forest does not know it, but he is haunted—hunted, even—by that shadow wolf in the shooter's head. "Humans do not live with biological creatures as much as they live with beings constructed within human cultural frames," wrote historian Erica Fudge. What shadows have we stitched for the wolf? This book is interested in the real life of *Canis lupus,* but also in examining the body of the "symbolic wolf," as veterinary anthropologist Elizabeth Lawrence dubbed it. That wolf is a piece of cultural taxidermy, fabricated by humans with parts gathered across time and space, and howling first and foremost in our heads. The symbolic wolf is enormous. She appears screen-printed beneath a gold moon on the tourist-shop T-shirt; in the "lone-wolf terrorist" headline; blowing down the straw house of the "Three Little Pigs"; in Adolf Hitler's Eastern Front headquarters dubbed the *Wolfsschanze,* the "Wolf's Lair"; in *Twilight* and *Game of Thrones*; in the Lakota term for "a wolf's day," called such because she has created the fog and wind desired by traveling warriors. Because this symbolic wolf roams inside our minds, she looks different to me than she does to you. We have all been taught a certain kind of wolf; very often we have absorbed her, like osmosis.

Perhaps the first bounty placed on a wolf's head was in the sixth century, by Solon of Greece. Many Indigenous tribes have had close bonds with wolves for thousands of years, including the Haida and Tlingit in the Pacific Northwest, where I grew up. In their 2017 book *The First Domestication: How Wolves and Humans Coevolved,* ecologist and evolutionary biologist Raymond Pierotti and Indigenous nations studies scholar Brandy Fogg turn to Indigenous testimony to argue that wolves and early humans lived symbiotic, entangled lives, with humans learning hunting techniques from wolves.

"Each species recognized a skill set and emotional capacity in the other that would allow both to maximize their chances of survival and leaving more descendants," wrote Pierotti and Fogg. They cite the language Indigenous peoples have used to describe wolves as evidence: "brother, grandfather, relative, companion, teacher, and even 'creator.'"

Despite this evidence to the contrary, the wolf's legacy as a symbol of danger—the beast to vanquish, the human foe—has persisted as the dominant Euro-American narrative. "The wolf is the only animal with a criminal reputation and record that has lasted for centuries and resulted in so many legal acts putting a price on its head," writes human-animal scholar Garry Marvin in *Wolf.* In 2021, the Norwegian Institute for Nature Research published "Wolf Attacks on Humans," a comprehensive report of what is known about alleged attacks worldwide. This report is the continuation of a 2002 report, where J. D. Linnell et al. surveyed some four hundred years of human history and concluded that attacks were "unusual but episodic," with humans "not part of their normal prey." Wolves, they had noted, are "among the least dangerous species for their size and predatory potential." In their updated report, which surveyed the years 2002 to 2020, Linnell et al. summarize their findings by writing that a "very large proportion" of wild wolf attacks appeared to come from rabid wolves, with a small number being "defensive." The remainder, clustered primarily in historic Europe and contemporary south Asia, were "predatory."

Though this last category is arguably what contemporary North Americans visualize when they say they are "afraid of wolves," the risk of death by wild wolf attack here is almost nonexistent. Most recorded predatory attacks have been on children, and isolated in specific windows of time and space, in areas "with almost no wild prey and poor, vulnerable, human communities," the 2021 report notes. With rabies essentially eradicated in North America and Europe, the last eighteen years here have seen only twelve wolf attacks on humans, with two fatalities. In a place where millions of people and close to 75,000 wolves share the land, widespread fear and persecution of the animal—especially on the grounds of threatening human life—are evidently misplaced. "It is apparent that the risks associated with a wolf attack are above zero, but far too low to calculate," the researchers note. They urge the public to consider wolves in the same category as large predators such as sharks, bears, crocodiles, and leopards. Worthy of caution, sure, but not execution.

Wolves have historically roamed nearly every ecosystem on earth, from the salmon-flush tidal waters of coastal Canada to the Indian subtropics, from the Italian Riviera to the Arctic Circle to the saguaro-strewn Mexican desert. Other than humans, wolves were once the most widely distributed land mammal across the globe. The Pacific Northwest's oldest fossilized wolf remains were found in Oregon and are over 300,000 years old; the area's archaeological signs of *Homo sapiens* are thought to be the oldest in North

America too, but that evidence is only 16,560 years old. The wolf roamed here long before humans did.

If I, like many children in North America, inherited fairy-tale stories that portrayed the wolf as a figure of fear, I was of a demographic that eventually absorbed the story of the wolf as a creature to fear *for*, less the hunter than the hunted. Though legislative policies and taxpayer-funded extermination led to their essential extinction in the continental United States by the mid-twentieth century, the environmental movement that followed ushered in a new lupine rhetoric. Beginning in the 1960s and 1970s, many conservationists, primarily in North America, espoused the belief that wolves held no danger to humans, a radical shift in the "symbolic biology" of the wolf, to borrow philosopher Noel Carroll's terminology. Rather than framing the wolf as beast, writers portrayed it as a totem of wilderness, a reminder of the wildness pulsing within the spine even as one commuted to a dead-eyed desk job. "Saving the wolf" became a strategic fundraising lever for nature-facing nonprofits, a way to plumb the "guilt, vague environmental concern, and resources of people, especially in cities, who wish[ed] to do something for wildlife and 'the environment,'" write Steven H. Fritts et al. in *Wolves: Behavior, Ecology, and Conservation.*

Farley Mowat's 1963 bestseller, *Never Cry Wolf,* framed as a non-fiction account of his time observing wolves in subarctic Canada, was the first piece of popular literature to cast the wolf in a positive light. The book and follow-up Disney movie stirred tremendous support for the persecuted creature, but they also furthered misconceptions, such as the belief that wolves eat primarily mice, not caribou. Such oversimplifications propped up the Western-centric mindset Linnell et al. describe as "overtly optimistic," rebutting "the historic or present day reality from other parts of the world" by suggesting wolves are incapable of harming humans. Mowat later admitted to fabricating much of his story to rally sympathy for *Canis lupus*. He excelled at shifting public opinion, and though some wolf advocates will argue his rhetoric was a necessary overcorrection—helping to pave the way for a climate where wolves could reestablish a foothold in the United States—the shadow Mowat stitched to the wolf replaced one myth with another.

For humans grieving the mass loss of other species on our warming earth, the return of the wolf can feel like a narrative of redemption, a promise that, like the tree that cracks through the concrete, "nature" will prevail. "The wolf situation in Oregon is extraordinary because the animals are coming back on their own—a rare example of a large predator actually expanding its range instead of, as is the more common pattern, diminishing ever closer to extinction," wrote journalist Alastair Bland in a 2012 *Smithsonian* article. What is at stake in this redemption narrative, though, is not just the animal's expanding population, but a particular fantasy of restoration-as-reparation. As if white man's state-sanctioned slaughter of the wolf in the twentieth century—not to mention continual habitat destruction and fossil-fuel production since then—might be remedied if he could only bring wolves back in the twenty-first. Whether stoking fear, anger, admiration, grief, or guilt, the wolf is a pressure point in our psyches. The real animal, of course, could not care less.

I began researching the repopulation of wolves through the American west for my undergraduate environmental studies honors thesis in 2013. I was attending Bowdoin College in Maine at the time, and I had heard from an acquaintance back home that a journalist had gotten a death threat for reporting on wolves who were reestablishing themselves in Oregon. I didn't understand how people were so riled up about an animal, and something about it made me—a conflict-averse, indecisive, weigh-both-sides Libra who had never thought much about the wolf before—decide to dive in. I understood the wolf had become a metonym for conflicts about public land, government intervention, and that oft-proclaimed cultural "urban-rural" divide, but I thought the riddle of cohabitation could be solved if I just shared the scientific reality of the "real wolf." It turns out, though, that many people have written books about wolves, and they had already done that extraordinarily well. It is almost a cliché to allude to this at the beginning of a new wolf book—"more books may have been written about wolves than about any other wildlife species," world-renowned wolf biologists David Mech and Luigi Boitani write in their introduction to *Wolves: Behavior, Ecology, and Conservation*—and a glut of lupine-related scholarship, journalism, and storytelling always begs the question: Why one more?

Like others in the canon, this book unspools the relationship between a writer and a wolf. However, unlike some of those authors, I have never weaned a wolf pup in my backyard, nor have I ever immersed myself beside a pack. The wolf whose story I center in these pages has never seen me, has never known of my existence. In Cathy Park Hong's essay collection *Minor Feelings: An Asian American Reckoning,* she quotes filmmaker Trinh T. Minh-ha's suggestion to "speak nearby" other cultures, not "about" them: "When you decide to speak nearby, rather than speak about, the first thing you need to do is acknowledge the possible gap between you and those who populate your [art]." The gaps in this book lie not only between me and the humans I speak with, but the wolves too.

Lakota hunters once stepped under wolfskins to hunt bison on the American Plains, but as historian Karen Jones points out, a writer can never step inside the wolf that seamlessly. I am not an academic nor a scientist, I am just one animal trying to see another. I may have approached the wolves first as an amateur, but the Latin root of "amateur" means *lover*. I, a person who loved animals but would never have self-identified as an "animal lover," could not at first explain why I began tracking the path of one of contemporary America's most famous wolves, and then not just him, but others too, right through the roadside body of OR-106. I became omnivorous for anything "wolf," aware that whenever I heard the word—so often pronounced *woof* by even the sternest-faced adults—a hundred other symbolic wolves raced through my head, jostling for attention. I realized the problems of animalizing humans and villainizing animals are not discrete; the violence of one depends on and reinforces the violence of the other; so much of Western civilization was built on both. The New York *Daily News'* 1989 headline that referred to the wrongfully convicted Central Park Five as a "wolf pack," for example, relied on readers visualizing a vicious pack of bloodthirsty beasts, not a group of creatures cooperatively caring for their young. Inversely, the early-modern Swedish organization Jägeristaten's choice to frame the civic fight against the wolf as a broader battle against foreign intruders depended on a baseline of xenophobia. This book believes we cannot untether the biological wolf from the stories told about it without also examining those associative, metaphorical stories—picking them up, holding them to the light, examining their seams. I am as compelled by the wolf as I am by the themes I grew up seeing the animal entangled with.

The late, renowned naturalist E. O. Wilson called this interdisciplinary approach consilience, the "'jumping together' of knowledge by the linking of facts and fact-based theory across disciplines to create a common groundwork of explanation." This book circles the wolf as I "jump" between lenses of history, ecology, biology, anthropology, fairy tale, myth, and journalism, motored by the conviction that the associative leaps of the brain—between self and other, past and present, symbolic and real wolf—are not a distraction from understanding *Canis lupus,* but the tunnel we must pass through. "Symbols are problems when they reduce what shouldn't be reduced, placing a significance not in what something is, but in what it brings up beyond itself," writes Native essayist Elissa Washuta in *White Magic.* To understand the "wolf," I look to what it brings up beyond itself. I cannot see the animal without seeing the dynamics of gender, race, colonialism, violence, environmental degradation, and capitalism that ensnare my conceptions of it.

If the wolf has often been a vessel for human fear, and more recently, a vessel for human grief about the environmental harm perpetuated by the globalized affluent West, this is a book that empties those vessels out. As Alfred Hitchcock told a biographer in 1970: "What frightens us today is exactly the same sort of thing that frightened us yesterday. It's just a different wolf." This from the man who knew just how much an audience would pay to watch a woman scream. Very often we speak of growing out of fears, as if the most important thing we can learn from them is how to slough them off, but stories about wolves are often stories about how we grow into fears and at what cost we bear them, both for the world and ourselves.

When I began writing this book, a storm of anxious fear had flooded my life. I couldn't pinpoint when or how it arrived, and I wasn't sure how to escape it. I kept writing because I was searching for the answers to those questions; I didn't realize then that research and writing would become its own answer. In pausing to reflect on my relationship with fear, and the ways the emotion can be inflected by shame, guilt, astonishment, excitement, loneliness, camaraderie, and so on, I've demystified and defanged its burden. This is a book not only about peeling back the layers of what scares me—what so many childhood stories said were "wolf"—but also about learning to evaluate and shed them. We bear our fear as individuals, but those fears are born from the world. If I once wanted to rewire my worried brain, I now know the first step is to trace those wires outward, through time and space and story.

The feeling of fear—like that of love—is innate and physiological, but also scripted, however unconsciously, by the culture we inhabit. In looking to bail myself out of my own fear, I went back to the beginning of those stories I had been told. Back to the big bad wolf. In *Caste: The Origins of Our Discontents,* journalist Isabel Wilkerson uses the metaphor of buying an old, crack- and leak-riddled house to describe America's inheritance of its racist past. The structural damage was not the homeowner's fault, perhaps, but sooner or later they must confront it. I could not engage contemporary debates about how to live beside the wolf without understanding the legacies of the symbolic wolf we tote—however unwittingly—through our hearts and minds.

One of the reasons I became interested in wolves was that I sensed "we" were too afraid of them, and I was interested in the (ir)rationality of fear. As poet and essayist Claudia Rankine points out, though, "Who is this 'we'? Is it even possible to form a 'we'?" To deny any predatorial potential from the wolf, as Mowat did, is to risk silencing the experiences and expertise of those living in what Linnell et al. define as "vulnerable, human communities." Contemporary predatory wolf attacks are much more common, for example, in parts of Iran and India; we can expect human fear there might be differently calibrated. In studying how women think spatially about crime risk, social geographer Rachel Pain found that those who most fear crime are often already suffering in isolation—women least integrated into their neighborhoods, already marginalized by poverty or disability, generally aware of their powerlessness in the face of an attack, not to mention society writ large. "'Fear' involves such a complex set of emotions and cognitions that to label it with polarities such as 'rational' or 'irrational' has little meaning," she wrote.

Her scholarship is a reminder that fear will not be monochrome within the body, but also not the body politic. Conversations around the wolf are often framed as either "pro" or "against," with media commentary spotlighting the polarization between the sides. This binary fails to capture the nuance necessary for sustainable relationships with the animal, which should acknowledge the biological "truths" of the species but also the effect local histories, cultures, and environmental factors have on how both wolves and humans behave. If fear occurs on a spectrum of rationality, the threat a wolf poses to a person—just like the threat a person poses to a wolf—is not a static thing. Wolves that live in colder climates, like Alaska and Russia, for example, are statistically larger than those in the continental United States; they may represent slightly more threat to humans. Just as there is no "one" human, there is no "one" wolf.

My wolf is not your wolf. My experiences as a cis white millennial woman with family in both city and country in the North American west have influenced the way I approach this animal and its symbolic representations, just as they have influenced my relationship with fear. Because the bulk of my encounters with predatory human behavior have occurred within heterosexual interactions, I feel most qualified to examine how popular language around the "wolf" informs and exposes those power dynamics, and vice versa. The book's skew toward wrestling with dominant Western, white narratives around the wolf similarly reflects the limits of my own background—these are the stories I grew up with—as well as the reality that these stories have tended to carry the most visible, material sway (though, as philosopher Amia Srinivasan critically points out, those "outside of the anglophone mainstream have never been invisible, or 'marginal,' to themselves or their communities"). I thread my own life into this book not because I expect my experiences will speak for yours, but because others' stories can be doorways. We step through not just to understand the storyteller, but ourselves. Consider this a chance for our minds to "jum[p] together."

Wolfish: Wolf, Self, and the Stories We Tell About Fear is the story of the hunter and the hunted. It is the story of the girl in the forest and the creature in the cage, about who gets to be predator and who gets to be prey. It is about my obsession with an animal, and about how it impacted my reckoning with the things that scare me, both personal and cultural, as I learned to live beside them. It is about growing up in increasingly unlivable habitats, and about the lies and lessons we tell about our fears, which is to say, about one another. "After decades of advocacy for wolf conservation using all possible means to sell the goal of wolf recovery, it is now necessary to start advocating for compromise between wolf and human interests," wrote Mech and Boitani. As humanity sprawls even farther from city centers, it is likely the wolves who prevail will be bold, exploratory, and adept at living in our shadow. Sightings of wolves will likely increase, as will wolves experimenting with anthropogenic food sources. This does not necessarily mean predatory conflict will rise, but it does mean our knowledge about wolves and how to live with them should increase. The wolf does not live apart from us, in some "pure" wild space, but, increasingly, beside us. To look at what it means to share habitat with the wolf is to consider how we share it with all fellow beings, human and animal and other.

Research suggests wolves howl as a mode of connection. A wolf will howl after feeding, but also, sometimes, out of loneliness. This book is both the howl you make when you think you are alone and the howl that answers to remind you that you are not. Let this book be an invitation. See the tracks in the snow, the size of your palm. Notice how they make your heart feel. Walk with me.

1

Adventure v. Wolf

I t was winter when she crossed. Maybe she found a bridge of ice, maybe she snuck across Brownlee Dam, or maybe there was only current. Maybe she just swam. At the depths of Hells Canyon, the river that separates Idaho and Oregon is milky and knotted with rapids. At one end, over the reservoirs just south of the dam, the water is nearly a mile wide. The wolf would have chosen her path carefully. She did not flirt with risk, not like a coyote; she knew what she could do. A wolf can swim up to eight miles at a time, paddling like a dog after a stick, the skin between her toes enough webbing to help push her through a current. The Snake is the largest tributary to the Columbia River, its waters an echo of the agriculture it has slipped through heading west from Wyoming. The wolf could not know it, but all through the river there were traces of cow. Fertilizer, sediment, manure. Water that had once been blue was now often sea-glass green with algae.

It was 1999, and the wolf was in the belly of Hells Canyon, the deepest gorge in North America, 2,000 feet deeper in some places than the Grand Canyon. From the sprawling plateaus and high pastures above, the canyon feels unfathomable, as if the northeastern border of Oregon has just unzipped rocky, sagebrush-strewn cliffs to reveal a world over a mile deep beneath mud-slick layers of limestone and lava, 300-million-year-old products of underwater volcanoes. This is the homeland of the Nez Perce, the *Nimiipuu*, who know the canyon as a place of shelter carved by Coyote. Their stories tell how Creator made wry Coyote the teacher of human beings, but the wolf, *hímiin*, belonged here too. This was her land. When white men appeared—those who would later hunt the region's wolves to extinction—they had taken this same route, and the Nez Perce named them for it. *Sooyáapoo*, they called the invaders. The ones who divide.

As the wolf shook the river from her back, droplets constellated in the frozen air. She was a yearling, nearly full grown, the runt of her litter. Almost waist high on a grown man, her weight around sixty-five pounds, her coat the gradient of stone, the color, perhaps, of that day's January sky. Her winter underfur was so thick the cold did not even reach her bones. She was a descendant of the Canadian wolves reintroduced to Idaho just a couple of years earlier as part of an effort to restore the American gray wolf populations that had been slaughtered to extinction in the early twentieth century. Around her neck, the radio collar given by the Idaho Department of Fish and Wildlife (IDFW) was a dull and nearly forgotten weight. B-45. That's what they were calling her. The forty-fifth wolf to be collared in Idaho, one node of a federal wolf recovery program that the Nez Perce tribe was working with the IDFW to implement.

With each step, her saucer-sized paws splintered the lattice of icy crystals that frosted the earth. Turning tail to the river, she climbed into the snow and the vanilla-scented air of hundred-year-old Ponderosa pines. If a bald eagle cut the sky above her, she heard it. If a rabbit threw itself into a snowy burrow, she smelled it. A wolf can average eight to ten hours a day of travel, often moving in the seams between night and day. Ten miles, twenty, thirty, forty, more. She had left her family in east-central Idaho to look for the three things any young wolf needed to survive—a mate, a meal, and defensible territory—and she did not know that in climbing onto this far shore of the Snake, she had crossed a border. Not just a state line, but a line of history. Because she had been fitted a year earlier with a radio collar, her movements were legible to humans, and she was now superlative: the first known member of her species to step into Oregon in over fifty years. As in much of continental America, wolves had not lived here since the state's last wolf bounty was paid to a trapper in the 1940s. When B-45 arrived, she came as both the dawn of the future and a relic from the past. "[B-45] seems to me a title ill-suited for a majestic animal, and more appropriate for a chemical used to color breakfast cereal," wrote one skeptical editor of an eastern Oregon newspaper. When the Nez Perce tribe and an environmental conservation group held a contest to name her, "Freedom" won. A local conservationist began to call her "Eve."

Though gray wolves were protected by the Endangered Species Act in 1974, law is a conceptual shield. It can mean very little in the quiet of America's trees, where the "3S treatment"—"Shoot, shovel, and shut up"—can reign. But B-45 was lucky. Even as she made headlines, she traveled on, leaving her scent against trees, telephone poles, and fence posts. She walked a hundred miles from the state line, up and over the snow-clotted forests of the Blue Mountains, back and forth across Interstate 84, somehow, then toward the headwaters of the John Day River. "She appears to be doing normal wolf stuff," U.S. Fish and Wildlife Rocky Mountain wolf specialist Ed Bangs told the *Oregonian*.

It should have been no surprise wolves would reenter the state the way B-45 did, just as guests will enter a house party if a door is ajar. Nearly a century earlier, after elk were driven almost to extinction by white settlers, their repopulation had caused a similar spectacle. "His place is in parks and museums, preserving the memory of Oregon undeveloped," wrote one northeastern Oregon sheep rancher in 1912. "Civilization and savagery cannot occupy common ground. The one must give way to the other." It had taken time—wariness from sheep farmers who worried about competition for their herds—but eventually, the elk had been reaccepted: a cherished Oregon citizen. Now the wolf was the trespasser. Specifically, B-45.

Looking back, Oregon biologist Mark Henjum saw her arrival as a turning point, not just for wolves but for how people talked about them. "[B-45] really tipped the scales to where wolves became a real issue," he told a reporter. Local officials struggled to know how to react. Could an animal be invasive if it had once called a landscape home? "She presents a somewhat odd situation for us because Oregon is not part of the wolf recovery effort," another ODFW biologist told a local newspaper. Officially, the state wasn't anti-wolf, but they weren't pro-wolf either. They urged caution: this wolf could get in the cyanide traps ranchers used for coyotes, or could mate with a dog, spawning a potentially dangerous dog-wolf hybrid. There was no management plan, but to do nothing, said livestock producers, was to let a predator walk free—toward their cattle, toward their lambs.

When B-45 stepped through the mountains, I was an elementary-schooler across the state in Portland, all braids and freckles and red Converse high-tops. I did not know a wolf had come back into Oregon because it had never occurred to me they had ever disappeared, that we had ever killed them off. In her *New York Times Magazine* article about mass insect extinctions, journalist Brooke Jarvis quotes a Danish bug-counting survey that describes the disorienting, indescribable sense that "something from the past is missing from the present." I wish I could say I felt the loss of predators from the forest, but born into the loss, I accepted it as the norm. We do not grieve the things we have never learned to love. Scientists call this inability to register change "baseline theory." Because I did not understand the ecosystems I hiked through with my family had been curated by a government-funded extermination campaign of native predators, I assumed wolves were out there in some distant shaggy forest, waiting with owls and bears beneath a peachy moon. The animals' presence seemed both distant and guaranteed. Like a soulmate, I assumed one day our paths would cross.

Fifteen years later, when I began researching the wolf, I felt motivated by a handful of factors, but none was instinctual awe about the animal. Mostly I had become jumpy, and because I did not trust my fear, I was ashamed of it. It struck me as supremely unfair that in so many stories and sayings, the wolf had been made shorthand for the threat.

The French have an old saying, *Entre chien et loup,* which refers to that dawn-or-dusk hour when it becomes hard to tell the difference between a dog and a wolf. That time when you cannot tell if the shadow on the road before you is familiar or strange, if it poses a threat. With roots in the Latin expression *inter canem et lupum*— that time "when the dog sleeps, and the wolf seeks his prey," as a seventeenth-century English treatise described it—the phrase connotes a threshold between known and unknown, that liminal zone where anxieties may be rational or unfounded. In the moment of *entre chien et loup,* it seems to me, the journey is as internal as it is external. What you see on the path is shaped not only by your eyes, but also by your mind: stories you have inherited, experiences you have accumulated, beliefs you carry about how the world will treat you. I began to suspect I would not see the wolf, never mind the fears it conjured within us, without first zooming in on this moment of identification. Every day we trace the contours of fear in our own lives, squinting for its shapes, listening for its creaks, evaluating if our hearts are right to pound. This is the tipping point where one creature might be tagged as predator and one as prey. It is the moment our eyes might first get it wrong.

Initially I believed I would be a good arbiter of *entre chien et loup*. Surely I could tell a dog from a wolf! I was mildly nearsighted but neurotic about detail. Rational, or at least attuned to the prospect of my irrationality. At the time, I was encountering stories about wolves both real and imagined with the cool, smug distance of a reader who could flip to the ending or turn away. But as I continued my research, driving into the mountains, sharpening pencils into little spears to take into the archives, I began to see that even if the stories I had heard about wolves were collected in the pages of folktales and old newspapers, their undercurrents were enacted in the pages of our lives. I wanted to consider the theater of predator and prey from the remove of my laptop screen. Life got in the way.

I had been studying the subject on and off for a few years when the jury of an artist residency granted me a cabin in the woods to write about it. I decided to travel west by train, alone. My second year of graduate school at the University of Minnesota was done and my students' grades were submitted. The Wi-Fi on the tracks would be bad. For thirty-six hours, I thought, I could disappear. Nobody would be able to ask anything of me. Like B-45, I imagined myself crossing the border into Oregon undetected.

It was eleven p.m. when the ticket-checker nodded at my phone and the gold-ceilinged Amtrak station gave way to a platform lit by buzzing fluorescent lights. Tiny bugs danced in the metallic glare as my fellow passengers volleyed cheery midwestern hellos. It was late May, but the Minneapolis night was defiant with chill. I hugged my backpack straps to my jean jacket, jostling the suitcase and tote bag I had packed with cheese, crackers, and apples for rations until the train reached Portland, a short drive from the cabin.

Since arriving at the station, I had surveyed my fellow passengers like we were in a reboot of *Lost*. Plane travel was so often frictionless, choreographed by the omnipresence of flight attendants, but traveling by long-haul buses and trains was a different game. Earlier that year, my then-boyfriend and I had spent a surreal day stranded in a train in Idaho due to some unforeseen malfunction on the track. We spent those fraught, bonus hours sitting beside Bakken oil field workers and sightseeing retirees. At one point, we called a pizza delivery to the train and split it with a nomadic octogenarian with a literal feather in his green felt cap; later the three of us took up Amtrak's offer to dine on free Kentucky Fried Chicken in the white-tableclothed dining car. We had fulfilled a certain archetype, then—the smiley young couple with laptops and a bottle of wine on our observation-car table—and only as I stood alone on the platform was I aware that I was playing a different role now. The only young woman traveling solo. Black jeans and short black boots, a big sweater beneath my jacket, my shoulder-length brown-blond hair typically unruly. Headphones, yes, but I listened to nothing. Music was good, but staying tuned to the present while maintaining a guise of unapproachability? Better.

"An insider tip for you," said a man behind me, tipsy with authority. "Minot's pronounced 'Why not.' If you pronounce it like a French guy you'll sound like a real asshooooole!" The smoker's rattle in his throat rose to a low howl. Beside him, two women who looked to be in their late sixties threw their heads back in laughter, jostling hand-quilted bags. I couldn't help grinning. I was a sucker for eavesdropping. It was like stepping into a room where a TV show was playing and trying to get your bearings. On the train, I'd be the audience. I'd watch the prairie buckle into mountain and read my books.

I was reading *One with the Tiger: Sublime and Violent Encounters Between Humans and Animals* by Steven Church, which opened with a chapter on a twenty-five-year-old man who, in 2012, had jumped into the zoo pen of a four-hundred-pound Siberian tiger. The man survived, giving little explanation for his actions. "It's a spiritual thing," he said. "I wanted to be at one with the tiger." Church was interested in what had drawn the man into the cage not because the feeling was foreign, but because he found it so familiar. I never wanted to face off with an animal, but I had long chased the tingle of launching myself into the unknown. Most of my friends were surprised I was choosing to travel solo without a bunk or cabin, but I'd heard a rumor that the new president, Donald Trump, was going to slash funding for the route, and I wanted to take the trip however I could afford it. I liked traveling alone. I surveilled the world more acutely. The volume turned up on my senses. My last solo train ride had been only a few hours on the East Coast, but I'd ended up getting looped into a game of Uno with a few guys from Toronto who were drinking Soylent on their way home from the Governors Ball Music Festival in New York City. We followed each other on social media at the end of the night, and every few months I would come across a photo of one and wonder who he was, how he had gotten into my feed and my brain. *The train,* I would remember with a twitch. *The train threw us together.*

Shuffling forward in line, I now watched a man in front of me maneuver two giant beaten bags forward. He was moving a life or something else. That was the thing about trains. No airport security, rarely dogs. You came with whatever you wanted. Each of the man's bags was the size of an ottoman, and he too seemed supersized. His bald white head and broad neck gave him the look of a giant thumb, one that now hovered nearly a half-foot above five-foot-nine me, his shoulders draped in what some people called a "drug rug," a term that stunk of Reagan-era bias. Something in his movements struck me as off-kilter, but I tried to squash the possibility of threat. *Don't judge people you don't know,* I thought just as he turned and caught my gaze with a thin line of smile. Were his teeth black, or was it the shadow? He gestured for me to board ahead of him while he put his bags in the external compartments. I nodded thanks. Was I an *asshooooole*? I shuffled on. The half of the car reserved for "Families/ Couples" was nearly empty, but I headed toward "Singles," where each row was occupied by a lone rider except the one I now claimed. Everyone had taken the aisle, so I did too. I would move if I had to. Dog eat dog.

The cabin I'd be visiting was at the base of a peninsula in coastal Washington where wolves had long held importance to Indigenous residents. Early twentieth-century anthropologist Alice Ernst wrote about visiting the winter ceremony she called "Kluukwalle" (tłókʷali), which was later referred to as Wolf Ritual, where members of a wolf society, probably hunters, captured young warrior initiates and took them to a wolf house for a night of rituals that challenged their mental and physical strength. If they passed the tests, the youngsters were said to attain new strength: the strength of a wolf. In the last decade or so, wolves themselves had begun re-populating this rain forest peninsula. I did not expect to see one in the wild, but its shores seemed like a good place to hole up, and there was a wolf sanctuary nearby where I could pay $30 for an afternoon tour. I never had a coming-of-age ceremony, no bat mitzvah or even graduation party, but the two-week cabin trip was beginning to feel like its own rite of passage. After a lifetime of never spending more than a day or two alone, I hoped the hurdles of loneliness would leave me stronger and more self-reliant. When I told people I was going alone to the woods to write, they joked I should try not to get murdered, *haha*, until it felt as if that was my goal. Not to work on my thesis, but to stay alive. *Haha*. I could do that.

The tall bald man walked slowly down the aisle. He was the last one to board, and thanks to his invitation for me to go ahead, every row was now taken. I ducked my head toward my backpack and began a theatrical search for nothing, determined to avoid eye contact.

"Mind if I sit here?" His shadow stretched across my seat.

"Sure," I said automatically, scooting toward the window. My voice wave-tossed. The man did not put anything in the overhead compartment. He shoved a bag under the seat and brought a thin leather briefcase to his lap. At rest, the side of his body touched mine. How, in my imaginings of the trip, had I not considered I might spend hours touching shoulders with a stranger? Folding his arms across the briefcase, the man stared at the seat back before him. A conductor with barrel-curled blond hair walked down the aisle, taking notes on where we were all headed; most passengers were exiting in North Dakota and Montana. When she got to us, the man and I spoke at the same time. *Portland*. It felt so shitty I almost laughed.

"What's in Portland?" he asked, after she passed. I did not want to share my life, but I had nothing else to say. Lying made me blush.

"From there," I said. "You?" The conversation was a reflex, my voice falling into that familiar groove of feigned interest. I had a high tolerance for talking to strangers, even if I didn't personally like them. It was why I had wanted to write nonfiction: to have an excuse to ask people about their lives. But now I was tired, and the only life I wanted to think about was my own. Though I learned cordial kindness from men—my father is notoriously helpful and courteous with strangers—it had been distorted by a gendered instinct to subjugate my comfort to those around me. Partly I did not want to sit with the sense of having hurt someone else's feelings, but partly I feared that if I did hurt this man's feelings, he could, hypothetically, hurt me in return. An unconscious calculus. To preserve peace in this dark and inescapable space, I spoke, straining to sound less annoyed than I felt. My father, I sensed, would have known how to make the conversation stop.

"Me—I'm going to Portland because I'm on the run!" The man exhaled a huff of laughter. Beneath us, the train jolted. The rails hissed. "My ex tried to fucking kill me, that's why. That's fucking why I'm leaving. Yeah, I'm from Iowa." He shook his head vigorously. Steam filled the windows as we began to move. "I'm moving to Portland because now I'm with her little sister. Wild, wild fucking world." I made a hum of acknowledgment, pressing my lips into what I hoped was neutral acceptance. I had just told my students I liked nonfiction because people said things in real life you couldn't make up, and this man's words fell in that category. They would be hard to pull off in fiction, but here they were, a pebble thrown into my night. True.

"A fresh start sounds good," I said. Inside, I raged. This man had hijacked my dream of a quiet night, the kind literally every other passenger in the car was having. I envied the man alone in front of me, then I felt bad for wishing a seatmate on someone else. Wasn't this just the contract of public life? Sometimes you were lucky and sometimes you were not? But was this luck? The man's eyes tracked

me as I stared at my book. Around us the lone men were balling up
sweatshirts as pillows, putting in headphones, falling asleep. With
six hours of darkness ahead, the discomfort in my gut crystallized
to dread.

Outside, the black boxes of the St. Paul freight yard popped in
and out of view. I tried to focus on city lights in the black milk of
the Mississippi, but the man's pale reflection wobbled atop it all. The
silver hinges from his briefcase glinted in his lap like blades.

"Hey, can I tell you something really honest?" His voice so close
I flinched. "Iowa kills. It fucking kills." He pulled up his sleeve and
showed me the inner crook of his elbow, skin full of track marks, a
constellation of bull's-eyes. Needles made me dizzy; I hadn't known
their marks would too. The man saw me trying not to look, and
started laughing, low and slow, moving jerkily, watching my reaction. I sucked in air, hoping to telegraph *Yeah, dude—addiction sucks,*
before turning my gaze resolutely back to the page.

My mind, though, lingered on the briefcase. What was inside,
and why wouldn't he take it off his lap? A gun? Or maybe just his
next fix? Was I paranoid to think these thoughts, or naive not to
think them? I knew I was prone to catastrophizing. I had recently
come across a French proverb in my research, *Quand on parle du
loup,* which is akin to the English "speak of the devil." When you
talk of the wolf, the saying goes, you see its tail—*on en voit la queue*
implicit at the end of the phrase. I understood the proverb to mean
a scary thing could appear if you conjured it. You could bring your
nightmare upon yourself. On a molecular level I did not believe this
possible, but I understood perspective shaped reality, and I wanted
to scrub my fears from the window of the future. "I will believe it a
good comfortable road until I am compelled to believe differently,"
wrote Meriwether Lewis in his journal as he came upon what he
thought were the Rocky Mountains in 1805. I prickled at the pre-

sumption of manifest destiny, but the Pollyanna-ish optimism of his words resonated. Should I try harder to see the path before me as smooth? Friends encouraged me to think less about earthquakes, cancers, car crashes, snakes. I got carried away! I knew I did. And now I was twenty-five years old—an adult! I had to learn to chill out. In this light, my worry with the man on the train seemed rude.

He interrupted my thoughts. "I've got a lot of games for us to play later." Did I imagine it, or were his eyes bulging, two veined grapes in his wide forehead? He lifted the briefcase. My fingers felt fizzy, a stranger's hands folded in my lap. Slowly the man creaked open the hinge, eyes tracking my own. Instead of a weapon, a back-gammon board and a Ziploc of cards and game pieces spilled out. "Wow!" I said, because I did not know what else to say.

A minute later, when the man stood to readjust his belongings, my overhead reading light blinked off in the process, throwing us into dark. "Sorry," he said, a grinning shadow. Newly aware I was going to have to keep the sickly yellow light on all night as vigil for my worry, I flicked it on, then gestured vaguely to the aisle. I needed out.

"Gonna explore," I said. He stood, silently. It did not occur to me he did not need my explanation. Walking to the dining car, I tried to ignore the eyes of those who traced my path. The men who tapped cans of beer against the plastic tables. The train was rocking, a rattle that matched my pulse, and when it jolted, I went with it, flying toward whoever was sitting nearby, barely catching myself as I did. In the closed cafe, a woman in a blue Amtrak uniform sat at a table surrounded by legal pads and charts.

"Hi," I said. "Excuse me." She gave me the tired smile of some-one who knew she was about to be asked for something. I apolo-gized for bothering her.

"Lay it on me," she said, amused.

"Can I go to the family section?" I scanned the empty car, then lowered my voice. "I'm not totally comfortable with the man who sat next to me. And there are lots of seats up there."

The woman waved dismissively, as if this were the most common question in the book. "Go up, honey. You'll be fine. Just move your destination tag." *Play it cool,* I told myself. *He won't care.* I thought about asking to move to another car entirely, then chickened out. I did not want my discomfort to look too obvious. I didn't want to offend.

When I returned, the man was eating chocolate cake out of a plastic container. It looked homemade. The tenderness touched me. Someone's hands had stirred oil into batter, set a timer, poked a toothpick in the top. His life had been hard, he told me that, it was obvious. Was that reason to fear him? Certainly not. Suddenly I saw myself as the last in a long line of those who had given up on him. I tried to keep my voice light as I explained there were extra seats up front.

"More comfortable for sleeping, you know," I said. Was my voice always this singsong? The man was silent, plastic fork quivering in his lap.

"I'm staying here," he said, after a second too long. "Next to this." He gestured across the aisle, to the staircase leading to the bathrooms, luggage, and exit. "In case I need to run."

His laughter was staccato. I tried to chuckle but it came out more like a gasp. Gathering my things, I went as far toward the front as I could go, maybe fifteen feet away. An elderly couple sat behind me. The man slept but the woman watched me, warily. Was I unnerving her, moving so close to midnight to a section where I clearly shouldn't be? I smiled but her expression stayed taut. As I put in ear plugs, inflated my cheap neck pillow, and pulled up an eye mask, I tried to imagine how nice it would be to wake to the mountains. I was floating toward a dream when movement woke me. The man was standing over me; I could see beneath my mask. A second later, he was gone. The flame of his red T-shirt down the aisle, toward the cafe. I waited, eyes cracked, for him to return to his seat, but he never came. The train tipped. Eventually, I slept.

Snow frosted B-45's tracks as she zigzagged the mountain logging roads of northeastern Oregon, weaving through spruce, tamarack, lodgepole, cedar, hemlock. One dark afternoon in February, a man was plowing an empty highway when a shape began to move below the timberline. He squinted. Blinked. "She had the prettiest hair coat on her that I had ever seen on an animal," the man later told a reporter, "and I said to myself, 'That animal has wolf written all over it.'"

What does it mean to have wolf written all over you? A thousand miles south in California, the San Diego Police Department and the Federal Bureau of Investigation were studying a spike in white supremacy–fueled hate crimes and calling their program "Operation Lone Wolf." When humans refer to other humans as "lone wolves," they tend to imply a perpetrator has appeared solo, as if by immaculate conception. It is an appealing myth, but as B-45 showed, every wolf arrived from somewhere.

Oregon's new wolf, that real lone wolf, did not want to be alone. As she stepped across pastures and into scrubby junipers, her nose rose like a lantern through the night. Twitching, wondering, waiting. Research shows that when a wolf moves through another wolf's territory, she tries to conceal her presence, less likely to howl and leave her scent. In a wolf-free area, the opposite is true. Her howl becomes a billboard: I am here. See me. In 1996, scientists coined the word "endling" to describe the last surviving member of a species. "The little sound of it jingles like a newborn rattle, which makes it doubly sad," wrote Elena Passarello in her essay collection *Animals*

Strike Curious Poses. The word was meant to describe the last of a species on earth, but when I think of the last wolf alive in Oregon in the 1940s—destined, like so many of its relatives, to die for a trapper's bounty—I want to let that animal be an endling too. As if to say: *Surely you were alone enough to be, certifiably, alone.* In a place with only one wolf, scientists are apt to classify the species as "functionally extinct," which meant no longer influencing its ecosystem. Enough extinctions and you reach our present day, what E. O. Wilson calls the Eremocine: the age of loneliness.

And now B-45. Fifty-some years after that last death, a new wolf, again alone. In his canonical global environmental history, *Something New Under the Sun,* J. R. McNeill suggests that since the mid-1940s—those years when Oregon's last wolf was killed—the global environment has changed more swiftly and dramatically than in any period before it. B-45, then, was entering a world that looked very different from when earlier wolves had roamed it, but she, much like me, would not comprehend it. There is no word I know of to describe the first member of a species who steps back after obliteration. A *startling?* Like a beginning, but also, I think, of being startled. Like entering a party you thought would be buzzing and finding you are the only guest there. With both the last and the first wolf, I wonder: *Did you know just how alone you were?* Beneath this question lay the other one, the same one that now flickered in my chest as I traveled alone for interviews and research. *Were you afraid?* I wanted to ask the wolf. *And if you were, how did you bear it?*

I woke to blotches of water in the fields outside Minot. *Why not.* A sign on the station said it was the geographic center of America. I bought a sour, lukewarm coffee from the same attendant I had spoken to the night before.

"Find another seat?" Her eyes were still tired. She had seen it all before.

"All settled," I said, and we shared a knowing glance, the one that said, *Men, right?*

Back in my seat, I tried to read more of my tiger book. "How many times have you, sir, ever been in a place where you are not the top of the food chain?" asked Church in one scene, playacting the role of a bear-attack victim being interviewed for a friend's journalism class. "Do you know what it's like to be prey?" he asked the would-be student journalist. "It's strange, really. And pretty cool. Kind of hard to explain. I guess it's a unique intimate experience, a chance to know yourself better." Fear as novelty, a thrill to chase. Huh. This was what I was mulling over when the bald man slid into the seat beside me. I startled.

"Hey," he said. "Remember me?" He did not know I was a writer or a teacher, but he now held a glossy three-hole spiral notebook up, thumbing the pages. His hands were huge, the knuckles looked swollen. "I have a bunch of letters for you to read," he said. "Letters to my emotions. I want to know what you think of them." I started saying I was busy, on a deadline, but he just smiled that thin line. "I need you to read them."

As he stood, he dropped the notebook so it touched my denim-covered thigh. "Also—I don't think we properly met last night. I'm Dave." He held out a hand. What to do? I met it. Mumbled *Erica* as I stared at my boots.

"I'll come back soon," he said.

The year that B-45 crossed into Oregon was the end of the millennium, early 1999. The national mood was twitchy. President Bill Clinton was on trial for impeachment in the Senate. Schools were already blocking out future vacation days to prepare for a Y2K shut-down. In early February, a 640-foot cargo ship sent from Japan for a load of timber ran aground in a storm on the southern Oregon coast. Nearly 70,000 gallons of oil leaked like molasses across the sand. Government biologists and cleanup crews, many wearing the yellow rubber of bathtub ducks, combed the beaches for life. They found a few hundred seabirds alive, but over a thousand were dead, wings mangled as blown umbrellas, bodies slick and black as some-thing coughed up by the dying. It was one of the worst environmen-tal disasters my home state had ever seen, and four hundred miles away, the wolf walked on, unaware.

They found her a month later. A dark spot moving across the snow. Officials had come to the consensus that Oregon wasn't ready for wolves, and it was time to send her back. ODFW officials were hearing from people worried the wolf was going to eat their kids; one woman called to say that if they didn't kill B-45, the blood of local children would be on their hands. The state needed a plan first, and more public education.

Tracking B-45's radio collar had taken days of coordination. A Cessna sliced through the air for a bird's-eye view and clear radio signals while a helicopter hovered below with a biologist ready to fire that nonlethal net gun. The first shot failed. For so long B-45 ran through the rolling hills and timber, away from the motor birds above her. They used the planes to flush her out of the forested mountain ravines and into a meadow. The next time they fired, a cloud of net rained down on the wolf. Bingo. On the ground, they shot her with a sedative, tucked her into a tall, dark narrow box so she wouldn't be too stimulated, and flew her to Idaho.

"She wasn't in very good shape when they caught her," Curt Mack, gray wolf recovery project leader for the Nez Perce tribe, later told writer Jim Yuskavitch. "They chased her too far with the helicopter, and I thought to myself, 'This wolf isn't going to make it.'" From the airport, they drove her into the mountains, opening her crate just as the light was disappearing from the sky. For too long she lay in her box, watching the door like a portal she couldn't trust. After they shook the crate and prodded her with a catch-pole, she eventually emerged, only to stand, frozen, in the dying day. "It was an awful feeling," an ODFW official later said. When B-45 eventually ran, it was straight to the creek. Frantic splashing, then eerie silence. When Mack climbed down the bank to check on her, B-45 was nowhere to be seen. It wasn't until the next day, when he logged a signal from her collar, that they understood she had survived.

Over the next decade, other wolves arrived in Oregon via that eastern corner. One crossed the Snake and was hit by a car on Interstate 84, not far from where the man with the plow glimpsed B-45 in the snow. One was found shot in the northeastern part of the state, and then another was found there, in that same cor-ner where OR-106's body would turn up that January morning in 2022. It is a federal crime to shoot an endangered species, even by accident, but when a wolf is shot in the forest, and if nobody sees it but the human who pulls the trigger, the fine—which could be up to $100,000—is not paid. According to ODFW Stop Poaching Campaign coordinator Yvonne Shaw, only a fraction of poachings are ever detected and reported. Few of those are prosecuted.

The subject of wolves returning to Oregon was so hot that pub-lic town hall meetings that usually draw a cluster of people were suddenly packed. Sixteen hundred oral comments arrived alongside fourteen hundred written ones. Like the wolves themselves, the po-liticization of the controversy had a precedent in the Rockies. "Kill all the Goddamn Wolves / and the People who Put Them Here," read a handmade sign in a Clayton, Idaho, restaurant window, according to Carter Niemeyer, the trapper-turned-government-biologist who helped spearhead reintroduction in Idaho and Montana. "Wolves: Government Sponsored Terrorists," proclaimed a bumper sticker I often saw while visiting family in Montana. Hating wolves was "a force more unifying than high school football games, church, art, the local watering hole," wrote Niemeyer in his memoir, *Wolfer.* "Being against wolves brought a certain solidarity even among lifelong enemies . . . reaffirm[ing] a collective neurosis among residents that the federal government was out to get them." Lupine enthusiasm was just as fervent as the hate. "I understand the issue with wolves killing," read one public comment, from a fourth grader in a town not far from Portland. "I find it appropriate to kill a wolf if that wolf is caught consuming a ranchers' livestock . . . [but] if we work hard, the wolf can roam freely in Oregon again." The ODFW employee responsible for writing the plan said he had "never seen anything like it. No one in the state had ever had any personal experience with this animal, yet there was so much emotion." The wolf was not like other animals.

A committee of stakeholders from across Oregon met to address how to manage Idaho's migrant wolves. The group had trappers, conservationists, educators, economists, tribal members, ranchers, hunters, urban and rural citizens. By 2005, they had implemented a management plan acknowledging that the spread of wolves into the state was inevitable and called for a conservation approach. The animal would remain classified as an "Endangered Species" by the state until its population reached seven breeding pairs of wolves for three consecutive years. At this somewhat arbitrary threshold, the wolf would stop being thought of as "endangered." A hunter would be able to take a shot and know the law could back him up.

A year later, in Idaho, an off-duty Wildlife Services officer found B-45's carcass while hiking through the autumn woods. By then it had been more than seven years since she had wandered into Oregon and been shipped back. This first wolf—Oregon's *startling*—was now nothing but a skeleton with a collar, grass growing through her bones. When the forensics lab examined her body, they found a trace of radio-dense fragments by her paw, but her death remained a mystery. When I spoke to Idaho Nez Perce biologist Neil Thagard about it, he told me the fragments were likely evidence of lead, suggesting she might have been shot. I asked if he thought it had been a mistake, a mix-up with a coyote, but it was a foolish question, and I knew the answer before he said it. *We'll never know.*

All through the 2000s, the web of wolf sightings in Oregon grew. *Entre chien et loup.* People called them in to fellow hikers, neighbors, ranchers, a government hotline. Depending on who was giving the account, sightings were labeled as either "possible" or "hearsay." "Man Spots Wolf—or Not—in Oregon," read one headline. In the corresponding article, even government biologists disagreed on whether the alleged wolf could be a wolf, on whether the real animal could have traveled hundreds of miles and not be glimpsed by anyone else at all. Russ Morgan, ODFW's first official wolf coordinator, began spending nights in the forest, eating peanut butter sandwiches and sleeping on the dirt outside his truck, waking every few hours to curl his hands around his mouth and howl into the night, breath misting his palms as he wished for proof of the creature he knew was out there.

Finally, in January 2008, a wildlife camera near Hells Canyon captured another wolf who had swum the Snake River, the same route B-45 had taken nine years earlier. This was B-300, a collared female wolf from Idaho. Her coat was the color of old snow, legs as white as skinned birch, eyes rimmed in inky black. Later that summer, when Morgan howled into the dry July night a few hours after midnight, he finally heard an answer. First one howl, then a deeper one, then a waterfall of yips. It was the sound of a family—the first evidence of reproduction the state had seen in more than sixty years. As one blog post noted, B-300 had just become "a proverbial mother for the return of wolves to Oregon." Like a body twitching awake from sleep, *Canis lupus* were coming back.

The first time Curt Jacobs saw a wolf, nobody believed him. It was the winter of 2008. He was returning from the reservoir in the mountains above his ranch, riding his Snowcat, hunched against the cold, and the wolf was standing in the road, looking at him, through him, as if right into his heart. Curt was in his fifties. He had been ranching in eastern Oregon for decades, just like his father and his father before him, turning cows and sheep to beef and lamb and wool, carrying on the legacy started in 1898 when his grandfather left Nebraska to come homestead a patch of dry earth near Baker City, a few hundred miles east of Portland.

When he saw the animal, Curt's spine went brittle. In the shadow before him he saw a new future flickering like a scary movie he couldn't pause. When he called in his sighting, he was told wolves weren't confirmed in that part of the country. Curt, by that point, had used a shovel to cut the iced paw print from the snow, brought it home, and set it in his freezer, a reminder next to those bright red hunks of frozen beef. He also set a picture as his desktop screensaver. Maybe you should come take a look at *that*, he told the official on the phone.

When early April 2009 rolled around, wolves weren't much on Curt's mind. He had loads of weeks-old lambs and ewes to take care of, to ferry them into trucks so he could take them off the ranch and into higher pasture for the summer. They had the trucks all in position, chutes open by the barn, when he walked out one

Thursday morning and stopped. Dead lambs. More than one, over ten, so many bodies on the ground and only a few actually eaten. Curt's breath caught like a bug in his throat. "I'm not just saying one here, one there, it was here, there, and everywhere," he told me later over the phone.

He started walking around with his brother and nephew, trying to track what happened. Their first thought was cougar. They had seen that before, so they figured they would call up a neighbor, someone Curt called a "cougar chaser." He figured they would take care of it quietly, the end. But that's when they noticed the tracks were different. Cougar tracks didn't have toenails. Curt made a plaster cast of a paw print. Not unlike the chunk of snow iced in the freezer.

"They don't want us using the 'Big W' word," Curt told a reporter a few days later, referring to the ODFW staffers who visited his farm to investigate the kills. "If we catch one or get a picture of it, then we can say it's the 'Big W.'" By that point, his lambs had been attacked twice. First Thursday night, then Sunday night—Easter Sunday, his daughter later told me. It would take days to confirm the depredations had come from wolves: twenty-three lambs, one ewe. The nonprofit Defenders of Wildlife, which had previously supported reintroduction efforts in Idaho and Montana, offered to reimburse Jacobs $7,300 for the losses, and Oregon wolf coordinator Russ Morgan installed fladry, a type of fencing tied with blowing flags that is known to deter wolves. Help was good, but what Curt really wanted was to feel in control. It was the first time a livestock kill had been traced to a wolf in Oregon in nearly sixty years, and while data suggests that wolf kills represent only one percent of total livestock deaths in the mountain west, Curt was pissed. Life as a livestock producer was hard enough without a new predator.

"I guess I'm not really happy," Curt told a journalist. Legally, he was allowed to "haze" wolves—to set off firecrackers or make other noises to try to scare them, or to shoot rubber bullets at them—but he couldn't fire a real gun at them. "My personal opinion is, if somebody is breaking into your house and stealing your money, you have the right to shoot."

My first thought was to ignore the notebook. I had already granted the man too much attention, either kindness or fear, and it didn't matter which. But what if there was something significant inside? A clue to his behavior? A warning for the train? Behind me the elderly man was discussing a crossword clue with his wife, who, from the sound of it, was cutting an apple with a pocketknife against the tray table. They seemed oblivious to what had just happened, but it was the butter in their voices as they spoke to each other that made me finally crack the cover, side-eyeing the hallway to confirm the man was not about to appear.

> I want to tell the girl that I sat next to the one thing that would complete her world but I scared her off . . . She's young. Maybe she won't meet Devils like me. Fear? I miss you where are you. You and Alive aren't here . . . Maybe she is a evil person, maybe she can help. Even if she does not want to . . . I think she will be the only other human to read these. It's worth a try . . . Ooh, fear hi!

A strange thing happened as I scanned his slanted writing. Adrenaline hit so fast I thought I would be sick. Meanwhile, my worry began to gloat, flexing like a long-idle muscle. It seemed suddenly clear the man could, in fact, be planning something. That my worry had been right. I felt like I was in a bad dream, the kind where I knew I was dreaming and still couldn't wake up. As I photographed a few pages—evidence for others or, really, myself—my hands and vision began to wobble. Behind me, ten or twelve rows, I imagined the man leaning into the aisle, watching the top of my head rise and fall. Closing the notebook on the seat, I took my phone and walked as if leaving for the bathroom.

What happened next matters in as much as it "resolved" my immediate concern. The woman from the night before saw my expression and knew, immediately, something was wrong. She found the conductor; I showed them the writing; they settled me in a curtained sleeping car, told me to lock the door, then radioed the police to meet the train at a station just past the next town. The man was escorted away, and eventually, I was returned to my seat. A few of the guys in the car approached me then, apologizing for their silence, saying they'd always thought that guy was a fucking creep sitting next to a girl when so many other seats were free, and what did he say, anyway? I didn't know how to respond. They had come too late, but also, had I wanted to be saved? Still, I listened when they told me how they'd watched the man fight with the police as they'd hauled him off. Arms flailing, shouting about meth.

This was an ending of sorts for those of us on the train, but it meant nothing to the story of the man. A police detective asked for my number and never called. Later I searched local newspapers and police logs and found nothing. I hoped he had not been thrown off and abandoned on the platform, as had happened when a friend dropped acid on the train then panicked when the oil flares appeared. I hoped this man had gotten help, but what did that look like out here? So much brown flat. That town, the next one we pulled into after I spoke with the conductor, was Wolf Point, Montana. It had fewer than 3,000 residents and was the hub of the Fort Peck

Indian Reservation, not far from the banks of the Missouri River. Lewis and Clark's expedition had passed by in 1804. Its namesake is disputed; the town website traces the most popular story to one William Bent, allegedly the nephew of the legendary Kit Carson and a Pony Express mail rider who spent the winter of 1868–1869 hunting wolves in the region. "Wolf Point got its name from the fact that one winter the wolfers killed such a large number of wolves that they froze before the skins could be removed," he wrote. "The frozen carcasses were piled near the river to wait the coming of spring and the pile was so high, it became a landmark for all the country around." I imagine the value of these pelts was not just in how they would be sold—fur for ladies' coats, say—but in what their presence represented. The loss of a wolf. Those trappers were paid not just for the token of the fur but for the perceived evil of the creature that once animated it. Wolf pelt as a symbol of vanquished fear.

Crystallized in the violent history of Wolf Point's name, then, was the idea that by eliminating the creature who threatens you, or whom you see as a threat, you have something to celebrate. This is a tempting story, but the expulsion of the man on the train revealed its shabby architecture. Sure, I wanted him away from me, but I also wanted to better understand his life, his brain, the mechanisms that led him to write such things to me, the mechanisms behind how I responded. "If you don't punish people who do unacceptable things," asks psychoanalyst Adam Phillips, "what else can you do with them, or to them?" Punishment, he writes, is so often a failure of imagination. When I looked out the window, I pictured one pile of wolf pelts after another.

In talking to the conductor, I learned the man had not been escorted off in Wolf Point as planned. Only one officer had been free when he called in, and the conductor thought they needed at least two to remove him in case he resisted. That impulse was, at the next station, proven right. But I was still thinking about Wolf Point as the train moved west, past beached school buses with punched-out windows, aspens quaking wet in the afternoon light. That night, I got a call from a number I did not know, and when I googled it, the area code read Wolf River, Wisconsin, a town I had never heard of. This was a coincidence that felt like a sign. A day later, when the train pulled into Portland, I hugged my parents for too long, and a few days after that, I picked up the rental car and drove north to the cabin. The house was not alone in the woods as I had imagined, but at the end of a long dirt road with only one other house in sight. A sign outside read Curly Wolf Gunsmiths. I looked for the bald man everywhere, but all I saw was the wolf.

When a wolf chews a kill, it can ferry the meat in its gut. This is how a parent feeds her young if they are older than about five weeks— belly full, running through the brush to the den. The pups bump their snouts into hers, licking her muzzle, signaling their hunger. When she regurgitates the meat, they pounce, jostling one another for the best bites, eating themselves into a stupor. This is how it works: an animal is killed, a pup is kept alive. There is no morality in the wolf's kill, only the blunt logic of animal life.

The same month a wolf killed Curt's lambs, in April 2009, another wolf in northeastern Oregon had pups. This was B-300, that new wolf who had swum the river from Idaho. She was the one whose first litter Russ had heard the previous summer, still the only wolf known to have pups in the state in decades. She gave birth in a den her mate would have helped her dig. It would have been near water, probably on a hill or a ridge—maybe a rut under tree roots, the natural depression under a boulder, the sandy dark of a cave. The entrance to the den was probably about the size of a desktop computer monitor, leading to a tunnel that hooked to a rounded hollow some six to fourteen feet into the earth. This was where the bodies multiplied. When they were born, her pug-faced pups could barely smell. They were deaf and blind for about two weeks, unable to regulate their own body temperature or support their own weight. Crawling meant pulling themselves with their front legs as they tipped into one another, each pup a mewing, tiny thing, about a pound in weight, the size of a Beanie Baby.

Pup mortality rates can be hard to determine in those first, private months, but research suggests it could be around fifty percent. Though some of B-300's litter likely died, many did not. One of those pups would grow into one of the most famous wolves in America, a wolf whose life would tug many into its orbit, including me—someone who had never thought much about wolves, or what learning to live with them might teach us about learning to live with ourselves. But that comes later. At first this wolf, OR-7, was just a pup. Still reliant on the kill his mother had spit up, until, somewhere after a few months, his milk teeth became strong enough to tear flesh.

Wolves may have been exterminated in America in the mid-twentieth century, but the wolf as symbol never left. The violence European settlers exercised while slaughtering the animal is now etched in the cartography of U.S. place names like Wolf Point, while the reverence still carried for its alleged "wildness" motors down the highway on RVs airbrushed "Gray Wolf." I knew the man on the train was not a wolf, but in so many fairy tales, his part would be played by one. I did not trust my culture's narratives about fear. I wanted to hold them up and light a match, first to illuminate and then to watch them turn to ash. At the same time, I could not ignore the thrum of panic in my own life. Not just for my own body, but for those of others, both human and animal. Little moments, like what happened on the train, were accumulating like sediment and throwing off the balance of my days. "My inner world had gone away," says the young protagonist of Anna Burns's novel *Milkman* after she is stalked by an older man. I knew growing up meant learning from the past, but it also meant choosing when to look away from it. I couldn't figure out how to decide when to do what.

Liana Zanette is a Canadian biologist who studies the ecology of fear, and whom I later interviewed for her research into dynamics of predator and prey. "Fear is not an emotion in my lab," she told me. "We think about it in terms of behavioral responses to life-threatening events." I knew an elk getting charged by a wolf was incomparable to one person being threatened by another, and I was wary of the metaphors that often conflated them. At the same time, I couldn't help acknowledging the wedge at the center of the Venn diagram: that in each case, a body can be transformed by its stress response to a perceived threat. Zanette studied psychology as an undergraduate, and her research now applied biomedical definitions of human PTSD to animal contexts. Everything changed after trauma, even plants, she told me. Responses to chronic stress were basically the same across species. "If you experience something life-threatening, you are a different animal the very next day," she said.

I doubted my life had been threatened on the train, but I felt something like validation from the other end of the phone. I appreciated visualizing my fear not just as a *feeling*—I could deal with those!—but as a set of responses, a row of dominoes that tipped outward into different spheres of life. "We need to form fear memories instantly to survive another day," Zanette said. "They are extremely difficult to get rid of because they have to be instant, and you can't afford to lose them." A fearful experience changes how a body moves through the world. She found that in high-predator environments, birds will forgo food. A recording of a barking dog was enough to scare raccoons off from searching for food on a beach. Audio of an English actor reading *The Wind in the Willows*—textbook terror—made nearby badgers forage more quickly, less frequently, and with increased vigilance.

During my time at the coastal cabin, I surprised myself by cutting afternoon hikes short, too jumpy of what might lurk behind the old-growth trees. In scanning for the man's giant shoulders in the grocery store and on the beach, I conjured him, again and again. *Quand on parle le loup.* When you speak of the wolf, you see its tail. I wanted my old self back. Describing a recurrent dream of home invasion, memoirist Melissa Febos writes that because she has never experienced such an assault, nor has she been raped, the feeling is "not a reenactment of such a trauma but a preoccupation with the threat of it, with the problem and necessity of refusing without ever saying no." The man had not violated me physically, but the tenor of his attention had reminded me the world and its inhabitants were, at the end of the day, unknowable. The word "fear" comes from an Old English word connoting sudden danger and ambush. As my sister Annika pointed out to me one day, maybe we try to defang the feeling by anticipating it. We cannot be ambushed by the threat we have been waiting for. And so I started looking differently at all strange men I encountered, expecting the worst. I no longer entertained Meriwether Lewis's words that it was a good smooth road ahead.

The man on the train would not leave me, but I did not want to imagine the man. The wolf would not disappear, so I began to imagine the wolf.

I read that in a corner of western Russia, wolves were killing dogs. They used to eat wild boars, but then there was an outbreak of African swine fever. The government implemented a boar-hunting program, and maybe, say the locals, that's when the predators grew bolder. A news article from 2018 reported wolves walking town roads as if they were in forests. Multiple villagers described searching for missing dogs but finding only their heads remaining. No humans had been hurt, as far as I could tell, but people were afraid. They built backyard cages for domestic animals. When summer passed, they abandoned the unpaved streets around five p.m., when the sun went down. Because the changing climate had made winter unseasonably mild, with little snow, there were few tracks for hunters to follow. If you do not know where a wolf has stepped, you imagine it could have stepped everywhere. In the face of this uncertainty, villagers created rules for safety. One town kept Christmas lights blinking in the streets from October to May, believing the flashing to be a deterrent. Another town's residents scattered pitchforks along its footpaths, for walkers to use in case of an attack. One schoolteacher invented her own ritual. "I walk to work in bright red mittens," she told the reporter. "I hold flashlights inside to produce a sort of red flare. Maybe that will frighten them." She does not have to say: maybe it will not.

Because many of our stories about wolves have been inflated for so long, it is a challenge to separate the being from the belief. But if it was a leap, at first, for me to imagine the reality of a twenty-first-century town haunted by fear of wolves, it was not hard for me to imagine how the schoolteacher felt. We invent rituals to shield ourselves: wear this, shout that. The systems become our stories. The stories become our lives. I am less interested in the villagers who are killed by wolves—there are so, so few in this age, especially in North America—than in how it feels to be the one who believes they can be killed. Who puts on their red mittens, takes a deep breath, and steps out the door. This book does not unfold in the aftermath of rape, or murder, or attempted murder, or any of the other horrors that constellate our world. It is not about waking up in the gut of the wolf. It is about the stone in the belly of the person who knows these outcomes are possible, who has experienced—haven't we all?—some shade of confrontation before, and now lives in the twilight zone between the anticipatory anxiety of *what could be* and the memory of fear that screamed *what now*. It is the story of a journey through *entre chien et loup*, that hazy hour where we not only evaluate our fear, but learn to question it, deny it, walk beside it.

2

Girl v. Wolf

The month before I began my senior year of high school, a teacher named Candice left her home near Pittsburgh and flew to Alaska. She took a photo from the airplane showing a silver creek dripping into a hilly green valley, and then a few days later, posted "The Journey begins . . ." on her blog. After an orientation with fellow teachers near Anchorage, she flew west again, this time south down the peninsula on a wobbly ten-seater bush plane, heart whacking as they soared across water-threaded forests down into the fishing village of Perryville, some five hundred miles south of Anchorage, along the sea.

Alaska was nothing like home, but she was good at starting anew. After graduating college in 2000, Candice had packed her beat-up Chevy and driven to California, living in her car and grooming at the local community center until she wrangled a job, her father later told reporters. Now, about a decade later, after getting a master's in special education, she'd found this gig at a job fair. Based in Perryville, she'd fly from one remote island village to another and teach a patchwork of special-education students, many of them Alutiiq, many of their parents subsistence hunters and fishermen.

Perryville was founded in 1912 as a refuge for the Alutiiq displaced after the eruption of Mt. Katmai, the largest volcanic eruption in twentieth-century North America. If Candice was homesick in that place born of disaster, she did not share it on her blog. She baked cookies for the bush pilots; she caught her first salmon then ate it grilled on the deck of the boat the same afternoon; she threw sea urchins into a campfire and waited until the spines cracked to start eating; she learned that bear grease made a pie crust sing. She befriended village dogs on her morning runs, feeding them milk bones so they would run beside her and chase off the ravens and foxes. The whole time she gripped her bear spray, like the hand of a friend, in her palm. There are so many brown bears in this part of Alaska that government biologists classify it as "high density," with approximately one bear for every ten square kilometers, like one bear wandering an area the size of three Central Parks. Candice knew about the bears. When they hibernated in December, she relished the chance to go farther on her morning runs through the moonlit bush. Nights in Alaska felt brighter than in rural Pennsylvania. Darkness was not real dark, just a monochrome glow lit by everything bright that hung above. Candice's ponytail swung as she ran, a gold flare beneath the moon.

Alaska delivered Candice her own heart—so human, so fragile—as if on a silver platter. Rarely had she been so aware of its thump. So much of life must have felt like the hike she went on one day through bear country with the friend who carried a .44 Magnum for protection—"a little nerve wrecking [*sic*], but exciting," as she summed it on her teaching blog. Still, she was against trophy hunting, even for a creature that made her jumpy. "I personally do not like the bears being shot," she wrote. "I think they're beautiful and amazing animals to watch." She knew that a bear who had been shot could still attack. There was no such thing as immunity, just head and luck and fist. So much of her life in Alaska could, suddenly, tilt into survival mode. You could leave for a walk on a mild day and find plummeting temperatures and forty-mile-an-hour winds on the way home. "At one point it was so windy, that I thought of waiting in the ditch for someone to find me, but then I realized there was no one around to look for me, so I got up and kept walking," she wrote. What else was there to do? Experience had taught her snow could blow on the carburetor and gas could freeze in the tank and she'd just have to walk home, extremities numb, only a small bubble of vision around her face. She knew she could surf a glassy twenty-second ride on those Gatorade-blue waves but if she hit trouble there was no lifeguard watching, no rescue plane waiting. "I hate to see nice waves wasted, but I'm not sure how safe the waters are," she wrote. One day, on a sunny Sunday back at her base in Perryville, a couple of students asked if she wanted to go for a hike. They climbed a mountain that jutted above the rock-strewn shore, watching the sun splay its last golden beams across the sea. Coming down she was acutely aware of what it would mean for a foot to slip. "Careful!! I must have said that a thousand times, it was a steep descent!" she wrote later. "To be a kid again with no fear . . ."

One of the towns she taught at regularly was Chignik Lake, population ninety-one. This was a place you could only reach by air, or, hypothetically, boat. Landing there meant wind tossing the plane, a captain searching for caribou bulls, a runway just a long smudge of dirt. When they didn't crash Candice remembered to exhale. The one road out of town led to the large blue swath of Chignik Lake, which led to the Chignik River, which fed Chignik Lagoon and Chignik Bay, and then you were in the Pacific, miles of salty blue so cold it would make you gasp like a trout off the line. The school mascot at Chignik was a wolf. There was a taxidermied one in the lobby, coat the color of Oreo ice cream, jaws swung open, who, through its blue-glass eyes, watched the twenty-some students pass in and out. "It's a great reminder of what lurks outside in the wilderness and to be on the alert at all times," Candice wrote on the blog. She spent Thanksgiving that year helping a fellow teacher with his trapline, piling halibut carcasses for bait beside the metal snare traps. "Next week we're hoping for a wolf," she wrote. She had seen the tracks, big ones, and converted them to pelt in her mind. She was learning this was how locals stayed warm in the minus-20-degree weather, but also that this was money and livelihood.

When the holidays came, there were blizzards, and the prospect of maybe five planes to go home was enough to make Candice stay. "It was hard to be away from family, but not having to go into a Walmart, Giant Eagle or deal with the hustle and bustle of Christmas came close to making up for it," she wrote. She sewed mittens and hats out of beaver and otter fur. She checked traps; she rode the four-wheeler. She watched her students' Christmas play in a school gym and ate grilled shrimp slick with seal oil at the potluck afterward.

In the new decade, Candice didn't update her blog at all. Maybe she was busy, or maybe the wind kept tearing the internet down, or maybe she just preferred sharing stories with friends and family over the phone, their voices entering her room as something rounder than words on a page. On Monday, March 8, Candice landed for a teaching stint in Chignik Lake. The day was overcast with a high of 24 degrees and a wind that averaged twenty-four miles an hour but was sometimes twice that, blowing the snow into a drifted topography of force. At 5:10 p.m., Candice faxed her timesheet to the district office from the school and changed into her running clothes. She told co-workers she was going for a jog, taking the only road in town to the mouth of the river. It was late enough in spring that the sky would be light for another few hours. And it was.

When four Chignik residents came snowmobiling down the road at around six p.m., the lead member was quick to see the red that streaked the snowy road, and when he followed the stain off the road and down the hill, he was quick to see the body. Did he suspect, in that town of under a hundred people, who the blond woman was? They were two miles east of town, flanked on either side by shadowy shrubs that formed dense canopies, any visibility kinked by the curving road. The snowmobilers rushed back to notify Alaska State Police. Later, the man who first found the body returned with two others from the community to guard and wait for instructions from authorities, but the temperatures fell, and at some point, two of them headed back for warmer clothing. The one who remained drove his snowmobile in circles around a clearing just downhill of the body, peering into the brush with his vehicle light, trying to catch a glimpse of who was there, or what was there, or why the body looked the way it did. That's when the wolf stepped into the spotlight.

"There are only two real plots," a teacher told me once. "The story of the stranger who comes to town, and the story of the one who leaves."

"All stories are about wolves," wrote novelist Margaret Atwood. "All worth repeating, that is."

When Joseph Campbell codified the concept of the "hero's journey" in 1949, he suggested a hero was made when he ventured out in the world, encountered wild forces, triumphed, and returned with new power. This was the scaffolding of boy into man, as heroes from Odysseus to Hercules, Luke Skywalker to Harry Potter will tell.

Nearly forty years later, in a 1984 interview, Campbell said a girl turns into a woman with "her first menstruation . . . it happens to her. Nature does it to her." Unlike the man's journey, Campbell portrayed the woman's as passive. She did not have to go looking for transformation because the seed of it was always inside her. "What is a woman?" asked Campbell. "A woman is a vehicle of life. Life has overtaken her."

The words first infuriated me for their flat essentializing of gender identity, then their naïveté. If my journey into "womanhood" had, at times, felt passive, it was not because I felt overtaken by my ovaries, but by forces outside my body. Forces I could not, with the right pill, control.

My favorite stories were the Campbell-hero kind. The ones about leaving. Of running into the forest and making a home in an old boxcar, or entering a wardrobe to lose yourself the way my friends and I did in Forever 21. I read these books while pretzeled in the tire swing on my grandparents' Montana lawn, palms sticky with berry Popsicle, my thick bangs a curtain between my brain and the world. These were stories of temporary orphanhood. Independence was a rainstorm that blew in and created good drama, allowed the green shoots to raise their tiny fists toward a sun that would, inevitably, return. At first the stories seemed ripe with the myth of universality. The child who set off from their parents was not boy or girl, they were runaway.

I identified first as an adventurer. It didn't matter how I appeared, I thought; it mattered what I did. I oscillated between overalls and dresses, sometimes brushing my long hair, other times tying it up to make it go away. I had been mistaken for a boy as a toddler, and though I would bristle at that later, taking pleasure in the twirl of my skirts, I sensed early that layering necklaces and pulling on tights meant others were more likely to pay attention to me. To appraise myself as feminine was to invite a certain kind of appraisal; its inverse was also true. By dressing in jeans and big, dark sweaters, my body could almost disappear. Become almost invisible when I walked down the street.

I did not realize then what a privilege it was to feel in control of how my body was read. "[E]ven dressed almost mannishly, I would be noticed ... I could not leave my race at home," writes novelist Min Jin Lee, recollecting her youth in an essay about violence against Asian Americans for the *New York Times*. My own ability to present my body according to mood was not just a privilege of my youth but of my condition, that cocktail of slow-blooming genetic scrawniness, cis-gendered heterosexuality, culturally sanctioned whiteness. "You cannot separate what it means to be a 'woman,' often used to mean a performance of acceptable femininity, from the conditions that decide what is and is not acceptable across time," writes sociologist, cultural critic, and award-winning writer Tressie McMillan Cottom. The same is true for girls. My hair and skin were light. I had crushes on boys. My body and its desires were mostly acceptable, the magazines told me. Across race and gender lines, society viewed Brown and Black girls as more adult-like than their white peers, but I was granted girlhood. I wore it like an accessory: a purse I could carry when I wanted to and drop when I did not. I could not imagine how such an accoutrement could carry danger. That one day I might see the purse fused to my skin, my female identity a costume I could not shake. Puberty is often described as growing into one's body, but I experienced it as slowly becoming trapped there, standing on a spit of beach while the tide rolled in.

I did not hate my changed body, but I mourned the old one, or rather the ease with which I once occupied it. "We're all stuck in our bodies, meaning stuck inside a grid of conflicting ideas about what those bodies mean," writes Olivia Laing in *Everybody: A Book About Freedom*. Society told me my new body had rules: shave this, cover that. I had become trapped in a tighter grid.

When did I see the sliver of divide? Wading through that canon of stories about young people leaving home, and there it was, a seam in the glass cup. The girls were going off, facing danger, and falling in love, always with boys. Sometimes boys were saving them from threats, but sometimes just from themselves. Love taught those girls they had been walking around like plastic half-heart necklaces, waiting for a union to click them into wholeness. To strive to be completed was to cede that you as an individual were incomplete, lacking. By the time I was in middle school, I had learned to wait for crushes the way I waited for sunshine in the spring. I did not think I needed saving from physical threats, but I absorbed the cultural message that I was unfinished. Raw as an undressed salad. I wanted adventure, sure, but I understood the finish line should be love. Still, I kept reading about boy adventurers, the self-sufficient ones who stowed away on boats and made homes in trees. Was I in love with them, or did I want to be them? The difference seemed negligible. Because my own bravery had rarely been put to the test, I sensed it was in the wings, folded and ready as an airplane life vest. To read stories of danger was to rehearse my escape.

Only now can I feel nostalgic thinking of that tween version of self, so outwardly independent, so inwardly boy-obsessed. A girl who craved the boys' company for fun, for attention, for a lark. Still oblivious to that dumb tick: fear.

The summer before middle school I went with two friends to a "girls' empowerment" camp in a meadow outside Eugene, Oregon. My friends went for a weekend the summer before and came back giddy with girl power and henna tattoos, but we weren't at the seven-day session long before they admitted this was a stronger brew. The teenage counselors waved us with sage smoke and robbed us of flip phones and watches, locking them in the white-haired director's ranch house. At night we slept in a giant circle of sleeping bags on the dewy grass of what was, I now realize, her yard. Activities included walking the labyrinth painted onto her driveway, passing around the cold beak of a cervical speculum, and crouching in the ferns, told not to come out until our "spirit animals" appeared. Without language to articulate why the camp felt so bad, I began to suspect I just didn't know how to have fun. At the buffet-style meals, I ate one plate of tofu pasta salad after another, desperate to feel soothed.

I left the camp with a turd of earthy clay strung on yarn around my neck and a bubblegum-colored T-shirt signed by my peers. GIRLS KICK BUTT, someone scrawled next to a peace sign on my shoulder. In the spirit of a lower-back tattoo, my friend Sharpie'd STRONG INDEPENDENT WOMAN right above the hem, where the shirt fell above my nonexistent ass. The camp strived, in admirable ways, to teach us feminist self-reliance so often missing in Western fairy tales. But the punch line that stays with me now was, I realize, the same as in "Little Red Riding Hood": that the boys are out to get us. We sat crisscross in a circle, wide-eyed as the counselors passed around a tube of pepper spray and told us to carry one at all times, especially on dates with boys we thought we might like. Just as the wolf knocks on the sick grandmother's door, feigning the disguise of Little Red so he can eat the geriatric and assume her boudoir post, so we were told boys would do anything to get us into bed.

I had grown up knowing not to get in cars with strangers, but I do not remember my parents giving a gendered shape to their warnings. It was the early 2000s, a time of glossy, commercialized girl power, of "Take Your Daughter to Work Day" and *Sabrina the Teenage Witch*. Of course I knew men could be creeps, but I was also wading into middle school with girls whom I had seen do pretty terrifying things. Camp was the first time a woman looked me in the eye and told me men were out to trick us. That, or it was the first time I wondered if I should listen. The lesson was delivered, like the a cappella goddess chants we sang to the stars, as a secret of our sisterhood. As with those lessons, I scoffed. I was a skeptic who missed her wristwatch, and deciding to fear men felt like deciding to put faith in the director's healing crystal. Until I saw evidence with my own eyes, I would continue to doubt its weight in my life.

I became compelled by the wolf because I was intrigued by the investigation of a body that could be both feared and feared for, sometimes simultaneously. I wanted to unspool the cultural narratives that constructed and concealed my layman's perception of it. At first I did think my body fit into this. But if all stories are about wolves, and all plots are about arrivals and departures, then there are two archetypal stories of leaving home I cannot ignore. One is history and one is fairy tale, but they are connected by a central metaphor: that the wolf is a violent man, and vice versa. Their language is bedrock for how so much Western thought conceptualizes the wolf, but the predator is not the only one implicated. We—me and you—are ensnared too.

First, take the story of a boy who leaves home. He has been leaving for thousands of years. Imagine him champing at the bit of his known world, sharpening stones in a starched animal-skin hut with his parents and siblings. The boy cannot be a hero in these walls. He wants to prove himself; he wants to matter. And so he leaves.

Thousands of years ago, boy-men often left home together and formed itinerant warrior packs. They did this all over Eurasia; there is evidence of the tradition in the Ancient Greek, Germanic, Indo-Iranian, Italian, and Celtic worlds. Sometimes they were expelled for raising hell in their home societies—in the words of anthropologist and archaeologist David Anthony, "These were young guys on the edge of society who occasionally would steal cows, and you'd rather they were off stealing someone else's cows"—but sometimes they just left because they wanted to. As if to grow into your body you had to grow out of your childhood home.

A young man had to earn his place in the roving war brotherhood, often called *koryos* in that Proto-Indo-European language. He had to train first, maybe for years. Look his fear in the face and prove himself through ritual. The Rigveda, an ancient Sanskrit text dated before 1000 BC, dictated that he must sacrifice a dog during a ceremony on a winter evening. North of the Black Sea, in what is now Ukraine and Russia and Kazakhstan, archaeologists studying Bronze Age nomadic communities unearthed dozens of butchered dogs and wolves and linked them to a similar tradition. The canines were too old to have been raised for food, and their bones were cut unusually, with snouts divided into threes. Scholars speculate the men sacrificed the canines, perhaps eating the meat as if to take its spirit on.

Historic conflations of young men with wolves extended in more symbolic directions too. In Ancient Greece, warrior-initiates were the only ones allowed to adopt wolflike traits in battle. To prowl at night, ambush, play tricks. They did not have to follow the code of older warriors because they were not seen as human. Free from the taboos of both childhood and adulthood, they were encouraged to live in their culture's vision of the predator, being strong, fast, conniving, promiscuous, ruthless, and resistant to pain and fear. Without remorse or second-guessing, they were engines of instinct; often, the instinct was blood. There is more evidence of "wolf-warriors" than any other animal-warrior in Indo-European culture. All across Eurasia, warriors were adopting names that included the word "wolf"—a reference to violent death in Indo-European beliefs—and joining local militias to become wolves. And so the *koryos* prowled.

Bands of young men pillaged, raided, and raped, killing indiscriminately and howling while enveloped in canine carcasses, one scholar of ancient Ireland and England said. The illustrious Norse warriors known as Berserkers were known to don wolf skins and wolf heads too, moving like rabid beasts, garnering the name *úlfheðnar* ("wolf-skinned"), as in *Look at that man going berserk, dressed as a wolf.* "To put on mask-clothing is not so much to conceal a human essence beneath an animal appearance, but rather to activate the powers of a different body," wrote Brazilian anthropologist Eduardo Viveiros de Castro. The Berserkers were known for finding ecstasy in violence. They danced and howled, often high. They took hostages, they killed. This type of wartime fury was called *lyssa* in Ancient Greece, from *lykos,* wolf, as if the young warriors' hunger for battle shape-shifted them entirely.

Scholars now suspect those warrior-bands were, implicitly, doing more than spilling blood. Their violence would likely have incentivized those they encountered to join their ranks for safety. Sometimes relatives from the men's homeland would follow, and new communities would form, leaching customs and habits and language. It seems possible the movements of these men helped start migrations across Eurasia, seeding the spread of Indo-European languages now spoken by forty-five percent of humanity. Similari-

ties between the battle behavior of the Berserkers and the Indigenous North American Aztec *quachics* have made scholars wonder if
their wolf-inspired rituals were just warrior coincidence, or evidence
of customs shared via contact across the Bering Sea.

In Navajo tradition, where wolves are held in high esteem as
leaders and hunters, the word *naatl'eetsoh,* which literally refers to
wolves, is used to encompass all human and animal hunters. Contrast this to findings from Ancient Norse, Sanskrit, Prussian, Ira-
nian, and Slavic traditions, where words for "wolf" are also words
for "robber," or "evil-doer," or "outlaw." When I learned about the
negative conflations, my impulse was to untangle the canine from
the ways we made it human. I thought if I went back far enough I
could find where the lines of language had crossed, where we began to refer to human enemies as wolves and vice versa, and that
by pointing it out I could sever the tie. "We have manhandled so
many words that I only dream of using them anew," wrote Chinese
farmer-poet Yu Xiuhua in an essay in her collection *Moonlight Rests
on My Left Palm.* This was what I wanted: new language for the
wolf. I once assumed we had feared the animal and raced to anthropomorphize it, but the more I read of these ancient traditions, the
more I wondered if our language was less metaphor than historic
reality—that thousands of years ago, men who might be dressed as
wolves had truly roamed the countryside, ready to kill.

I do not mean to suggest all young men who conflated themselves
with wolves were doing so because of unbridled bloodlust. Warriors
have long looked to the wolf as an icon of loyalty, skill, bravery, and
community. "There was no talking, no laughing, but only carefully
suppressed excitement while our teacher painted our bodies with
the mud ... set [ears] on our heads, so that they were like the ears
of wolves ... [and] cover[ed] our backs with the wolf skins we had
stolen out of our fathers' lodges," recalled Plenty-Coups, a chief of

the Crow in Yellowstone River country. "Ho! Now we were a real party of Crow Wolves." These sorts of kindred relationships—as in many animist cultures, where animals are viewed as spirit reincarnations of humans and vice versa—have kindled legacies of holistic respect for the creature around the globe. But what of the residue left by the other wolf-warriors? Might today's anthropomorphized metaphor of Big Bad Wolf have roots in a real-life legacy of masculine violence?

"The first subject matter for painting was animal. Probably the first paint was animal blood. Prior to that, it is not unreasonable to suppose that the first metaphor was animal," wrote art critic John Berger. I am not a linguist or archaeologist or ancient historian, but I recognize a story, and it seems the conflation of human and wolf is one of the Western world's oldest, perhaps predating the English language itself. One of the stories seeded in my blood like some unseen parasite: the fact that when we say we fear one animal, we allude by proxy to the other, and vice versa, in a vicious loop that can be unfair to both.

You know the story. Once upon a time a boy left home. At some point on the road he became a man. At some point he became a "wolf."

When I think of the girl who leaves home, I think of that story that begins in the fairy-tale village. I see squat smoking chimneys and hear a mother raising her voice, rousing the girl from her place by the fire as she asks her to run a quick errand. Unlike the boy, the girl does not leave the house to find herself, or prove herself to herself. She leaves to prove her love to those around her. She fills a need.

In the earliest printed version of the story, written by Charles Perrault in 1697, the heroine goes to her sick grandmother's house with a homemade cake and a pot of butter. Their love language is gifts. When she steps into the trees, she is wearing a ruby cape the grandmother has made for her. Like so many future female-identifying politicians, she is defined by her dress; Perrault calls the story "Le Petit Chaperon Rouge." Later, the moral implication of her costume becomes clear: she has been "spoiled" in more ways than one, as if one sort of attention invites another. The girl does not walk far before she runs into the wolf. The animal wants to eat her, but he restrains himself because woodcutters are working nearby. If Little Red remembers her mother's warning not to talk to strangers or stray from the trail, she does not heed it. When the wolf asks where she is going, she tells him it's to grandmother's house.

"Well, and I'll go and see her too," says Perrault's wolf. "I'll go this way and go you that, and we shall see who will be there first." The girl dawdles in the forest, and by the time she reaches the house, the wolf has eaten his meal. Disguising his voice as that of the granddaughter, he had stepped into the cottage, where the older woman lay ill in bed. "He immediately fell upon the good woman and ate her up in a minute," wrote Perrault. When Little Red knocks on the door, she hears the wolf answer, but her fear gives way to reason, as she convinces herself the cold has transformed her grandmother's voice into something hoarser. The wolf is under the bedsheets when she walks in. Watching her approach, he tells her to put the gifts on the stool then crawl into bed. If Little Red is hesitant, Perrault does not voice it. Taking off her clothes, she crawls under the sheets.

"Grandmother, what big arms you have!"

"All the better to hug you with, my dear."

Their dialogue continues in this pattern, the spotlight of Little Red's skepticism slowly illuminating the wolf's whole form: his ears, the better to hear her with; his eyes, the better to see her with; his teeth, the better to eat her with, the end. The wolf "fell upon" the girl, just as he did with the grandmother. You could say the tragedy was math. Where there had been three bodies there was now only one.

Perrault did not invent this plot, he just hammered an oral folktale with roots in the Middle Ages to the page. In the process he built something new and fossilized his own place in history. A similar story had long been told in China, Japan, and Korea, under the name "The Tiger and the Children," featuring a tiger who entered a house of unprotected children, taking the form of a mother or grandmother, and representing not just male power but, in the words of folklorist Wolfram Eberhard, that "region of death"—the West. Unlike the Brothers Grimm version that would appear in 1812, Perrault's initial story had no deus ex machina. There was no huntsman to perform the strange cesarean and free the girl's pale flapping arms and the soggy raisin of her grandmother from the belly of the beast, just a pretty girl who led herself astray and died. Instead of a rescue for Little Red, Perrault's version ends with a punch line:

"Moral: Children, especially attractive, well bred young ladies, should never talk to strangers, for if they should do so, they may well provide dinner for a wolf. I say 'wolf,' but there are various kinds of wolves. There are also those who are charming, quiet, polite, unassuming, complacent, and sweet, who pursue young women at home and in the streets. And unfortunately, it is these gentle wolves who are the most dangerous ones of all."

There is the boy who leaves home and becomes the wolf, and there is the girl who leaves home and meets the wolf. But there is a third story about leaving home. It is hundreds of thousands of years old, older than the others, and though it is at the root of each, it is the least sung of all three. The story of *Canis lupus,* the gray wolf, begins each year in spring, when a pup is weaned by her mother and moved out of the den to the rendezvous site. This is where pack members gather to eat, play, and sleep before an evening's hunt. When the pup's parents leave to procure food, an older sibling watches her, and in return, she clambers over them, paws like tiny fists. As she grows, blue eyes turn to gold. The adults carry her like a rag doll when her wrestling becomes too much, milk teeth like needles in their scruff, her first attempts at a howl a high-pitched whine. By the time fall arrives, she is nearly full-size, old enough to learn to hunt. For up to a few years she will travel with her family, mapping the terrain of her pack's territory, learning the high plateaus and forested ridges and meadows that appeal to a lupine eye. The better hunters are often the young females. A scientist will say this is because they are slimmer, smaller, faster. I want to believe there is something more.

After a year or so, around the time the pups are ready to breed, some will choose to leave. These become dispersers. They are both male and female, and they are looking for independence. Not just for a mate, but for land free enough for them to start their own pack. This was why B-45 braved the Snake River crossing, and why B-300— mother to Oregon's first twenty-first-century wolf pups—did too.

Wolves have scent glands beneath their toes; they leave olfactory breadcrumbs wherever they go. A wolf who travels alone is always constellating the paths of those who came before her, traveling the buffer zones of overlapping territories. Dispersing is risky: it is harder to catch bigger prey, and besides the increased chance of malnutrition and meeting territorial wolves, there are those regular risks of hunters and bears and illness and roads. Anyone she meets is a potential foe. But a disperser walks despite the danger. Not because it is an adventure, but because it is simply the thing she knows

to do. Nobody knows what makes an animal a long-distance traveler, but it's probably best understood as a personality trait. There
is some evidence that the behavior might run within bloodlines.
That some force tugs her from her family, and there she goes.

I wanted only to go far. All but one of the colleges I applied to
were closer to the Atlantic than the Pacific. I cried when I thought
about leaving Oregon, but angst was welcome. I did not want to
sustain comfort, which gave me no excuse when the inevitable anxiety showed up, and I had nothing to blame but myself. I wanted to
be somewhere so strange it would distract from myself. I wanted
to stand out enough to be seen. Mostly I wanted to feel slightly
unmoored, and blame that on my surroundings not the voice that
whirred somewhere above my ears, telling me even when I was
laughing with friends that I was still alone, ringed by some moat of
unease that could never be breached. I was ready to shake the gray
sky, the giant old-growth firs that seemed perpetually wet, sticky
with either rain or sap, their green branches like shaggy claws. I
craved brick buildings flanked by well-pruned shrubs. The tidy silence of snow.

My parents had met as freshmen in the laundry room at the University of Oregon, my mother having arrived from a small town near
Missoula, Montana, and my father from a sheep-filled farm less than
a hundred miles from their dorm. Two years in, he dropped out to
teach himself to code. By their midtwenties, they were married, and
then a few years later, I was born. My father did not talk much about
regrets, but he felt strongly that my sister and I not only enroll in
college but stay. I did not know what to do with the privilege of their
support but fly as far as I could. Neither of my parents had applied to

school on the East Coast, and as the oldest of all my cousins, I was first to look that way. I was ready to blaze the trail. I knew how to bushwhack, that if you kicked through the bramble you could figure it out, legs scratched but everything fine.

"I guess we'll let you go east," my maternal grandfather told me with a wink the summer before I did. He was splayed on a lounger on their Montana porch, a beer snug in the crook of his hand as the sprinklers tossed themselves back and forth behind him on the lawn. "You just have to come back when you're done." He squinted at me, set down the bottle, and grabbed my arm—*Gotcha.* He had recently given up his karate studio, and the man I had known growing up—a ski racer and instructor with a PhD in botany, a black belt, a marathoner who often started the morning doing crunches while hanging upside-down on a basement machine—was dimming. His opinions softer, drawn in pencil not in pen. Still, his calloused hand was iron. I wriggled out of his hold and told him I couldn't imagine it any other way. His lip curved beneath his baseball cap, as if trying to decide whether to believe me. I smiled. A few seconds later, he did too.

The Russian language has different forms of the verb "to leave" depending on whether one intends to return. In truth, I was skeptical I would. Oregon felt both too socially restrictive and too geographically wide, like standing before packed bleachers in an otherwise empty field. I believed that to enter a place where nobody knew me was to take full responsibility for how I would be perceived, and that—narrative control, free from the hieroglyphic of the past—was what I craved. I did not want to be shadowed by the frizzy pyramid of my seventh-grade haircut or the way my parents danced after margaritas at the block party. Though I told myself I did not want to follow in their footsteps, deep down, I hoped I too might meet a man in a strange dormitory laundry room. That he would see me in my entirety, and ask for my number, and transform me into something whole.

In one way, the now-infamous story of roaming wolf OR-7 began when he was born into Oregon's second litter of wolves in over sixty years, not long after wolves killed Curt's sheep. On the other hand, the story we know is not the story of OR-7's life but of how we witnessed it. That story began when we were able to track him, a day like a second sort of birth. The day he got his name.

It happened in early 2011, the winter of my first year of college. The wolf, B-300's offspring, was just under two years old, and tensions around wolves in Oregon were running high. Two pregnant cows had recently been killed by wolves in northeastern Oregon, and in the eyes of the rancher who owned them, the loss included their two unborn calves as well, wrote Aimee Lyn Eaton in *Collared: Politics and Personalities in Oregon's Wolf Country*. Advocating for government biologists to hunt down and kill the wolves, the head of the Oregon Cattle Association described the cattle depredations like murder. Bodies ripped open, fetuses dragged across the ground. Ten days later, ODFW employees followed the signal of a wolf's radio collar to the nearby Imnaha pack. Their goal was to collar more adults so they could keep watch when the pack neared livestock.

The temperature that late February day was below zero, Russ Morgan later said in an interview. He was the ODFW wolf coordinator who had howled into the night. Now the chopper's blades would have shaken skeletal branches as the team zeroed in on the wolves among the trees. Russ leaned into the cold, sky whipping him from all sides, and pointed his tranquilizer at the wolf's hip. Telazol, the drug in the darts, could take five to twelve minutes to hit, longer if the wolf exerted enough energy to metabolize it faster. In that time, it was easy to lose the wolf in the trees, and hard to figure out where to descend to safety. And that's assuming you hit the animal. A dart gun needed a trajectory. A moving plane, a moving wolf, the swirling rotor wash of chopper blurring the sky. Everything could affect a dart's path. You didn't want to hit the animal's lungs or head or spine or belly, so you aimed for the hip and hoped you made it before the wolf was in the trees again. A shot, a stagger, a wolf on the ground.

By the time they located the two darted wolves through the deep snow, Russ and Roblyn Brown—then his assistant, later his successor at ODFW—could see they weren't the adults they were expecting, but a pair of pups just under two years old. Still, they did the dance. Drew blood, measured the bodies and paws, hoisted the wolves onto the scale, placed the tracking collars around their necks. The male, the seventh wolf collared in Oregon, thus OR-7, weighed ninety pounds. Later, when reporters asked, the answer would always be no: they hadn't taken any photos of him that day, it was too hand-numbingly cold, all they could think about was doing their job and motoring on.

Wolves often wake fifty to sixty minutes after being tranquilized, but they can be slow to resume activity—one biologist told me he sometimes referred to their behavior after capture as "sulking"— but eventually both pups began to move. Every few hours, OR-7's GPS collar tagged his location and stored it in a black box about the size of a computer mouse. Each day it beamed those signals to a satellite orbiting the world, which bounced them to a computer in Germany and then back to the ODFW office, all in a few minutes. If the collar had been stationary for more than eight hours, a sign that the wolf wasn't moving, it sent a mortality signal, alerting biologists that the wolf had likely died. If, as sometimes happens, the wolf had been poached and its collar destroyed, no signal would come. The silence was information too.

Most wolves survive the hangover stress of capture, but some do not. Biologists train themselves to steward a population, not an individual. They try not to get attached. Russ and Roblyn could tell from the signals that OR-7 had rejoined his pack, but his sister had not. A few days later, just five miles from where they had released her, they logged it: the rapid beep that meant a collar was working but a wolf was dead. Later Roblyn told me that while a "live" signal registers as forty to fifty pings per minute, death sounds twice as fast. With a collar registering eighty to one hundred beeps per minute, they knew the journey of the female pup was done. OR-7's, though, was just beginning.

How does a disperser know which way to go? In the end, I saw two paths. One was a college in Maine, with a quad full of Frisbee players and a dining hall that felt like a ski lodge. The other was in the Midwest, and it had Jack.

I met him during a campus visit a month after I was admitted, in the twenty-some hours I stayed to shadow a high school acquaintance. All her friends were beautiful and hip, like extras in an indie film I would have never known to see. I felt like an anomaly, though I wondered if I might be acquiring shine by proxy, if this was the place that would finally deliver me to full potential. That first Friday afternoon we stopped by the track to cheer him on. Jack was a few years older, a friend of my friend's, running toward us in a shimmering uniform. He was tall, with a dark aura of hair flapping above his cheekbones, arms loping beside his chest like two golden dogs. Was he winning? It didn't matter. His face wore, beneath the ache of fight, something else. Some curiosity that found my eyes, hooked me behind the knees and tugged. And then he was gone. For hundreds of yards, he would be a smear, and then our eyes would meet, and for a second, he would be crystal, and then he'd be gone. My face was a white flag, an open door. After the race, we held our hands out for him to slap. His attention was a heat lamp. I didn't want to turn away.

When we ran into Jack again, it was night, and he was wearing a plaid shirt and a cape someone had given him at another party, flapping toward us through the shadowy quad, a ghost flanked by a dark wing.

"You again," he said, matching his stride to mine. I glanced at my friend, and she grinned, peeled off to talk to someone else. Jack's words felt like a kind of miracle. On a campus of beautiful strangers, someone was seeing me. Unlike the high school acquaintance I shadowed, Jack had no obligation to talk to me. He was wry and self-deprecating and teasing and smart, and he had picked me on his own. "Tell me about my beloved school," he said, offering me a sip from the red cup that suddenly appeared from beneath his cape. "What do you think?" How did I answer him? I had just watched as my friend talked one of her friends down from swallowing too many pills; someone else she knew had just been carted away in an ambulance because she'd had a bad reaction to the afternoon's LSD. I was thoroughly overwhelmed by the prospect of making this place my life, but I was also swaying drunk, the first time I had been like this around strangers, the first time I realized doing this made them not into strangers at all.

By the time we kissed, we were on a makeshift dance floor in some wood-paneled house. My friend was long gone when Jack pulled the cape over our heads and socked us in black nylon. It was the first time I had met and kissed someone in the same day; the first time I kissed someone whose last name I did not know. As he pulled me into a back room and tipped me into an armchair, I began narrating our meeting to my friends back home, and then to Jack's and my future children, the way my parents had told us about theirs. We couldn't have been kissing for more than a few minutes, his hands up my shirt, when he started asking me to go down on him. Was this the normal college thing to do? Already? In this weird public room? My skin prickled, as if someone had opened a door, let in a draft, and walked away. I shook my head in a way I hoped was coy.

Describing her adolescence, Katherine Dykstra writes that she was "afraid of being beautiful, afraid of what it might inspire in a man . . . but . . . equally afraid not to be beautiful, to be a disappointment." I felt a rush of each at that moment, both the acute vulnerability of my situation—drunk and unmoored in a foreign place with an older man I did not know—but also the power that came from having been selected. For the first time in my life, a stranger had made his night about me. When I looked at my bare arms, they seemed to glow with the residue of his choice. "Victimized and seductive . . . is it disordered, in a sexually disordered world, for a woman to feel something of both?" asks critic Jacqueline Rose in her book *On Violence and On Violence Against Women*, swiftly deciding it is not. Each feeling brought a head rush; I could not disentangle them.

Elle a vu le loup, the French once said. She has seen the wolf. An idiom for a girl losing her virginity. And what then, I wanted to ask. Did she run away? Or did she chase it? Later I would think of the moment in the forest where Little Red first saw the wolf walk toward her. Not because Jack was a wolf, but because he, like the wolf in the story, was a stranger. What if Little Red had felt both wariness and interest in that moment? Could it be she saw the wolf and could not decide how to feel? I wanted only to make out with Jack, but also I wanted to dodge the weight of his disappointment.

It would be nice if he could fall a little bit in love with me before I left. To see the wolf not as flesh-and-blood but tracks in the snow, the specter of something that might, at any moment, come back.

And so I tried to ignore the things he asked me to do. Eventually his palm just found the top of my head and pressed. It felt like we were floating on a large lake, playing that game where I tried to keep my head above the water while he tried to make me sink. My neck ached. Still, some desperate lizard in my brain kept narrating romance—the immediacy of our connection, the way we had found each other, not once, but twice, on campus—while trying to just clip out this part of the plot. All day I had wanted to be confident and blasé, but my repetitions of "no" punctured that. Later, I would realize a part of me started hating him then for making me feel like a prude, for making me hate myself.

Eventually he gave up, or I said I needed to go home. I don't re-member. When he insisted on walking me back, I agreed. I wanted to be witty and fun again; also, I was lost. Once we were on the quad, he swung an arm around my shoulders, behaving as if nothing had soured. Had it, in his eyes? Every few seconds I remembered the frustrated whine of his voice and the pressure of his palm, but it was easier to forget. He asked me what my future was going to hold, as if it were a package I had ordered online that would be delivered any day, and whatever I said made him laugh. The laugh buoyed me. By the time we reached my friend's dorm, I felt sure I had crawled safely out of the lake. As if now I was lying beside Jack on the dock, body flayed to the stars, listening to the lap of water and wondering how it had ever felt too deep.

A few days later, Jack found me on social media. A few hours after that, I wrote back. Soon we were chatting on the phone, me in my childhood bed, him wandering the campus I wondered if I should join. Jack was both attentive and cheeky, a listener and a confessor, a reader and an eater. We talked about being from the West Coast, about having siblings more glamorous than us, about the incomprehensible kindness of our mothers. Early on I had written him a message calling him out for preying on younger women in his cape, but it was more flirt than reprimand, my only acknowledgment of the discomfort I felt that night. "He says he likes me more than anyone he's ever met. (I say he doesn't know me)," I wrote in my journal as he floated the idea of coming to Portland, or me flying to visit him that summer at his childhood home.

One day, I told him I had never really had negative adolescent experiences with men. Later he would lord this over me as proof of my naïveté, insinuating feminism was a club for prettier, worldlier girls. Only now can I look back on my teenage years and see how narrowly I defined—and thus narrated, to myself and others—"negative experiences." Operating in the logic of Little Red, I believed threat implied stranger. Someone who would shout or grab me off the street. The boy from school who kissed me while I pretended to be asleep at a party, his hands searching, my body frozen—what was that? I did not feel traumatized by moments like this, only woozy with shame to be locked inside a skeleton I was not sure how to steer. I tagged those interactions, like Jack's unwavering pressure on the dance floor, as blips of poor judgment. They were not *threat*, they were *boys being boys. Drunken mistakes.*

When it came time to decide on a college, I was careful to make excuses. It was geography, academics, a scholarship. What I did not say was that I could feel Jack's expectation and it worried me. I wanted to go far for college because I craved a story I did not know the ending of, and Jack, it seemed, had already conjured a happy ending with me. I moved to Maine.

In the months after he received his collar, OR-7 watched his parents. The breeding pair in a pack will most often initiate a kill, leaving the younger ones to trail and occasionally help. OR-7 might have helped the charge. Wolves want their prey to run. To flee, so they can corner it and rush its legs, trap it to the earth with their jaws. Sometimes the prey tries to buck a wolf, the canine's teeth still attached as she leaves the ground, sails into the air. But say the wolf wins. She will open the body cavity with teeth and claws. She pulls out the large internal organs first—slick purple heart, starchy lungs, nutrient-rich liver—then eats the stomach lining and the honeycomb of the intestinal wall, saving the smaller organs and marrow-filled bones and hide for last. OR-7 would have learned to kill, to eat, to cache food for later.

And then—on September 10, 2011, a warm day as far as I can tell, sky sun-bleached metallic blue, blades of cheatgrass rusting with autumn—OR-7 left home and didn't come back. Russ and Roblyn were monitoring a handful of other collared wolves by then, all over the state, so they weren't paying too close attention as this one crossed one county line after another, zigzagging southwest toward the Pacific. When they checked the computer in late October, though, OR-7's path began to stand out. The wolf had gone over 250 miles. Suddenly he was the first known wolf in western Oregon in seven decades. Walking toward that half of the state crowded with people and empty of wolves. Howling, alone.

A few weeks into my first semester, I left the college library around eleven p.m. to walk to my dorm. The quad of the snow-globe campus was quiet. The air smelled like pine trees and old rain, and my mind was full of Robert Hass, the California poet whose words I had been introduced to in class that week. His poems were full of droopy trees and fog-soaked mornings, and I was surprised how swiftly my longing for Oregon had gotten caught between his words, gathering like lint in a comb. The nostalgia flustered me, revealing a homesickness I had so far kept tamped down. That was what I was thinking as I kicked my sneakers through the moonlit grass: how sorely I wanted a sign. A sign I belonged here, in a dining hall of lacrosse sticks and pastel shorts embroidered with tiny lobsters; a place where people referred to "the city" and only meant one place, New York, even though many took planes to arrive, passing over other cities as they went.

As I rounded the curve of a shadowy path about two hundred yards from my front door, I saw a pack of guys walking toward me through the trees. I do not know whether to call them men or boys. I could not tell if they were talking, but they had the straight gait of people who were not engaged in conversation but purpose. Their bodies were muscular, solid as a wall of trees. "We are what we can imagine," wrote Hass in the poem "Winged and Acid Dark." Some spark plug in the root of my spine told me to panic, but I was what my parents called "jumpy" and I was trying to learn to control it. Besides, this was a small town of students and retirees on the coast. I was used to seeing others returning from the library at this hour, and I imagined the group would murmur hello as we slouched past each other.

They did not. When we were a few feet apart, the line of guys formed a tight semicircle around me. They did not speak, but they stared, and when I looked back, I saw their faces were masked in white cotton T-shirts, with slits for eyes and mouth. The white athletic socks they wore on their hands turned their fingers into paws. I do not need to tell you what my heart did in those moments, or for the rest of the night, or for the nights that followed. What happened to my body is that it froze. The men were fro-

zen too. It was a terrible dance. The moon gaped above us. *Pray*,
I thought. Also: *Prey*. Nobody talked. I waited for their hands to
reach for me; they did not. Finally, my body pushed through their
bodies and ran. Nobody followed.

Though I knew the story of Little Red Riding Hood as a child,
it did not make a big impression on me. My interest was held by
stories about those who defeated the odds, not those who were
defeated. I wanted stories I could live inside.

The version of Little Red I knew was some iteration of the Brothers Grimm telling. In that version she is still a damsel, but with the
addition of the huntsman she becomes salvageable. He is the friendly
passerby who heard loud snoring coming from the grandmother's
house and entered to find that "old sinner" of the sleeping wolf.
Sensing the grandmother is inside, the woodsman scissors the wolf's
belly open, and out tumble two victims. There will always be evil,
this story says, but that's where man steps in. In defining the wolf
as someone to fight and the girl as someone to save, the fairy tale
offers up the hero of "male governance," as fairy-tale scholar Jack
Zipes writes. It is as if this savior springs from the bone of a wolf
and the bone of a girl. He is nothing without them. In my memory, a man was always rescuing Little Red and killing the wolf, but
in the original Grimm version, she is the one who, once cut free,
gathers rocks and places them inside the sleeping wolf. He wakes to
a belly of stones "so heavy that he collapsed at once, and fell dead."
The huntsman walks off happily with his pelt, and the girl goes
home, flush with new resolve to obey her mother and heed the path.

You could say writing about the story today is, to take one cliché
to describe another, beating a dead horse. This is because the most
common iterations of the fairy tale, which stem from Perrault's and

the Grimms' derivative version, feel so obviously rotten from the root. Just as girls should not be punished for stopping to stuff their fists with bright sprays of flowers, so *Canis lupus* should not be vilified for the predations of two-legged males. Perhaps the thing I hate most about the story is that there is no coexistence, no restorative justice, just two creatures in moral opposition. Only one ever makes it out alive.

Because I was so sick of it, I was surprised to realize the further I got from girlhood, the more I thought of Little Red. At first I believed it was because the story carried all the lessons I needed to ditch. "Wolves are trapped in folkloric narrative that defines them just as firmly as women, and, like women, they are feared and reviled for their potentially predatory power," writes South African fairytale scholar Jessica Tiffin. If I just untangled Little Red's story, I thought, maybe I could free us from it—free the women, free the wolves. I could be the huntsman, smirking with my axe. I see now this was wishful thinking. In a fairy tale of regressive lessons, it was not the lies in the story that tugged me back. It was its bulb of truth. That fear, some fear, was maybe useful after all.

There is one more part of the story with Jack. A jagged corner of the puzzle—a piece I am not always sure fits into my life. It begins when a girl—I'll call her Anna—leaves home on an errand. She is not delivering a cake to grandmother, but she is picking up some papers for her mother, who works downtown. She is not in the woods, she is in Jack's Vancouver hometown, and it is a warm June afternoon, the summer before both Anna's and my last years of high school. Exactly one year later, to the day, I will fly there to meet Jack, and later, I will think: Would this day have happened if that one, a year earlier, had not?

The man who confronted Anna beside her car had just left a rehabilitation program. In the security footage taken a few minutes later, he was the one driving the car, with Anna in the passenger seat. When he pulled up to an ATM, she tried and failed to withdraw cash with the cards in her wallet while he stood beside her. Anna called her parents and said she needed money to buy food. They told her the credit card couldn't give cash, and she should come home. Later they would say they heard no fear in her voice. Sometime in the next few hours, her captor snapped. When police found Anna the next day, she was dead.

It was easy to read about the murder. I saw her face: I clicked. From the articles, and the photograph her parents released, I learned Anna and I were both seventeen, wore scant makeup, and had freckles and wavy dirty-blond hair. Newspapers described her as "bookish." I couldn't think of a time when I had read an obituary for someone who resembled me so much, and tracing the outline of her life electrified and horrified me. "It felt good, in a bad way, to think about my own proximity to violence. To imagine my life as a near miss," writes Rachel Monroe in *Savage Appetites,* her book about women's fascination with true crime victims. My comparison to Anna was superficial; it said less about knowing her than about the media's uneven coverage of the missing and murdered, that preference for white middle- and upper-class female victims who were conventional enough to be respectable, what journalist and PBS news host Gwen Ifill coined "missing white woman syndrome." Because women like this—Little Red, Anna, me—are most likely to be cast as innocent, we are more likely to be seen as worthy of public protection and, hypothetically, grief.

When did Jack tell me about their relationship? Some night over the phone in the weeks after we had met, probably, while I was procrastinating the conjugation of French verbs and sprawled on my rug, eating chocolate chips that melted into my sweating palms. He must have just said it: last year, a friend was murdered. He did not know what to do with his grief. They had gone to school together, and though he was older, they had been close, or something. I wanted to know if he had had a crush on her, or vice versa, if they had ever had too much plastic-handle tequila at a high school party and made out in someone's kitchen, or just had one of those moments I knew from my own life, where one friend drives another home and there's a minute in the dark, parked car where time slows and hearts speed up, but then someone opens the door, and the spell breaks—but in my memory, I asked nothing at all. I told myself it was because it did not feel relevant to his grief, but really it was because I could not bear to know.

The night before I graduated high school was the night Anna should have turned eighteen. A year earlier, she and Jack had celebrated the day with grocery-store cake. He told me this in a long, meandering email I woke up to the next morning. I read it repeatedly, trying to figure out how I fit into it and how I should respond. Here was someone he had cared about, perhaps just platonically, but deeply, on some sharing-birthdays level, and now, less than a year later, she was dead, and I was here, and now he cared about me. She should have been the one whose graduation he was celebrating: it seemed so obvious. I could not help wondering if Jack had seen a flash of Anna on the track when he ran toward me, or if he had just found me at the right stage of grief, someone who could adore him, or who represented enough of the same things to be worth chasing, to keep talking to even after I decided to go to school a thousand miles away. Unsure how to support him in his grief, I wallowed in horror, and also, unspeakably, envy. Not because of what happened to Anna, but because of the real estate I imagined she now held in his mind. I was greedy. I wanted to be the sole girl—the sole woman—in his skull. I sensed this made me a terrible person. I did not know what to do with the shame.

A month after I spontaneously traded my ice-cream shop wages for that ticket to meet Jack in Vancouver, we flew our different ways for college, and not long after that, when he offered to visit me in New England, I said no. It was not that Anna had come between us, but that I did not want to think about her at all. I wanted to fall in love without being reminded of other women dying. I wanted a world that, as the night on the quad would soon remind me, did not exist.

Within minutes of arriving back at my dorm, I called campus security and reported the masked men. The next day, an officer called me to confirm their identity on camera footage. Their headquarters was behind the little white house where I had just attended my first student newspaper meeting, and I kept my head low as I walked down the driveway, trying not to feel like a snitch. The security director was a tall, jovial Mainer with silver hair and a low baritone. He was so popular among students that he had become a sort of college meme, handing out plastic wristbands with Security's number and cheerily posing for photos with anyone who asked. Everyone wanted to be friends with him, not just because we thought it would get us out of trouble if we got busted for partying, but because being liked was anointment by the institution, and in a bubble of overachievers, that was a badge you couldn't turn down. If your nineteen-year-old friend was puking in the hallway, Security wouldn't get you in trouble; they would make sure your friend was safe. I didn't know if the masked men were a legitimate threat, but I trusted Security would solve the problem. Now, sitting on the edge of a plastic office chair, I watched a stream of silent video that showed the men keying into one of the dorms, jostling one another in the foyer like herded cows.

"That's them," I said. The officer, one I didn't know, ran a hand through his hair, shaking his head. "Creepy as heck with their faces and hands covered like that." I nodded. What else was there to say? These were the faces I would think of, years later, when reading about the ancient warrior men who, when masqueraded as animals, did things they would never do as men. The officer told me these were first-year soccer players who had been initiated. That is code for drunk. Hazed. Security staff had already spoken with the guys: they were very sorry about their inebriated "prank."

"They meant no harm," he said. That did not make me feel safer, but it did make me feel foolish: like I should have been in on the joke. When he mentioned some names, I recognized one as some-one who sat behind me in microeconomics, a guy who had already smiled and retrieved a pencil that I had dropped on the floor. He wore the sweatshirt of his boarding school and had the blunt, for-gettable attractiveness of a Ken doll. Then the officer told me the soccer players did not know whom they had scared, but they wanted to apologize face-to-face. I thought about it. I wanted to see how the men wore sorry across their lips. But some shard of my teenage self did not want to interfere with the equilibrium of that afternoon economics class, or anything else. I said I didn't need a personal apol-ogy. On one level, it seemed only fair. They had had their masks, and now I could have mine. I wanted to let them think I could be any woman on campus. That I could be anywhere, watching them. That at any moment I might step toward them, collapse the space, open my mouth. That the hunted could play hunter. Mostly, though, I did not want to be known for my tattletale fear.

In her book *Complaint!*, queer theorist Sara Ahmed notes that while a complaint is often necessitated by a crisis, it often becomes part of the crisis too. At some point after leaving Security I got a call from a campus dean, who apologized for what had happened and mandated that I see a campus mental health counselor. I began to wonder if, in the college's eyes, it was I, and not the boys, who needed fixing. Later that day, I called my mother. We were close, so I told her almost everything. Still, with a country of new distance between us, I wanted to frame things in a way that wouldn't worry her. I mentioned what had happened with the soccer players, but I spent more time making an anecdote of my visit to Security head-quarters, with its burnt coffee smell and its wall of little screens. She laughed when I laughed, and then apologized.

"I'm so sorry that happened," she said. We both knew that what this really meant was *I wish I could protect you from everything*. We were silent for a second, then I said, "It's okay," which we both knew meant, *I know you can't*.

Evenings were different after that night. Even once I learned the group had meant no harm, I called the campus shuttle to ride a few blocks, or I left the library whenever a friend left, or I did home-work in my dorm. Logically, I understood nothing about the state of campus safety had changed. The only thing that had changed was my capacity to understand life at the brink of terror. That, it seems, was enough. It was a waiting room I dreaded returning to. Inevitably, I thought of Anna. Of how she had been stuck in another waiting room, a room that had gotten so much worse. Melissa Febos makes a point not to say "trauma" in her memoir *Girlhood*, using "event" in-stead, a word that, while making me think of a conference hall and nametags, also carries an "etymology [that] suggests consequences rather than wounds . . . experiences that separated rather than inte-grated." We might have better language to define these moments, muses Febos, if they occurred less frequently. Every day men did far worse things than the soccer players did to me; I had been, for so many years, luckier than so many. But that night on the quad was the first brick to smash the glass, shattering the window between my lived experiences and my anxieties of what the world could be. It was the first time I accepted that the stranger coming toward me down the street might not just nod or ignore me; that he might be wearing a mask when he blocked my path. It was, in this way, a night for growing up.

I cannot remember what happened to the soccer players, or if they received any punishment. I am not sure what the charges would have been because I am still not sure how to narrate that night. "The limits of my language mean the limits of my world," wrote philosopher Ludwig Wittgenstein. Some moments I wondered what would have changed if I had screamed when the men surrounded me, making my fear and rage into a sword, or if I would have let them apologize in person, and then made small talk for four more years by the salad bars and library stacks. Some moments I wondered if I should forgive them and blame instead the "polluted and inescapable air of social instruction we receive from childhood," to extend Isabel Wilkerson's language about racial caste to the scaffolding of patriarchy. Should I let myself see the masked men as unwilling perpetrators, pressured into a drunken initiation ceremony by older men they felt they had to impress? Other days I wondered if I should try harder to erase the whole night from my mind. Not because it was the right thing to do, but because it might make nights easier. "Looking on the bright side of things is a euphemism used for obscuring certain realities of life, the open consideration of which might prove threatening to the status quo," wrote Audre Lorde. At the time I did not want to change the status quo, I just wanted to feel at home on campus. To wish less to fly home so I could lie on my childhood bed, silent beside our family dog.

The word "victim" has its roots in the Latin *victima*, meaning sacrificial animal. Could I be a victim if the boys had not meant harm? I did not feel like one, not exactly. I felt like a girl who had left home and learned a lesson. I had this in common with the boys. They who had just left home too, they who, like me, were learning their thresholds. What we could get away with. What could break us.

As the months passed, I wondered if that night stood out for them at all. In the college's eyes, they were just sheep. Sheep in wolves' clothing.

Years later, in graduate school, I found an old version of "Little Red Riding Hood" in the University of Minnesota archive. The library said it was from 1911; online someone estimated it closer to the 1890s. The book had a Kewpie-like girl on the cover, someone described inside as "rather forgetful, as you know, she did not think enough when she was told to do, or not to do something, that was why she was naughty sometimes, she did not mean to be, but she 'forgot' . . ." She reminded me I could not see the "symbolic biology" of the wolf without seeing what—whom—the "beast" was supposed to be chasing.

"The prey controls the predator," a biologist who worked in government wolf management once told me. It was a well-known maxim in the field, that you could not study one without the other. This meant one thing in an ecosystem such as Yellowstone National Park, but his logic could be applied to stories about other species too. In Perrault's telling, where Little Red is punished for being spoiled and gullible and absentminded, the wolf is animated in her inverse. He is scrappy, wry, cunning. Little Red's problem, as Perrault depicts it, is not that she has happened upon bad luck, it is that she has bad wiring. The villainy of wolf is propped up by the foolishness of girl.

And yet, in most retellings that have evolved from the Brothers Grimm, Little Red's wiring does not cost her her life. "The power of the damsel is that she provokes the protective urge," writes Ruby Hamad in *White Tears/Brown Scars: How White Feminism Betrays Women of Color*, a wide-ranging historical deconstruction of white womanhood and its long legacy as a form of oppression. White women prop up this privilege by performing the role they have been cast in: someone good and virtuous, ultimately, powerless. "It is this powerlessness—or, I would argue, this APPEARANCE of powerlessness—that governs the nature of White Womanhood," writes Hamad.

To be powerless, and to have someone see you and want to help you, is to have your humanity confirmed. Being helped, however condescendingly, is better than being stepped by on the sidewalk. Traditionally, white men's defense of white women's bodies has been less about inherent respect and more about the maintenance of alleged property. As pioneering Black feminist academic Hazel V. Carby said, "White men used their ownership of the white female as a terrain on which to lynch the black male." The white damsel is valuable to the white man not just because she is "his" but because she, in her constructed victimhood, supports his rise to hero. Her own power is limited.

The innocence of Little Red is, like the innocence of all children, more a projection than an innate reality. In *Minor Feelings*, Cathy Park Hong reminds us "the alignment of childhood with innocence is an Anglo-American invention that wasn't popularized until the nineteenth century"—around the time the Grimm Brothers' telling of the story was first published. Australian philosopher Joanne Faulkner notes three problems with the way this innocence is popularly conceptualized: it's a fantasy created by adults; it causes adults to demote children who have lost their innocence; and it keeps children from participating fully in society. In thinking of Little Red, I am most compelled by Faulkner's second point, that "innocence"—which we should see as both a protective shield and a handicap—is doled out unevenly by adults, metered by the codes of a justice system that, in America, still carries the DNA of the slave era in its bones.

Draped in this "innocence," Little Red becomes one of the first victims that American children may encounter. Her shadow looms large. "Eventually, we'll forget the thing . . . that changed us," writes essayist Matthew Gavin Frank, on the lasting power of cultural works. "We'll just be changed." Little Red is girl-as-prey at its most literal. In nearly every artistic rendering I have seen, she is also white. In books she is drawn like Shirley Temple; in a 2011 film adaptation, she was played by blond, big-eyed Amanda Seyfried. Whenever the story features a huntsman or a woodcutter—or, as in the propaganda version circulated by the Nazis, a man wearing the SS uniform favored by Hitler—Little Red seems to live. She is prey, yes, but also worthy of protection. This bears out in the contemporary United States, where the greatest predictor of who will get the death penalty is not the race of the perpetrator but of the victim. If a victim is white, their attacker is more likely to be killed. "Blackness . . . is already a stain and therefore unstainable," wrote Toni Morrison, referencing an October day in 1991, a day millions of Americans tuned in to watch the Clarence Thomas and Anita Hill hearing aired on live television. The day I was born.

"I was never taught that the world would nurture me, so I perfected the ways of hiding," writes poet and essayist Morgan Jerkins in *This Will Be My Undoing: Living at the Intersection of Black, Female, and Feminist in (White) America.* Because Little Red was nurtured—because she was seen, and fought for—her adoration separates her from arguably a majority of women, even white ones.

Maybe a woman is seen to have been unmarried too long, or had a child the wrong way, or sex the wrong way, or be incarcerated, or too poor, or not fit that narrow feminine ideal of beauty a man believes she should. A woman's "disobedience," in any of these cases, is not only a threat to the nuclear family but to the broader institutions of white male power that prop it up. It should be noted that when I write "woman," I lean on Ahmed's fluid definition of "all those who travel under the sign *women*," with the understanding "no one is born a woman; it is an assignment," and often an arbitrary one; it can change. According to a 2021 study by the Williams Institute at UCLA School of Law, people in transgender populations are more than four times more likely to experience violent victimizations than cisgender people, including rape and sexual assault; these numbers are highest for people of color. Though undoubtedly victimized by the storybook wolf, Little Red's identity inoculates her against systemic violence perpetuated by society and state. "Violence hovers around the deviant," wrote Ahmed. What I mean is that for all her victimhood, Little Red has power too.

What is easy to ignore amid the opera of wolf-in-drag and huntsman's axe is that Little Red is a story about a mother who has tried to warn a daughter and a daughter who has disobeyed. The child who reads the story may leave unduly afraid of wolves, but she may also leave sensing that the "naughty sometimes" Little Red has brought the predators upon herself. When her mother sends her off with cake for grandma, she does it with full knowledge beasts dwell in the trees. "Do not loiter on the way," she tells Little Red in the 1911 picture book. Her advice suggests the wolves—and we should read these wolves as men—are not the real danger. The danger lies within the girl's capacity to wander from the path. Perrault's story is not meant to teach boys. You cannot train a wolf. Only the girl has the lesson to learn. Only the girl can keep herself safe.

I had a middle school friend whose mother told her not to wear makeup on public transportation because she'd be more likely to attract unwanted attention if she looked pretty. When I asked my mother if this was good advice, she scoffed. Soon I was riding the bus downtown with a pocket of peanut M&M's and a backpack of library books. I barely wore makeup anyway—a swipe of mascara and lip gloss, maybe—but nothing happened to me, and I began to wonder if it was because my hair was too frizzy, or my body's angles too awkward. I suspected my mother knew this, and this was why she was not more worried about my safety. It never occurred to me to wonder if she just thought it more important to insulate me from fear than from the things that might spark it. In her book *Rape: From Lucretia to #MeToo*, cultural critic Mithu Sanyal writes that anti-rape activists have, paradoxically, at times achieved what some men want: "For a significant part of the female population to live in constant fear." I now see my mother just wanted me to walk, head high, into the woods.

What are the ways a mother can and cannot protect her child once there? Should and should not, will and will not? The mother in that 1911 version of Little Red bakes a cake for her own sick mother, bundles it in cloth, then sends her child into the trees with a kiss on the cheek before retreating "to get dinner ready for when she came back." This is the blunt ritual of a woman who has seen the wolves and lived to tell. But what to make of what happens next? Can we fault her for letting the leash too loose, if indeed, it was? Can we fault Little Red for stopping because she saw "a dear little mouse climbing a wheat stalk?" Can we fault the ill grandmother for letting in the wolf after mistaking his voice? In the right slant of light, the most prolific tellings of Little Red Riding Hood can seem less like a fable of predator and prey and more like a fable of a flock unable to protect one another. Maybe it is not fair to rob them of all responsibility, but neither is it fair to blame them for what happens next. The forest is already rigged.

Because the logic of "Little Red Riding Hood" is built on binaries—wolf versus woman, wild versus domestic, forest versus cottage, knowledge versus innocence—the girl's rules for survival are deceptively clear. The stranger will be the wolf, while Little Red's unnamed father, for example, will not. If men induce such warnings, the mother in Little Red is a reminder that women often enforce them. The advice we give is a story we tell about the choices we have made for ourselves. I think of that other heroine, Rapunzel, who was told the reason she lives in a tower is so no harm comes her way. Grow up as a girl, these stories say, and you better learn to dig a moat. They never mention you might be so busy digging to keep the bad things out that one day you may realize you are trapped. The stories reintroduce the wolf to make you feel the entrapment is for your own good.

Fear becomes a lever of social control, a tool of both solidarity and silence. If the shepherd in "The Boy Who Cried Wolf" is eaten because he has been too eager to imagine danger in the trees, Little Red and her grandmother are eaten because they are too reluctant to do so. They are not cautious enough. Maybe they are gullible, or maybe they are just wired with the optimism of the very young and the very old. It is a feeling I now miss. The ability to imagine, above all else, the best in the stranger at the door.

The part of that old picture book that sticks with me now is a page before the wolf opens his mouth. It's right after Little Red leaves home, when she stops for the mouse, and then, even after meeting the wolf, pauses for a "little squirrel seated up in the tree." I want to pickle her curious gaze. I want her mother to let her make this walk many, many times again, and I want Little Red to want to make it. Because we can't deny the presence of risk, the story carries a salvageable lesson of *be careful.* This is the truth that troubles me within the fairy tale. I am still learning what *be careful* means. How careful one must be, or should be, or can be. There is so much I want to throw out about the story, but I want to take a lesson too, from how the mother sends the child out, knowing predatory behavior exists out there but also knowing that to keep a kid out of the forest is to keep a kid at home, and what kind of life is that?

The animal most deadly to a wolf is a human, but the creature most deadly to a human is the mosquito—not the insect, per se, but the diseases they carry. The second most deadly animal to both wolves and humans is, in each case, another member of our own species. According to Ancient Greek scholar D. Steiner, "in myth, men who commit cannibalism routinely turn into wolves—not because wolves eat men but because such men have, like wolves, eaten of their own kind." A wolf will kill another because it is fighting for territory, or attacking a transient disperser, or, occasionally, in a struggle for power within the pack. It is harder to explain why a human kills a human.

There is no state in the United States more dangerous to be a human woman than Alaska. Its murder rate is around double the national average; the sexual assault rate is nearly four times the average, reported Alaska Public Media in 2019. These percentages skew higher for Native women, many of whom live in towns in the western part of the state, like Chignik, where Candice lived: towns inaccessible by road, where sex crime rates run twice that of the rest of the state. On paper, Alaska has the fourth highest rate of missing and murdered Indigenous women in the country, but experts in the field know it's higher, and many of these cases are essentially ignored. More than two-thirds of sexual assaults against Native women in the

United States are perpetrated by men who are not Indigenous. If, say, a white man commits rape or murder against a Native woman on her tribal land, the tribe cannot prosecute it, and it gets bounced to federal jurisdiction, where, per a 2010 study, around half of the cases were declined by the U.S. Attorney's Office. Imagine Little Red missing, and the woodcutter waving off the mother's cries as he sharpens his axe. In November 2018, the Urban Indian Health Institute reported that 153 cases of missing and murdered Indigenous women simply did not exist in local law enforcement files. As an epidemic of violence, these statistics suggest two cruelties. First assault—a life gone missing—and then silence. "The removal of evidence of something is evidence of something," said Ahmed. "And so: our evidence is often evidence of the removal of evidence." The lack of investigation and news coverage becomes a second form of erasure.

To talk about a woman dying by the teeth of a real wolf and not a metaphorical one is to talk about a statistical sliver of occurrence robed disproportionately in fear. After mosquitoes and other humans, people are most likely to be killed by snakes, and then dogs, which kill an average of nineteen people in America each year. Domestic dogs kill "orders of magnitude more children than wolf-dogs have ever been accused of doing," write Pierotti and Fogg in *The First Domestication*. To call a death by wild wolf a freak accident is almost to understate it. Throughout the twentieth century, there were no authenticated reports of healthy wolves seriously injuring or killing people in North America, not until November 2005, when a young man died in Saskatchewan. What those snowmobiling Chignik residents saw that March evening was that Candice had just become the second.

She was far more likely to have been killed by bears on that road, or to die from the cold. More people are killed each year by cows, by toddlers who pick up guns, falling vending machines, lawnmowers and lightning and ladders, autoerotic asphyxiations. And yet, I imagine Candice's death was covered in newspaper after newspaper because it was both exceptional and, for ears tuned to the song of Little Red, familiar. A bell we had been told to expect had finally rung: the wolves had killed the woman. Not just any woman, but the petite blonde one, grinning on the deck of a boat as she held up two freshly caught crabs, as the photograph accompanying a Reuters story depicted her. The BBC put "killed" in quotes when it headlined the death, as if trying to differentiate between the killing an animal and man will do.

In the toxic sediment of blog and newspaper comments that accumulated after news of her death, Candice—like Perrault's Little Red—was blamed. She was blamed for daring to run alone ("a big risk . . . she paid with her life"), for not tracking the season's dip in moose and caribou populations, for running without a "sidearm or some loaded weapon," for wearing headphones. The wolves were blamed too. For being bloodthirsty, for being "destructive intrud-er[s]," for stoking fear. The follow-up governmental report and bi-ologists' investigation was over forty pages long. It found that the two, three, or maybe four wolves who attacked Candice were not afflicted with any of the things that make a wolf most likely to be aggressive. They were not rabid or sick or starving, they had not been habituated to humans, they were not defending their food or young. Officials know this because, in the aftermath of her death, locals were told to hunt wolves. When efforts failed, bans on killing wolves in wilderness refuge areas near Chignik were lifted, and even the Alaska State Troopers sent in an officer to play assassin. Eight wolves were killed in the area, but when their bodies were examined, no identifying triggers were found, and no clear DNA match was found, though the report's authors speculate that at least one of the killed wolves may have been present during the attack. "This case represents one of the best documented cases of a predatory attack by wolves," wrote Linnell et al. in their most recent overview of global wolf attacks, adding that it "stands out from all others in that there were no warnings or underlying risk conditions."

Government biologists found, similarly, that Candice was not at fault. She was not carrying food, and sure, she was listening to music—headphones were found in the snow fifty feet from her body—but even if she had not been, she would likely not have been able to hear their progress. A wolf in the snow can move silently, appearing as quickly as a summer squall. The attack on Candice defied the statistical logic of those thousands of encounters where wolves have, upon seeing humans, fled. Tracks in the road revealed both were running toward each other down the curved, brush-flanked road, but the wolves would have smelled her long before she saw them. Footprints show that she sensed their presence at some point and turned around. The wolves would have easily collapsed the distance. Her death, the evidence shows, was quick.

It feels important to clarify neither Candice nor Anna are Little Red. They are just two young women who left their homes and were killed by forces beyond their control within eight months of each other, both within that first year I too was leaving home. The mechanisms of their deaths are, adamantly, not the same. "I do not consider the suffering that prey experience from a predator a form of cruelty," writes psychoanalyst Jeffrey Moussaieff Masson. The difference between humans and other predators, notes Masson, is choice. The animal predator does not decide to draw blood: he just kills so he can stay alive. Humans, of course, are different. This is why most wolf metaphors go slack.

I did not hear about Candice's death when it happened, and I avoided reading about it for years afterward, even when I started studying wolves, even when I was trying to understand the legacy of human fear in the face of them. I did not want to look at her death because it was such a freak accident. I did not want to privilege this wolf story above others. But now, reading Candice's blog, I am drawn to it as I am drawn to so many stories of those who vault themselves into the unknown. I found her story because of how it ended, but I stay because I am intrigued by the motor that made it go. "[F]eminism has nothing to gain by seeing women solely or predominantly as the victims of their histories," writes Jacqueline Rose. As she notes, the key question is not "How did she die?" but "How did she live?" With Candice, I return to her awareness of risk. "To be a kid again with no fear . . ." she had written after that cliffside hike, words heavy with an all-too-familiar longing. Her strength and courage did not negate her fear.

What made her do it? What made her go? Not just to Alaska, but into the wilderness, alone? Candice knew how many ways Alaska could kill her, and still she woke to jog through the frozen black, lashes iced, headlamp a little sun, the dogs she had befriended warm shadows beside her. "Why does the chicken cross the road?" asks essayist Lily Hoang. "Because I can't stop walking." Speaking to a reporter after her death, Candice's father described her as "small and mighty," someone who lifted weights and liked to box and was training for a race. When she ran, he said, she entered a meditative place. She died doing the routine she always did. When asked if the attack had changed his perspective of wolves, her father answered similarly. They too were just "doing what wolves do . . . Their nature happened to kill my daughter, but I don't have any anger towards wolves."

The aberration of Candice's death is what makes it hard to look at, but also, it seems to me, somewhat essential. Being human means learning to evaluate risk, but also learning to exist beside the statistically improbable. We cannot dwell on those stories, and certainly not sensationalize them, but what is lost if we erase them entirely? Now, when I think of Candice, I think of how many snowy miles she must have run in the months before that March afternoon. I imagine all her frozen footprints strung together, a shimmering rope of curiosity, the trail for someone fierce.

The year OR-7 left his pack, his travels were traced by collar, by camera, by witness. It was common for a young wolf to make a short, pre-dispersal journey before heading home, returning to his pack before leaving on a longer trip. OR-7, though, wasn't turning back. One day he walked near Crater Lake, the deepest lake in North America, banks frosted with snow. Another day he fed on a young elk calf who had died after catching its legs in a wire fence. One afternoon, former Iditarod racer and bed-and-breakfast owner Liz Parrish saw him at the end of her driveway. Standing beneath a fifty-foot cedar tree, his coat was dark and mottled.

"I was stunned—it was such a huge animal," she told a reporter. Liz knew wolves—she had seen them before in Minnesota and Alaska—but she wasn't afraid of them, even though she, like Candice, was small, five feet tall, nicknamed "Little Musher" in her races. Now, woman and wolf watched one another, unblinking. "We had a stare down that seemed like a long time, but was probably just a few seconds," she told the reporter. She reached for her camera. By the time she looked up, the wolf was gone.

After watching *Vertigo*—the Hitchcock film where a man becomes obsessed with a living woman because she reminds him of a dead one—writer Maggie Nelson asked her college film professor "whether women were somehow always already dead, or, conversely, had somehow not yet begun to exist." When I read this, I felt a thud of body truth. The insolvability of patriarchal violence is at its crux. "There was no adjustment I could make in my psyche or my life that would make this problem acceptable or nonexistent, and there was nowhere to go to leave it behind," writes Rebecca Solnit in her memoir *Recollections of My Nonexistence*.

When we feel powerless, we look for who to blame. I knew "Little Red Riding Hood" had not created what the World Bank would dub a "global pandemic" of violence against women and girls in 2019, but it seemed the popular versions of the story shouldered some responsibility for how I experienced it. They seemed like origin stories for a dominant narrative about predator and prey, one rehashed so often as metaphor. Not only do they unfairly vilify the wolf, they teach girls that to grow up woman is to grow up inside its belly, as if, in Anne Carson's words, "the entire female gender were a kind of collective bad memory of unspeakable things." In Perrault's and the Brothers Grimm tellings of Little Red, "the heroine [became] responsible for the violence to which she is subjected," writes folklorist Maria Tatar.

More than two hundred years after Perrault's publication, though, French folklorist Paul Delarue collected and studied the original oral storytellings that would have inspired the nobleman's curated adaptation, publishing a story—now the more historically accurate one—called "The Story of Grandmother." There are several differences between his and Perrault's, but the most important is that after the exchange about the wolf's teeth—in this story, he is a werewolf—the girl butts into the plot. Her fate swerves.

"Oh Grandmother, I need to go outside to relieve myself." The interjection is so surprising I laugh the first time I read it. The (were)wolf's response? "Do it in the bed." But the girl is persistent. Finally, he agrees. He ties a "woolen thread" around her ankle and sends her out. Once in the yard, she unties the thread and knots it around a plum tree. By the time he realizes she has taken too long, she is gone. He follows her home, but she is safely inside. The only hero is the girl, who outwits her captor then hightails it to safety.

In "The Tiger and the Children," the iteration of the story told in Eastern Asia, the child also frees herself with the excuse of needing a bathroom, and scholars studying the evolutionary route of folktales now believe it evolved from the same early oral storytellings Delarue later traced. Unlike the Brothers Grimm story where the girl lives but the wolf dies, in the original oral versions of Little Red Riding Hood, both walk free. "All fairy tales are about survival," says fairy-tale scholar Kate Bernheimer. In those oldest tellings, it is not just the girl who survives, but the wolf too.

The first storytellers of Delarue's iteration were likely peasant women, clustered in France and northern Italy through the late Middle Ages. In Europe, the fifteenth to seventeenth centuries were a time of skepticism and fear, a place where people were tried as witches and werewolves, where anyone's neighbor might one day be accused of eating children. Early tellings have been traced to regions where trials most proliferated. The stories passed on to young girls were meant to imbue resilience and strength in a world often inexplicably cruel. Perrault, though, was not a peasant. Life was easier for him. He was a civil servant, a staple at literary salons, a full-hearted proponent of King Louis XIV's absolutist regime to colonize the continent. In penning the story, he followed the established tradition of men hijacking a female-centered oral folktale long spun by rural women and stylizing it for a bourgeois audience, portraying both forest and girl as unkempt and in need of civilization. Characterizing Perrault's mindset, scholar Zipes writes in *The Trials and Tribulations of Little Red Riding Hood*: "Inner and outer nature must be brought under control, otherwise chaos and destruction will reign."

In rehashing Little Red, Perrault and the Brothers Grimm codified the male Western imagination of female victim. She is the girl who so often dies in horror movies, adored and innocent but streaked with a coyness and curiosity so often made to be her downfall. Someone who needs to learn a lesson. This male-sewn archetype was, admitted Charles Dickens, his first love. "I felt that if I could have married Little Red Riding Hood, I should have known perfect bliss."

When I think of my first flight from home, I think of Jack, and when I think of Jack, I think of Anna. I worry that to dwell on her death without knowing her life is to co-opt a tragedy, stitching her story to my side like another stolen shadow. In an op-ed written after Anna's murder, a journalist pled with readers not to co-opt her death to derail prison reforms. Her words made me think of one of the final sentences in the report on the Alaska Department of Fish and Wildlife investigation into Candice's death. "In spite of the findings in this report," the biologists wrote, "wolves are no more dangerous than they were prior to this incident, and people should not be unnecessarily fearful." Whether about wolves or men, the takeaway was the same, and I agreed with it heartily. *Do not become irrational. Do not make these deaths about your fear.*

I never wanted to dwell on fear, but I was not sure how to stow it either. I knew I was unlikely to die in a freak accident or a random murder; statistically, I had to be living one of the safest lives in history. The thing I could not accept during those years as I was leaving home was that so many others who died too young were, until their last minutes, also unlikely candidates. Someone is always about to become a statistic. Sometimes there is a moral, like *wear your seat belt* or *be careful hitchhiking alone* or *carry bear spray,* but sometimes there is very little. A man is suddenly violent. Wolves suddenly, improbably, attack a human. To draw a lesson from death is to milk a moral from it and make it something useful. A moral, by definition, teaches us how to live, but it never gave me what I wanted—a tonic to help me face the fact that I could, on any given day, die. As Anne Boyer wrote in *The Undying,* her memoir about being diagnosed with breast cancer in her thirties: "Every person with a body should be given a guide to dying as soon as they are born."

That night after I graduated high school, the night after Jack wrote me the long message about Anna's birthday, my classmates and I stayed up until dawn. We signed yearbooks and cried into one another's necks at the rec-center party our parents organized to keep us sober. When I finally got home and fell asleep, I dreamt I had been attacked. I entered the dream from above, as if my body were a corpse and I the spirit coming back to greet it. Lifting myself off the ground, I walked to a bathroom mirror and ran a finger across my forehead, stopping at a slash of claw marks. Somehow I knew what animal had done it. The wolf's cuts weren't fresh, but they were deep, a rake of red flesh already starting to scab. In between, my bangs sprouted through my wounds. My skin was growing over the claw marks and over my hair, the way a tree grows through the fence that restrains it. My body's resilience had made me into some sort of monster.

Overwhelmed by the gore, or by the sense of having survived something I shouldn't have, I woke up. "Wolf-bangs," I wrote the next morning in my journal. "Crazy." And then, a few lines later: "I am always anxious, worrying, scared." I felt haunted, but it wasn't from having narrowly escaped. It was from understanding that to be lucky enough to grow older is to learn how to be one of the ones who is, for now, still alive.

By my second semester in Maine, I felt rounder. I had stopped texting Jack on Friday nights and missed home a little less on Sunday mornings. I hadn't met a potential husband yet in the laundry room, but I no longer expected to. I had friends I loved. On the weekends we sometimes crawled into one another's twin beds and giggled until we fell asleep, dressed in the costumes of whatever theme party we had attended, bodies side by side, warm as dogs. It was exhilarating how quickly we became one another's harbors. Because the sun was usually down when I got out of class, I was often walking campus in the dark, and I grew used to my shadow stretching in and out of pools of lamplight. I learned to trust the groups of young male athletes who walked toward me would, a few seconds later, pass. That I would not flinch when they did.

I did not then know about dispersing wolf OR-7, so I did not see when, in early November of my sophomore year, the two-and-a-half-year-old walked into the eye of a trail camera outside the southern Oregon logging town of Butte Falls. A deer hunter had placed the camera on a forest tree. The black-and-white footage showed him with his nose to the ground and a cape of dark fur across his shoulder blades as he stepped through fallen logs. It was the wolf's first known time on film.

When people called in reports of OR-7, as a hiker on the Pacific Coast Trail did one day, ODFW biologists confirmed sightings by matching the rough coordinates received from his collar. As word of sightings grew, so did the aura of potential awe. "Wandering Wolf Inspires Hope and Dread," read one local headline. OR-7 wasn't the only wolf in Oregon, but he was becoming the most well known,

and media coverage of his long-distance journey was stoking conversations. Seeing a wolf—which had been near impossible in so
much of the northwest for decades—began to feel increasingly possible. As if the clouds had been scrubbed away, and now you might
walk outside and glimpse a shooting star where before there had
been nothing at all.

And then, one day, it looked like OR-7 walked very near where
the state's last wolf had been killed for a $5 bounty in the mid-
1940s. An endling; a startling. The thing about being a wolf was
that this information did not and could not land. It was outside the
realm of grief. It meant nothing at all. Whether the path of this
new, young wandering wolf inspired "hope" or "dread" in Oregonians, that last wolf would always be by his side. Less a ghost than a
shadow. If fear had led settlers to slaughter American wolves en
masse, the reminder of that legacy—embodied by OR-7's return—
was now, for many onlookers, alchemizing grief. A shame and awe.
A hope for the wolf that was coming back.

In the subsequent journalism and books that mention OR-7,
the detail about this new wolf crossing paths with that last bounty-
killed one is often noted. It wasn't until later, when I was tracking
OR-7's route, that I understood that to follow the story of a wolf
like this was to follow the story of our human reactions to it. We
were the ones who knew that to be born was to enter a world filled
with the shadows of those whose lives had ended too cruelly and
too soon. That to grow up was to learn to keep walking. Not away
from the shadows, but between and beside them. Into the woods to
grandmother's house we must go, and go, and go.

3

Town v. Wolf

When I was four years old my grandmother died on the Oregon farm my father grew up on. She was sixty when the pancreatic cancer landed like a witch's curse, turning her skin the papery yellow of a carbon copy receipt and shrinking her body down to bone. After one surgery, she declined treatment, aware it would bring her no more time, only diminishing the days she had left. In two and a half years, she was gone. An anti-nuclear-war activist and progressive organizer, an English teacher, a mother who raised her four young children abroad in India for two years in the mid-1960s while my grandfather worked as a doctor for Peace Corps volunteers. I knew none of those identities. I knew only Grammy.

In the cruel economy of childhood memory, I see her only twice. In one glimpse, she lies on the burgundy sofa in our Portland living room, framed in soft spring light, her arms nearly as thin as mine. In the other, she has health, or the appearance of it. She guides me to a dining table strewn with fire-colored maple leaves, each one flattened after being pressed inside the books that lined their living room walls.

Laying a square of white paper above the leaf, she rubs a crayon over the surface until its outline and veins emerge in color. *Now you try,* Grammy says. Trying to conjure her now—someone who disappeared when I was too young, who I did not have enough time to know—is like gripping that old crayon. The spine of her appears, a frilly outline, but it is a flat approximation of the life that once gusted through her being.

In the years after Grammy's death, Gramps traveled often. He learned German, then Spanish. Always, though, he came back to the farm, walking the dirt road to the sheep barn in his tweed hat and rubber Wellington boots, border collies leaping by his side. I grew up believing that because my father had roots on this farm, the farm had roots within me. Its moss a marrow in my bones. The fifty acres of land were outside Corvallis, hub of Oregon State University, about a two-hour drive from our Portland door. When I thought about being from the Pacific Northwest, I thought of these trees and the sheep that grazed below them, as if I had inherited their legacy the way I had inherited my father's toes.

It was one thing to fantasize about seeing a wolf streak a distant mountainside while I was hiking in eastern Oregon, but to think of one strolling the dirt road toward Gramps's sheep pasture? I couldn't help it. My pulse quickened. Not for my own body, but for the lambs. And not just for them, but for the people whose labor had kept them alive for so many decades. People I loved and didn't want to see hurt, or stressed out, or scared. My young father helping to carry sheep that coyotes had attacked into the garage so that Gramps could try to stitch them up; Grammy in her faded jeans, singing as she refilled their trough; Gramps nudging their wooly rumps with his hand-carved walking stick. Would the return of wolves threaten that herd? My earliest reflexive answer was so strong—surely!—that when I began to peel off the shingles of its construction, layer after layer of history and narrative appeared. The story of the wolf as threat to farm, family, and small-town American livelihood is, like the story of wolf as threat to girl, stitched into the fabric of national and regional history. Not a decorative stitch, but the very thread of its construction.

Because both my parents left rural homes to launch lives in an urban area, the days we spent between their own parents—at the farm, and at the house my mother's parents had recently built on land a half hour outside Missoula, Montana—gave me a sense of quilted identity. Everyone talked about the cultural divide that jagged through Oregon and the wider West, the headline-grabbing polarization of "us" versus "them," urban versus rural, but to me it never felt like a gulf, only a ditch to be jumped. When we went to Montana, I dropped the g's from verbs without my even knowing, stepping into the staccato of my cousins' speech. Mostly I felt proud. To have roots outside the city was to belong to something deeper than the cracked streets I biked. My relatives in the country possessed a DIY mentality that was easy to marvel at: deer made into sausages in freezer Ziplocs, giant gardens, neighbors helping neighbors care for sick animals and dig cars out of the snow. This wasn't my life, but it was adjacent to mine, and I could claim its ethos. Hidden beneath my tween sailor stripes and flare jeans and plastic choker necklaces, there was, I sensed, a tiny, plucky homesteader.

With its canopy of old-growth Douglas firs strewn in lichen the color of cucumber flesh, and those clusters of Lisa Frank–hued foxgloves, Gramps's farm felt like a sort of paradise. Trees so large they might take six or eight of us finger-to-finger to hug the knobby trunk. The gnarled arms of the white oaks twisting into leafy umbrellas that scattered sunlight into shiny pennies at our feet, illuminating the oaks' fallen galls, those dusty marbles that popped underfoot but glowed like lanterns when held to the light.

I had always assumed these galls were some kind of fruit or nut, so I was surprised when my father told me they were parasitic growths—the place a gall wasp has laid eggs inside the plant. As the eggs grow, they release chemicals that cause the tree to produce extra tissue, swelling into the protective "gall." The orbs can be striking ornaments, but even when their presence is harmless to the tree, their beauty is not the miracle I once took them to be. A gall is not a nest born just from labor alone, but from nutrients leached. When did I begin to see in the gall the story of so many American farms? Life is born—family cultivated, beauty sown—but to make room for it, life has been displaced.

Not far from the grove where we scattered Grammy's ashes, a pioneer cemetery hid beneath a plumage of blackberries and encroaching sword ferns. It wasn't much—a small plot of time-rounded gravestones enclosed by a low wire fence—but to the child in me, it felt like both an inheritance from, and an invitation to, history. Sometimes Annika and I acted like stewards to its nearly illegible stones, peeling the damp moss from the headstones until our fingers brittled in the cold. Later we learned this was the burial site for nine of the fifteen children born to the farm's first white inhabitant, the daughter of an Oregon Trail pioneer. The oldest gravestone was for a girl who died at fifteen after falling from her horse; the youngest for an infant boy.

Because we could not forget the sight of those stones, we could not stop imagining the heartache of those who once loved the bodies beneath them. The farm was a place of verdant growth, of chicks and lambs and golden plums, and the relentless life was matched only by a drumbeat of death. A channel seemed to run beneath the gummy red clay soil, bubbling up every now and then to claim the lambs born maimed whose mothers would not feed them, the raccoon whose still-fuzzed skeleton appeared in the clearing one rainy afternoon, a mystery we could not solve. I knew the channel ran through Portland too, claiming birds who had smacked windows and bicyclists hit by cars, but it felt more obvious at the farm, that site of the first grief I knew. Witnessing the "slow transformation of [a] landscape over time" transforms it into what naturalists call "a local patch, glowing with memory and meaning," as writer Helen Macdonald puts it. So much of the memory I read into the farm was melancholy. Sometimes when I walked the land, my hand jumping from splinters as I brushed the fence Gramps had built with hand-split cedar, I tried to welcome the dead. To find Grammy's dark strawberry hair in the light that buttered the daffodils. To imagine the pioneer children who had once carried water from the stream, laughing and crying until, one day, they stopped.

Psychologist Paul Bloom describes empathy as a beam that illuminates the suffering of some while leaving others cloaked in shadow. I see now that my childhood obsession with imagining the lives of the land's first pioneers was not just curiosity but unintentional erasure. Describing the European vision of the world that my child self had, by osmosis, inherited, James Baldwin wrote that it is "as remarkable for what it pretends to include as for what it remorselessly diminishes, demolishes, or leaves totally out of account." To lose so many children, so young, was an unfathomable tragedy, but it was not an invisible one. The headstones demanded my remembrance in ways the forest floor could not.

If I thought of the farm "before" that pioneer family, I thought of how dense the Douglas firs would have been without paths cleared to walk between them. An unruly place; a home for wolves and not sheep. Once a cousin and I tried to bushwhack a path up a hill behind Gramps's house, and a turkey launched herself out of a fern and into our faces, protecting her nest. We turned, screaming, her dinosaur wings and mother's shriek burned into our brains. We had known to be wary of the bull snakes underfoot, but giant birds? I never walked the hill again.

The years before white men forced themselves across America are often colloquially thought of as "pure" nature, the paradigm of "wilderness." But the Americas, of course, were already home to millions of human inhabitants working the land. By the time Christopher Columbus arrived, ten percent of the land was already settled or being intensively farmed, a reality that colonizers often failed to recognize—not just because settlements looked different than they did in Europe, but because they did not imagine Indigenous inhabitants were capable of such management. Gramps's farm is located on the unceded territory of the semi-nomadic Kalapuya people, "almost a pre-agricultural society," according to regional tribal scholar Henry Zenk. The Kalapuya slash-burned forest to create open pasture, creating habitat for elk and deer as well as for plants like camas and hazelnuts, which they ground and pressed into cakes for the winter. It seems plausible many of the area's sunny meadows, like Gramps's sheep pastures, were not cleared by industrious pioneers, but by those whose land they stole.

"[T]he 'end times' arrived for millions in the Western Hemisphere with the arrival of Columbus and countless species and ecosystems were condemned to make way for the 'progress' enjoyed by the Global North," writes Eddie Yuen in *Catastrophism: The Apocalyptic Politics of Collapse and Rebirth*. Throughout the Americas, 90 percent of the pre-Columbian inhabitants died before 1600, a number totaling some 56 million people. The Kalapuya population is estimated to have numbered 15,000 before contact with white explorers, traders, and missionaries, but by 1849, only 600-some peo-

ple remained alive. One estimate is that only ten percent of inhabitants along the whole Pacific coast and Columbia River survived
the spread of disease. Grief alone may not change an ecosystem, but
such death can. As human populations diminished, forests spread,
their greenery inhaling enough carbon dioxide to lower the Earth's
temperature by 0.15 degrees Celsius. "In many places, it was this
apocalyptic aftermath of the plagues that got codified as the 'natural'
state," writes Oregon journalist Emma Marris in *Wild Souls: Freedom
and Flourishing in the Non-Human World.* What settlers viewed as
"wilderness" was not a landscape *before* human influence, but after it.

Visit someplace you have "roots" and it is easy to encounter the
landscape as strata of story. At the top is the pulp of your own
sense-memories and lived experiences. As a fraction of the whole,
this is deceptively small; like the crust of the earth, perhaps only one
percent. Beneath it are those tectonic plates of ancestral gossip and
anecdote, the fossilized lore of family arrival. At the center is the
mantle of the past. Though this bedrock is the majority of total volume, it is too often seen only in glimpses, if at all. "To not remember
is perhaps not to feel touched by events that don't interfere with
your livelihood," wrote Claudia Rankine. In a country built on
colonization, resource extraction, and exploitative capitalism, un-
earthing the core means confronting the stories of those—person,
plant, and animal—who were forced out.

What, it seems worth asking, is a wolf? The Oglala believe all animals are members of their own nations, with wolves thus deserving
of "recognition as nations with full rights to live and move," beings who are "relatives" and "equals" to humans. To the Cherokee, a
wolf is a watchdog and hunter for Kana'ti, the power spirit of game
animals and insects. To the Pueblo, a wolf is a gift sent by their

creator, a magical spirit often represented as female with an ability to heal and instill courage, to know the night around her as easily as she knows her own bones. "In our astronomy / the Great Wolf / lived in sky, / It was . . . the mother of all women, / and howled her daughters names / into the winds of night," writes Chickasaw writer Linda Hogan in her poem "The Fallen."

To Swedish botanist and zoologist Carl Linnaeus, in 1758, the wolf was a creature to classify beside coyotes and jackals under the Latin genus *Canis*, for "dog." While *Canis lupus* were wolves, *Canis familiaris* were our pets. Linnaeus's main distinction was that the wolf was the one with the tail turned up at its end, like a comma flipped on its back. In recent years, after finding genetic differences between dogs and wolves to be negligible, scientists renamed dogs *Canis lupus familiaris*. The wolf in our family. Despite the challenge of biologically parsing wolves and dogs, mainstream Western views continue to champion the divide, persecuting one to the edge of extinction while the other becomes "man's best friend."

In Japan, traditional taxonomies once classified animals based on their relationship to human needs, organizing them by assumed medical and culinary properties. Wolves, unlike "mountain dogs," were edible, argued taxonomist Hitomi Hitsudai in 1695; though the meat was "tough" it would make its eater "courageous." These canines were further sorted by emotional and social context. There were different words for wolves, for mountain dogs, for honorable dogs, for wild dogs, for bad dogs. Unlike in historic Europe, where dogs might be groomed for royalty, dogs here were left to run and beg for food in the streets, blurring the distinction between domestic dog and wild wolf. The same canine could be a dog in the street and a wolf in the woods. Both canines lived at the fringe of human life, and because traditional livelihoods did not depend on livestock but on hunting and the production of grain, the wolf-dog was the one who protected their fields. Eighteenth-century Japanese geographer Furokawa Koshōkan explained that when the people of one village in northeast Japan spotted a wolf in the wild, it was common to say, "O lord wolf, what do you say? How about chasing the deer from our fields?" The predator was someone to be thanked.

Wolf as savior, wolf as mother, wolf as predator, wolf in brain. "If the definition of a dog is simply a wolf that lives with humans, we have a conundrum, because different cultures define their canid companions according to their own experiences, and the question becomes, who gets to make this distinction?" write Fogg and Pierotti in *The First Domestication*. They argue that the boundary between wolf and dog has been porous for the last 40,000 years, when coevolutionary relationships between Indigenous peoples and dogs likely began. In *The Lost Wolves of Japan*, historian and philosopher Brett Walker's chronicle of shifting Japanese perspectives around the predator, he argues that the distinction between the two canines did not calcify until cattle farming ramped up around the mid-twentieth century. That's when the Japanese government began importing wolf-killing techniques from the American west; the "father of Hokkaido agriculture," Walker notes, was an Ohio rancher who introduced strychnine to poison the region's wolves. The main thing that had changed about Japan's wolves was the economic world they existed in. Capitalism, among other things, had made the wolf a wolf.

Just as I cannot see this wolf without seeing the girl the fairy tales say he is chasing, so I cannot see the wolf without seeing the town—my town—that marked him as evil, chased him away.

One morning in the soggy winter between 1852 and 1853, Mr. James Ingram, a settler who lived with his family in the Willamette Valley not far from where I grew up, found that wolves had attacked his ox. The animal's ear was gone, and its insides were splayed, but its heart still pulsed. Ingram shot the ox, then dressed its corpse in poison. Strychnine is white, odorless, granular, somewhere between cane and powdered sugar. Within 10 to 120 minutes of first bite, the wolves that ate it would be seizing, their limbs and torsos locked into rigid sawhorse stance, followed by respiratory paralysis and asphyxiation. If the animals were lucky, death would come quickly, in one to two hours. If they were unlucky—if the dosage was small, or unevenly chewed across the pack—it could take up to two days.

The wolves did not return to feed on Ingram's ox for two months. It seems impossible other scavengers would not have fed on it, also that he would have recognized *those* specific wolves' return, but James Richey, the man who records the story some thirty years later, is sure of it. These are "monster wolves," he writes, and his account has the silvery sheen of a dragon slaying, of man-versus-nature at its most mythical. The "beasts" acted "crazed" after ingesting the poison, approaching Ingram's house "as if to hunt him who gave them the fatal poison." They made "night hideous" with "dying groans and howlings," footprints a frenzied music in the snow. Writhing with pain, the animals rolled against the front door. Their bodies slammed against the cold wood until, with a heave and a creak, the door fell open. The wolves were in no condition to attack. Whatever their jaundiced eyes saw, it didn't hold them, and the animals turned from the doorstep. When Ingram found them the next morning, they had made it less than a quarter mile from his house, their bodies crumpled shadows in the snow.

Lewis and Clark's expedition killed thirty-six wolves on their overland journey, but none were west of Montana. Lewis wrote that wolves were "not abundant" near the Pacific, "because there is but little game on which for them to subsist," likely due in part to the hunting pressures of various tribes. Still, the wolf as threat, at least rhetorically, persisted. In 1812, one man reported traveling through the Oregon territory, lost and starving, when a wolf ran before him and paused some twenty feet away. His account of the incident was frenzied—"I redoubled my cries, until I had almost lost the power of utterance"—but the wolf never attacked, only watched him silently then trotted away. In 1841, another settler described wolves as "very numerous in this country and exceedingly troublesome." By the time wagons of white faces began settling in the Willamette Valley, run-ins between predators and livestock had increased. Unlike early Texas and Colorado ranchers who raised herds of longhorn cattle— bullish and aggressive, with horns extending eight feet tip-to-tip— pioneers entering Oregon brought quieter, short-horned cows. These were bred for higher milk and beef yields, but floundered in the face of predators when let loose on the open range; one 1860s-era rancher called them "as helpless as most duchesses would be if left on a desert island." Though previous attempts at organizing a provisional government had splintered in the face of factionalism between the French Canadian fur-trading Catholics and the English pioneer Methodists, wolves provided a common enemy.

Two meetings in early 1843 were called to discuss the problem of predators threatening livestock. Though bears and mountain lions were included in the agenda, the gatherings are now referred to exclusively as the "wolf meetings." They were held in Champoeg, a town about thirty miles outside Portland. A mural in our capitol's House of Representatives chamber honors these historic meetings. In the foreground, men in tall boots take off their top hats and set aside polished rifles to shake hands with one another. Beyond them, in green pastureland punctuated by furrows of stumped trees, a crowd pumps both fists and guns in the air. "We deem it expedient for this community to take immediate measures for the destruction of all wolves, bears, and [mountain lions], and such other animals as are known to be destructive . . ." read an accompanying report.

These meetings catalyzed an executive committee to collect the territory's first local tax, which in turn created a bounty on dead predators. Put another way: my home state's first law was to incentivize wolf killing. Delegates set the bounty at 50 cents for a small wolf, $1.50 for a lynx, $2 for a bear, $3 for a large wolf, and $5 for a mountain lion, with Native Americans receiving half the payment of their white counterparts. By today's currency rate, a large wolf would be worth just under $100 to a white hunter. To get paid, you had to bring in a skin with the ears still attached. The bounty system exemplified what the slow-forming administration could do for its citizens, and in May, a majority of Oregon's settlers voted to approve the creation of a formal government. Hegel wrote that a threat of death has often been used to keep citizens in line; as Claudia Rankine later added, the minute one stops fearing death is the minute they stop being controlled by civil institutions. With the animal predator cast as a specter of death, central government in Oregon could take root. "The situation was wholly unlike that pertaining to the early occupancy of any other portion of our entire country," wrote Oregon's governor T. T. Geer in 1901, likening it to "a well-prepared romance." I can only imagine he meant, *Slay the beasts, take the virgin land.*

Was the story of wolves knocking open Ingram's door true? In the end, as with early moments in any dramatic "romance," the facts matter less than how they are remembered. Ingram's story entered the current of frontier history: that this is what it was like to be a man among the beasts. The teeth at your doorstep, even as you had the upper hand. A page later, the same account mentions Ingram guarding his home against "marauding Indians." His stoop, it seems, is perpetually under threat. The phrase "keep the wolf at the door" has its roots in the peasant poverty of medieval England. If you were hungry, the wolf was said to be at your door—hungry, implicitly, for you. In this light, the wolf was the arrival of starvation, of hunger taken to its highest pitch. To see the wolf walk over your doorsill was not to see yourself as a passive victim, but as someone who had already failed to enforce a boundary. Someone unable to provide for, and protect, their family.

In his novel *Mating*, Norman Rush describes the concept of a "lore package" as that narrative shield we carry for safety, to make sense of the world. By choosing to believe that lions are "torpid during the day," Rush's narrator buys herself a break from fear. When I read this, I underlined it: I liked the idea of limiting lore to a package. Our arms can only carry so much. When I am camping, I need to believe the tent is my safe zone. When I am road tripping, that space becomes the car. My lore package is that I will be safe in those thin walls, that things like hail and snakes will obey the boundary I have made. The idea that wolves could open Ingram's door was the idea that wilderness could breach the walls of so-called civilization. Not only did it threaten family, it threatened the lattice of control settlers had created. "Killing wolves, of course, was a sign of progress . . . such work implied extending the bounds of civilized space," wrote environmental historian William Robbins in *Landscapes of Promise: The Oregon Story, 1800–1940*.

To have control is to create and enforce expectations for acceptable behavior. It depends on sorting, and on labels. The dog let into the house; the wolf kept out. Walker chalks Japan's vernacular distinction between "mountain dogs" and "wolves" up to "some last-ditch effort to distinguish humans, the creators of artifice, from the rest of the natural world." But how different are we? A body can be porous. Many Indigenous cultures see the spirit world and the natural world as so interconnected that a body might move between them, the way a candle can slip back and forth between liquid and wax, the self able to move between human and animal forms. You might see a wolf and know it to be your sister.

The wolf is central to the creation story of the Kalapuya, on whose homeland the "wolf meetings" unspooled. Tribal elder Esther Stutzman has shared the story publicly, describing a world once made entirely of stone. One day, the top of a mountain came to life to reveal earth's first woman, Le-lu, with two babies by her side. As she walked down the stone mountain, grass and rivers appeared. At its base, Le-lu met Mother Wolf, who offered to watch her children while she explored the world. Le-lu felt a bit afraid, but she wove a pack basket and strapped the babies to the wolf's back, weaving a thick band around their foreheads so they would not fall out. She was gone a long time, but she returned to find her babies safe. As she unstrapped them from the basket on Mother Wolf's back, she noticed her children's heads had been flattened from the band. "From now on our people will flatten the foreheads of their babies in honor of Mother Wolf, who took such good care of my babies," Le-lu said, in Stutzman's words. This Kalapuya story emerged from the same ecosystem as that wolf-killing "creation story" of Oregon's statehood, the same landscape as the fern-dense, mossy forest of my grandfather's farm. Both stories hinge on an interaction between local humans and wolves, but their outcomes could not be more different.

Colonization not only dampened such modes of Indigenous knowledge, it attacked them, displacing and killing the people who spoke them. Until the 1978 passage of the American Indian Religious Freedom Act, it was against the law for Indigenous peoples to share stories or songs. "They are intrinsic to cultural sovereignty," writes U.S. poet laureate and Muscogee Nation member Joy Harjo. "To write or create as a Native person was essentially illegal." A decade after the "wolf meetings," the Kalapuya and other area tribes were made to cede the entire Willamette River drainage area to white settlers; relocated to the Grand Ronde Reservation in the Coast Range, tribal members were pressured to take up farming. Barred from U.S. citizenship, they could not step off the reservation without a pass. "This country is not good now," said John Hudson, a Kalapuya member thought to be the last known speaker of the language. "Long, long ago it was good country."

In the settlers' wake, and with the nuance of Indigenous wolf stories essentially silenced, the stark binaries of Christianity prevailed. Wolves, mentioned thirteen times in the Bible, appear primarily as a metaphor for greedy destruction, a foil to triangulate one's own "good" identity off. "Binary oppositions, oversimplified as they are, leave no room for individual distinctions and complexity," wrote Ruby Hamad. "The existence of a binary means that one pole in the structure is always going to dominate."

For as long as white people have been coming to America, they have been kindling the story of their own belonging, erasing the stories of early inhabitants, in part by conflating them with animals. One piece of seventeenth-century legislation in Massachusetts said that "[w]hoever shall shoot off a gun on any unnecessary occasion, or at any game except an Indian or a wolf, shall forfeit 5 shillings for every shot." As if shooting a wolf or a Native meant nothing at all.

The work of statehood is at first the work of boundary creation. Not just erecting a border but policing it, deciding: Who do you let in? Who do you push out? If I once thought these questions were posed in one way about humans and another about animals, the wolf has shown me otherwise. Often, it is only by anthropomorphizing animals and animalizing humans that the fictions that necessitate human borders can be propped up at all.

One of the first white naturalists to carry animal specimens east from the Pacific Northwest was an ornithologist named John K. Townsend. Traveling through the Columbia River valley in the 1830s, he wrote that the "depopulation" of Indigenous peoples due to European-borne illnesses in the area was "truly fearful": "[I]n a very few years the race must, in the nature of things, become extinct; and the time is probably not far distant, when the little trinkets and toys of this people will be picked up . . . as mementoes of a nation passed away for ever from the face of the earth." Their expedition trespassed on.

Townsend became a celebrated naturalist, selling many previously uncategorized species to John James Audubon, who put them in his canonical *Birds of America*. Did Townsend understand, then, that his own work was endowing him with a textbook immortality? Over a hundred years later, wolves like B-300 and OR-7 had likely crossed paths with creatures who carried his name: Townsend's mole, Townsend's vole, Townsend's pocket gopher, the white-tailed jackrabbit (*Lepus townsendii*), and any number of others.

What is in a name? Taxonomy—the classification and organization of organisms based on shared characteristics—is the language of biology. It is how scientists track what species exist and how they are connected to one another; increasingly, it also tracks what is disappearing. But taxonomy reveals more than bodies. As a map made by humans, it also reveals culture. "The ways in which scientific research is implicated in the worst excesses of colonialism remains a powerful remembered history," writes Indigenous scholar Linda Tuhiwai Smith in *Decolonizing Methodologies*. Knowing the name "Townsend's ground squirrel" does not help me, an amateur, identify the squirrel; it helps me identify the white man who shot the animal down.

Carl Linnaeus, that grandfather of the field, was not only responsible for first classifying wolves and dogs, but for sorting humans as well. In publications between 1735 and 1759, he listed six subdivisions of *Homo sapiens*: *H. americanus, H. africanus, H. europaeus, H. asiaticus, H. monstrosus*—which posited various remote tribes of allegedly monstrous "exotic" peoples—and *H. ferus*, the so-called wild men. His classifications included information about physical traits as well as behavior and custom, the sorts of things we would now recognize as learned action—as culture—but which fed the idea that groups of humans were internally different. His 1753 description of African women as "without shame," for example, persisted for centuries, buttressing antebellum laws that legalized the rape of Black women. In Linnaeus's view, a distinction between "them" and "us" was indisputable, as objective a difference as that between a flamingo and an owl. Though biologists and geneticists no longer believe in the idea of distinct physical races, they still believe in the legacy of racism, seeded by the "belief that races exist, and that some are better than others," as Nell Painter writes in *The History of White People*. Linnaeus's definitions of race, which for so long organized social and cultural differences under the disguise of biology, persist today.

Townsend, meanwhile, plundered skulls from Native American gravesites, subscribing to the belief that the measurements of a man's head could reveal the traits of the human it belonged to. At forty-one, he died, poisoned by the arsenic he insisted was the "secret" ingredient to his taxidermied specimens. I suppose he was good at his job: his writing vibrates with reverence for the creatures he encountered. Hidden, though, are the hands of the Indigenous people who helped him find the most elusive specimens. Though Townsend was not the first white man to write about Oregon, his perspective speaks to two engines of imperial inquiry. The pursuit of knowledge, sure, but also control. As if the way to make a new world was not just to break the old one but to deny the breakage altogether. To deny there was anything to break. In relegating a place's local inhabitants to past tense, the colonial mind transforms the evidence of life—Townsend's "little trinkets and toys"—into tokens to pocket, to ship home, to put behind a glass case, eventually to forget.

Constructing a boundary is always a form of shaping selfhood. In defining what is "inside" territory, you are also defining what—who—sits in the shadow beyond. Many of the borders we encounter are spatial, like the road or river turned to a thick line on a map, but many others are unseen. The neighbor's dog who used to run across the lawn at me, and just when I thought he would attack, leapt back with a yelp at the invisible current of a fence, as if smacking a glass wall. In researching perceptions of wolves in Albanian villages, anthropologist Garry Marvin found that canines who wandered into human settlements were considered rude travelers. They showed up unannounced, failed to obey the rules of hospitality, and ate what they wanted. In disavowing local custom, they would never be "guests." The boundaries those wolves bumped into were not only unseen but cultural—fictional—determined by laws, traditions, emotions, and etiquette. Though such borders can be matters of life and death, they can also, paradoxically, change on a whim.

It wasn't until I began thinking about wolves moving into "human land" and vice versa that I began to consider how quiet the breaches of boundaries can be, unknown even to those who are doing the breaching.

No human witnessed that tipping point where OR-7 became "at least temporarily, a California resident," as a local newspaper put it the following week. The wolf had been walking three hundred miles when he crossed the southern border of Oregon somewhere in the shallow freshwater marshland of the Lower Klamath National Wildlife Refuge. In the three and a half months since he had left his family, he had cut a diagonal across one state, and was arriving now at the lip of another.

On December 28, 2011, the temperature hovered around 40 degrees. The air was sodden with a damp chill, no snow, just the hulk of Mt. Shasta iced white in the distance. There was a poetic justice to this roaming wolf crossing the border here, on land designated by Theodore Roosevelt as the nation's first refuge for migratory waterfowl once nearly hunted to extinction. Winter at the refuge was the season for bald eagles, their wingspans wider than my six-foot-something father is tall, silhouettes unzipping the sky as they searched for fish made sluggish in the cold waters below. Beneath them the grasslands of the refuge would have pulsed with tundra swans, their necks the bright white of plastic clothes hangers in the soggy gold fields, their thin black beaks rising and falling to the grain like the jumping needles of a thousand sewing machines. Like wolves, these swans are known to feed in moonlight. Though that night of December 28 brought just a fingernail moon, imagine if that wolf had suddenly appeared, running toward them at eleven miles an hour: the scalloped shells of their wings unfolding as they rose, en masse, into the air.

Once again, OR-7's route had led him into human superlative, becoming the first wolf to enter California since the last one had been killed in 1924. On January 5, the California Department of Fish and Wildlife (CDFW) created a website for him and began posting about his status. "This animal can easily cover more than 40 miles (straight line distance) in a day, and of course, an even greater distance as a wolf travels," noted the first blog post. The words were matter-of-fact, but they seemed to hum with unmentionable possibility, as if any Californian might soon wake to find a paw print in the yard.

"He remains in forested habitat providing both cover and food resources," wrote the CDFW dispatcher. Three days later, just one line appeared: the wolf had moved only a few miles. The next update, which came two days later, had even less information. Cloudy skies were preventing his collar's GPS from transferring data. Over the border but under the radar, OR-7 had disappeared.

In the legend of Saint Francis, a wolf is said to threaten village life in the medieval Italian town of Gubbio. This is a town of orange-tiled roofs and stone houses, many of which still contain two entrances side by side, with one just a narrow opening a foot or so above the street. No one quite knows why Gubbio's houses have two doors. Some say one door was for lifting coffins out of the house, but it seems more likely it was an act of security. You could barricade the main door and defend the small one, peeking down onto the stranger below. It was in this village, amid this architecture of defense and doubt, that a wolf began to prowl.

First the animal preyed on livestock, but eventually it prevented people from leaving the town at all. Flush with belief that God would protect him, Saint Francis ignored the warnings of his fellow townspeople and exited the walled town, hiking into the forested mountains beyond. According to some Catholic accounts, the wolf charged toward him, but when he raised his hands into the symbol of a cross, the creature went slack, "meek as a lamb" at his feet.

With a notary as witness, Francis offered the wolf a now-legendary pitch: residents would feed him and let him roam the village in peace, but in return, he must never harm a human or animal inside. This conversation and its aftermath are now memorialized in Western art. In a painted altarpiece displayed in London's National Gallery that shows Francis introducing the wolf to the town, he holds the animal's paw with the tenderness of a parent bringing a small child to school, trying to coax her to trust the teachers.

In the legend, their trust is mutual. Francis becomes known as a patron saint of animals, and the people live happily ever after, leaving scraps each morning for the wolf. Evil wrangled. What the story suggests, but does not say, is that the wolf has just become a dog.

Short of saintly intervention, what explains the trajectory from wolf to dog? Did certain wolves choose us, or did we choose them? Details around the forks in canine lineage are still contested by scholars and scientists, but the divide between dogs and wolves likely stemmed, at least in part, from fear. Most wolves would have been afraid of humans, skittish and aggressive. Not only were we predators, we competed with them for big game. In one hypothesis, those wolves who acted differently—the brave or the brash, those who approached humans for food, circling encampments for scraps—would have gained what evolutionists call an "advantageous foothold." In the words of Brian Hare, director of the Duke University Canine Cognition Center: "We did not domesticate dogs. They domesticated themselves." It was, in his view, "survival of the friendliest."

I understand his evidence, but a part of me questions the value it puts on domestication, as if becoming a dog was the smart way to go. Evolutionarily, sure, there are more dogs than wolves. For centuries, humans have poisoned, shot, trapped, caged, and skinned wolves, one tortured verb after another, while dogs have been thrown bones, cocooned in pleather raincoats, welcomed into human beds.

But is the easier life always, unequivocally, the better one? There is a proverb from the Eastern Caucasus, spoken by the aboriginal Dargva people, which translates to "A wolf does not bark like a dog, but searches for his sustenance." The Dargva identify with the wolf, taking pride in the distinction between the canines. They are proud to be the self-sufficient ones. It makes me think of a study where researchers gave both dogs and wolves a locked box full of food. The dogs soon stopped trying and looked at the humans, pleadingly, while the wolves tried to open it until the test ran out. Dogs have lost up to thirty percent of their brain size compared to wolves, as relative to body weight. They rely on us to eat. "Man took the (free) wolf and made the (servant) dog and so made civilization possible," wrote Donna Haraway in *The Companion Species Manifesto: Dogs, People, and Significant Otherness.*

When I think of Hare's theory for those first dogs, I imagine a fire. Humans swatting mosquitoes, drinking something fermented, tearing at a leg of deer blackened on a spit. Somewhere in the shadowy brush, two wolves. Smelling man but mostly the salted char of meat, noses twitching more than 10,000 times better than our own. One of the humans picks the gristle from the ditch between his yellow teeth and throws a bone over his shoulder. On the outskirts, one of the wolves stamps his front paws, a nearly inaudible whine. For a minute, maybe, there is the suspension of fate: Will he, won't he? Then he does. Darts toward the fallen bone. So easy to grab the food and come fold himself back in the shadow, to return night after night. Evolution is far from a clear flowchart of cause-and-effect—as paleontologist Stephen Jay Gould once said, it is more like "a drunkard's walk"—but we can imagine how she might have learned life at the edge of camp. Archaeologists call this the "trash pile theory" of canine domestication.

This trajectory is all well and good, but it is not the canine I am interested in. I am less curious about the one who joined than the one who did not. The one who shunned our protein, our heat. Because I do not want to see the wolf as some less-evolved dog, I wonder: Might there be the sting of rejection in the reigning Western treatment of the wolf? I think of the phrase that has echoed through the centuries, from the Hebrew Bible's Book of Joshua to the words of Matthew, Mark, and Luke; from Russia's Lenin to Italy's Mussolini to America's George Bush and Sarah Palin—"You're either with us or against us."

In my favorite childhood Disney movie, *Beauty and the Beast*—never mind the depictions of killer wolves, I liked that Belle had a ladder on wheels to reach walls full of books—Gaston, that arrogant hunter with oiled man-bun, shouts those same words as he incites the townspeople to raise their pitchforks and enter the woods. Their mission, ostensibly, is to save their "Beauty," but it is clear their red-eyed giddiness bubbles more from loyalty to one another than to her. It is a familiar story of white womanhood, with Belle's body a terrain for killing the "Other." The men are drunk on self-righteousness and that shallow adolescent confidence of knowing who you are because you have ostracized who you are not. "Kill the beast!" cries the mob behind Gaston. "Kill the beast!" And so they light their torches, and walk into the trees.

A year after Oregonians passed the wolf bounty, that same provisional legislature passed a bill that required settlers holding enslaved people in Oregon to remove them from their land within three years or see them freed. This sounds progressive, but its goal was not to reform slavery but to eliminate Blackness entirely. As noted in the historical archives on the website of Oregon's secretary of state: "The great majority of . . . new Oregonians simply wanted to create an all-white society free of the racial problems threatening to cause an American civil war." Under the new policy, "freed negroes" over eighteen were told to leave the state or face trial. If they lost, they would receive "not less than 20 nor more than 39 stripes." This punishment, referred to as the "Lash Law," would be repeated every six months until the person fled. No evidence exists that the law was enforced, though I am skeptical evidence would have ever been collected. Historians agree the law was a powerful deterrent to potential Black settlers.

Fifteen years later, in 1857, and on the brink of joining the union, Oregonians voted on two unique clauses in the fledgling constitution. First, they rejected slavery by a vote of 7,727 to 2,645. As a child I believed this happened on moral grounds—that it was because the canyon-carved west, as a landscape and a state of mind, was more free—but I saw what I had been taught to see, which is what so many white Oregonians wanted to see. It was not the truth. "In arriving at this conclusion we are not influenced by hostility to the institution of African slavery per se . . . [W]e think that our climate, soil, situation, population, etc., render [it] to any useful extent an 'impossible' institution for Oregon," wrote Asahel Bush, an editor of the *Oregon Statesman* newspaper.

Second, citizens voted to exclude free Black people and "mulattoes" from the state by a vote of 8,640 to 1,081. "We were building a new state on virgin ground; its people believed it should encourage only the best elements to come to us," said one commentator at the time. Chief Justice Williams urged his colleagues to use the constitution to make Oregon a state exclusively for white inhabitants, excluding "the negro, Chinaman, and every race of that character." Two years later, my home state joined the union. It was the only one ever accepted with a Black exclusion clause in its constitution. As South African journalist Mark Gevisser would later write: whiteness is a world defined "by what it ha[s] been walled against."

In the years after the Civil War, Oregon's pro-South weekly the *Democratic Review* published a tirade against the state's remaining Black inhabitants. The editor described them as, among other things, "wooly headed, [and] animal jawed." The animalization of the Other and the humanization of the beast have long gone hand in hand, but it wasn't until reading those settlers' accounts that I realized just how deep in Oregon's bedrock the conflations went. To think about the plight of the wolf was to think about the people who had created the bounty laws incentivizing its persecution, those same people who then laid the foundations for the state, deciding who could root within its borders.

In 1850, the U.S. Congress passed the Oregon Donation Land Act, promising 320 acres to any white settler who could farm it. Hawaiians, Native Americans, and African Americans were excluded; Black settlers on the Oregon Trail tended to branch south to California. That question of who could till the land, tend the farm, die old beneath the trees—it was not, as the pioneer wisdom I learned as a child proclaimed, just about the strongest ones surviving. It was about who was allowed the chance to try.

I was a teenager before it sunk in that my father's parents did not, in fact, have Oregon roots. My grandmother, born in Queens, New York, to a homemaker and minister, had gone to high school in San Diego; my grandfather was born in Berkeley. They were married in a stone church in New Haven, Connecticut. For the first time I felt a shudder of dislocation from the farm. Surprise at how quickly I had come to feel as if the land, after just a few decades, had always been ours. It was easy to collapse the pioneer gravestones and my grandfather's muddy boots into the same legacy of toil and renewal, that slog to cultivate life beneath dripping trees. To sum the sweat and soil as if it meant that we belonged—as if it meant the land belonged to us.

When not raising sheep or working in town as a pediatrician, Gramps was a dedicated environmentalist, and a longtime member of the Sierra Club, the largest grassroots environmental organization in the United States. In 1968, at thirty-two years of age, Gramps's younger brother Phil was elected the organization's youngest-ever president. That was the year the Environmental Protection Agency was established, the year the first Earth Day was celebrated. Phil went to the White House to shout at Nixon about energy use, and he attended protests at the Standard Oil building, his arms holding a poster with a photograph of oil-slicked birds sprawled on the beach with the words STOP DRILLING IN THE GULF drawn under it in capital letters. In 1991, he was elected to a second term. I never knew Phil well, but I imagined his fingerprints when I read about the organization in history class: how they had blocked dams and coal-fired power plants to expand parks and protected areas, indelibly shaping the scope of not just the American wilderness but environmentalism writ large. Gramps was involved in the organization too, frequently attending trips in the years after my grandmother died. I thrilled at the chance to tag along, marveling at the giddy, canonized nature writing of its founder, John Muir.

"When we try to pick out anything by itself, we find it hitched to everything else in the universe," wrote Muir in *My First Summer in the Sierra*. I first learned his words as a testament to ecological complexity, an ode to the inextricable symbiosis of an ecosystem. Only later did I read, in Michelle Nijhuis's history of modern conservation movements, *Beloved Beasts: Fighting for Life in an Age of Extinction*, that while hiking in those mountains Muir had come upon a group from the Mono tribe and decided they "had no right place in the landscape." He did not understand that their labor had made the meadowed terrain he so loved. It was as if he had forgotten his own observation, as if the Indigenous inhabitants of a place might just be picked out, unhitched to anything at all.

Human control over wild animals has always been a way of controlling the land and the humans who share that habitat. Exterminating the bison of the American west would indeed "confine the Indians to smaller areas, and compel them to abandon their nomadic customs," as President Ulysses S. Grant's interior secretary had projected. Not long after the founding of Montana's Glacier National Park in the early 1900s, one warden patrolled its trails with a wolfhound, a dog once used for catching enslaved runaways. His goal was to scare away not only wolves but also the local Blackfoot, both of whom he wanted to prevent hunting within park borders.

Indigenous populations suffered indirectly from wolf extermination as well. Poison killed more than just the predator; it was a domino toppling lives throughout the ecosystem. Songbirds like juncos and horned larks were killed for use as bait, but bison were too, the crystals dissolved into incisions that seamed their skinned bodies. Each dead animal was a bomb, its poison detonating in the bellies of wolves hours later across the prairie. One late-nineteenth-century night in Montana, seventy-eight wolves died off the carcass of one bison. Other animals fed on it too, dogs and coyotes and vultures and bears. Their deaths, like the wolves', were not quiet. Slobber could dry on the grass, crusting in the sun, holding the poison for months or, in some accounts, years, killing the ponies, antelope, elk, and deer who tried to graze. "The Indians losing their stock in this way feel like making reprisals," wrote one trapper in his 1891 biography. Who could blame them?

American taxpayers would go on to fund a mass poisoning

campaign made up of many deaths like this in the twentieth century, all under the benign-sounding umbrella of "predator control" or "Animal Damage Control." These words disguised the scale of violence enacted. The agency, Animal Damage Control, did not say "kill," they said "take"; someone who hunted wolves was "a wolfer." In his memoir *Wolfer*, Carter Niemeyer describes how every township in Montana once maintained a pole of about ten feet in the center of a field with a bright-orange top. Every year, trappers would inject some 100,000 pounds of horsemeat with poison and dump the meat around each pole. Come spring, they'd count the bodies in the thaw. An estimated 18,000 to 20,000 coyotes died this way; I can only imagine the number of wolves.

By the time Oregon set its first bounty on wolves, similar laws had been in place in other American states for over two hundred years. Some laws relied on Indigenous labor, weaponized not only to kill wolves but to undermine traditions that saw the animals as sacred. The Massachusetts Bay Colony instituted one such law in 1630, later paying Native Americans three quarts of wine or a bushel of corn if they delivered a head. Virginia's policy required tribes to participate in the slaughter, and to deliver wolf hides as a form of tribute. Except for a small remnant population in the upper Midwest, wolves were extinct in the lower forty-eight by the mid-twentieth century.

Removing a body does not remove the specter of it. After controlling what roamed within national borders, authorities' anxieties about wolves radiated outward. Officials in the United States worked with Canada to collaborate on fighting the so-called wolf menace; in the words of the Glacier Park superintendent, "our efforts to destroy these animals will help each other." Though they found camaraderie in trading tactics—to disguise human scent on a trap, he recommended treating it with a cocktail of urine, extract of anal gland, glycerine, and corrosives—mistrust and fear still bobbed beneath the surface of cross-border interactions. U.S. authorities depicted our northern neighbor as an "infested territory," expressing fears of Canada's "canine peril" sneaking across the border. The logic was familiarly xenophobic: insecure boundaries would permit the entry of illegal migrants, who would endanger America's hard-earned economic resources. That latitude line of the 49th parallel, wrote Wallace Stegner, was "an agreement, a rule, a limitation, a fiction perhaps, but a legal one." But what does legal mean to a wolf? In some parts that line was nothing more than a swath of cut trees. The story was the same along the southern border, where an inspector responsible for hiring hunters in the New Mexico and Arizona district referred to the border as a line that would be patrolled lest "animals . . . drift in from Mexico."

The national narrative of invasion changed in the mid-1990s, when the U.S. Fish and Wildlife Service's Operation Wolfstock airlifted thirty-one wolves from British Columbia and Alberta into Yellowstone National Park and Idaho, including the parents of B-45, that first wolf known to cross the river and reenter Oregon. "The fact that Canada had something the United States did not, and something of considerable value, proved a matter of patriotic report," wrote historian Karen Jones, as explanation for the red-carpet reintroduction of an animal that had, fifty years earlier, been brutally exterminated. The listing of the wolf under the Endangered Species Act had created a legal imperative to reintroduce *Canis lupus*, and children waved flags when the motorcade entered Yellowstone; President Clinton later posed for photographs as he fed the wolves in holding pens in the park's Lamar Valley. Though official perspectives warmed to the idea of cross-border wolves, emotions ran high through the communities adjacent to their new homes. Some commentators compared the wolves—who had no say in their reintroduction—to welfare scroungers.

The wolf was back, but once again, the wolf was not a wolf. Decades earlier, now-revered conservationist Theodore Roosevelt had called them "black-hearted criminals," an association that stuck. As a fearmongering metaphor, it mischaracterized and flattened not only wolves, but also the humans they were compared to. Nobody, after all, is born with a black heart.

A few months after OR-7 wandered into California, the sheriff in his pack's home territory of northeastern Oregon ruled that any rancher who suspected a wolf had killed one of their cows could choose to report it to either the ODFW or to him directly. The police would treat the area as a crime scene, explained a local newspaper.

"Wolves are a public concern and this is an issue of keeping the peace," Sheriff Fred Steen told a group of citizens gathered at a community meeting in that spring of 2012. He made little effort to hide his bias. A few years earlier, he had told a reporter that wolves ("a very efficient, four-legged piranha") were being reintroduced in what was "essentially a social experiment" in the county. Now, at the community meeting, Steen recounted a story from earlier that month, where a woman who suspected a wolf had been on her property called his office to file a police report. Her five-year-old son and their malamute had been playing in the yard, she said, and when the boy ran in, upset, telling his mother there was a monster near the house that had scared the dog, she sat him down with a series of images: coyotes, dogs, and wild wolves. The boy picked the wolf from the lineup—*Guilty*—and Steen filed the woman's statement alongside dozens of other accounts in his office. The crime? Being born wolf.

Meanwhile, OR-7 zigzagged back and forth across the state line. Nearly a decade later I would visit some of the ranches in Oregon and California that he likely traveled through, including the Hart Ranch, run by a sixth-generation ranching family committed to stewarding the land as a conservation easement and wildlife corridor. To them, their cattle were not just a commodity but a tool to habitat management. Multiple university researchers were studying the biodiversity their properties supported. From the window of the Harts' pickup, I witnessed the passing checkerboard of private and public land. The Forest Service land that abutted theirs was overgrown, seemingly not burned or tended in years, a thicket of spindly lodgepole pines turned copper with beetle kill, the floor crowded with brush. We saw six deer on that afternoon drive, but all were on the Harts' property. Where would I go if I was a wolf? The answer seemed easy. Surely I'd pick their thinned juniper grove, or the meadow stubbled with lupines and the occasional Indian paintbrush, skunk cabbages sprawling by the stream.

Beneath the prehistoric squawk of passing sandhill cranes, Blair Hart told me that if their land was good habitat for cows, it was good for deer and elk, which meant it was good for the creatures who preyed on them. By the time I met the Harts, they had hired a part-time employee whose sole job was monitoring and tracking predators on their land and shepherding the cattle accordingly. They wouldn't have chosen to add wolves to the equation—ranching with no antibiotics, no growth-hormones, minimal cattle, and no government land allotments was already very expensive, they told me—but the presence of a wolf was a sign that their ecosystem was healthy. It meant they were doing something right.

It was easy to imagine how OR-7 had walked their land. He

would not have known the difference between public and private, between one ranch and another, between where he might be sheltered and where he might be shot, shoveled, and shut up. He would have known the smell of a deer. The swoop of a ridgeline. The ease of movement on a dirt road. By that spring of 2012 when he crossed into California, OR-7 had walked hundreds of miles from home. If he was indeed a "four-legged piranha," he had gone a long way without a single livestock attack confirmed along his route.

After my grandmother died, Gramps's new girlfriends came and went with their pie-baking and spaghetti, and in between, he subsisted primarily on things born on the farm. There was a pond edged with scum the color of Mountain Dew, banks full of breeding newts. We'd dodge them when we brought an old coffee can full of sour-smelling fish feed down to the trout Gramps filled its waters with every spring. Up by the house, he kept a large garden enclosed by an eight-foot fence, rows bursting with fuzzy rhubarb leaves, towers of beans and lemon cucumbers, beets lurking beneath the dirt. Near the gate was a flock of hissing geese, necks thick and gray as vipers. They laid eggs the size of pears that Gramps would push into our hands. "Omelet!" he'd say in his jovial, gruff way, and we would nod, pretending we had the gall to crack them open.

The chickens Gramps owned were some sort of fighting Russian kind, birds with combs like Mötley Crüe, a breed supposed to be meaner to the predators that lurked, always, just beyond the fence. I didn't like imagining Gramps walking the driveway to find a pen of half-eaten chickens, but it felt worse if the attacked ones were sheep. Each one a birth he had touched. To tend sheep is to be someone who "holds a cigarette paper to the mouths of 'stiff, clammy' lambs to see if they're breathing, warmed them in basins of hot water, feeding them drop by drop for hours," wrote Montana shepherd Bill Stockton in his book *Today I Baled Some Hay to Feed the Sheep the Coyotes Eat*. Though my involvement with the sheep was cursory, I always felt a tender patronage toward the messy world they inhabited, from the rolling meadows lined with towering oak trees to the sagging, lofted barn Gramps insisted on building the old-fashioned way back in the 1970s. No power, just a chainsaw and wood pegs, my school-age father and his siblings peeling bark and splitting it into boards. Still, steady as the seasons, the predators come. Raccoons, coyotes, cougars, badgers. During the spring of my senior year of college, wolf tracks appeared on the flank of Mt. Hood, a few hundred miles from the farm, but closer than they had been in decades. Wolves in places people thought they'd never see them again.

Gramps had long owned sheepdogs, border collies with glossy tongues and burr-flecked coats, but when they didn't intimidate the coyotes, he got a llama and named it Pajama. He knew herdsmen relied on them for protection in South America, but the animal he bought was too true to its name, the sleepy chaperone on the school trip. We'd see Pajama when we drove in, filling his mouth with grass then raising it to the sun to chew like someone already stoned. A dud guard from day one.

I did not hate the predators on the farm, but their appetites could feel like a violation, a feeling I later recognized when a friend described learning burglars ransacked her childhood room. A farmer knows better than anyone that he cannot tend all of nature, but to wake each day he must believe he can protect his little patch. These depredations breached the boundary between wild and domestic. Any logistical failures of llama or barn paled in comparison to the emotional ones. There seemed to be a shame in being unable to protect the things you loved, a cloud that crossed Gramps's face when he mentioned he'd found another dead lamb. The way he could then turn his back, wave his hand, dismiss it like the deaths had been no tragedy at all.

Gramps is old now. His bald head is spotted with age. A ram knocked him over in the wet pasture last year, and for too long he lay in the mud, eighty-nine years old, unable to move. I wince and marvel at the pride that continues to drive him to the barn. *They keep me alive,* he says. *They need to be fed.* His new wife, a Salvadoran woman he met while they were both working in Guatemala on one of his traveling-doctor stints, prefers a cabin near town. It's possible this iteration of farm will die with him. I do not know if he will be alive if—when—a wolf pack settles in the Willamette Valley. The wolf and my grandfather could be ships in the night. I am spared something by this possibility. Not just because I do not want to imagine what could happen to the sheep, but because I do not want to imagine what might happen to the wolf.

When scientists talk about animal territory, they are talking about the swath of land an animal will defend against other members of its own species. To a human, the boundary between one animal and another's territory is often indecipherable. It is piles of dry scat mossed with mold, the needly duff kicked up at the foot of a tree, trails of urine like invisible ink.

"How do I mark my territory?!?!" typed looneyanimal25 as the title of a fourteen-minute video he uploaded to YouTube in late 2013. He was recording himself playing a game called Wolf Quest, and his voice was lisped and nasally, the sheepish cute of someone's little brother hunched over a computer in flannel pajamas. "Pshh—" he said, his childhood laughs reverberating through the background of the game. "I just keep peeing all over the place . . . How much does she have liquids in her?" His avatar, which he referred to alternately as "I" and "she," was thin and black, sleek as a housecat, and as the wolf walked against the snow-spotted rocks of Yellowstone National Park, she lifted her leg: to a pillar of aspen, a mound of white snow, a lichen-smudged boulder. Each time she did this, yellow looneyanimal25 got 10 points, and also increasingly frustrated with Wolf Quest Level Two. "I'm still trying to mark my territory and it doesn't work, I'm just peeing everywhere," he said. He sounded embarrassed.

Launched by a grant from the National Science Foundation and produced by an educational game developer in cohort with the Minnesota Zoo, Wolf Quest has existed in various iterations since 2007. The "3D wildlife simulation video game" seeks to translate the adrenaline of a wolf's life into both single and multiplayer play. You compete with bears and coyotes to hunt elk and hares and mule deer, try to find a mate and establish a den, shuttle your pups as the season changes. It is impossible to play and not want your avatar to survive—for the wolves to win. At the same time, looneyanimal25's frustration was testament to the challenge of translating one animal's logic to the body of another. For over ten minutes, his avatar circled the same rocks, urinating on the same trees, while he asked new versions of the same earnest question: "Hold on, did I mark my territory?"

When a strange gray wolf appeared, twitching and tiny in the corner of the screen, looneyanimal25 inhaled sharply. "No, no, no, no," he said. He wanted to protect his pack and deter outsiders, but he was a tourist in the body of a wolf. He didn't speak their language. He wasn't sure how to broadcast that the land beneath him was "*ours*," and any wolf who breached it was going to be a "*them*." Looneyanimal25 seemed unaware that peeing was not a distraction, it was the point. If you were canine, urine was the spell you cast to claim possession, the way my mother once wrote initials on the tags of my coats before I left for school.

Just as many humans would not recognize a wolf's territory, a wolf does not understand the lines we humans draw in the sand. Wolves dwell across ecological zones, chasing deer and elk through low country in winter, making dens there to rear pups, then following their prey toward high country as the weather warms. As the old conservation motto "saving the last best places" suggests, human borders around wilderness and national parks have often sought to sequester the most aesthetically striking landscapes for protection—glacial peaks, cliff-clipped canyons. We evaluate a landscape by human metrics, then expect animals to thrive tidily within our boundaries. Wolves ignore our logic; it is not theirs.

A wolf's ideal territory often sprawls from mountains into low-level pasture or prairie. Though the size of the territory will depend on several factors—pack size, competition from other packs, the terrain, the density of food sources—they have averaged from over 850 miles in northeast Oregon down to 200 square miles in northeast Montana and Idaho. The word "ecosystem" comes from *oikos,* the Greek word for house. To survive in-breeding, disease, and inclement weather, a wolf must be able to roam its corridors, out of alpine areas and into the wetlands and meadows so often used as pasture. To map its territory over the blueprint of our own.

Within a week or so of OR-7's crossing into the state, the California Department of Fish and Wildlife created a Twitter account for him, sharing rough plot points of his journey while hiding his locations. Their @Wolf_OR-7 ("2 y.o. wolf from Oregon. Left family to find wife & new home") was joined by fan accounts too, mostly run anonymously, like the @WolfOR7 Twitter (bio: "Native Oregonian; California tourist. Grew up in troubled family . . . Hobbies: wandering, ungulates . . .") and Facebook pages that classified him as a "Public figure," where fans came together to comment things like "He is an amazing symbol of hope and strength" and "Too cool! He's a beaut."

By mid-January, the *New York Times* had published an article about the wolf's "almost cultlike status." They quoted a senior policy advisor for the CDFW who said random citizens were suddenly calling the office, "saying we should find him a girlfriend as soon as possible and let them settle down." Others wanted to expunge humans from parts of the Golden State and revert the land to wolf sanctuary. "People are going to get wolf tattoos, wolf sweaters, wolf key chains, wolf hats," a board member for a California wolf advocacy organization told the *Times*. The *National Enquirer* wrote about OR-7. There was even a bumper sticker: "OR-7 for President." The swag made me think of a line about fandom from critic Michelle Orange's memoir: "Claiming and being identified with a love of this or that is integral to the pleasure, to the experience of loving it." People wanted to be identified by their love of wolf.

That same month, environmental nonprofit Oregon Wild sponsored a naming competition. They wanted to publicize the animal, to make him so famous nobody would try to kill him, and to promote him as a figurehead for wolf recovery more broadly. Hundreds of children submitted ideas to name him, from as far as Finland and Nigeria, and when two girls picked the same name—a seven-year-old from Idaho and an eleven-year-old from North Dakota—the name rose in an online poll. *Journey*. "Don't Stop Believing," read subsequent headlines. For the third time, the wolf had been reborn in human minds. First he had been wolf, then he had been OR-7, and now, for a new audience, he was Journey, the lovesick wanderer.

Scientists avoided romanticizing the new figurehead. They knew no amount of fame could give a wolf immunity from the muzzle of a gun or the tire of a car, much less from the risk of an animal passing, alone, through another wolf's territory. When a human refers to himself as a "lone wolf," as an ex-boyfriend once muttered in the moments after we broke up, he seems to be suggesting it as a static state of identity. That he will walk alone, eat alone, sustain himself on the back of himself. While it is true a wolf who is alone has left his pack, he often does it in search for companionship. He goes it alone so he might find another. His period of aloneness is not only liminal, but a period of increased danger. As a biologist quoted in the *Times* put it: "OR-7 is unlikely to survive long hunting alone without a pack."

When OR-7 left his home territory, he left Wallowa County, a mountainous sprawl of prairie, peak, and ranchland in the northeastern corner of the state. The Cascade mountain range bisects Oregon near the coast, dividing the state into two distinct climates. The west is a belt of dense, mossy old-growth rain forests, where waterfalls can spill icy water all summer long. Geographically speaking, this slim strip represents the minority of the state, but it is home to the capital, Salem, the two main state universities, and Portland, that manic pixie dream girl of the public eye. The western wedge of Oregon holds most of the population, money, Democratic voters, and national gaze. The landscape to the east is drier: shrubby high desert and arid pine timberlands beneath a sun-bleached blue. When I share photos, friends from other places ask if I'm traveling in Montana, Colorado, Wyoming. Here Hells Canyon plunges into the Snake River, and the Wallowa Mountains rise above 9,000 feet, referred to locally as "the little Alps." The county is a place of extremes, in more ways than one. Cows outnumber people nearly four to one. When I decided to start researching rhetoric around recovering wolf populations, this was the first place I went. One livestock producer I interviewed told a journalist, "Wolves are about as welcome in Wallowa County as a 9/11 terrorist at Ground Zero." Not everyone felt that way, but the ones who did made their feelings clear; so to maintain neighborly relations, others kept quiet.

I had been to the county once before. May 2009, the spring OR-7 was born. The spring the wolf killed Curt Jacobs's lambs, those first confirmed wolf depredations since the species had returned to Oregon. I knew nothing of wolves then; I had driven across the Cascades for a long weekend of mountain climbing with a group of other high schoolers, all but one of whom were boys. I started climbing on the weekends because I liked showing my body it was capable of things it did not know. To see a summit in the distance and be eating Thin Mints at the top a few hours later was to reset my perspective on what it meant to move through time and space. In the vertigo of squinting down at tiny trees, I'd feel a strange mix of pride and humbleness, my body as mortal as ever, but strong too. Back at the car, I'd feel recharged, reoriented, ready to climb whatever "mountains" awaited in Portland. I wasn't always sure how to steer my body on the weekends I spent at home. A teenage friend had been drugged at a bar and awoke in a room she did not know. Was this growing up? Just waiting for the bad stories we had heard to manifest in the lives of our friends, our own lives? I wanted to bring everyone I loved into a room and douse them with some magic oil, casting a spell of protection. Because I could not do that, I relished the chance to turn off my phone. To snap crampons onto my boots.

I loved the mountains, and loved the person I became there, but that weekend in the Wallowas, I struggled. We spent one seventeen-hour day "bagging summits," ascending and descending on rock and ice, taking turns punching footsteps into the snow at the front of the rope we tied our bodies to. My body had never worked so hard. When you are strung to other bodies across a glacier, you cannot stop walking. You grip your ice axe, and at some point, beneath your gloves, your fingers go numb. My self-pity was a broken siren in my brain. Every now and then we saw the top of a pine tree sprouting from the snowfield like some overgrown crocus, and this reminder that there was a world beneath the snow—that our reality would melt—felt unfathomable. We each carried a few water bottles, but even though we kept stuffing snow in to try to melt it down, they were empty by afternoon, and the remainder of the day was lit by thirst. Delirium cobwebbed my brain, my tongue leaden and sweet in the wind, the edge of my vision swirling. We had started climbing at dawn, but it wasn't until a few hours after dark that we found the tents. I crouched in the snow and steadied a match above my camp stove, watching the thin flame shiver to life. "Will I look back on this and see myself as strong?" I wrote later in my journal. I had never felt so physically weak.

The other girl on the trip was asleep beside me within minutes, and across the glacier I heard the boys zipping tents, whispering with occasional laughter. Sometimes I felt like one of them, full of coltish ease and banter. *You're like Wendy and the lost boys,* a friend told me after seeing us all together one day at school. I snorted. I loved the camaraderie, but some days I felt unshakably self-conscious and alone. While the boys cracked jokes on the rock face, tossing their T-shirts to belayers below, I clung to the cracks, armpits steaming. I couldn't tell what was harder, finding fingerholds or trying to stop my legs from shaking. The other girl in the group was muscular and enthusiastic, and my anxiety felt like a blight, a failed representation of our identity. To admit I feared dying on the mountain felt like admitting I was too much of a scaredy-cat to be up there at all, an affront to the legacy of those who had fought for a place on the rock.

In committing myself to concealment—not just of my fear, but my shame about having it—I signed up for trips like I was taking a vitamin. Because I didn't feel authentically brave, I wondered: How many summits do I have to reach before I'll trust myself up there? On that climbing trip in Wallowa County, I had worn a wolf-and-moon T-shirt I bought at a tourist shop in Montana, cashing in $20 from a great-uncle's trivia tournament about "The American West." Slipping into my sleeping bag after that seventeen-hour day, I couldn't help smiling at its glow-in-the-dark face. So there was the beast who howled against my chest.

By the time I went back to Wallowa County, OR-7 had already left Oregon, and it was the summer before my senior year of college. I had first seen the headlines about him leaving his family and starting to walk just months after I too had left home, but I paid them little attention. I had always wanted to spend hours whispering into the neck of a furry creature, but it never stuck. My friends had been girls like this—horse girls, cat girls, dolphin girls—but it was clear they were native speakers, and I was a tourist, trying on the rote language of devotion as I squealed for what they loved. I loved our dog, but I loved her as part of the family, not just because she had four legs. Valuing animal life felt like the best way to be in the world, but it came as much from my head as my heart. I wanted to preserve habitat, kindle respect, and check the human ego. I had read elephants could communicate underground through foot vibrations and smell water from up to three miles away, and I thought: Who could argue those are less-evolved creatures than us? Who could sum the facts and come up with anything less than reverence and awe?

By 2013, when I became interested in the controversies over wolf repopulation in the American west, it was easy to feel there were only two types of citizens: those who loved the wolf, and those who loved to hate it, as the truck-stop T-shirt emblazoned with "Smoke a pack a day" suggested, with its family of wolves framed in the sight of a gun. My mother's sister in Montana had, a decade earlier, married a taxidermist with an anti-wolf bumper sticker on his baby blue pickup, and though I wondered about it, he was smiley and kind and I was too shy to bring it up. Later, on social media, I would see one of my cousins posing for prom photos with a rifle, and, years after that, grinning with a boyfriend as they held up the freshly killed carcasses of what looked like two dead wolves. In the caption, she suggested they were coyotes; I had rarely wanted to believe something so badly.

All my life I had tried to clear up misunderstandings with family and friends, smoothing the kinks from the cords that connected us. Naively, I believed writing a thesis about wolves could accomplish the same thing. By studying the polarization, I thought, I'd learn how to crack it. "The story of the wolf is . . . a compelling example of how Western myth and folklore overtook scientific fact to shape legislative policies in the early 20th century," I wrote in a summer funding application. Weeks later, a lump of money arrived in my checking account. A professor suggested a list of environmental nonfiction books that would be relevant for me to read, each one written by a man. Flush with new cash, I ordered them all.

I talked my parents into letting me borrow their old minivan, then I loaded it with camping gear and notebooks and drove six hours east. I was twenty-one years old by then, just back from a semester abroad, and already I loved my parents more for how good they were at letting me go. I was not going into the mountains this time, I was camping beneath them, near the one-strip ranch-slash-tourist-town of Joseph. I'd spend a few days joining a wolf-focused workshop led by an environmental nonprofit, then a few days talking to locals about the wolves reestablishing themselves in their midst. Since my high school visit, my own experiences in the mountains had shifted. While studying in Scotland that spring, two friends and I spent a week trekking part of the West Highland Way, a long-distance trail that zagged through boulder-strewn hills and heather-swept moors. It rained on us for hours at a time, but hiking was the easy part. The group of walkers whose path we crisscrossed day after day were older men in yellow rain jackets who would call to us whenever they found shelter ahead on the trail. We'd see them peek from beneath the roof of a covered bridge, whistling to us, raising their whiskey bottles in our direction. "Join us, girls," they'd slur. "Or do you girlies like getting wet?" The sound of their low laughter was rockfall as we trudged past them. We sang ABBA beneath our hoods and tried to distract ourselves with marvel—the way the mountain shuddered when the wind blew in, flattening the amber grasses as if by an invisible hand. By the time I returned to the Wallowas, I feared the wildness of the mountains less than the humans they might hold.

Joseph belongs on the front of a gift-shop postcard. A town abandoned by the fallen timber industry and propped up by a bronze foundry that helped make the World War II memorial in Washington, D.C. The cars on the main street are mostly pickup trucks and Subarus, tourists and locals, those who have lived there since before the terrariums began to fill the shopwindows and ex-urbanites who moved in from the coast. There's a new, white-walled hotel that serves Stumptown Coffee and rents rooms on Airbnb. There are, proudly, no fast-food chain restaurants, but you can buy handmade CBD truffles and chai body butter and fishing tackle and IPAs named after the local mountain passes. The town itself is wedged between the snowy hulk of the Wallowa Mountains on one side and the rolling patchwork of what some city people would call "endless" ranch land on the other. The roving presence of wolves has proven that any boundary between these two landscapes is not just permeable but fantasy.

That day in 2013, I passed a billboard that read, "How Do Wolves Affect You?" Paid for by local property owners, the giant sign showed the sharp-toothed snarl of a wolf framed by snapshots of a wide-eyed fawn, a cluster of calves, a mother elk with two babies, and a "Private Property Rights" sign stuck into a sunny field. The website in the corner of the sign (OregonWolfEducation.org) listed grievances that included "a constant threat to our livelihoods . . . livestock, working or hunting dogs, and our families."

I was thinking about threats and how we decided when to heed them when I pulled in to use a public restroom just off Joseph's Main Street. On a wooden display board in the parking lot someone had painted a map of the town. One side showed trails and campsites through the county, labeled "WALLOWA RECREATION" and marked by miniature stick figures carrying hiking poles and riding horses. The back of the sign had the same black county outlines, filled with state highways and splintering rivers, but instead of humans, the blank space was filled with animals: speckled fawns, leaping elk, cows on the Zumwalt Prairie. There, in between Swamp Creek and Crow Creek, was a small gray wolf. The animal had no face, just a black-tipped tail. Surrounding its body, a constellation of bullet holes splintered the wood.

That year, ODFW officials sent more than 83,000 automated

messages to local livestock producers to notify them of approaching wolves. Oregon confirmed thirteen wolf kills in 2013—cows, sheep, and one goat—in a state with over a million cattle; this was just a tiny fraction of livestock deaths, yet the deaths occupied a large psychic space. Though both my parents had grown up in rural areas, I now checked all the boxes for a certain kind of environment-studying city liberal. *Better keep your own life quiet,* a friend who lived in the eastern part of the state told me. *Word travels fast around here. Just say you're in college in Maine.* I buttoned my flannel and tried to keep my cards close.

One night I went to a dive bar called the Hydrant, its front draped with a vinyl banner that said "Hunters are w[ELK]come." I was having a beer with a Joseph local and the mutual Portland friend who had introduced us when one of her neighbors came over to chat. I knew, by then, that you couldn't arrive in town by accident. You couldn't "pass through" Joseph. You had to leave the interstate and follow signs for a good fifty-five miles. You had to drive over "Deadman's Pass," a notorious stretch of mountain road where seventy-eight percent of the crashes were out-of-state ve-hicles. You had to take hairpin turns on a little riverside highway where it seemed like the sun was always screaming in your face. This neighbor knew my friend and I weren't locals when he asked what had drawn us in. He was a big guy, with a jaw like a pit bull and a smell like a beer-stained leather couch, and he cupped a hand on our shoulders as he leaned in too close. I was trying to figure how to respond when my friend outed me in a boozy, flirty giggle. *She's researching wolves.* The man slammed his pint glass on the table and leapt back. I instinctively jumped too. He asked who in the govern-ment had sent me.

"So what, you think wolves are cute?" He cracked his knuckles against the table. "You're tryna snuggle them?" I shook my head, trying to keep the horror out of my cheeks. Suddenly the man's fingers narrowed into a crude pistol, and for a minute, his voice softened. Behind him, the few drinkers in the room had turned our way, pints frozen amber in the air. "It's just not that complicated, sweetheart," the man said. Then his voice grew louder: "Boom, boom, boom, boom." He waved his arms around the bar, spraying spit while miming gunfire. "Boom, boom, boom."

In her essay "The Gender of Sound," Anne Carson writes that the wolf is a well-trodden symbol of marginality in Greek poetry, "an outlaw." Through this ancient lens, the animal has much in common with the woman, seen to possess "a 'natural' female affinity for all that is raw, formless and in need of the civilizing hand of man." Carson describes a poem where a man, far from home, listens to the sound of both wolves and women howling in the night. She writes that in Aristotle's "The Pythagorean Table of Opposites," the side with female on it is also the side of "dark, secret, evil, ever-moving, not self-contained and lacking its own boundaries." Women, like wolves, have long been faulted not only for crossing the boundaries made by others, but for lacking boundaries themselves. For being too loud, too big, too scattered. A problem to solve.

Sitting on the beer-stained vinyl of that high-top chair, I understood that to this man I had breached an invisible boundary. I had left academia and landed in his bar. He would welcome me, but only if I played by his rules. To drink, smile, flirt, defer. To ask questions about wolves was to fail the test. Now, like the predator, I needed to be scared out. I understood that no matter what I wanted to be inquiring about in interviews, part of my subject would always be fear, the potential for male violence a smear of grease I could not wipe off the lens. At the same time, it was too simple to say I was "prey." The man could sense I was an outsider. Urban, educated, aligned in some way with systemic power. My interest in the wolf threatened him; my fear, then, was a response to his own. We make others predatory to justify our own predations. As Linda Tuhiwai Smith writes, that legacy of research supported by "traveller's tales" has long involved "represent[ing] the Other to a general audience." Was I the beast who sunk my teeth into his story, then ran for home?

OR-7 moved toward the Nevada border and away from it, his path a ball of yarn strung across itself. Nevada hadn't seen wolves in years, and across the internet, spectators pleaded for him to avoid what would surely be a romantic wasteland. "A radio-collared wolf's historic journey across Oregon and Northern California now plays like a country song as he goes looking for love in all the wrong places while an important Valentine's Day looms," wrote a reporter on the beat for the Medford, Oregon, *Mail Tribune*. Mid-February was the peak of wolf breeding season, and if OR-7 hadn't found a partner by then, he'd likely have to wait another year to start a family.

"His mind right now is on love, and the clock's ticking," said Ed Bangs, the veteran who had spearheaded wolf reintroduction for the U.S. Fish and Wildlife Service for twenty-three years. But Valentine's came and went, and still the lone wolf walked on, crossing the 1,000-mile threshold. In early March, he returned to Oregon, and then a few days later, to California. "He's baaaaack," wrote the *Mail Tribune* reporter when OR-7 reentered the state. Russ, the ODFW's wolf program coordinator, released a statement reminding people that land was land, and that "while wolves crossing state boundaries may be significant to people, wolves and other wildlife don't pay attention to state borders." The following spring, when OR-7's collared three-year-old sister OR-5 stepped over Oregon's eastern border and died in a foothold trap on the next-to-last day of

Idaho's legal trapping season, she was killed by the cruel metric of a boundary she could not see. "Crossing the border . . . was a death sentence for this wolf," said spokesperson Amaroq Weiss in a Center for Biological Diversity press release. A wolf traveling through this patchwork of state and federal protections is like a person playing pinball with their eyes shut. It doesn't matter how smart you are: the landscape will confound your logic.

Dispersing wolves have been observed crossing four-lane highways and circumnavigating large lakes and cities, traveling hundreds of miles over months in their search. During those days OR-7 wound through the borderlands, the CDFW's alerts sounded like my old basketball coach summarizing a poorly played game, acknowledging OR-7 was "covering some distance, but not in any specific direction." Nobody could say why this wolf stayed longer in one location than another. I can only imagine he knew the importance of territory. A wolf does not take settling lightly. Maybe OR-7 slowed when he found somewhere promising, leaving his scent and waiting to see if anyone would walk his way, said Bangs, or maybe he befriended a dog or another canid. Either way, he wandered on. "He'll go until he finds a female or dies," said Bangs.

In Joseph, I spoke with a field ecologist, a few livestock producers, an anti-trapping activist flanked by a wolf-dog hybrid, a government biologist who said the wolf conflict had "turned him gray," and a conservationist so worried about our collective future he and his wife didn't want to have kids. At twenty-one, the idea had never occurred to me before. Because the conservationist was an outspoken advocate for wolves, I wondered if his love for the animal had tainted his ability to love being human. Did I love being human enough to create another one? I couldn't decide.

One sunny afternoon at a coffeeshop downtown, I met Joe Whittle, an enrolled member of the Caddo Nation of Oklahoma and a descendant of the Delaware Nation of Oklahoma. He had grown up in Wallowa County and spent childhood weekends backpacking in its mountains. At the time he was a freelance photographer and Forest Service ranger in his late thirties, with a faded baseball cap and a neat triangle of hair on his chin. "I was always conscious and aware that the landscape was somewhat sterilized," he told me. He grew up in the years before wolves were reintroduced to Yellowstone, before they crossed the river into Oregon. "I grew up imagining all the things that used to be here, including Indians, not just wolves, being native myself." He paused, then mentioned that the county now had far more wolves than Indians, and that he was one of only a few local enrolled tribal members. "They've suffered the same oppression that we have."

There are no migration stories for the Nimiipuu, the Nez Perce whose homeland encompasses Wallowa County. "If science suggests Nez Perces migrated into their homeland, the theory would have to be about a time . . . before writing, before history, before time mattered," wrote historians Allen Pinkham, Steven Evans, and Frederick Hoxie. The town of Joseph was named after Chief Joseph, the man forced to lead some eight hundred Nez Perce men, women, and children away from that homeland. On June 15, 1877, thirty-seven-year-old Hinmatóowyalahtq'it—"Thunder strikes out from water"—had no choice but to leave. Pursued by over 2,000 soldiers of the U.S. Army, he guided his people across 1,170 miles of Oregon, Idaho, Montana, and Wyoming, hoping to reach the camp of Sioux chief Sitting Bull in Canada. They fought four battles and numerous skirmishes along the way, traveling within miles of where my grandparents now live in Montana's Bitterroot Valley and winding among tourists in the then-five-year-old Yellowstone National Park.

Finally, on October 5, starving and freezing after a five-day battle
that had left leaders and children alike dead, the man who would
become Chief Joseph—later referred to as the "Red Napoleon" in
American media—was forced to surrender just forty miles south of
the Canadian border.

As legend goes, he handed over his rifle and spoke some of the
most canonically romanticized lines in the American west: "Hear
me, my chiefs! I am tired. My heart is sick and sad. From where the
sun now stands I will fight no more forever." In reality, a young white
aide, Lieutenant C.E.S. Wood of the 21st Infantry, stood nearby
with a pencil and a notebook, chronicling the course of events. In
the margin of a long-forgotten first draft, he put a reminder to
come up with something poetic later. "Here insert Joseph's reply to
the demand for surrender."

As Joe told me about his dream to offer wolf-tracking expeditions for tourists in the backcountry, drawing a livelihood not from
extracting the land but witnessing and learning it, I thought of how
the wolf was forcing Oregon to confront its myths of founding and
belonging. Beginning in the 1990s, the Nez Perce tribe's Wildlife Division had overseen the recovery of gray wolves in Idaho,
giving the animals equal status to that of human beings; director
Neil Thagard described their management as an intentional rever-
sal of colonial practices. "Their summer range, transitional range
and winter range has been disrupted by man," he told a journalist,
speaking about the wolf. "Today, we [Natives] don't have a lot more
space on the ground—at least in the Lower 48." In the Nez Perce
language, there is no word for "eradication," whether in reference to
the intentional annihilation of humans or animals. As tribal cultural
resources ethnographer Josiah Blackeagle Pinkham—a descendant
of Chief Joseph and the son of Nez Perce historian and storyteller
Allen Pinkham—told a journalist: "That concept [of eradication] is

foreign to us." Familiar given what they had witnessed by settlers, perhaps, but culturally anathema. The wolf, like the tribe, would always belong.

To be from Oregon, I once thought, was to be at the end of the Oregon Trail. In those days the nice restaurant a few streets from my parents' house was Meriwethers; the one they liked to go to on date nights was Clarklewis. So much frontier pride lay in the myth of being from a place that had not just been founded but "found." But to tie the narrative of progress to the narrative of arrival is to ignore the tug of history. Speaking to Toni Morrison, Homi Bhabha once said that "remembering is never a quiet act of introspection or retrospection. It is a painful remembering, a putting together of the dismembered past to make sense of the trauma of the present." To make sense of the poacher who killed the wolf, one must confront Oregon's history not only with the animal, but the people so long conflated with them, and the land that held them both.

I thought of a conversation I had with a government biologist, one of those called to the scene after livestock producers report finding a carcass believed to have been attacked. His job was to perform the autopsy and jigsaw the past. If he determined a wolf was accountable, the government would reimburse the producer the market cost of their animal. "Cougars are ambush predators, jumping on their prey and leaving constellations of distinct claw marks. Bears attack between the shoulder blades. But wolves don't always draw blood," he told me. "They bite on the armpit, the groin, the back of the hind legs, but sometimes the skin is free of puncture wounds, hiding the trauma below the surface." Some kills, he suggested, did not look like kills at all. The trick was to always cut the cow open. It wasn't pleasant to do these autopsies, crouched in the frozen mud of a pasture while an upset producer paced around you, maybe, but going deeper was the only way to understand how the animal had gotten to where they are now. If the first step was to admit something was wrong, the next was to excavate the source of the wound. The Greek word for "not forgetting" translates to "it does not escape notice," which suggests it is a thing that cannot be hidden. The past—its fear, its grief—a hurdle we cannot dodge.

A forest that had not seen wolves for a hundred years was still the habitat of the wolf, just as the street I parked on outside the Joseph coffee shop was still the land of the Nez Perce. "The European newcomer . . . drove the Wolf and the Native American from ancestral homelands, disrupted their lives, and upset their balance," Lakota author Joseph Marshall told the audience of a 1992 lecture. "They also shared the same fate. Life was never the same." In the years since I first met Joe, though, the Nez Perce tribe has reclaimed more land near Joseph through purchase and donations, becoming one of the county's biggest landowners. In late 2020, the tribe announced the purchase of one of the area's oldest farms, formerly the site of a Nez Perce village and a council site for Chief Joseph. A few months later, they received the title to the now-former Wallowa Methodist Church. "The Nimiipuu—the people—are tied to this land . . . the Nimiipuu are here to stay," tribal member Mary Jane Miles told a crowd gathered outside its doors.

When I caught up with Joe in mid-2021, he told me he'd never started that guiding and tracking company, and his gaze had shifted farther away from the wolf. He was still a ranger with the Forest Service, and a freelance journalist and photographer, but wolves were less of a hot-button issue in the county now. The racism and xenophobia no longer needed to "hide" behind the animal as a symbol, he said: after the 2016 election, they had come out into the open. "The new wolf is the face mask," he said. His freelance work and advocacy now engaged more directly with issues of social and environmental justice. He showed me cell phone photos of an interpretive sign he had just finished collaborating with Nez Perce elders on. The sign would be waiting for tourists at the Wallowa Lake trailhead, letting them know, as Joe told me with a shake of his head, that "this land is Nez Perce land, not theirs." However much I might feel like prey if I went hiking and encountered mountain lion prints in the mud, as a descendant of American settlers, my presence on stolen land also came from a lineage of predation. To restore the landscape as a habitat for wolves without thinking about redistributing resources to the people who lived beside them for thousands of years is, it seems to me, to miss the point. "Conservation is a Western construct that was created as a result of settlers overexploiting Indigenous lands natural resources, and depleting entire ecosystems," writes Jessica Hernandez, a Maya Ch'orti' and Zapotec environmental scientist, in her book *Fresh Banana Leaves: Healing Indigenous Landscapes Through Indigenous Science*. There was no need for conservation precolonization, she writes, because Indigenous peoples viewed the natural world communally and through a model of kinship, not as property or resource. Conservationists today must pause not only to consider what species or ecosystems they are working to conserve, but what histories and voices too.

The traumatic expulsions of humans and animals from an ecosystem are not analogous, suggests critic Carla Freccero, they are connected. If the contemporary ethos of Oregon has been defined by those who walked in, its future is being shaped by those once forced out. See OR-7, ears flattened, tilting his head for the sound of another wolf. Is she there? And if she is, will he hear her? Will you?

4

Truth v. Wolf

There's a story Gramps likes to tell about one of my early visits to his farm. I must have been two or three. Toddling. We are walking toward the barn, and I am running ahead in grass already mowed to fuzz by the herd, probably chasing butterflies, those ones that appeared each spring to surf the breeze like shreds of torn lavender tissue paper. I turn a corner, round a hill, and stop. I've seen something. Made eye contact with it.

"Gramps!" I say, breathless, running back to his ambling frame, his boots nearly my height. "A wolf!"

There's an animal ahead, eyes glassy but alert, neck hooked in a metal snare trap. As an environmentalist Gramps believed in the conservation of wild spaces and their inhabitants, but here on the farm he was a tender, and he reckoned those two aims with little angst. His responsibility for the sheep was love but also business. His job was to keep the flock alive.

On the ground, from a distance, the animal is my size. For a second we watch each other. Her breath surely labored. Did she know she would die? Did I? Gramps will shoot her, or he will call ODFW, or she will die on her own, the blood at her neck already thickening in the fur where she has tried to tug away.

It's not a wolf, Gramps knows that immediately. There are no known wolves in Oregon at this point in the early 1990s. My wolf is just a coyote. But I am a child and I know only stories, and the wolf in my stories looms big. The wolf is the beast that gets the sheep, and I love the lambs, I lean over the rose-colored bathtub and help bottle-feed the ones whose mothers have, for whatever reason, turned away. What did I feel watching the predator? I would like to think I cried on instinct, aware I was witnessing a brink of death, but I'm not sure. There is a chance I may have felt like we had won. Like this was the last threat; like we had saved the lambs. Or maybe—and this is worse to consider—I saw the animal I thought was a wolf and I did not realize that we had won. Maybe I thought the animal was still a threat, so I ran to grab my grandfather's hand. Maybe I saw panic in the animal's eyes and mistook it for my own.

Gramps does not have answers to tell me about what happened after I got him. When I asked, recently, he waved it off, eyes floating elsewhere. He began to tell another story. So many of his stories are tall. Stretched, sculpted. Does it go without saying I have no memory of the encounter with the trap? No memory of the creature I thought was wolf. No memory of what twitched inside me when—if—I rounded the corner, alone, and looked her in the eye.

In French, the word *loup* means wolf, but in other contexts, it can also mean other things. An error in calculation, for example. Pluralized, it's the black velvet mask worn at a costume ball. Both definitions suggest one's first impression of a *wolf* is wrong, or rather, imperfect. The truth is not always what it seems.

When I began researching wolves, I believed my first wolf sighting was in the Lamar Valley. Snaked by the Lamar River and rutted by creeks, this Edenic prairie is sometimes referred to as America's Serengeti. It's the part of Yellowstone National Park you don't go to if you are playing geothermic bingo, where it's harder to find a lodge to sell you hot chocolate than it is to see a herd of pronghorn. I now know it as the part of the park where wolves were flown in from Canada in the 1990s.

The sighting was on my first trip to Yellowstone. I was eleven, waiting for middle school with the resignation of a sailor facing hurricane season. Self-consciousness radiated from my fuzzy legs, the choker necklace I had clipped together with bead-strung safety-pins my only talisman. That week my parents had left my sister and me with my maternal grandparents in Montana, so my then-fifty-something grandmother, Sally, loaded us into a car with her own mother, then drove us to the park. For a day or two, she rustled us from dark motels in pastel hours, telling us if we wanted to see animals, we had to get on their schedule. I was skeptical. Witnessing an animal had rarely left an imprint on my own life.

The last morning started before sunrise. We hadn't been driving long when Sally pulled to an overlook above a cliff and shook our ankles. *Enough dozing. Out.* In the brown grass below, a herd of bison inched toward the growing orb of sun across the valley. Through the aura of dust that followed their path, it became clear that two animals were staying behind. The smaller one lay like a boulder in the grass. I don't remember if she faltered and failed to get up, but something radiated life. A larger bison stood above her, craggy as a statue. Every few seconds she would pivot between the body and the departure of her herd. It wasn't until she, too, started to follow the crowd that I understood what was going on.

How could I forget that mother bison's dance? Grief swung a pendulum between what must have been her sick calf and her herd. She turned multiple times toward each, swinging the tank of her body a few steps in one direction before her hoofs would kick back, clumsily, to correct herself. Attributing human emotion to another animal has traditionally been a scientific minefield, a stance ecologists like Carl Safina now resolutely challenge. "When someone says you can't attribute human sensations to animals, they forget that human sensations *are* animal sensations," he writes in *Beyond Words: What Animals Think and Feel*, noting that if we can detect hunger or exhaustion in an animal, surely we can detect joy when they are playing with their children too. And what is the inverse of joy but grief? The opposite of playing with a child is surely abandoning it. I was no scientist, but I was a daughter. I had little doubt what was going on in the mother bison's mind.

As the sun eased over the mountains, a saccharine, yolky glow leached across the grassland, illuminating the ever-widening expanse between mother and child. Beneath the self-pitying glaze of my preteen self, I felt a surge of sadness so great I thought I would shatter. If the mother's pain was one reality of what it meant to occupy a body on this earth, the dumb distance of our gaze was another. We could play no role but witness. Perhaps because it was all we could do, we could not look away: my great-grandmother in her plastic visor, Grandma Sally in her Tevas, my sister and me in our jean shorts, mouths ajar with city-girl sadness. It was the day I realized watching non-human animals could make you feel things that weren't about being human at all.

Even as the space between bison stretched into what must have been a football field, the mother continued to pause, turning back and forth. I don't remember the questions Annika and I surely asked—*Why do you think the herd had to leave now? Do you think the baby was just born sick? Could the mother survive on her own without the herd if she stayed?*—or maybe I just don't remember Sally's answers. The memory has taken on the silent Technicolor of a Disney movie, the ones I grew up hating because the mother always died. It felt as if I still owed the calf my gaze, or owed it to the mother. As if we had promised that though she had had to turn her back, we would not turn ours. In truth, of course, there was no etiquette. We were just animals who had stumbled into another animal scene.

If the memory were a movie, the violin would suddenly quicken. The camera would pan. As the mother shrank into the horizon, the wolves appeared on a nearby hill. They were beady, sunlit, and impossibly fast, like shadows of death itself. At that time, the Lamar Pack would have been in the valley less than ten years. As Nate Blakeslee later wrote in *American Wolf,* his nonfiction epic dramatizing the life of this very pack, food could be hard to come by. It was common for wolves to follow a herd for days, waiting for someone to get left behind.

When I told people I was writing about wolves, they often asked if I had seen them in the wild. *Oh,* I used to say, *did I ever.* And I recounted this day. My punch line was unsatisfying, though, because I had no memory of the wolves reaching the young buffalo, only the fact that at some point, like the mother, we had turned away. Clicked ourselves into seat belts and driven home.

It is one thing to reference the memory, but in pressing it to the page, my image of tiny running wolves has begun to fray. To stumble out of a car into a big-game feeding is a bit like opening the door to a meteor shower. It is the pulse of nature documentaries, not everyday witness. If we were watching the wolves run toward the calf, I do not think Sally would have let us walk away before we saw what happened. And if we had seen them feed, I am sure I would not have forgotten. Years later, when I asked if she remembered wolves that day, Sally laughed, shaking a head still naturally sandy blond in her early seventies. She's sensible, her matter-of-fact rationality often throwing the spiraling inquiries of my sister and me into relief.

"I guess they could have come," she said. "I've seen them there before."

"But you don't remember seeing them eat, right?" I felt a creeping dizziness as she shook her head. "I wonder if you just mentioned they could come and my brain filled in the rest—" She raised her eyebrows at me, then, slowly, her head bobbed.

"Yeah," she said, laughing as realization bloomed on my face. "Sorry!"

Whether on Gramps's farm or in Yellowstone Park, my first wolf sightings were only in my mind. I never meant to lie. How had it happened? Even as I understood wolves were not "bad," I had, in fixating on their prey, conflated them with everything that was, anticipating their arrival with the dread-soaked familiarity of all possible endings: illness, heart attacks, house fires. It had been easy to identify with the helplessness of both mother and child, and to want to protect them at all cost. Still, as Yellowstone Wolf Project coordinator Doug Smith told Safina: "There is no peace for prey in a land without predators. There are only alternate sufferings." In this light, death by wolf can be a form of mercy.

Though I never meant to "cry wolf," I had absorbed a certain type of Big Bad Wolf story so many times it became reflex. The day I realized I invented the Yellowstone sighting was the day I knew to doubt the stories I had been told about fear. Stories about real wolves, but other ones too. Those fictions that rippled through my body as fact, even as I tried to guard against them. I began to mistrust my instincts around the truth.

As a kid I grew a slight reputation as a chirpy exaggerator. I didn't lie blatantly, not like the kids who invented pet parrots and private jets, but I sanded the edges from reality. My loyalty was to the story, its spirit. "I spun the stories golden," writes poet Catherine Pierce. "I iced them, I spiked them . . . I never lied, / exactly." Once, a teenage friend and I ran into the lead singer of a popular band on the sidewalk, where he was holding a box of takeaway cake from a local restaurant. When we asked, he took a photo with us, but did he really offer us his cake? It seems possible, but I don't remember; I know only that, in some later tellings, I said he gifted it. That we had eaten the pop star's chocolate cake. "You're kidding," friends would say, and maybe I'd cop to it, and we'd laugh, but sometimes they wouldn't doubt me, and the moment would pass. Why did I lie? Wasn't the photo enough?

It wasn't until a year or so after college, sitting in a bar with old friends as we updated one another on lives that had split on so many different tracks, that I recounted a nearly catastrophic health scare and, instead of sympathy, was met with disbelief.

"You're kidding," one friend said, grinning. "That didn't happen." She shook her head, eyes narrowed. "You're exaggerating, right?" It didn't take long to convince them, but the lag in belief clung to me like body odor. I had grown up so much, but to those old friends, that earlier version of me—jumping onto the bed at a slumber party to recount a caricatured encounter with a crush—was still there. She had never meant harm, but her stories had stained. Her truth had been burnished. What amount of truths now told could rub it out?

From California, OR-7 crossed over Wolf Creek, named for his ancestors, and then, back in Oregon, he managed to cross all lanes of the I-5, moving northeast into the Rogue River-Siskiyou National Forest. Suddenly, after years of wandering, he began staying put. The Rogue-Siskiyou mountains are a biologically rich volcanic region, the largest swath of serpentine soil in all of North America. The flowers that grow there need little soil, and can thrive in drought, filtering out the heavy metals of millions of years of accumulated sediment. It's one of the richest temperate coniferous forests in the world, but the region also has dry oak savannas and Alpine grasslands and cranberry bogs. During his years of travel, OR-7 had scavenged from roadkill, the carcasses left by other predators, and the bone piles livestock producers might leave on the land. His hunting would have been primarily for small creatures, but now, as he learned the human and animal rhythms where he was settling, it became likelier he could take deer and elk calves. This choice to localize, as biologists call it, can be evolutionarily smart. OR-7 was no longer crossing busy roads. He was becoming an expert in place.

Then, in early 2014, the GPS collar on OR-7's neck passed its three-year life expectancy, and state and federal biologists said they had no plans to replace it. There were other wolves to track; priorities went elsewhere. His "very public and historic trek . . . could come to a blipping halt any day now," wrote a reporter who had been following him for years. "When that collar dies, we'll never know his fate," said the director of conservation group Oregon Wild. "But that could be OK. It's good to have a little mystery in the world." Another writer imagined the collar dying as a sort of departure, when "like Voyager, he'll leave the boundaries of our universe."

Without a collar, the wolf would become, again, illegible. If a witness thought they saw him, there would be no easy way to back it up. There would be no GPS coordinate to say, *You are right. A wolf is really there.*

"The Boy Who Cried Wolf" has its roots in Aesop's Fables, that collection of oral tales attributed loosely to a freed slave named Aesop, who lived in Ancient Greece some 2,500 to 2,600 years ago. Wolves appear in at least twenty-five of the stories, some of which have echoes in Jewish and Indian folklore that trace even farther back in time, but the most well-known wolf story is probably "The Shepherd Boy and the Wolf." Aesop's version of the fable is short, only eight lines in the anthology I find at my library, so my brain fills in the rest. See the boy outside the village with his flock, bored. Maybe chewing grass, maybe thinking of some girl. He thinks it could be fun to pretend a wolf is attacking: to feel something, anything, in the flat lull of afternoon. He cries "Wolf! Wolf!" and the villagers run toward him. Imagine their faces stretched with anger and fear, motored by the adrenaline that pulls one away from the washing or the fields. When they arrive and see there is no wolf, the boy laughs. This, he decides, has been a good time, so he plays the trick again and again, and over and over, the people are fooled. Then, one day, a wolf does appear. "Wolf! Wolf!" the boy cries, but no one runs. His words are threadbare from overuse. In Aesop's version, the story ends there. The slaughter is unspoken but, at least for the flock, implicit. In later versions, the boy's punishment is clearer. He dies at the jaw of a wolf.

Over the hundreds and hundreds of years that this story has mutated and persisted, "crying wolf" has become essentially synonymous with lying, while the "boy who cried wolf" has, in many cases, become a girl. "A girl who cried wolf is an all too common occurrence in today's society," reads a 2008 entry on the crowdsourced *Urban Dictionary* website. "If a guy makes advances towards a girl that likes him, he's a hunk, cutie, or sweetiepie. If she doesn't like him, even with the exact same advances, he's a creeper, stalker or loner. The girl will often retaliate by seeking to embarrass and spread all kinds of cruel rumours about the poor sap. . . . #liars #bitches #nerds #geeks #doublestandard."

Not long after arriving in Minneapolis for graduate school, I biked too far across the city to attend the birthday party of an acquaintance. Underestimating the length of the journey on unfamiliar roads, I arrived late, sweating in a new sundress. I had a beer, but after an hour I knew I had to go. The sky hummed with low light, and I didn't want to navigate a five-mile journey in total dark. It was August, and the air was so humid it felt swaddling, protective. I hugged my friend on the patio. I went inside to pay.

Watching a bartender escort a belligerent white man out, drunk or high or both, my mind raised a familiar red flag of vigilance. Still, what to do? That flag rose so many times a day. I signed the receipt and walked outside. Now the man was arguing with the guy who checked IDs at the door. I headed down the sidewalk, pilsner softening my limbs. I was dreading the ride home, annoyed at the stubbornness that had prevented me from driving. When I heard the thunk thunk of footsteps behind me, I told myself to be cool, to keep walking, to chill out. A split second later, I changed my mind, turning just as the man flung his arms around my neck and pressed his body against mine.

He did not threaten me, not exactly. He told me he thought I was someone he had loved, someone who had left him, and now he did not want to let me go. His breath was hot against my cheek. My back bent under his leaning weight, and I wondered if we would both fall to the ground, and what would happen then. My future appeared like a multiple-choice question, and I knew I had to act—to scream, scold, punch, kick, grab the pepper spray in my purse—but my body felt immobile, my throat dry. In France, a hoarse voice can be called "*le loup*"—you have been silenced by the fear of a wolf. This man was not a wolf, but his action had cast us in an all too familiar story, one I had rehearsed internally on so many nights. Now the improbable had happened: the strange man had grabbed me on a dark street. It was a shock to be held by a stranger, but also to realize my reaction. Shame floated above my body, judging it: my slack limbs, my quiet mouth. *This is a moment where you could try punching someone,* I thought, but the man was making yowling noises as he screamed, and I thought: *Can you punch a whimpering man?*

I tried to shrug away his arms, but when they did not move, I walked ahead. Staggering, dragging. A man stood on the sidewalk ahead, a decade or two older than me, about the age of my assailant, and he watched us for a beat before asking if I needed help.

"It's fine," the man behind me slurred. He was shouting, but he also sounded near tears. "She left me and now she hates me. Everybody does." I shook my head, the most I could do to rebuke his claims. I pitied the man more than I hated him, but I didn't want to fight, I wanted to disappear. Splinter, evaporate, like the video I'd just seen of fainting goats. They trot blissfully through the grass until the human they are with pops open an umbrella. One by one the animals freeze then fall. Fear overwhelms their bodies as heat overwhelms an engine. Movement and mind stop.

"Help would be great," I said, as if I were in Home Depot, trying to find a strange tool. As the second man began to pry the first off my back, the first started fighting with fists and yells. For a moment I stood in the glare of a streetlight, watching them twist, the first man still shouting that he knew me and I'd done him wrong. It seemed I should help the second get free. That we should continue this seesaw of intervention until the first tired out.

"Run," the second man said through his teeth. "I'm calling the cops." Or did he say that? How did he get his phone out while they were entangled? Was there a third person who appeared and said they were calling? I don't remember; I didn't see. I was already running across the street where my bike leaned in the shadows. The lock was jammed. I rattled the key and shook the frame, adrenaline radioactive in my palms. In the distance, sirens. The red-blue lights were glowing on distant buildings by the time I was on the bike, but by then I was pedaling as fast as I could. I had no direction. The only destination was away. I did not want to talk to the police; I was not sure what I would tell them. The man had not been, explicitly, violent, but he had violated my body and space. Did that make it an assault? I felt like a victim, but I did not want to testify as one. What if the man was not drunk, but suffering from some mental illness? Either way, I did not trust the carceral response.

Later the parallel would emerge, inescapable. Just as with running into the group of masked men on the college quad, this encounter had happened in my first weeks in a new place I was trying to make home. A Wednesday in September, to be exact. Just as then, I was unsure how to narrate what had happened. Had I ever actually been in real physical danger? *Entre chien et loup?* Was it a dog or a wolf? I wanted to know if my body's reaction was earned, because that night, as the one years earlier, clung to me. Or not me, but the city I was in. I no longer wanted to walk or bike if it wasn't daylight, even just a few blocks. I stopped wearing the sundress, wondering if it might have always been too short, subscribing to the broken belief that the right hem might protect me. I gripped the key to my old car. When I couldn't find parking within a block of wherever I was going, my breath quickened, pepper spray in palm. I sensed I was being irrational. That the odds of my being grabbed by a stranger were still ridiculously low. At the same time, my body held a memory, and the memory would not go.

A few years later I published a short essay online about the difference between lone wolves and men. At the end, I mentioned briefly what had happened with the stranger on the street, that it had recalled that old myth of girl-in-forest, wolf-in-trees, and the comparison had bothered me. Someone named Wild Swan left a comment beneath the essay, recommending a local martial arts studio where I might "purge [my] fears rolling with that awesome bunch of guys." This suggestion was preceded by a caveat, an assumption that "the attack on you wasn't just a literary addition."

I knew online comments were often the scum curdled on the pond of the internet, but these words slid under my skin. Wild Swan did not call me a liar, but they floated the possibility I had lied. That I had invented an attack for attention; to make a rhetorical point. My fury radiated out to all accused of making up "literary additions" and much worse. Internally, I carried so many questions about that night—about what had been coursing through the man's body and mind, what would have happened if I had tried to fight him, if someone else had not intervened—but the possibility that someone else would question my account came, this time, as a surprise.

I was naive. Anyone who has experienced something on that spectrum of harassment and microaggression to assault and physical aggression will recognize those two phases of gut acceptance. First you learn the chemical power of your body's fear, how swiftly it can light up every joint and vein like the fluorescent gene scientists splice into monkeys to make them glow. Next you learn the loneliness of it. Not only will you be alone in your fear, but you can also be alone in your belief of it. Another's doubt can be viral. You can see it in their body and stay away, but though you never catch it, not really, still your life is infected by the possibility. The question of *What if?* That you have overreacted, that you have misjudged, that you are wrong to feel so much. A buzz in the skull, a twitch in the throat. Soon the call of doubt begins to ring from inside your own house.

After that long-ago April day when Curt Jacobs walked into his pasture to find so many bodies of dead lambs, the ODFW installed a motion-sensor wildlife camera near the scene of the deaths. In one black-and-white still, two wolves and two lambs are visible in the frame. A time stamp reads 3:05 a.m. The grass is silver, splotched with a dark Rorschach of what must be blood. In the center of the frame lie the lambs, bodies apparently intact. They are back-to-back and almost touching, heads at opposite ends, the way Annika and I used to pile into one of our twin beds and pretend we were eighteenth-century English orphans. The most visible thing about the wolves is their eyes. Four fluorescent marbles trained on the camera, as if someone has just yelled "Gotcha!" One wolf stands behind the lambs, spine bowed and head low, stooped perfectly between the bodies as if about to take a bite. The other is in the background, side profile facing the camera, head swiveling toward the lens. Has the camera made a noise? Something to draw their gaze?

The photo makes me think of that old idiom, "caught red-handed." As if the animals could be indicted as killers by presence alone. Use of the phrase "red hand" dates to Scottish legal proceedings from the fifteenth century, an allusion to the moment when a killer has blood on his hands. The prospect of "catching" red-handed evidence is a detective's or prosecutor's fantasy. That red means guilt is black-and-white. In their public release of that April 2009 photo, ODFW wrote a caption explaining that the wolves were returning to the site of their previous depredation. Entering the world the same month OR-7 was born, the photograph became evidence of Oregon's first confirmed wolf kill of livestock since the species was eradicated from the state in the 1940s.

There is, however, an alternate world, one where truth is not revealed by the footage. It is possible a wolf could be photographed eating an animal it did not kill. Wolves will feed on a carcass regardless of whether they have brought the body down. If a livestock producer finds a gutted cow with tracks circling the carcass, the state official who comes to peel the skin and investigate could find a body that tells a different tale of death. Sickness, bear, dehydration, weather, old age. A wolf likes to attack its prey from behind as it flees, so there will be evidence tucked behind the front legs, or the front of the hind legs, where it's easiest to lock on. Even when the hemorrhage of the bite fades, a trace remains, "tucked away under the putrid skin along with several tooth marks," wrote Carter Niemeyer, the wildlife manager who skinned every animal that wolves were accused of killing in Montana between 1987 and 2000. Those marks could be better evidence than a photo of a wolf snout-deep in a lamb.

In the earliest historic usages of "red hand," there were no cameras. The only evidence was eye. Say a witness goes to authorities to report what they have seen. It is not hard to imagine how selectively the term "red-handed" might then be legally applied. To note that someone had been caught red-handed said perhaps less about the person with bloodied hands than who spotted and reported them. To speak the phrase is to confirm your belief in the teller's story. This is a reflection not just on the eyewitness but the world they are living in. About whose stories are heard; whose are believed.

I used to believe truths were objective. Each one the opposite of false. But Hannah Arendt wrote of the difference between "rational truth," which is proved by axiom, and "factual truth," which depends on experts: witnesses, historians, scientists. When tied to a witness, it can mean only that a third party has chosen to believe and bestow trust. "Evidence has to be spoken of: the crumbs do not speak for themselves," writes Sara Ahmed. Factual evidence is as much a trace of history as of how that history has been interpreted. A nurse is only allowed to note a bruise on a battered woman's body, for example, if it can be seen with the naked eye. "What if your skin is too dark to show the bruises that the police often require to believe that you were abused?" writes Tressie McMillan Cottom. Sometimes the procedures for hunting evidence innately conceal the evidence.

Like a badge, belief is a thing conferred. Though it can be given mistakenly, it is almost always received as a gift. A thing you should not squander.

If you claim to see a wolf that is not actually there, and if you dread the arrival of the animal, then surely you are crying wolf. This is an injustice both to truth and to the predator. But what if you cry wolf, and what you really mean to cry is life itself? Or what if, through the sediment of years, you have come to believe the wolf is present? "A lie is not a lie if the teller believes it," writes Maggie Smith in her poem "Parachute." I want to believe her, and yet.

Nineteenth-century Swedes once used the concept of "a wolf story" to describe the popular genre of juicy stories with "somewhat weak credibility." Historian Karin Dirke cites the example of a Swedish woman who, in 1888, claimed she saw a wolf. Twenty-three armed men went after it, and what they first thought could be a bear turned out to be only a large rock. Because the woman's fear was unfounded, the anecdote suggests she was made a fool. But if a "wolf story" connoted a certain kind of storyteller, it also suggested how readily the wolf became a vessel for other fears. "A wolf story was obviously understood as a story about humans' general fear of nature," writes Dirke. Writing about seventeenth- and eighteenth-century Germany, historian Martin Rheinheimer came to a similar conclusion: "Every threat that issued forth from an all-powerful nature could now be given a name: the name of wolf . . . The entire fear of death was thus put into the wolf hunt." To talk about seeing a wolf has long been code for talking about seeing fear itself.

The bluntest definition of "crying wolf" is inventing a wolf from thin air for attention or entertainment, conjuring a potential threat where there is nothing at all. But the act of "crying wolf" can occur on a spectrum of truth and intent. A lie can just be vocalizing that you are in danger when you are not, regardless of whether you are aware of it. "Calling something a lie implies that one has the truth in one's mouth and swallows it," writes Cyrus Dunham in *A Year Without a Name,* a memoir about his gender identity and eventual transition. "What if one can only speak—only think—what one suspects another person wants to hear? Then where is the truth? How does one learn to think it?" For Dunham, the lies come not only through the lips but through their body, a body born girl that feels, so often, boy. Dunham does not mean to deceive the world; he just cannot, at that point, imagine another way to be.

That French phrase *entre chien et loup* has roots in the Latin idiom for dawn, *inter canem et lupum.* What is true and what is false; what is dog and what is wolf; what is rational fear and what is nerves; what is learned and what is inherited. The lines are rarely clear.

In the decade since I began hunting the stories of the wolf and its stories began haunting me, the world around me seemed to be shrinking. The truly livable parts were disappearing. One day Cape Town, South Africa, seemed about to run out of water. Not long after, temperatures in Arizona climbed so high construction workers began to pour roads at midnight so the concrete wouldn't get too hot and crack. During the summer, my family in Montana evacuated their homes as a wildfire charged toward them, and then a week later they evacuated again while the fires zigzagged back and forth. Soon the smoke was its own season. Fires are an essential part of an ecosystem, and Indigenous communities have long practiced controlled burns to help revitalize soil and make way for new vegetation. But the winds and droughts of climate change, combined with high fuel loads from decades of fire suppression, have created new and unpredictable fire behavior. During the year the flames arrived in rainy western Oregon too, threatening my apartment near downtown Portland, I packed my own bags. I understood the wolf's plight in a new way: my habitat was under threat.

All the while, loud voices on television and in statehouses and in my nation's capital were saying the evidence we saw—the natural events outside our windows—was an aberration and not a larger problem. Our fears about the livability of the future were irrational; we were stirring up drama for attention or money. This reflexive answer, which said the reality I was experiencing was nothing to get worked up about, echoed the responses so many marginalized groups have come to expect when voicing how the status quo is not okay. *Relax, you're overreacting!* say the voices of those in power. Beneath them, that familiar taunt: *Stop crying wolf!*

A few weeks after I moved to Minneapolis in a car stuffed with clothes and books, an assailant violently sexually assaulted a young woman sometime around one a.m. a few miles from my new house, putting her in a coma. I had been at a bar that same night with my grad school cohort, and I had left to walk home alone at a similar hour. After my encounter leaving the brewery across the river, I thought of her attack as confirmation for my fears. Maybe I wasn't paranoid to refuse to walk a few blocks in a poorly lit neighborhood. Maybe this was what people meant when they said "street smart." It wasn't until I came across her obituary a few months later that I learned Rebecca Rose Anderson was a mother of five children and a member of the Red Lake Nation. According to the Centers for Disease Control and Prevention, murder is the third-leading cause of death for Indigenous women. Biologically, our bodies might be the same, but centuries of colonial racist power in America had rendered our "symbolic biology" differently in the eyes of society and, very often, the state. Fearing too much for my own body was not only projection, but distraction.

Those days I lived in a leafy neighborhood full of big houses mostly converted to apartments. It was a street full of renters, where few people landscaped their lawns or knew each other's names, and where plastic moons of broken foam plates and fluorescent chip bags often wind-tunneled their way to our front porch. The neighborhood was full of old trees and dogs and clumps of orange daylilies and garage sales and progressive lawn signs, and every few hours the preschool down the block opened its doors for recess and the air filled with yammering joy. Every few months we received photocopied notices in the mailbox from the police department, alerting us that a man with a criminal history of sexual violence toward women had moved in nearby. Politically, I was pro-rehabilitation, and against the policies that made it so hard for sexual offenders to find property companies that would rent to them. Still I studied the pages for a second too long, as if the mug shots would reveal some clue I could apply to a conversation if an encounter occurred.

Communications professor George Gerbner coined the term "mean world syndrome" in the 1970s, arguing that people who consumed more media were more likely to believe the world was dangerous. My parents raised my sister and me adrift from media, somewhat unintentionally. The television was tucked in a far upstairs corner of the house, where the connection could wobble and the futon sagged. In the car, rather than listen to the radio, they acquiesced to our pleas to harmonize to the soundtrack for *Shrek*. Though the local newspaper was often splayed on the kitchen table, I once caught my mother prepping the table for an elementary school craft project by flipping over the pages that featured images of planes crashing into the World Trade Center. I didn't feel sheltered—they answered our questions in slow, frank conversations at the dinner table, my dad pulling us out of school to protest the Iraq War downtown—but the world's heartache and horror was filtered. I suspected they had done this on our behalf. Later my mother just suggested it was all she could bear for herself.

Now, in Minneapolis in my early twenties, I was on my own for the first time in a large city, newly aware nobody was watching out for me, much less what tabs were open on my browser. I was supplementing my grad school stipend with freelance journalism, so educating myself was, more than ever, my duty. I never considered what I could bear. I read, I monitored, I digested, I discussed.

"See the new flyer?" a friend who lived a block over asked me one twilight evening as we strolled back from the grocery store. "I googled him," she said, her face flush with guilt. "Couldn't help it. But it was really violent. Like, I had to stop reading. Though god, this is awful to say . . ." We were alone on the sidewalk, but she leaned close, voice low. "His victims were all girls under the age of twelve." She did not have to say what we were both thinking. Horrible: unspeakably, unimaginably awful. At the same time, shit. For our own twenty-three-year-old bodies, this seemed a little like immunity. One threat to check off the list.

Two years into my time there, in the spring of 2017, while walking back from the bus stop, I came across a man wilted against my neighbor's fence. The man was white and in his early thirties, wearing a leather jacket and jeans. His body was tilted outward, half slouched against the chain link and half leaning up to the sky, but mostly his body was on the wrong side—the inside—of the fence. The property belonged to a man with hair the color of sardines, a man who smoked and watered his plants in a terry bathrobe and white tank. I wondered if it was some long-lost son, and then some part of my brain slapped the other part of my brain, and because I knew this leather-man did not live next door, I wondered if he was okay.

By that point I had lived in snowy states long enough to know that the first warm days thawed all sorts of ebullience you forgot you had. So my face was already lodged into a crack of a smile when I approached the man. Our eyes collided, and I tipped my head forward in a little nod, as normally as if he was just standing there smoking a cigarette or watching a dog. One part of me wanted to check in with him—to prod at his lucidity—but another part figured he was bigger than me, and my arms were full with groceries, and he was probably just having a little pause amid a kaleidoscopic acid trip. I walked to the adjacent house, unlocked my own door, and told myself to chill out.

A few minutes after I dropped my groceries on the front table, my door began to shake, the bolt-lock thunking in the wood. I imagined the pale sun of the man's face, and from the dining room I tiptoed to the corner of the wall and peered around it, where—

sure enough—his leather-covered torso was pressed to the glass. He had opened the screen door, and was now standing against the inner door, one hand shaking the handle while the other rapped a staccato on the full-length glass panel inset into the wood. He hadn't seen me, I was sure of it. I slunk to the floor and reached for my phone.

Beneath the haze of shock and fear, I felt a sprouting shame. It was the crystallization and clash of two deep impulses—the ropy tethers of some long-ago-taught female self—and I was not sure how to square them. On the one hand, I felt a compulsive urge to make sure the guy was okay. To help him, to comfort him. I also felt the rattle of self-protection when I wondered, If I opened the door, would I be able to keep him out? "Fear is a cruelty to those who are feared," wrote essayist Eula Biss in *Notes from No Man's Land: American Essays*. I believed this wholeheartedly, but against it I felt the tug of my adult life, all the interactions that had escalated when I believed so fervently that they could not. As I listened to another few minutes of tectonic door shaking, I did a thing I'd never done before, and have never done since. I tallied all the ways the man's appearance might protect him from police violence—his white, well-shaven face; his clean clothes; his able-looking body—then I called 911. I said a man seemed to have followed me home, that he looked under the influence, confused and mad, that he might need medical help I could not provide.

"Does he look dangerous?" asked the female dispatcher.

"I'm not exactly sure . . . It's just—he won't leave and I'm alone and I don't want to open it." I paused, listening to the hammer of his fists. "The door is glass. I'm worried he could break it."

Suddenly I felt sick. Sick with fear and sick for calling, sick I hadn't known some other hotline to dial instead, sick I was hiding behind the couch instead of asking if he needed help. "A medical check is probably all he needs," I added, fervently.

"We'll send someone over," the dispatcher said. My door shook again.

A few minutes later, an ambulance and a police car arrived outside my house. From what I could overhear, the man was polite to the officers, and they were polite to him. He believed my door was a door to the halfway house he needed. It was clear he was confused, but—the male police officers determined—not dangerous and not in danger. They walked him out to the sidewalk and drove away. A few seconds later, he was back on my porch, knuckles on my door. Now he was shouting. I reached for my phone. When the officers cajoled him into the squad car, they told him they would help him find his home. They spoke to him with kind pick-yourself-up voices, like fathers consoling sons after a lost basketball game, and for a minute I felt I was watching cops on an old television sitcom, not the cops I was used to seeing on screen, filmed on cell phones holding guns and shouting in terrified boy-man voices.

As they drove into the sun, my chest throbbed with relief, but I could no longer tell if it was because my own body was safe or because the man's was too. On the one hand, he was getting help, which he might not have gotten if I hadn't called. On the other hand, could I have given that help on my own, or called a friend for assistance, or snuck out the back door and waited for him to leave? The answer was obviously yes. I had feared for my own body, but how easy it had been to endanger another's too, someone I deemed, right or wrong, a threat.

That evening, stumbling over how to narrate the experience to a friend, I realized this was not a story about my being scared. It was a story about the power of my white female fear, a fear that could ignite the apparatus of a police state I had long ago come to doubt. Less than a year earlier, police officer Jeronimo Yanez had shot and killed Philando Castile at a traffic stop across the river in St. Paul. A few years before that, Yanez was one of countless police officers nationwide who attended a police training designed by self-proclaimed "killologist" Dave Grossman, a method he pitches as the study of destruction. "Some people may be destined to be sheep and others might be genetically primed to be wolves or sheepdogs," wrote Grossman in his book *On Combat: The Psychology and Physiology of Deadly Conflict in War and Peace.* "When the wolf comes, you and your loved ones are going to die if there is not a sheepdog there to protect you." The sheepdogs, preached Grossman, were the police. The heroes, the woodcutters. A few years later, in 2020, an officer in the same police force would murder George Floyd outside a grocery store two and a half miles from my former front door, while Floyd—pinned down despite posing no threat—repeatedly gasped "I can't breathe." Hearing the news, I thought of Grossman, and then of the sheepdogs I had grown up with on Gramps's farm. They would never do such intentional harm.

By the year of Floyd's murder, my fears for my own body had quieted, settling like sediment in a tank. By then it would be hard to conjure what I had felt during those years in Minneapolis, years when my encounters with relative strangers collected like splinters in my palm. It wasn't the place that was doing it because the encounters happened everywhere—while traveling, while abroad, while at home. "The well adjusted seem to distribute their fear across their lives, not just keep it in one area, so it seems to disappear," wrote Sarah Manguso in her aphoristic book *300 Arguments.* I suspected I had become obsessed with stories told about wolves because my fears of the forest had begun to clot. I say "forest" and do not mean "forest." I mean the world outside my house, a world I was becoming less and less comfortable in. My fears no longer the haze through which I saw the narrative of my day-to-day but the narrative itself. Being alone on the sidewalk or bus or hiking trail or house no longer felt like the absence of other people; it felt like the presence of dread.

At any moment there was the possibility of a hijacking. The man who sat beside me on the bus and squeezed me toward the window, staring at the thigh visible through my checkerboard tights before whispering what he wanted to do to me, his voice so low a hiss I could almost convince myself I was hearing him wrong, even as my joy in my new skirt curdled, even as I decided to ignore him, more committed to keeping the peace than my own dignity. Or the man who approached while I read on a blanket in the park, followed when I got up to leave, chased when I began to run, telling me what he wanted to do, his language studded with vulgarity and smooth with conviction. These men thought they knew me, and in some way, they did. They knew I would not talk back. Why would I not yell? Why did I not trust my reasons to?

I did not know how to weigh who was worthy of my fear because I knew the stories I had inherited about it were false; born of bias. I did not trust men, but also, I did not trust my gut. Even just to say I was scared—no, to be heard saying it, and believed—could be pulling a trigger, endangering the life of another body, awakening that old binary of girl versus wolf, sheep versus wolf, girl as sheep. "Where is the moral?" asks Anne Sexton in her 1971 poem "Little Red Riding Hood." "Not all knives are for / stabbing the exposed belly."

I had felt "brave" as a child. When had I lost it? I could not tell if I had let it happen or if it had happened to me, but I felt robbed. Not of anything tangible, but of pleasure in a public sphere I had once loved like an off-leash dog. I struggled to sleep in tents while camping, so much that I began to avoid their fabric walls entirely, eschewing the wilderness I had once felt most free in. I began to see a therapist because I told her I was finding it hard to run outside. It was no longer possible to see where my fear ended and my grief over what it was doing to me began. Because my body had not, in any literal sense, been violated, I was overwhelmed by my own mind. Ashamed of what I perceived as irrationality. "Fearfulness obscures the distinction between real threat on one hand and on the other the terrors that beset those who see threat everywhere," wrote Marilynne Robinson. Later: "Fear operates as an appetite or an addiction. You can never be safe enough."

During those years in Minneapolis, people suggested I was prone to "bad luck," as if the encounters I had were mistakes, aberrations, not just blips in the field of female—of human!—life. And because I chafed against this way of living—because I wanted to be the sort of person who reveled more in freedom than safety—I daydreamed about what could be different. Because I felt powerless to change the world, I fixated on how to change my mind. I was supposed to be studying an animal predator, not dwelling on my own potential to be prey. I thought of the summer camper who had once scoffed at pepper spray and missed her with an ache.

During my last months of graduate school, there were a spate of purse-grabbings-with-stabbings in my part of the city, so on one Saturday morning, a neighborhood group organized a free self-defense training with glossy pastries and boxed coffee. Meeting up with a friend who was also living alone in a first-floor apartment, I told myself I was going for research. About twenty of us were there, on folding chairs in a store now empty in a nearby mall. We were all ages, mostly women, mostly white.

The instructor was a spry woman who looked to be in her sixties, wearing white cotton karate garb and the telltale black sash cinched around her waist. She greeted us by saying it would take a while for her morning voice to warm up. For the first fifteen minutes, we leaned forward as she croaked introductions; for the last eighty-five,

I gripped my chair as she shouted commands with the aerobic gusto of an elementary P.E. teacher.

The workshop was helpful in that I learned where to put my thumb to throw a punch, and that sometimes the best thing to yell if you are attacked on the street is just commands to a bystander: *Can someone call 911, now.* Still, I left the workshop uneasy. I had hoped we would talk about sizing up the legitimacy of our anxieties, but the handout she gave us held no such nuance. "You don't need to wait to find out why you feel uneasy before acting!" read a note beneath a bullet point headed "Trust Your Feelings." The gist, the instructor told us, was that there was no harm in saying you were scared, even if the threat turned out to be benign. "If you hear someone running behind you, just pull your safety alarm," she said. "Chuck it at whoever is back there." The veins on her neck popped as she mimed a toss behind her shoulder.

I wanted to raise my hand—"But what if it's just a jogger?"—but I knew the question was beside the point. She was teaching us to recognize fear, to trust it. To cry out, and to not be afraid of crying out at the wrong time, as if embarrassment would, implicitly, be better than whatever physical harm might come our way. But because there was no mention of what harm this fear, real or perceived, could bring to anyone else, I wasn't convinced. Because my fear was residual from a world that told me I was a victim, it seemed safer to absorb it than lob it outward. I did not want to cry out. I did not want to risk crying wolf.

The shepherd in Aesop's fable is lucky. When he cries, someone runs. When he cries again, they run again. His fear is heard; his voice is too. For so long his lies are met with belief. Imagine another version of Little Red's attack. In the woods or in her house. A wolf or a woodcutter. Her father's old friend, a schoolteacher, an uncle. When the girl decides to speak up, or is finally able to speak up, her mother tells her to stop reading so many books. Her grandmother hugs and hushes her and tells her the worst things are best forgotten. Her father rages. How dare she suggest he did not protect his own daughter—as if he was not a man!

Little Red, that canonical victim, could so easily be cast as liar. The wolf she reports just evidence of her fantasy. Victimhood withheld; reputation tainted. The red cape now a symbol of the spark that has caught the grass and grown. In opening her mouth, Little Red would become dangerous. Not feared but hated. Someone who slanders the man who cuts the wood to keep the people warm. *She just wants attention,* the townspeople might say. *She's crying wolf.*

When I think of "crying wolf," I think of those whose lies are believed, but also of those who tell the truth and are thought to be lying. It would be nice if these people existed in two camps, but the former harms the cause of the latter, and they teeter-totter together. Both fates are tied up in audience. Sometimes "crying wolf" is less about the wolf or the crier than who it is cried to and how they respond.

"What is the value of proof?" writes Carmen Maria Machado in her memoir *In the Dream House.* "What does it mean for something to be true? If a tree falls in the woods and pins a wood thrush to the earth, and she shrieks and shrieks but no one hears her, did she make a sound? Did she suffer? Who's to say?"

Every storyteller has an audience; every audience is a jury. I cannot look at those whose truths are doubted while ignoring the ones who disbelieve them, just as I cannot look at the liars without looking at those who choose to believe.

———

A woman goes jogging alone in Central Park on a clear, moonlit night. The path is sparse of streetlights and shadowed with trees. It's April 1989, just after nine p.m. The woman is white, twenty-eight years old, a financial advisor. She does this often, "relishing the solitude and a feeling of ownership," feeling, as she will later write in her memoir, "indestructible, omnipotent." Her headphones are on and it is thought unlikely she hears the man behind her as he brings the branch to the back of her head. She falls, bleeding. Though the attack is not at all like Candice's, there is an eerie echo of choreography: each time, the lone jogger's headphones hit the road as her body is dragged into the trees. When two passersby find her a few hours later, she has lost between seventy-five and eighty percent of her blood. At the hospital, she is given last rites, and her attack is treated as a probable homicide, later found to have included a rape as well. Twelve days later, her eyes blink open from the coma. She remembers nothing.

Two days after the attack, on April 21, the New York *Daily News* prints a cover story headlined "WOLF PACK'S PREY: Female Jogger Near Death After Savage Attack by Roving Gang." These wolves, according to the lede, are "more than a dozen young teenagers . . . at the end of an escalating crime spree." The next day, the headline reads: "Park Marauders Call It 'Wilding': And It's Street Slang for Going Berserk." "Going berserk," that old shorthand for those ancient Norwegian warriors who draped themselves in wolf skins before they killed.

Deputies soon apprehended five boys: four Black and one Hispanic, all found in Central Park around the same time. I say boys because they were on the cusp of high school. They could not legally drink alcohol or vote. They were fourteen, fifteen, and sixteen. There was no DNA evidence to indict them, no witness evidence, just their bodies in the woods at a similar time, and, later, confessions now known to be essentially forced. At first they were given no legal representation, with some of their parents not even allowed in the rooms where they spoke, a baseline when apprehending anyone under sixteen. "Whose boys get to be boys?" wrote Claudia Rankine. The male students who surrounded me on my college campus, white T-shirts masking their heads with holes sliced for their eyes: they had been allowed to roam the night as a pack of boys.

"[One officer] told me the others admitted raping the woman and said I was there and that if I didn't admit it, he couldn't help me," a police report quotes one of the Central Park Five as saying. "So I made up the story you see on the tape to satisfy them." He lies because he is trapped, because he wants to save himself.

Two weeks later, then-real-estate-mogul Donald Trump paid $85,000 to buy full-page ads in four New York newspapers. The headline: "BRING BACK THE DEATH PENALTY. BRING BACK OUR PO-LICE." Beneath it, he wrote of a place where "roving bands of wild criminals roam our neighborhoods," adding, "I want to hate these murderers and I always will. I am not looking to psychoanalyze them or understand them, I am looking to punish them. . . . How can our great society tolerate the continued brutalization of its citizens by crazed misfits?"

Eight years earlier, at the annual meeting of the International Association of Chiefs of Police, President Ronald Reagan had evoked the idea of a superpredator, conjuring the image of someone "stark, staring . . . a face that belongs to a frightening reality of our time—the face of a human predator." A wolf mapped onto a man. In describing the political creation of the American victim, Rachel Monroe pinpoints a "radical ideological shift" in the 1980s and '90s, where victims and criminals were sorted into two distinct categories of beings. There were no blurry lines, just those who were helpless and those who were irredeemably bad, a delineation often determined by racism, with zero-concession policies and a ramped-up carceral system seen as the only way to protect the former.

And the "wolf pack" who were accused, arrested, convicted, charged, jailed, and vilified? They were unilaterally exonerated in 2002 and paid $41 million for wrongful prosecution in 2014. The woman's real attacker was outed by confession and confirmed by DNA, a serial rapist and murderer already incarcerated for killing another woman.

In both "The Boy Who Cried Wolf" and the Central Park Five case, a canine predator is conjured—one by a shepherd, another by a newspaper—and made to be a threat. A chase ensues. In each case, the word "wolf" is a flare thrown to gather attention. There are no real wolves. With the Central Park Five, one lie told is that the boys are guilty and bloodthirsty criminals. Another says they are a wolf pack, and that a wolf pack equals rape and murder. Neither is true. The press, politicians, cops, and courts indicted the Central Park Five as if they had been caught red-handed, when in fact the boys were framed through bias. Did all who cried wolf that spring know they were lying about the boys' involvement? It seems unlikely. I imagine many just failed to recognize that the stories they had so long been told—about who would be a "predator," and what that even meant—were askew. You cannot trust a "gut impulse" if it rings from a system wired with prejudice. Ignorance of the wiring, of course, is no excuse. When those with institutional power cry wolf, the accusation becomes a bigger comet. The claim of "wolf" blazes longer, moving farther and faster. In the folktale, the shepherd is punished for his lie, but in the case of the Central Park Five, the victims and those who look like them suffer far more. Those who lie barely take a hit.

A year before I went to the self-defense class, *Vibe*, a music-and-entertainment publication owned by *Billboard* and aimed at millennial hip-hop fans, featured a year-end slideshow of "The Women Who Cried Wolf in 2016." The introduction cited the wrongful accusation, and subsequent lynching, of Emmett Till. All the women in the slideshow were white, those often presumed to be telling the truth by both police and a majority-white public. One slide told the story of a twenty-five-year-old Michigan mother who testified that she was forced into a car trunk by four Black men. She claimed to be held for days, beaten and raped, and she sent photos to her boyfriend as part of a supposed ransom: her own body bound and gagged, her head bloody. A few days later, she confessed to fabricating it all. She gave no motive. The price of her lie? A year in jail and a $1,158 fine.

"Much of social programming is an education in fear," wrote Alice Bolin in *Dead Girls,* an essay collection that investigates the title trope. The white woman who cries wolf is not innocent, but neither has she acted alone. She, like her audience, has absorbed the fears she has been taught, fears handed down to her through centuries, often articulated to consolidate white power. Up until the mid-nineteenth century, white people used the term "Black Peril" to describe the specter of Black male desire for white women, a fear acknowledged as being so wildly disproportionate to real threat that it is now considered a form of psychopathology.

To feel you are under threat when you are safe can be to tell a lie. To believe so fully in one's own victimhood that you do not realize you are lying is no excuse. Ignorance in white women is often read as innocence, but as Afro-Surinamese Dutch scholar Gloria Wekker writes in her book *White Innocence*: "The claim of innocence is a double-edged sword: it contains not-knowing, but also not wanting to know." Of choosing to look away from the truth, or from the tunnel one must travel to get there.

I once envied the techniques behind a good lie—the flair,

courage, spunk—more than the skills required to unearth something true. I now see the bravery in trying. Not just in digging for
the truth but owning what you find there.

Why do we lie? A liar knows the truth, weaves an alternate possibility, and sells their new version of reality to the world. This takes a
certain gall. "Lying is related to intelligence," explains Dr. Victoria
Talwar, one of the world's leading experts on children's lying behavior, to science journalists Po Bronson and Ashley Merryman in their
book *NurtureShock: New Thinking About Children.* They chronicle an
experiment Talwar and her team of researchers did where they read
either "The Boy Who Cried Wolf" or "George Washington and
the Cherry Tree" to young students. The latter is rooted in the myth
of a young Washington damaging his father's beloved cherry tree
with a new hatchet. When his father confronts him, asking if he
knows who has cut the tree's bark, Washington breaks down with
confession on the spot.

All the kids who heard the George Washington tale in Talwar's
study subsequently lied less in tests (boys by seventy-five percent,
girls by fifty percent), but those who read "The Boy Who Cried
Wolf" lied more. Why? In the version Talwar read, the boy and his
sheep both end up dead, fluff and blood along the hillside. There is
no reward. George Washington, in contrast, has tasted the frosting
of his father's praise. "Glad am I, George, that you killed my tree; for
you have paid me for it a thousand fold. Such an act of heroism in
my son, is more worth than a thousand trees . . ." his father says in
one version of the anecdote, detailed in a Washington biography
in 1809. Perfection does not make the boy a hero, but truth does.
Admiration, the researchers found, was a better motivator than fear.

In the absence of validation—or the absence of its prospect—kids will lie to stay afloat. "Lying," concluded Talwar, "is a symptom."

The summer OR-7 became the only known gray wolf in California since 1924, the land around him began to burn. This was not uncommon—by August there was often lightning, dryness, low humidity, wind—but the scale of those 2012 fires was unprecedented, and a harbinger of what would come. That year the amount of ground burned in the United States broke a record: 7.72 million acres, an area about the size of Massachusetts plus Connecticut. Though animals have long existed beside wildfires, scientists are now studying how heightened burn patterns affect wolf populations. Researchers in Portugal have found that in burned areas with limited refuge, wolves have become more vulnerable to human persecution.

But that comes later. First there was OR-7, his collar showing him walking extremely close to the Chips Fire, a blaze that began in a steep canyon in the remote, rugged northern Sierra Nevada. What was the calculus that played out in the wolf's head as he entered the smoke? His fur would have been good insulation, providing armor against the heat. Unlike small mammals, whose bodies heat up quickly, his bulk would have bought him extra time. Biologists speculated he approached the fire because he was looking for prey.

At first the possibility surprised me. I had sold him short, never imagining he could be so opportunistic. How smart to wait in the smoke for prey who thinks she has escaped. How brave to flirt with flame. I now wonder if the wolf's bravery was not choice, as I know it, but body instinct. A sign of how hungry and desperate he might have been. A body will move toward danger if it feels like the best way to stay alive. True with fires, but also, perhaps, with lies.

In her international 1997 bestseller *Misha: A Mémoire of the Holocaust Years,* Monique "Misha" Defonseca compares her Jewish identity to that of *Canis lupus.* "I was like the wolves, a hunted animal, one that would be killed on sight," Defonseca writes. Her story begins when she is a young Jewish girl living in Brussels, sent to live undercover with a Christian family after her own parents are taken to Auschwitz. Defonseca knows only her parents have gone east, so one day the six-year-old sets out to find them. Cutting her hair to try to look like a boy, she punches a hole in a loaf of bread and strings it around her neck, brings a compass embedded in a cowrie shell, and tucks a knife into her jacket. Thus begins her journey on foot across Belgium, then Germany, then Poland.

One day, stumbling famished into a shady glen, Defonseca lets out a howl, "a long involuntary cry of distress." While she sits on the ground, cradling her head in her arms, a female wolf appears. Through the coming days their paths zigzag until they eventually overlap. Soon the wolf lets Defonseca sleep back-to-back in hollowed ground with her, nudging raw meat in her direction. When a male wolf appears, the child becomes their surrogate pup, rolling onto her back to welcome them home from the hunt, and naming the female Rita after her own grandmother. When Rita is shot and killed by a hunter, a devastated Misha batters him with a metal pipe, tossing his rifle in a well as she travels once again east. Stumbling into another cluster of wolf pups in Ukraine, she finds another ad hoc home. Her trek has been unimaginably cruel, and life with the animals is a relief. "Transformed by injustice, I was reborn in a form I understood and respected," she wrote. "No longer human, I became in my heart an animal, a wolf."

Eventually World War II passes, and Misha traverses back across

Ukraine, Romania, and Italy to Belgium. Defonseca will never see her parents again. The memoir ends with a flash forward into her move to Boston, forty years later, accompanied by her husband, son, and a menagerie of pets. Though Defonseca's first name was Monique—from *monos*, she notes, the Greek word for "alone"—she went by "Misha" in America. Her family bought a house in the suburbs and joined a conservative synagogue, where Defonseca identified herself as a survivor, and where, when a few years later, a rabbi asked her about her past, she said she had been "saved by animals." When Holocaust Remembrance Day came, the rabbi invited Defonseca to ascend to the platform where the Torah was read to bear public witness. Defonseca agreed, requesting that one of the six memorial candles be devoted to animals. Her gesture warmed the congregation. Locally, she gave talks about her wartime past.

Photographs show Defonseca with a deep tan, hair the color of September straw, and blue eyes stalked by a swash of aquamarine eyeshadow. When she met Jane Daniel, a Newton mother who had launched the publishing imprint Mt. Ivy Press out of her house, Defonseca said she had no plans for a memoir. But Daniel was hooked on the commercial glitter of the saved-by-wolves lore, and after repeated visits, she managed to sell Defonseca on the idea too.

When *Misha* came out in 1997, the memoir was blurbed by Elie Wiesel, who called it "very moving." Working with a Boston literary agency, the independent press sold a film option to Disney and foreign rights to several countries, including a reported six-figure deal for a German translation. In America, the book sold some 5,000 copies, but in France, where it was titled *Survivre avec les Loups,* it sold over 30,000; in Italy, over 37,000. "Her statement that the Nazis killed like humans not animals was so profound and true," wrote one Amazon reviewer the year it was published. "Animals would never kill in masses as the Nazis did." "Will be read and reread in 1,000 years," wrote someone else.

Even before publication, the memoir raised doubts. Before its release, Daniel typed a wary note on the Mt. Ivy website. "Is Misha's story fact or invention? Without hard evidence one way or the other, questions will always remain," she wrote, after listing all the reasons why she held faith. Interviewed for the *Boston Globe* a few years after publication, she said, "I have no idea whether it is true or not. My experience is that all Holocaust stories are far-fetched. All survivor stories are miracles." At the end of the piece, the *Globe* reporter weighed in with his own belief. "Misha Defonseca makes a compelling impression, and does not sound like an untruthful person," he wrote. When he asked Defonseca why she thought people were voicing skepticism about her story, she told him it was because her survival story featured animals. "People are afraid of animals," she said.

In the prologue to *Misha*, Defonseca herself addresses the question of belief. "Who can believe that so many could become killers without a conscience and so many, victims without a protest? Who can believe the Holocaust?" she writes. "And yet it happened. I believe, because I am a witness."

In detailing the clinical phenomenon of "The Boy Who Cried Wolf Effect," *Psychology Today* notes that in real life, "shepherds" are "mostly women" who "aren't acting out of boredom." Instead, these "damsels in distress are very often motivated by an intense desire for attention and may feel unfairly neglected by those close to them, often romantic partners. Others are simply crying out to a world they feel ignores them."

Twelfth-century French cleric Marbod of Rennes saw deceit as elemental to female experience. A woman, he believed, was "a shameless liar who is by no means innocent of the crime of in-trigue." She is, at root, "a babbler, and unreliable." He gave no basis for his grotesque assumptions; he did not need to. His prescriptions were accepted; too often, they still are. Though his words are easy to swim against—punching against the eye-rolling dismissals of so, so many Marbods—it is harder to know what to do with the women who do, in fact, lie. When you cry, you carry the flag of victim. You are not beyond criticism, but the one who criticizes you must cross a higher threshold to open their mouth, swatting away the possibility that you have been hurt. That you have earned your tears.

In her essay "Women and Honor: Some Notes on Lying," Adri-enne Rich argues that our world does more than ignore women: it expects us to lie, to not only "wear clothes that emphasiz[e] our helplessness" but to "tell lies at different times, depending on what the men of the time nee[d] to hear." In this sense, the performance of lying is not different from the performance of a socialized fe-male self. A woman's survival depends on her maintaining control, however false her source of power. "Her lies are a denial of her fear," wrote Rich.

If the first wave of emotion for the shepherd who cries wolf is power—she has swollen the truth and gotten attention with it—the next phase might well be shame-laced fear. When she is really in danger, nobody will believe her. "When a boy cries wolf, he alone is punished," my graduate school advisor Kim Todd once told me across a wood desk. "When a woman cries wolf, all women are pun-ished." The credibility of all women's fears and experiences—that's what erodes when the shepherd opens her throat to lie. Not just the fate of whatever or whoever she has lied about, but the fate of those who come after her.

Monique De Wael was born to Catholic parents in Belgium on May 12, 1937. In the fall of 1943, when Misha was said to be living with the Ukrainian wolf pups, Monique was enrolled in a Belgian elementary school and being raised by her grandfather. Though her mother died a loyal member of the resistance, her father had turned in the names of his fellow fighters. Both died in Nazi custody. As a teenager, Monique applied to declare her father a political prisoner, which would have granted her financial benefits. Because her father was classified as a traitor, the appeal was denied.

A decade after publishing *Misha*, facing pressure from a global web of journalists, historians, and genealogists—not to mention the private investigators hired by her publisher—the author confessed through a lawyer to the world. "Yes, my name is Monique De Wael, but I've wanted to forget that since I was four years old," Defonseca said in her statement. *Misha*, she continued, "is not actual reality, but it was my reality, my way of surviving . . . I ask forgiveness of all those who feel betrayed, but I beg them to put themselves in the place of a four-year-old girl who had lost everything, who had to survive, who fell into an abyss of solitude, and to understand that I never wanted anything other than to ease my suffering." In the final pages of *Misha*, Defonseca refers to her childhood story as "a stone I drop into the lake, never knowing where the ripples will reach." This feels like a preemptive dodge, as if her problem stems from a lack of information, not a lack of imagination. And what a poor oversight: to see oneself as so *monos*—so alone—as to be incapable of rattling the lives of anyone else. Claudia Rankine wrote that her therapist revealed that some of her white patients who identified with trauma would dream they were Black or Jewish, as if their pain was only legible through the institutions of near-universally accepted tragedies. "What is this particular fear that possesses the liar?" wrote Rich. "She is afraid that her own truths are not good enough."

Defonseca cried wolf, but rather than vilify the animals by lying about them, she cast them as heroes. Did she lie because of her love for wolves? Love does not exonerate you. Intention only sometimes matters. Defonseca's story not only created cartoon wolves, it created a cartoon self. In becoming the trekking child with the knife, she cast herself as that near-mythical interlocutor between the species. Somehow wounded enough, special enough, to net a wolf pack's gaze.

Less than two months after the flurry of news articles predicting OR-7's collar would die, two remote motion-sensor wildlife cameras picked something up. A picture of a black wolf, a female, in the same area where OR-7 had started sticking around. What had he felt when he learned he was not alone? He would have smelled her approach long before he saw her. Heard her, maybe, through the breeze. Can a wolf feel relief? Can a wolf crack open into joy?

"Oregon's Wandering Wolf Finds a Mate," read one headline. "Love Finds a Way for OR-7," read another. When DNA samples showed the new wolf was related to the Minam and Snake River packs in northeastern Oregon, some joked OR-7 had crossed the state only to end up with "the girl next door."

It had been more than two and a half years since he left his pack, walking over 3,000 miles. John Stephenson, the U.S. Fish and Wildlife Service biologist who had been following him for years, said OR-7's collar showed signs he might have denned down. "If that is correct," he said, "they would be rearing pups at this time of year." It would be the first pack breeding in western Oregon's Cascades since the early twentieth century. "I'm very surprised," Stephenson told another reporter. "I didn't think it was going to happen."

He wasn't the only one. "The cute story of OR-7 and his female friend is so obviously contrived it feels as phony as a Walt Disney movie," read a letter to the editor published in the *Oregonian* in 2014. "After 100 years of zero wolf population, she wandered into the scene all by herself? No question there's a human hand at work here." It was rare a wolf like OR-7 would stay alive, alone, for so long, just like it was rare an eligible female would suddenly appear, so many hundreds of miles from those other wolf packs in northeastern Oregon. Sure, wolves could follow the scent trails of another's tracks, but this encounter felt almost as close to a miracle as could happen in the wild, Stephenson thought. Others had less faith.

"They thought we planted her," he told me half a decade later, knuckles guiding the steering wheel of his dusty government truck. "It just seemed too unbelievable. After that long . . ." He trailed off, shaking his head, eyebrows rising in wary disbelief. For some viewers, OR-7's journey as marriage plot sounded too good to be true. As if the beautiful thing had to be a lie. In a world full of so many harmful lies about wolves, skepticism—normally, I think, such a healthy reflex—can corrode the truth too. Lying is so often a habit of the young, a rhetorical cheat code that allows attention to linger, a little longer, on yourself. There is stress in lying, though, because there is always the potential of being unmasked. Doubt, in contrast, is easy. It insulates. You do not have to say what you believe in, only what you do not. The older I get, and the more I see of our bruised world, the more I feel myself bend toward doubt, and the more I must remind myself that skepticism, like lying, can become just another tic. A story we tell to avoid the truth—a story we tell about the wolf.

———

The summer after my first year of college, I took a job guiding adolescent girls on outdoor trips through Montana, Wyoming, and Idaho. I was eighteen, the only staffer not allowed to drink at our orientation, and at the beginning I tried to conceal my age from the girls. I wanted them to see me with authority, not as someone just a few years older, sneaking into the outhouses when we had cell service to see if the boy I liked had texted me.

One early morning, packing up camp on the outskirts of the Grand Tetons, less than a hundred miles from Yellowstone, I sent a group of girls to the faucet to fill up water bottles. They were giddy at that hour, cheery with puppyish delirium, the hangover of late-night whispers in the tent. Their bodies bumped as they walked, arms linked with easy camaraderie. They hadn't been gone a few minutes before they ran back, fists pumping the air.

"You won't believe it," said one, panting. "We just saw a pack of wolves, running in the field by camp. Come! Come!" I dropped the granola bars and followed them through the loop of the campsite, toward the sun-sliced field the girls were pointing at across the road. Specks of indistinguishable dark disappeared in the distance.

"You sure they weren't a herd of deer or elk? We're pretty close to the campground for wolves." Years later, rancher Kim Jacobs—the daughter of Curt, who had that first confirmed Oregon livestock kill—would call wolves "pretty ghosty." "You hear them," she told me, "but you don't see them." Now, behind us, an RV dragged a rack of bikes, its driver throwing us a hand of cheery hello.

The girls looked at me, not just exasperated but wounded, diminished by my disbelief. "We know what wolves look like," said one, and the others joined her, hands floating to hips. I wanted only to stay in the heat of their enthusiasm. A sighting wasn't impossible, was it? I woke up each day hoping the girls would witness wildness, and now they had led me to the field as if to say: *Here. We did.* They looked transformed, cheeks flushed and chests heaving. I sucked my lozenge of doubt, pushed it to the side of my cheek.

"You definitely had a better view than I did," I said, holding up a hand in high-five. "Way to be on the lookout." They beamed at my praise, and one by one they slapped my palm. As they turned, the tips of their braids swished like horsetails in the sun, and I hoped I was not wrong in giving them a wolf story—in giving them my faith.

5

Country v. Wolf

A month after my encounter with the man on the Amtrak train, I flew to England to watch wolves. I had received a two-week research stint at the UK Wolf Conservation Trust (UKWCT) and a grant from my graduate school to fund it. Founded in 1995, hundreds of years after England exterminated its last native *Canis lupus*, the UKWCT aimed to debunk "the myths and misconceptions" around the big bad wolf, showing the predator "as it really is," as I read on their website. Unlike many other wolf centers, the Trust didn't care that I wasn't a scientist or a teenage intern. The nonprofit would let me stay two weeks, the minimum length of time required for visiting scholars to gain a relationship with the wolves and the maximum amount of time the grant I had received from my university would cover. After half a decade thinking about the animals, watching them wherever I could in zoos or sanctuaries, the prospect of a prolonged visit left me tingly with anticipation, as if I was about to get face-to-face with someone I had been talking to online for months. I had no expectations for what sort of "relationship" we might develop, but I wondered if it would surprise me—if I would feel scared where I thought I would not, or fervor where I thought I would feel flat.

Did I deserve to fly across the ocean to chase these revelations? "It is, I promise, worse than you think," wrote David Wallace-Wells in the lede to "The Uninhabitable Earth," the viral *New York* magazine cover story he published about the climate crisis a few days before my flight. My Portland education had long ago pickled me in a brine of my own guilt—a slurry of the trees, water, animals, and air that my very existence continually compromised—but Wallace-Wells's article pelleted me with new facts and adrenaline. After a decade spent seesawing between denial and acceptance of my own inevitable punch line, global warming had lit a new mortality crisis within me, one that extended beyond my fingertips and out to everything we shared this earth with, a place I feared would soon embody the middle word of Wallace-Wells's title. The problem was systemic, but even if one person's actions wouldn't save or ruin the world, our choices were raindrops. I hated the puddle at my feet. *Don't beat yourself up over a flight,* my parents told me, perhaps sensing the way my anxious misanthropy reflected on them. *Relax.*

It was easy to envy the wolves. To want my human body to turn invisible—not only so the resources I used could disappear, but so I might disappear on trains and empty streets too. What was supposed to be a summer for solo inquiry and research had turned into a summer of fear. The man on the train had confirmed a worry in my brain, and all around me, now, the potential for other untapped worries bloomed. My suspicions bled outward, tinting one experience after another like a red sock in hot wash. Darwin wrote that fear was "often preceded by astonishment," as "in both cases the eyes and mouth are widely opened, and the eyebrows raised," but astonishment seemed like the right word for what trailed fear too. I

was astonished my anxiety had me checking inside closets and under beds when I walked into a house, just as I was astonished some
of my fears about my Amtrak seatmate's intentions had come true
after all. *Entre chien et loup*: I hadn't been able to tell.

When I thought of the man, I bobbed between two teams of
worry. On the one hand, I worried he had not gotten the help he
needed. On the other, I worried about how the conductor had visited my locked cabin to ask if my luggage was still back in my seat,
and if my address tags were on the bags, and if there was a chance
the man could see them. They were; there was. The conductor didn't
want to alert the man anything was wrong, so they'd never moved
the bags, just sent a staffer to periodically walk the aisles. Presumably the man had come back to get his notebook. Had he noted
anything else? Did he now know my name, my address? Was it irrational for me to wonder this, or wise?

The pitter-patter of my questions spiraled between self and
planet. As my mouse hovered over the flight-booking website, I
thought: What could I observe about the wolves to justify two
pickup-truck-beds worth of sea ice melting, the amount the emis-
sions from my round-trip seat will hypothetically finish off? None
of this was a useful frame for my trip, any more than it was a useful
frame for my life, but it was an accurate window into the mosh pit
of my brain in the summer of 2017. How should a person be on a
planet that might not support life much longer? And how to make
sense of the wolves? They who had been facing the dissolution of
habitat for so long. I didn't have an answer, so I ate a hunk of soft
bread then went for a walk in the sun. My shadow looked large
and indefinite on the sidewalk. Eventually, I packed my bags. In
her book *Insecure at Last*, V (formerly Eve Ensler) describes making airplanes a time for "fac[ing her] fear of death," a place where
she can "lear[n] to die i[n] the turbulence and hours suspended in

space." Inspired, I told myself traveling back and forth from England would give me practice living with death. Not just mine, but others' too.

I had learned about the murder right after committing to the trip. I'd been sitting at my kitchen table, googling the town where the UKWCT was located, when I saw her photo, still alive in black-and-white, a scowling teenager sprawled in the grass with a thick headband and a plaid skirt. My brain instantly mapped the similarities between Yolande and myself—within eight years of age, both outsiders arriving solo for new work in this town of Beenham—and then it was done, her story stitched to me like a new shadow, one I might outgrow but would never shake. That was so long ago, my boyfriend at the time told me, and he said it kindly, but what I heard was, *To let yourself be afraid because of one night in 1966 is to make yourself a fool.*

He was right. Didn't we move every day across a fossil bed of other people's tragedies, often just blissfully naive to the stories any given landscape held? As Anne Boyer writes in *The Undying,* "having a body in the world is not to have a body in truth: it's to have a body in history." Wasn't so much of my anxiety a product of projecting both the past—its murders and violence—and the future—that hologram world of sunken cities and deadly pandemics—into whatever blue-sky present I was currently sitting in, like a series of videos playing all at once across a white wall? I closed the browser window. I had already learned Yolande came to Beenham to be a farmhouse nanny; that a few days later she walked to the local Six Bells Pub for a pack of cigarettes around ten p.m. on the Friday before Halloween; that a farmer found her naked body in a ditch a few days later, near a barn locally known for harboring "courting couples"; that her killer, a man who had been drinking at the bar when she walked in, was now in jail. Wasn't that enough for a mind to hold? My knowledge would neither increase nor decrease my safety.

Later, though, when I found just two accommodation options within my budget, and when one was a room above the Six Bells Pub, I committed almost instinctively to the other. I told myself it was because I would have a mini-fridge and a microwave, but really it was because Yolande's murder had flash-flooded my brain, swamping me with everything I wanted to forget. Choosing to see an omen in past events and then to shape your path around it does not make you safe, but it does make you feel in control. I thought if I avoided the pub I could avoid conflating my trip to Beenham with hers. After all, I was making the trip to think about wolves and not about murder. At the start I believed this was a worthwhile distinction to make.

I arrived in London two weeks after a white man drove a white van into a crowd of worshippers leaving a mosque in the Finsbury Park neighborhood. The morning after the attack, *The Times* of London published a front-page headline referring to the driver as a "jobless 'lone wolf.'" The man, critically, had not been called a terrorist. He was one, but this was a label often reserved for those with darker skin. I hated when terrorists were referred to as wolves, just as I hated when wolves were referred to as terrorists; it surprised me the metaphors still stood up at all. In the weeks and months prior to that mosque attack, men in London had perpetrated a van attack on Westminster Bridge, a van-and-knife attack in Borough Market, and just over two hundred miles away, in Manchester, a suicide bombing at an Ariana Grande concert. I didn't believe these attackers were wolves, but they did make the rest of us into something like sheep. We squinted at one another as we shouldered by on crowded sidewalks then jerked our heads up when big trucks rolled by. Once the road had quieted again, we shared quick flat smiles that felt like cheers to our mutual powerlessness. The city's nervousness felt as communal and tangible as its sunshine. It was so easy—near inevitable in the 24-hour-media ecosystem—to fill one's brain with the statistically improbable, overlooking the steady drumbeat of mundane, everyday deaths. In lingering on headline-snagging ways to die, I convinced myself I was always one swerve away from being meat.

With a few research days in London before my train to the country, I dedicated myself to hunting wolf-related material in the archives of the British Library. Every morning I joined a swarm of other scholars to flash photo-ID badges then take a marble staircase down to the lockers where we would trade our backpacks for the clear plastic bags allowed in the archives. These bags acquired the sleek minimalism of museum cases, each of us carrying our exhibit of self: lip balms and laptops, the German notebooks and Japanese pens I immediately coveted as I opened my own helplessly American composition book, its cover so worn it looked practically edible. I had to force myself not to rubberneck my fellow researchers. They walked briskly up the stairs, unblinking scholars with round glasses and cashmere sweaters and what seemed to me a statistically improbable concentration of beauty. I was so afraid of death, and all around me were these professorial youth, with coral lipstick and Hugh Grant accents and little paper shots of espresso, telling jokes I strained to hear as they stepped outside to smoke. Had they dressed up to come to the library? I crossed and uncrossed my Levis, as if the friction of discomfort would turn my mom jeans into gold.

One day I surrounded myself with early drafts of Angela Carter's *The Bloody Chamber,* the English writer's 1979 collection of macabre feminist reimaginings of fairy tales. Carter's stories are full of women, wolves, and the contortions of power between them. There is the girl who "howled a little, in a firmer, deepening trajectory, to obtain the inscrutable consolation of the wolves' response," and the runaway husband who returns to his abandoned wife years later as a bloodthirsty werewolf. Her current husband attacks the werewolf, and as his pelt falls away, out comes that young man "just as he had been, years ago," causing the woman to weep and her new husband to beat her. Now, reading Carter's typewritten drafts scrawled with pen, I watched how her wolves crystallized on the page. In one moment, she slashed out "wolves are cowards at heart" to pen "wolves are less grave than they seem." Surely every living thing was a coward beneath it all, but in shifting the emphasis off the predators' own fear, Carter chided them for posturing and us for judging them incorrectly. It reminded me we all carried fear, but like one of those scarves you can twist and knot in twenty-something variations, we all wore it differently. Swaddled in our own, it was easy to miss the way it looked on others.

I had rented a room in the East London apartment of a young family, and though I had a few meetings and friends in the city, I spent most hours alone. I had imagined parking myself in the dark wood booths of pubs and the sunny tables outside them, but my solitude felt like a fluorescent spotlight I could not step away from. I longed for company, but instead I had Yolande, her ghost beside me with a pint. I didn't know if it felt worse to walk into pubs or worse to walk out, eyes at my back as I stepped into the night and tried to find my way home. Always I told myself it was narcissistic to believe anyone cared what I was doing at all.

On the Amtrak train I had told myself nobody was watching and had been wrong. I was still searching for that man's specter in the eyes of strangers everywhere, the same way I now scanned the faces of all who drove white vans through the crowded streets. *What are you capable of?* I thought, on loop. It was a hungry question, and it had no payoff; it brought me no answer and no peace. I became acutely aware of the brute logic of my own anxiety, only able to conceptualize "intellectual" anxieties if my body felt secure, a twisted version of Maslow's hierarchy of needs I had learned about in college sociology class, where emotional needs are tended to only after physiological ones are met. "Worry, like attention, is a limited resource; we can't worry about everything at once," writes poet-essayist Elisa Gabbert in *The Unreality of Memory*. I tried to convince myself the world was not, in any new way, ending. Here was a city where air pollution had been so thick at the end of the nineteenth century that people had walked into the Thames, while the "acid fog" burned eight millimeters a century off the stone body of St. Paul's Cathedral. Still, my dread about London sinking under rising sea levels pumped on, only stepping aside when I thought of the pre-departure articles saying MI5 had categorized the city at the highest terrorist threat level ("critical," defined as "highly likely in the near future"); those worries stepped aside when I was out for a jog and a car of men stopped to heckle me. On and on this went, a Russian doll of worries encasing my pleading heart.

By the time my week was up, I was ready for the country. Newsstand headlines told of a spate of acid attacks perpetrated by men on motorbikes, and it had taken only a few clicks online to see the attacks were—of course!—occurring in the neighborhoods around my rented room. I loved London, and I had spent giddy afternoons browsing charity shops and drinking cider by the canals, but I had always been acutely watching, watching for who might be watching me. I was ready to surveil another kind of animal.

A village parish some fifty miles southwest of London, Beenham looked like the paper pop-up town from a storybook. Flanked by sheep-freckled fields and stands of skeletal hawthorn trees, it has one pub, one primary school, one medieval church that was re-built after being set ablaze by lightning, and rows of quaint brick houses with windowsills frosted in white. The resident wolves lived on a fifty-acre private estate less than a mile from the town center. Though only a few of the ten-wolf cohort I met were born at the Trust, all of them were born in captivity—mostly in other zoos and wildlife parks—and if things went according to plan, all would die in it, likely in one of the four spacious, double-fenced enclosures they now shared with either their siblings or their mate.

The conceit of the Trust was that these "ambassador wolves" could provide a sort of inoculation-by-exposure therapy to curious visitors, much as my parents dragged me through the hot-sock stench of the python room at our local zoo. Writing about the biopolitics of such sanctuaries, anthropologist Austin Hoffman describes ambas-sadors as "canines that are uniquely social with humans and who gain enrichment from interspecies interactions with them." Every Wednesday, visitors paid £10 to watch wolves sleep, eat, and play, and to take photos through holes in the fence, hear volunteers share anecdotes about lupine matchmaking, and buy furry tchotchkes in the gift shop. The public would leave realizing that the wolves were not bent on killing them, and the profits would be sent to vetted wolf reintroduction and conservation projects abroad, from Bul-garia to Ethiopia to India. In a banner on their website, the Trust said they had donated £395,000 overseas. It seemed that if you wanted to believe wolves were "Government-Sponsored Terrorism," as a familiar brand of bumper sticker in the American west liked to assert, the Trust could be an international headquarters.

Alice was worried about me from the minute I texted her from Paddington Station. We'd had a mix-up about my arrival schedule and now she couldn't pick me up because she had to watch a Wimbledon match. Could she order me a car manned by a nice driver, a man she trusted, would I forgive her, would I be okay? I had booked a room in the converted thatched barn of the B&B she ran some miles from the Trust. On the phone a few months earlier, she had sounded plucky and optimistic. *Maybe you can borrow Peter's bicycle to reach the wolves!* Her accent was pruned, the syllables tidy. I pictured the scene in the film *Sylvia* where Gwyneth Paltrow and Daniel Craig bicycle down an English country lane. *Lovely*, I told her.

By the time I arrived, Alice was far from reassuring. They had decided the bicycle was a no-go on the slim sidewalk beside the screaming A4, and though I could take a plush commuter bus a few stops, I would still have to walk a few miles through the sprawl of an industrial park and up a few steep, poorly marked dirt trails.

"It's just not ideal," she said, glancing me up and down. She was an empty nester with the energy of a terrier. "The weather is fussy and the walk is just a bit . . . wild." As she talked I saw Yolande's face bobbing at the corner of my periphery like a deflating balloon. Blinking it away, I summoned the brassy American confidence I had learned to fake from boys back home. "Don't worry, I have a good raincoat," I told her with a smile. "And I like a good adventure." Her eyebrows skidded across her forehead.

The next morning, I let Alice drive me to the Trust. She pointed out landmarks while her rescue hound sat at my feet and watched me with heavy, sad eyes. When I asked Alice about the walking route, she paused, confused, before letting out a strangled laugh. "Goodness dear, you have to say '*root*' here. Nobody will have any idea what you're talking about." For the next two weeks, I was on my own. I took a bus six minutes down the A4, and then, at an unmarked road that led into the sprawl of industrial parks below Beenham, took off on foot. From there my walk was less than two miles. It was mid-July, but the weather was often cool and damp, the sky hanging like a dark, wet towel. There were no sidewalks and no pedestrians, and the few vehicles that passed were mostly trucks and unmarked white vans that rattled to the surrounding warehouses. I wondered if it was better to make or avoid eye contact with the drivers, but mostly I tried to be economical with my nerves.

Soon the road narrowed to gravel and the hedges on either side grew taller, forming a sort of chute. Here I tried to think of cheery explanations for why a soggy ballet flat was in a bramble-filled ditch. *Don't think of Yolande, don't think of Yolande,* my brain croaked. After a few minutes I veered onto a path that climbed above a pasture of big-eyed cows and into a thick, damp grove of trees. "The forest closed upon her like a pair of jaws," wrote Angela Carter of one nameless Little Red–inspired heroine in her short story "The Company of Wolves." I had always loved hiking alone, but something in those hills—or in Alice's anxiety, Yolande's story, or my summer brain—unnerved me. One day I heard the staccato of feet behind me and turned just as two horses galloped by, spraying dust as their suited riders disappeared down the hill. Had I fallen into some distant feudal era? I was used to seeking forests as refuge, and though I thought Carter's simile seemed too easy, I recognized the sense of stepping into some dark place you only hoped would spit you out.

Because I did not first arrive on a Wednesday, the "public" visit day when interns splayed sandwich-board "Welcome" signs on the street, the Trust itself was easy to miss. Hidden among Beenham's narrow neighborhood roads, its entrance was just a car-shaped pause in a hedgerow marked by a small plaque reading "Butlers Farm." A quarter mile or so of driveway wound past fields of perfectly shorn grass, a wooded stream with a sign for "frog and toad habitat," a side road pointing to the founders' stately brick manor house, and, finally, the one-room visitor center that flanked the towering chain-link fence of the first wolf enclosure. Reaching the Trust felt less like entering a zoo than entering a fairy tale. Here I let the trappings of the genre amuse me. I had ignored the mother's warnings, walked through the woods, and arrived at the wolf.

My days at the Trust were blissfully unstructured, a luxury of observation where my biggest concern was figuring out where to put my eyes. I was expected to stay on-site between nine a.m. and four p.m. with the interns and staff—later if there was something like a "Howl Night" for the visiting public—but within this window, I blocked my own time. Unlike my first weeks of summer, where the academic hangover faded into bright formless days that spread like a field for anxiety to bolt, the Trust grounded me in present tense. Walking down the concrete path that skirted the enclosures, I squinted at the wolves and tried to memorize their names. Mosi and Torak; Mai and Motomo; Sikko, Pukak, and Massak; Tala, Tundra, and Nuka. Everyone spoke to them, so I did too. *Hey Mai,* I whispered to the quartz-colored wolf with the sooty streak on her nose, mother to Tala, Tundra, and Nuka. *Where's Mr. Motomo?* My questions would hang dumbly in the air, the wolves' names melting like strange candy on my tongue.

I liked the Arctics best. Sikko, Pukak, and Massak were siblings, and they were the biggest wolves. Unlike the others—European wolves whose fur fell on a spectrum of dirtied snow to cookies-and-cream to the gray brown of a sparrow—these three were white tinged with gold, the color of milk gone sour, with sandalwood eyes lined in black that beaded in teardrops toward their snouts. Each enclosure carried a photo and profile for each wolf, written in first-person like a dating profile. "I am the smallest with a very pretty face," said Sikko's. Also: "I get very excited with my handlers and I become submissive by making squeaky whimpering noises." Both hers and her brothers' signs explained that they had been born into a snowstorm in a Quebecois wildlife park in 2011, trapped in their den and found barely alive. When they were flown to England ten weeks later, they were the first Arctic wolves to arrive on the island.

One morning I heard growling then watched as one Arctic put its head on the rump of another, stretching its neck like a saddle blanket across its sibling's body. I couldn't yet differentiate between the wolves, all scraggly without their winter coats, so I struggled to suss their social dynamics, but I wrote in my notebook that I had seen a snarl evolve into a tender moment. Later I realized that what I had witnessed was not an affectionate lupine hug but a show of reasserted power: that a dominant wolf will rest its head on the back of a submissive one as a reminder of hierarchy. A volunteer who had been at this a while shared it offhandedly, and when I heard it, I blushed. I felt like a foreign tourist in the land of the wolves, only capable of mumbling "Bathroom?" in their language. Aware I had much to learn, I steeped myself in the Trust's library, in the collection of wolf books and the archive of the Trust's quarterly *Wolf Print* magazines. I learned that like penguins, the Arctics had "counter-current heat exchangers" in their paws, which circulated blood and kept their feet from sticking to the frozen tundra. Everything I read was a reminder of how unnatural their current situation was: that these wolves—whose nails grew faster than any other subspecies of gray wolf because they had evolved to dull on permafrost—were now penned "ambassadors" in the dewy pastureland of southern England, scratching their paws against a food-filled chrome tube in a concrete base.

My instinct was to look to the wolves for my mirror. When two siblings circled one another, I longed to call my sister. When two mates nuzzled, I longed to call my boyfriend. Philosopher Suzanne Cataldi writes that respect for non-human animals means letting them "live a life fitted for [their] species-specific nature," and not, in other words, mapping a wolf onto how it reminds me of a human. I didn't want to anthropomorphize this creature that had so long dragged the baggage of human fantasy and fears, but to studiously avoid the comparison was "to risk falling into the related fallacy of mechanomorphism—the assumption that animals are machine-like creatures," as critic Amitav Ghosh writes, citing the work of ecological sociologist Eileen Crist. I was not a biologist nor a real academic; I had no real lens. I was just one animal watching another in the heat.

I propped my gaze on simile. Sometimes the Arctics walked with tails raised like scorpions; other times they dragged them like old rope. After the rain, their fur lay matted in creamy spikes like fresh meringue. When they rolled into the grass, their bodies fell like Slinkies, first front and then back-half lolling into the sun. In these moments they reminded me of my family's old Australian shepherd, but later, when I stepped through the outer fence to join the other interns and researchers for the afternoon feeding, lifting a bleeding hunk of cow from a plastic bucket and holding it against the fence for one to grab, I could feel a quick bump of tooth against the blue plastic of my glove and hear the clamp of jaw through another creature's bone. These weren't your average house Fido. The noise of a crunched femur sounds like rockfall, and always sent a zing of awe shooting up my spine. *What big teeth you have,* I would think, instinctively running my tongue over the smooth row of my own. The wolf, of course, would not respond. He was just a carnivore being a carnivore. Those teeth were not for eating me.

With so many blank hours to fill my notebook, my eye turned to the humans I shared my days with. Mike, the Trust's site manager and wolf keeper, was in his early thirties, smiley with scruffy ginger facial hair and a rain-or-shine uniform of khaki shorts and a forest-green staff polo marbled with indistinguishable stains. He reminded me of Winnie-the-Pooh, if Pooh gave impassioned lectures on predator mating rituals and stashed roadkill for the wolves in his car before work. Tsa, the wife of the Trust's late founder and its current director, was his aesthetic inverse. Short blond hair as straight as her spine, Wellingtons and pearls and crisp Oxford shirts. She lived on-site at Butlers Farm in the stately brick house that, Google Maps showed me, abutted tennis courts and an outdoor pool. Her companion was a Jack Russell terrier, Parsnip, a squirt of a dog who took unmistakable pleasure in peeing at the edge of an enclosure then kicking bark chips at the chain link while a wolf lunged and whined at the metal. Tsa, like her dog, expressed herself freely. "I'm not particularly obsessed with wolves," she told me when we sat down one afternoon. I knew Mike would echo the statement—he had told me that for an animal behaviorist, any creature that shows interesting behavior is interesting—but Tsa's reasoning didn't seem intellectual, just blunt. She liked to go foxhunting with dogs and wished England had not outlawed it. She thought the country had become too politically correct; she told me there were still mixed messages about the reality of global warming. "I'm not really a conservationist. I'm a watcher."

Except for one college student working on a thesis about wolf behavior, the five other "Work Experience" student researchers were all unpaid interns assisting Mike with farm maintenance as much as animal upkeep. The slots had been highly competitive, and the recipients knew they were lucky. One intern, a college student who arrived promptly each day with eyes painted like an Arctic's and lipstick the color of their dinner, had moved back with her mother to take the position. Another woman, a few years older than I, with a flamingo-colored ponytail and a heroic tolerance for the muckiest tasks, drove forty-five minutes each way to university accommodations where she had rented a room so she could make this work. The lone guy, a long-haired nineteen-year-old, biked an hour each way to and from a tent he had stocked with canned food. He was perpetually soggy from the rain, but he told me he loved it so much he was going to ask if he could come back during the Christmas break. That was the thing about the Trust. People fell in love. The wolves ran circles in your head.

On "Public Days," while the interns directed parking and led arts activities for kids, I lurked by the enclosures to chat with the visitors. Mike had told me that when student groups arrived for tours, half raised their hands when he asked who was afraid of wolves, but nobody raised them when he asked a few hours later. This was testament to what the Trust was trying to do—to slim the adjectives from the "Big Bad Wolf"—and, perhaps unsurprisingly, most visitors who made the pilgrimage seemed already ecstatically onboard. An elderly man in a Celtic-motif T-shirt told me we feared snakes instinctively from birth, spiders because we learned it from our mothers, and wolves only because we thought we should. "I'm on the side of the wolves," he said cryptically, tipping his head toward me in a little nod. "You know, I hope they win." A father who had come from Sweden swallowed shyly when he said his name was Ulf, the old Viking word for wolf, and his blond daughter, who stood beside him like a little echo, was Ylva—female wolf. "It's an honorable warrior in our culture," he said as they watched a wolf root the ground with a crumpet-sized paw. Except for a few children hiding behind benches while they peeked at the enclosures, fear seemed very far from the headspace of most visitors. One woman told me it would be amazing to be a wolf; another said she wanted to hug one because it looked passive; another watched one pace the fence line and then, shifting in her espadrilles while she nodded at her husband, told me, "We'd love to have one at home."

The visitor interaction I remember most clearly was when a man in a leather jacket and hair like a wet gray cat approached a wolf lazing with one eye open just beyond the fence. I couldn't help thinking of Bumble, the golden retriever who lived down the block from me growing up, who spent his days dozing in the driveway, looking stoned, a knockoff sentinel lion. The man leaned toward the wolf, rocking on the balls of his feet. "I've got a pocketful of sausages, come on back with us," he said, his voice the sort of hiss some men mistook for alluring. "That's right, come into my trunk, pretty." He was joking, but it wasn't clear to what end. The man seemed blisteringly aware of the power differential: a female predator caged at his feet. His face twitched with a waxy sneer. The woman who was with him snorted and stepped away, but the man didn't move until the animal, after what seemed like an interminably long stare, blinked her other eye shut. In some Japanese and Inuit beliefs, wolves are revered as judges of human character, possessing an ability to parse good humans from bad. After the man left, I lingered beside the wolf for a minute, watching. I half expected to share a look—to enact that old knowing eye roll—but her eyes stayed shut. In his research about wolf sanctuaries, Hoffman cites the work of Stefan Helmreich and Eben Kirksey, who "have noted [that] nonhumans may also act as anthropologists by studying the actions and mannerisms of humans." The wolf, in other words, was evaluating us. She smelled the man, she smelled me. It was unclear what difference, if any, she noted between us, but my reparative intent did not register. I was just one more two-legged beast beyond the fence.

It was impossible not to think of Yolande. I thought of her in the mornings when I tunneled through the empty fields and in the evenings when I walked the empty sidewalks. I thought of her because I was trying not to, and because as with most victims of murder, her only memorial was the thing I had built in my screaming brain. "Perhaps we have to dwell on the worst in order to keep it at bay; to imagine it in order to will it away, to pre-empt it and ward it off," wrote critic Katherine Angel in *Tomorrow Sex Will Be Good Again*. Did I pass the farm where Yolande had worked as a nanny? Had the killer seen her around before that night? Did I walk by the field where the farmer had found her body? And that night, had she relished that moonlit walk alone to the pub? At what point in the evening did she feel afraid?

Finally, on my first Saturday at Alice's, I gave in. There were so many things I would never know about Yolande. Why not chase the things I could? The rain was gravel on the crofted roof. Armed with a stack of chocolate digestive biscuits, I curled on the wicker couch and typed her name. *Yolande Waddington.* That's when I saw the *Telegraph* headline from 2002 that asked, "Can a Village Ever Get Over a Trauma Like This?" That's when I understood Yolande hadn't been the only one.

Roger Palmer, the late founder of the Trust, had always been an animal person. As a kid, he tended a menagerie of pheasants, parakeets, snakes, capuchin monkeys, and white rats in his family's ancestral Buckinghamshire home, an estate used in films such as *Elizabeth: The Golden Age*. His family had lived there for thirteen generations, once overseers of the cultivation of England's first pineapple, and now stewards of what its visitor website referred to as a "timeless rural bastion confronted beyond its watery borders with encroaching suburbia." How could you grow up in such a place and not inherit a sense of your own sway? A conviction that you, like your regal ancestors, had not only the power but the duty to steer your country?

When Roger went to school at nearby Eton, he brought the rats with him. They escaped and made a home beneath the floorboards of the science laboratory, but Roger was the sort of guy who could get away with it. After Cambridge, where he stoked a lifelong love for hunting, he spent a year chasing animals around Africa then began work as a stockbroker in London. While on vacation in Alaska in his early twenties, he had his first encounter with a wolf. Less than a year later, in 1972, he adopted a pup from a wildlife park in Norfolk and brought it home. Multiple people told me Roger had seen it advertised in an aviary magazine and bought it with a wad of cash.

Separate a wolf from its mother when its eyes are pink slits and you can be the first thing it sees when it opens them. Imagine seeing Roger: milk bottle in hand, hair like young Lennon, brows like dark hyphens. He named that first pup "My Lady." Three months later, he asked a blond teenager on a date, offering to make her dinner while she played with the pup. I had thought the Trust might conceal this story because I didn't understand how an international wolf conservation group could own its roots in a gilded history of wolves-as-lapdogs and romantic barter, but I was wrong. In the informational movie that played for visitors in the Trust's barn, Teresa "Tsa" Palmer tells the story of their first date with shining eyes. The promise of the wolf, she says onscreen, made it "irresistible." Roger went on to breed the first European wolf cubs born in Britain since their extirpation in Scotland over two hundred years before.

A large black-and-white photograph of the couple hung in a corner of the Trust's gift shop. Tsa and Roger are each crouched behind a wolf and holding a tether of rope. Tsa looks delighted, young and glamorous in light flare jeans, a black turtleneck, and a boyish 1970s chop. Roger wears a tweed Sherlock Holmes hat and an expression steeped in something harder, one hand perched atop each wolf. Somehow, six eyes are on the camera. Only Tsa looks above it, presumably at the face of the person taking it. The photo seemed to suggest two possible conclusions: one, that wolves can be gentle pets; and two, that these humans are powerful, superlative animal whisperers. Though I was aware this had all happened long ago—in an era where you could buy a tiger cub in Harrods department store, say—time did and did not neutralize the evidence of a very particular kind of coexistence. Of a wolf like a dog and a human possessing it.

"He's mad that trusts in the tameness of a wolf, a horse's health, a boy's love, or a whore's oath," wrote Shakespeare in *King Lear.* I thought of the blind faith of the visitors who had told me they wanted to hug the wolves or take them home. These feelings seemed as dangerous as vilifying the wolves, but I couldn't entirely blame visitors for having them. The wolves did seem especially doglike at the Trust, a place where they had once lived with Roger and Tsa, and where I heard fond recollections about volunteers cuddling and feeding them ice-cream cones or taking them for walks to the Six Bells Pub, or of Tsa keeping a pup in a cardboard box under her office desk. Though the Trust was clear the wolves-as-pets legacy was past tense—that visitors should, under no circumstances, try to replicate the founders' early lifestyle—the history was neither hidden nor particularly accounted for. I thought of that line from Antoine de Saint-Exupéry's *The Little Prince*: "You become responsible, forever, for what you have tamed." The wolves at the Trust weren't tame, but they were captive. Their enclosures had been specially constructed with mounds and viewpoints and dens, but run far enough and you'd still hit a fence. In the wild, wolves move through feast and famine, gorging themselves one day then sleeping it off for the next few. Here, their starve days and times of feeding were indeed randomized, but still, like children, they watched us, waiting to be fed.

"I think the best thing about this kind of place is being incredibly transparent or open and honest," Mike told me one afternoon. He acknowledged the rhetorical challenges, but he didn't see the Trust's past as a liability. "We have nothing to hide." Still, he admitted that since Roger had founded the Trust on a principle of de-mything the monster side of the wolves, the pendulum had started to swing. "We've done such an efficient job of dispelling the stories about wolves being these big monsters that it's almost swung the other way back to 'I want one in my home.' That's a bit of a problem now." He rolled his eyes and mentioned some guy named Rick Miracle, who had recently made headlines for owning a wolf-dog hybrid that bit a kid's arm off. "If you have a wolf for a pet, it never ends well. Ever. There's not a single case of it ending well." The captivity of a home did not agree with the instincts of a wolf. When I brought up Tsa and Roger, Mike raised his eyebrows, half a grin and half a shrug. Roger had understood wolves weren't meant to live fully in houses, Mike told me, and he had never forgotten what they were capable of. Roger didn't demonize them, but he didn't forget their wildness either. "They didn't so much have problems with them, but they were really, really good about looking after them."

This was the slippery paradox of the Trust. The organization was built on an exception to a rule. Visitors walked past a photo of the owners' leashed wolves and were told the animals were not evil but also not gentle, not enemies but also not pets. To understand an animal exists neither to kill you nor cuddle you is to untangle your ego from its life—to see it as complex and wild, worthy of existence independent of your feelings about it. This requires reframing the world into something less human-centric, reimagining both animal and self. Maybe it was reverence the Trust needed to cultivate, or maybe it was just an open-minded tolerance toward sharing habitat with a species so often seen as human competition and threat. We needed a spoonful of empathy, a spoonful of curiosity, a spoonful of healthy fear. The Trust's main challenge was in dosing that last emotion. I knew the challenge well.

They were nine years old and had gone to pick primroses. All of April 1967 had been an exceedingly chilly mess in Beenham, but the afternoon of the seventeenth was sunny, almost balmy without the wind, and Jeanette Wigmore and Jacqueline Williams set out on their bicycles, the earth turning and warming beneath their rubber wheels, the sky a dumb blue witness above them. I wonder if one of their mothers had been there when they left. *Be careful! Be back soon!* As if a parent's warning could be a flare, something that could help you, something more than just a fading sound.

How to live in the shadow of your history? That was the question of my summer. It was the question of the Trust, of Beenham; of the wolves, of our changing climate, of my own reactive anxiety.

"I trawled my body along behind me like a drift net, hoping that I wouldn't catch anything in it by accident," explains the narrator of Alexandra Kleeman's novel *You Too Can Have a Body Like Mine*. I was thinking of Kleeman's metaphor a lot that summer—about the things we could not help snaring and dragging around with us—but when I got to England, the image metastasized in my brain, becoming not just about one's personal history but also about the broader social and environmental histories we grew into, or tried to hide, or just hauled beside us. The things that were or were not our own faults but had happened or happened to us. That stuck to us like burrs.

The legacy of the wolf in Britain was knit with violence. How could you untangle that? Henry III had granted tracts of land to those who could kill the wolves upon it. The last English wolf was likely exterminated when Henry VII was in charge. Wolves survived a bit longer in Scotland and Ireland, perhaps another few hundred years, as late as 1743 and 1770, respectively, but it wasn't much. In a climate where the countryside could see twice as much crime as the city, slaughtering wolves had long been viewed as a step to both financial and emotional security. As geographer Yi-Fu Tuan writes in *Landscapes of Fear*, his exploration of the spatial aesthetics of fear, Europe's deeply lopsided wealth distribution had created a plenitude of "vagrants and vagabonds, beggars, thieves, cutthroats, and bandits." It could be terrifying to travel through the countryside, but ameliorating poverty was not only hard, it was, to the ruling classes, a loss. Better to make the enemy non-human. Better to make it wolf.

Memories of the animal's presence lie across Britain's cartography like a faded tattoo: Wolfmere, Wolferton, Wolfscote, Wolfhamcote, Wolfstones, Wolfenden, Wolferlow, Wolfs Castle, and Wolfpits, the last a likely burial place for Welsh wolf carcasses. In Beckermont, Cumberland, there's a hill called "Wotobank," allegedly named when a lord, lady, and their servants went wolf-hunting, realized at some point that the lady had disappeared, and eventually found her lying on a bank while a wolf shredded her body. "Woe to this bank," called the lord. And thus it was.

I read these details in the Trust's library, a corner of the educational barn with a few bookshelves stuffed with international wolf-related texts and a blue plastic chair where I could drink PG Tips tea and take indecipherable notes. Many of them were gleaned from a slim 1880 book, *A Short History of the Wolf in Britain,* by James Edmund Harting. It was hard to believe the story of Wotobank, but it was also hard to imagine the Saxons had called January "wolf month" because "people are wont always in that month to be in more danger to be devoured of Wolves than in any season else of the year," or that, in the mid-1600s, an Irish woman walking home with a new griddle stopped to chat with a friend, heard a rustle behind her, and, in the words of the newspaper Harting quotes, "brained" the wolf as it ran toward her, delivering "a blow on the skull with the full swing of her iron discus." The allegations of mutual violence in these stories awed me. As I watched what looked like a dog-and-human cuddle-puddle of Mike doing a health-check on one of the larger wolves, I could almost trick myself into thinking I was witnessing a long-awaited truce: the cease-fire between two carnivores who had once kindled an equal desire to kill one another. This narrative, of course, was wrong.

Large-scale wolf reintroduction in Britain was a distant prospect, and not even the Trust's conservationist goal. It was not just a question of if the wolves were good for a place, Mike told me one day, it was a question of if the place was good for the wolves. "They would get hit by cars here. We just don't have the wilderness for them yet." Ocean on all sides, too many highways, too many sheep, too many us.

Tsa was a bit franker, referring to English reintroduction as "detrimental.""It's trying to re-create something that was here 500 years ago," she told me. "It's better to work with what we've got." I didn't bring up that this same argument might be made about some of the foreign countries where the Trust was helping to fund reintroduction, especially former British colonies like India. The question of "rewilding" such landscapes will never be a neutral issue, especially given residual links between fascism and conservation, from Mussolini's pledge to reforest so as to make Italy colder and the Italians more "warlike," as J. R. McNeill writes in *Something New Under the Sun*, to the Nazis' dream of converting Poland into an extension of tribal Germany, filled with primeval forest and animals. To rewild is, by nature, to "rewind" time, often in an effort to "undo" human influence, but as with rewinding a tape to record over it, the act necessitates an erasure. Whose influence are you erasing, and whose are you "going back" to? It is acceptable to aspire to the 1872-level of "wild" in places like Yellowstone, writes Emma Marris, but advocates should be "honest about the fact that this date emerges from history, not ecology."

The question of contemporary English reintroduction is influenced in large part by public opinion, which, for wolves, is still largely about inherited fear. Surveys revealed that the older a person was, the more likely they were to view wolves negatively. It seemed likely that, as with exposure to a toxin, those individuals had just consumed more outdated fairy tales and fewer reparative retellings. "Traditionally, people with the most positive attitudes toward wolves have been those with the least experience," wrote a group of transatlantic researchers, reviewing surveys about attitudes toward wolves conducted between 1972 and 2000 in the United

States and Europe. By this logic, I assumed the Brits would feel rosy about a creature that had not only been gone hundreds of years but now existed only across the cold artery of the English Channel. I was wrong. Though Europe has seen almost no wolf attacks attributed to non-rabid wolves in the last century, in a study from 2009, about fifty percent of teens in the mainland United Kingdom self-reported being afraid of wolves, and sixty-five percent in Northern Ireland, compared to only thirty-five percent of teenagers in the "wolf regions" of rural Spain. In general, people were more afraid of wolf attacks in those parts of central and northern Europe where wolves had recently returned, as opposed to the southern and eastern parts of the continent, where populations never disappeared.

When I read these statistics I felt a blooming pride for the students who visited the Trust and, according to Mike, changed their minds about whether the wolves were out to eat them. The children had unlearned their fear. But one day, watching a wolf toss a stick with a noise that sounded almost like a whinny, I realized that English visitors to the Trust could decide wolves were not scary without ever having to really consider encountering one in their yard. A visitor's monthly donations to "adopt" an ambassador wolf could fund foreign rewilding efforts while the visitor remained, even unconsciously, in a hypothetical Not-In-My-Backyard nest. The wolves could come back, but they would come back on someone else's turf. They could become someone else's worry.

"A wolf may be more than he seems. He may come in many disguises," Angela Lansbury's character says to her adolescent granddaughter in the 1984 cult film *The Company of Wolves*, co-written by Angela Carter and based on her story of the same name. Framed within the dreams of a contemporary preteen who falls asleep in her family's gothic English country home, the film corkscrews into a fairy-tale dreamscape of stone huts and peasant skirts, snakes twisting in the trees like some medieval Eden. The girl's nightmare begins when her older sister, wide-eyed in a gauzy white dress, wanders off the path and meets a pack of wolves. When the animals emerge from the shadows, their Maraschino cherry eyes are the only thing visible, like headlights on a road where you have thought yourself alone. The girl is dead within seconds.

"Why couldn't she save herself?" the younger sister asks her grandmother after the funeral. "You don't know anything," Lansbury says. "You're only a child." She explains that there are two kinds of wolves: those with "hair on the outside," and, even worse, those with "hair on the inside," who want to lure women into the forest. This grandmother doles out warning stories the way mine does wool socks, each story unspooling a cinematic vignette within the larger dream. Men are often deceiving women. People are often turning into wolves. There's the man whose human face rolls off like strips of Twizzlers to reveal the snarling carnivore within, and the man whose wedding banquet is interrupted by a woman he once wronged, now a witch who turns the whole party into wolves, their furry bodies splitting through silk suits.

Most of the canines in the film are malamutes with fur dyed the purpled black of a bad wig. Some of the close-up shots, though, feature real wolves, some of the first to have lived with Roger and Tsa, the would-be stars of films such as *An American Werewolf in London* and *Dracula*. Tsa told me she accompanied them while Roger was in London or traveling for work. While filming scenes between the wolves and the young red-caped actress, the crew of *In the Company of Wolves* had a man with a shotgun, a man with a net, and a vet with a tranquilizer at the edge of the set, poised in case the wolves turned on the heroine. Instead of attacking, the animals spent their time afraid of a nearby duck. "They're terribly shy," director Neil Jordan said in an interview with an Australian broadcaster. "When you want them to look vicious, they don't look vicious, and when you want them to look calm they bite your arm off." Except they didn't. No arms were harmed. The wolves were distractible, squirmy. I could imagine they wanted to run from the villainous roles they had been cast in and would thus perpetuate, but that would be projecting. The wolves just wanted to run.

One day Mike brought in a deer scavenged from the side of the road. He cleaved it apart and tossed a quarter of the rib cage over the fence. Listening to the bones split like fireworks, it was easy to forget I was watching eaters who had been born in captivity. The wolves ate the way I tried and failed to dance: without self-consciousness, ruled by instinct alone. Was watching wolves in an enclosure like watching humans in an airport, poised between anticipation and relaxation but essentially inert? Unless something flew over the walls of the enclosures, they did not stalk or hunt prey. They did not disperse, or roam for mates, or colonize uninhabited territory because their pack size was increasing, or travel an average of twelve miles per day. I speculated what this did to the wolfishness of them, just as I speculated what eating three meals a day of pre-frozen plastic supermarket bundles or sleek bottles of Soylent did to the humanness in us. All the while I rebuked my own romanticism. Surely food tasted no better for a wolf if she had procured it herself. Wolves were scavengers; they ate meat others had killed all the time. Meat was meat, bone was bone. And yet, might the wolf taste the chase inside the deer?

According to Joe, a self-identified "nice Somerset boy" who was getting a PhD in behavioral biology and who overlapped with me for a few days at the Trust, captivity had likely shifted the innate behavior of the Trust's wolves. Joe's movement-sensing wildlife cameras showed these wolves rarely used the area in front of the fence when we were not around, coming to drink from the trough but not to stretch their bodies as they did when under our gaze. He thought the daylight feeding schedules were probably altering their circadian rhythms, in turn influencing their hormones. I had come to observe wolves, but I was seeing them through the fun-house mirror of their own captivity.

Joe told me he thought the Trust was doing a good job, and was an invaluable resource for research and observation, for the public, and for these animals, who had become accustomed to humans in their first months of life and would thus never be able to live in the wild anyway. Still, it felt complicated. I read a story in a back issue of the Trust's quarterly, *Wolf Print*, about a wolf who had crashed into one of the fence posts while playing with his sisters and damaged the top two vertebrae of his spine ("the same two as the late Christopher Reeve," wrote the wolf handler who covered the incident). Instead of killing the wolf, the Trust had rehabilitated him with the aid of a hydrotherapy center designed for horses. The designated volunteer sat in the pool "with a huge wolf who when tired wrapped himself round [her] and held on for support," in her words. The Trust, in this case, was both the indirect cause of the injury and the direct cause of its recovery. The volunteer called it one of the most surreal moments of her life.

When I interviewed Pat, one of the Trust's longest-standing volunteers, a septuagenarian with ivory hair spraying like uncorked Prosecco from his well-tanned skull, he told me the special thing about the Trust was it was one of the few places you could interact with a wolf where neither of you would have to feel much fear for the other. It was easy to forget about the fire extinguishers painted green to camouflage along the enclosure fences, which we intern/ researchers were instructed to employ with loud noises if "something turned" while a staff member or volunteer was in a wolf pen. "Never say never," Pat told us during orientation. Still, at the Trust, it was easy to think, *Well, probably not.* Perhaps the biggest thing Western folktales had distorted, Pat told me, was the fact that wolves were afraid of humans too. A young wolf will think everything is life-threatening until she is proved wrong. I thought of Angela Carter's crossed-out line: "Wolves are cowards at heart."

Fear is as primal as hunger. We are all born scared. The wolves at the Trust had grown up to believe they did not need to fear us, just as humans who reared wolf pups often believed they did not need to fear them. So often this instinct was wrong. I had heard about several Trust volunteers bitten by wolves over the years. And I had read about the wild wolves who, after previous exposure to humans, now approached the very hunters who shot them.

How much fear should you stoke to stay alive? How much trust can you afford before it kills you? My nerves were their own form of captivity, the summer days ghoulishly contorted through my own speculative anxiety. I didn't like to watch myself recoil or change my pace on the dark roads, but at the same time it felt naive to just walk and whistle. How could I pretend the earth could never quake, the stranger could never follow me home, the wolf would never bite?

After returning to Alice's in the evenings, I often jogged on a towpath along the Kennet and Avon canal. Constructed in the eighteenth century to expedite safe travel between Bristol and London, the wooded waterway had once been an artery of trade, but it now existed mostly as part of the UK's vast "heritage tourism" network, carnival-colored residential houseboats tethered to the shore. The whole place felt like something out of *Watership Down* or *The Wind in the Willows*, a stage set for talking rodents drinking afternoon tea. One evening I decided to jog toward the Trust along the canal, then take the bus back along the highway. Twenty minutes in, giddy on endorphins and the purpling sky, I paused to take a photo on a bridge. I hadn't seen a boat or a human in a while, and the canal was quiet except for the shuffling of poplar leaves and sprays of high-pitched birdcall. Raising a bare leg to the banister, I leaned in for a quick stretch.

The whistle hit me like a spitball. It is unmistakably human, this thing we call the wolf whistle. As I swiveled, trying to spot who had capsized my peace, my nerves tipped into rage. I wanted to run from the whistler and toward someone else, but I was in the middle of the bridge, and which way was that? I had no idea. Over a mile of woods sat on either side of me. The whistle came again, now fol-lowed by a low laugh. Someone was watching me panic. *Just a dumb human finding entertainment,* I told myself even as I started sprint-ing, turning in time to see two empty blue folding chairs partially tucked under the bridge. *Probably just bored teenagers,* I thought, and I told myself this for the rest of the run, heart yanking limbs through the darkening trees, as if it was any consolation, as if a teenager was too young to harm anyone at all.

David Burgess had been the kind of kid who would pull the wings off insects while their bodies still moved. He had grown into a dump-truck driver with brows like slugs and a glass eye from an air-pistol accident. "The man with the staring eyes," the press would call him. He was nineteen years old, working a shift at a Been-ham dump pit, when Jacqueline and Jeanette went for their bike ride. Had he just watched them pass and decided on a whim? He was gone from work for twenty minutes. In that time, he sexually assaulted and drowned Jacqueline and stabbed Jeanette before casting their bodies into a gravel pit at the Beenham Quarry. Soon after, his brother found him reading calmly in the staff hut.

When searches began for the girls' bodies, Burgess joined in. He spoke with television reporters about the tragedy. He gave his condolences to Jacqueline's father, the owner of the local garage. Months later, in July, a jury sentenced him to life in prison. "The 'Average' Boy Convicted of Savage," read one local headline.

Once behind bars, Burgess confessed to a guard that he had killed Yolande the previous fall as well. When the officer asked why, his answer, allegedly, was "Because I felt like it." He would go on to confess and deny her murder multiple times, as if even he could not decide what version of reality he wanted to endorse.

The English countryside was supposed to be peaceful. That was the story I told myself, that I confronted as early as my first sunset at Alice's, when my jog to a nearby pasture ended after a herd of thundering cows chased me under a barbed-wire fence and into a ditch of blackberries and stinging nettles. As a kid I loved England like a lazy groupie. I knew very little and felt very much, referring interchangeably to "England" and "Britain." In sixth grade I bought a Union Jack–printed sweater and pinned its miniature flag above my bed. It didn't matter I had never been, at that point—I had read *I Capture the Castle,* the first novel of *101 Dalmatians* author Dodie Smith, falling in love with the life of its young protagonist, Cassandra, who lived in a decrepit Suffolk castle with her eccentric family in the 1930s. Published in 1948, Smith wrote the book while living abroad in California with her husband during World War II.

Longing for her native landscape crawls like a vine through its pages. "What is it about the English countryside—why is the beauty so much more than visual? Why does it touch one so?" muses Cassandra's father one day. We don't get a clear answer, but later a character notes, "So many of the loveliest things in England are melancholy."

I wistfully agreed, though my preteen self wasn't sure why. I had always felt a kindred spirit between the gray drizzle of Oregon and England, but while the Pacific Northwest was shaggy and slightly monstrous—banana slugs the size of bratwursts, fifteen-story Douglas firs that dripped with acid-yellow lichen—the hilly patchwork of England allured me through its illusion of safety and order, its rolling pastures cut by low stone walls. Human touch was irrefutable in that cultivated landscape, but it was so obvious as to be almost beside the point. Any curiosity I felt about the state of England's former wild was overshadowed by the fantasy of imagining myself as another, more mythical creature of the country's heritage—an Austenian heroine running to meet a forbidden suitor through poppy-blown fields. Unlike Montana, where I spent so many of my childhood summers, I had no expectations for gawking at lightning or bison. In England I did not want the sublime; I wanted waves of sheep and bluebell-scented lanes. I wanted the gauzy golden days depicted in the first half of the Keira Knightley film *Atonement*—an effect, I later learned, achieved only by pulling a Dior silk stocking over the camera lens.

When scientists talk about the importance of predators in a landscape, they often mention the ecology of fear. It's a concept that refers to findings that carnivores may be more environmentally critical for their nonlethal effects on prey than for their direct culling. Wildlife ecologist Joel Brown coined the phrase in a paper in 1999, four years after wolves were first reintroduced to Yellowstone National Park, and, incidentally, four years after Roger founded the Trust. It wasn't until I read scientist Cristina Eisenberg's account of watching a wolf pack move at a "slow lope, tails high" through a herd of watchful elk that the concept clicked. Because those Yellowstone wolves were not then hunting, the species could warily coexist. But in the moments after the wolves disappeared, the elk regrouped in a tighter huddle, heads raised and watchful as they resumed their meal. "Where wolves go around, the forest grows," writes Eisenberg, summing a Romanian proverb. When they sense they have a reason to be afraid, deer and elk often change behavioral patterns. They may gather in clearer areas free of impediments for their escape, spending more time watching and moving and less time eating. Where fear shapes the herds, the herds can shape the landscape. Some willow trees in Yellowstone are stumpier in open areas compared to where terrain has visual obstacles. Songbird populations were shown to rise with the growth of new trees. Wolves don't take full credit, but their return to Yellowstone probably helped. Scientists might disagree as to whether wolves deserve the label "keystone species," but it seems clear their presence or absence combines with other factors to reverberate through, and shape, the landscape. This feedback loop is called a "landscape of fear," which science writer Ed Yong defines as "psychological topography that exists in the minds of prey, complete with mountains of danger and valleys of safety." One study found that after the wolf reintroduction to Yellowstone, elk herds nibbled shrubs less, leaving more berries for grizzly bears to bulk up on pre-hibernation. In certain places, and at certain points of year, these berries represented over half a grizzly's diet. It looked like an increase in wolves could lead to an increase in bears.

Can you apply what has happened in the managed ecosystem of

Yellowstone to the larger North American, or even global, landscape? Multiple biologists I spoke with were wary of how conservationists and the media oversimplified the "landscape of fear" narrative, referring to the wolves-singlehandedly-restoring-Yellowstone story as a form of "reciprocal myth making," as virulent as the idea that predators are a violent scourge, field biologist Arthur Middleton wrote in a *New York Times* op-ed. Elk populations dwindled because of other reasons too, he wrote, citing severe drought, record-breaking warm temperatures, beetle infestations killing trees en masse, and the effects of natural gas drilling on migration patterns. Sure, trophic cascades existed, and in some places they were easy to trace, but to trumpet the wolves as a panacea to the land was to overlook problems that still needed to be solved. Environmental groups might spend more time helping local landowners live beside wolves, and less time talking about how the songbirds were being saved, he suggested.

When I spoke with Arthur, he told me he was particularly frustrated by how the story about wolves as big bad actors in the landscape neglected to acknowledge how powerful prey could be too. "Give the prey more credit," he told me over the phone. "They can kick your face off or poke an antler in your guts." He had walked into a snowy field once to find a big male wolf he'd been tracking dead in a splatter-paint of blood, with two clean holes through its body, one in the groin and one in the shoulder. It took him a minute to understand the "predator" had been skewered by the "prey," the elk spinning its attacker around and around on its antlers. "The prey is pretty badass," Middleton said.

I had learned about the idea that fear could shape a landscape while studying the effects of wolf reintroduction in the American west, but in England I began to wonder how ecologies of fear extended to human communities too. Of course some environments felt safer than others, and of course we carried ourselves differently in those places, but if I had once thought prey was a particular kind of animal, I now saw it as a particular state of being, one that could come across you as swiftly as a passing cloud. If fear was a shadow, what might flourish in its shade?

My most memorable day at the Trust was when Mike shuttled the three Arctics into a holding pen, opened their empty enclosure for routine maintenance, and ushered me inside. "Take a look," he said. "Watch for holes, they get busy back there." It was an extremely hot day. Wolves cannot perspire through their fur, and these wolves lay in the shade, barely willing to acknowledge one another, much less us humans. Skirting the edge of the enclosure, I walked past thick stands of long-needled pines and toward a cluster of aspens, their leaves gossipy with wind. I held my breath, aware I was trespassing and aware that somewhere the real inhabitants were watching me do it through a chain-link fence. In the middle of the grove was a hole, its opening nearly wide enough for me to slide through, a trapdoor to a chain of caverns below. I kept walking, counting the steps to the hazelnut trees at the very back of the pen: seventy, eighty. From there you couldn't even see the visitor walkway. The Trust had designed it so a wolf could hide here from humans almost entirely. Queen Anne's lace and nettles wrestled through the holes in the back fence, while, beyond it, that record-breaking sun seared a distant pasture, upon which mounds of hay sat swaddled in black plastic, like giant licorice candies.

Stepping beneath the branches of a blushing apple tree, I eyed scattered gray feathers, a pile of dry wolf scat sugared with white, and a clump of vertebrae still furry with flesh. Just as I turned to circle toward the center of the pen, I felt that old cliché: eyes on

your back, steady as two thumbs. Spinning, I jumped. "Fear makes
for a redeemed ecology, one into which the reality of violent death
injects a kind of health and vigor," wrote English author Adam Nicolson in a *Granta* essay about wolves in the American west. I knew
I would not—could not—die in the pen, but I did not know what
else to chalk my vigor up to. Novelty? Awe? Behind me, not more
than a foot away, one of the Arctics was watching me through black
lozenge eyes, tongue out like a piece of sashimi. The fence felt irrelevant. I swallowed, instinctively glancing to see who had seen me
flinch. No human was there: we were alone in the trees. My mouth,
like the wolf's, hung open. For a minute we stood, two animals, and
watched one another.

It was tempting to label this the *heiliger schauer,* what zoologist
Konrad Lorenz called the "holy shiver" of awe that predators inspired in prey. In *Of Wolves and Men,* Barry Lopez explains that the
initial moments of eye contact between predator and prey facilitate
an exchange of information that either ignites or defuses a chase. "I
call this exchange the conversation of death," he wrote. But in this
case, who was predator, and who prey? At the Trust neither wolf
nor human feared the other. The conversation our eyes were having
was, very likely, not about death, but isolated from other members of our species, it still felt—to me—revelatory. In an interview,
poet and novelist Ocean Vuong said that to look at a creature is to
"decide to fill our entire existence, however briefly, with that very
thing." In looking at the wolf, I felt a part of me becoming him, the
heat a heavy hand pressing against our collective fur coat.

You're in my space, I thought, because it seemed possible the wolf
was thinking that too. Just as I had snuck into the animal's enclosure, he had snuck into my quiet. Because I knew they were penned
in the adjacent enclosure, I was less surprised by his presence than
that I had not heard him approach. I had prickled with awareness,

but the wolf had out-tiptoed me. Biologist David Mech writes that both a wolf and its prey may hesitate in the moment where they realize the other is aware of them. In our communal pause, I felt the whoosh of possibility: that a sneak encounter like this could happen when I was hiking back in Oregon, without a fence between us. It made me feel woozy, which is another way of saying it made me feel more alive, like all my senses had received prescription eyewear. "Eventually, to behold is to become beholden to," writes artist Jenny Odell in *How to Do Nothing*. This was where the Trust had excelled: at getting humans to imagine, albeit through a fence, how it would feel not just to behold, but to be a wolf. The projected feelings might have been overly romantic—"rugged," "free," "loyal"—but at their best, they could still nudge the anthropocentric brain aside. Remind the human that the world existed for bodies beyond themselves.

Later Mike would explain that the problem with contemporary wolf conservation was that some people thought it was the whole battle. There's no point trying to conserve an individual species, he told me. The thing we need to conserve more than anything is the habitat within which the species exists. It's one thing to stop hunting an animal, but it's another entirely to stop building subdivisions and highways that bisect the habitat predators and their prey need. Wolf habitat is human habitat too. Their landscape of fear bleeds into our landscape of fear. Both wolves and humans could be scary, but both of us could also be scared, and both of us were now faced with the strange reality of sharing ever-dwindling space as the forests burned and the sea levels rose. This was a world defined not just by the present, but by the violence of the past—a past only we, the humans, could conceptualize and, thus, face.

Geographer Tuan wrote we are wrong to see the study of fear as merely the study of withdrawal because though anxiety drives us toward security, it also ignites the curiosity that drives us to adventure and knowledge. As in: *What animal is making that rustling noise? Let me go look.* Wolves might be afraid of everything until proven otherwise, but fear did not have to be deadweight, it could be a motor for inquiry and creation too. If one form of fear had carried me over the ocean, another form had perhaps brought the wolf to my face that afternoon.

A starling fell toward us like a Frisbee. We both looked up. The bird peeled up, away. When the wolf and I turned back to one another, the moment had tipped. It feels important to remember who first stepped away, but I don't recall. The thing about love and fear is both will make your knees weak. I was as aware I had had a moment with the wolf as I was that the wolf had not had a moment with me. In *On Looking*, John Berger writes that in the wild, the stare between man and animal is "attentive and wary," with each "looking across ignorance and fear." In a zoo-like environment, like the Trust, this sort of encounter was impossible. As Berger would say, the animals were "immunized to encounter." I was just another tall body in the grass, damp gathering like dust in every crease of my limbs.

The heat was obscene. The day was not like England and yet, as the interns discussed over mandarins at lunch, it was the new, globally warming England. Sun like a fat pearl, which is to say like a gift we had to accept. When the wolf began to walk away, I did not hear a thing.

The month after I flew home, English writer Robert Winder published *The Last Wolf: The Hidden Springs of Englishness,* a book proposing England started on the path to becoming England when, in 1281, King Edward I gave a Shropshire knight a royal edict to rid the land of wolves. Even in remote parts of the country, sheep populations subsequently boomed, a transformative feature that "most persuasively describes England as a land cleansed of wolves," wrote Winder.

With sheep essentially the fossil fuel of the English Middle Ages, wool funded the creation of the picturesque manor houses and churches that linger as quintessentially "English" today. Citizens hunted wolves with bounties on their heads, but widespread decimation in some places came also through the cutting and burning of the forests that had once sheltered them. The landscape I had fawned over as a teenager was not just a bucolic place where wolves happened to no longer exist; it was a place that likely looked the way it did in part because wolves had been driven out. "I wish that we would not fight for landscapes that remind us of who we think we are," wrote English writer Helen Macdonald in *H Is for Hawk*. Though Winder cited other factors besides wool in England's rich ecological dowry—coal and wheat, for example—he pins the extinction of the wolf as a national genesis point. If sheep were money, wolves were man's main competitor for it. With the species' collapse, humans could transform the "wolf-haunted heights" of *Beowulf* into quaint profit-making pastures. What he did not say was that without wolves to fear, humans could turn on one another.

In *Landscapes of Fear*, geographer Tuan maps aesthetics of human horror while paying particular attention to the English countryside. "The farmstead is a haven, we say, but haven implies threat: one idea leads to the other," he writes in the introduction. I, for one, cannot look at a slate-smooth sea without imagining it frothing into cream. "Reading about murder in a country vicarage sends a special thrill through us, because the juxtaposition of violence with rose gardens and cow pastures seems so incongruous," Tuan wrote in a chapter devoted specifically to rural life. It was as if our minds were always bending toward some terrible equilibrium of peace and terror, searching for the silver lining in the cloud even as we waited for the rattle in the closet. Miss Marple, Agatha Christie's oft-knitting and oft-eavesdropping elderly sleuth, maintained a gleeful realism about the darkness that stalked her own Beenham-like town, St. Mary Mead. "One does see so much evil in a village," she said.

I started reading Tuan because I was thinking about the legacy of wolves in England's countryside, but I kept reading because I was thinking about the legacies of human violence too. The things our bodies and the land carried; the things our bodies and the land forgot. The wolves and the women who disappeared; the wolves and the women who came back. Tuan quotes the academic Raymond Williams writing about how swiftly the social exploitation of England's peasant-class "dissolved into the landscape" beneath its neat hedgerows and profits. "Behind it lay numerous tales of deprivation and fear which, but for the literary record, would have faded from our consciousness because they left their mark largely on the perishable bodies and minds of the people," wrote Tuan.

It felt impossible—no, not impossible, just remiss—to view Beenham's histories as discrete. Like having a headache and imagining it as only a nerve problem, and not that you might also be thirsty, or anxious, or tired, or you've just eaten too many snap peas, as I did once by a pool. No place has a single story, and in England, I finally understood. Black American theorist Saidiya Hartman writes that this "sense of temporal entanglement, where the past, the present and the future, are not . . . cut off from one another, but rather that we live the simultaneity of that entanglement" is "almost common sense" to descendants of slavery, those who both live in, and *as*, its afterlife. It was my privilege that I had so often been able to see the decades as history textbooks, each bound, each discrete. When I thought of the pastures around the Trust now, a thousand images flashed through my head. I saw the shadowy groves of beeches that once thrived there; I saw the wool sweater in my closet at home; I saw the oil-fueled tractor dragging across the horizon; I saw Colin Firth as Mr. Darcy in his wet white shirt; I saw the wolf eating the woman on Wotobank; I saw the wolf walked on a leash by a Trust volunteer; I saw Yolande in the farmer's ditch; I saw Alice laughing on the phone while she watered petunias at the B&B. I closed my eyes. I couldn't blink any of it away.

I hadn't told anyone at the Trust I had learned about the year of Beenham murders. I wore the knowledge like a rash, aware of its itch beneath my sleeve but unsure what to do with it. By the time Roger and Tsa had brought the wolves to Butlers Farm, over a decade had passed since the traumatic events. Both Jacqueline's and Jeanette's families moved away after the murders, and because they said they didn't feel welcome, David's had too. The gravel pit that once hid the girls' bodies had been filled. "All you can see is a splodge of green grass," an elderly Beenham inhabitant told a *Telegraph* reporter in 2002.

It felt cathartic to itemize the physical aftermath of the tragedy, if only because it was so dwarfed by the trauma that couldn't be tallied—the half-life of nerves that lingered, radioactive, as years passed. One local woman remembered the day of the kidnapping perfectly because Jacqueline's older sister had wanted to go out too, and she had persuaded her to stay and play instead. "Ever afterwards I've always thought, 'God, what would have happened to her if I hadn't done that?'" she told a reporter. For years afterward, her own sister had requested their father tie the bedroom window shut with a rope.

I wondered if, or how, the wolves had entered the psyches of those who dwelled around them. Soon after Tsa and Roger moved to Butlers Farm, the BBC came to film a fantasy TV episode with the wolves, for an adaptation of John Masefield's 1935 book *The Box of Delights*. They brought smoke and wind machines, a fire engine with fake snow, and long-horned cattle to create an Iron Age encampment where the show's time-traveling young lead could witness a wolf attack. The filming went on all night, and according to *Wolf Print*, the bright lights in the sky alarmed nearby neighbors, who walked across the fields in the middle of the night suspecting UFOs. What was the landscape of fear in Beenham? Maybe the wolves had truly brought no new fear to the village. Maybe they just provided a new identity. The primary school had decided to adopt a yearly wolf and start an after-school wolf club. Before you scroll to the murders on Beenham's Wikipedia page you learn that the howls of the Trust's wolves can be heard within a three-mile radius. The page doesn't hold much else.

Twenty-nine years after David was jailed for killing the younger girls, in 1996, he absconded from the open prison to which he had been transferred. "I thought you could only go through hell once," Jacqueline's father said. "But now we are going through it again." David was found and arrested seventeen months later, after being caught committing an armed robbery, but almost two decades would pass before a jury would convict him of Yolande's murder. By then he was in his sixties, a white-haired man who refused to take the stand, who cleaned his glasses while the jury deliberated the use of new DNA findings. A former Beenham resident testified that three years before Yolande's death, she too had been attacked by David while walking home one snowy night from the phone booth, his hands around her neck for "four or five minutes" until she could escape. In response, the cross-examiner suggested maybe she had provoked David by ignoring or swearing at him when he tried to chat.

It wasn't until I left Beenham that I learned about two headstones in the church graveyard I had passed on each commute. "A tiny flower lent not given to bud on earth but bloom in heaven," read Jeanette's. "In ever loving memory of our darling daughter Jacqueline Ann Williams, taken from us 17th April 1967, aged 9 years 10 months," said the other. I spent too long staring at maps, trying to confirm whether my forest path looked down to the farm where Yolande's body had been discovered, or if I walked past the quarry where Jacqueline and Jeanette had died. Realizing that the landscape of my Beenham commute had been the landscape of their murders felt like a strange kind of validation—a confirmation that my worries those weeks were right to leap so high. If my nerves hadn't been rational, at least they had been reactive. And yet. "How do people carry on? They just do," a Beenham local told the *Telegraph* reporter in 2002. "It has happened, life goes on."

In the years immediately before I went to England, Oregon's own wolf population grew. OR-7 had indeed found a mate, a disperser from another northeastern Oregon pack. "We . . . have been nothing more than raving peeping toms and yentas when it comes to OR-7's sex life like a veritable TMZ of the wildlife world," wrote the columnist for the Medford paper, not unhappy about the fact. OR-7's first litter was soon captured in a photograph on a trail cam, a couple of fur-balls playing in a hollowed-out log. Their pack was the first in western Oregon since the mid-twentieth century. Officials named them "The Rogue Pack" for their location in the mountainous Rogue River drainage east of Medford, a city twenty-seven miles north of the California border. Some wolves, like some penguins, will co-parent and mate for life. Trail cameras showed OR-7 hauling an elk leg back to his den, "bringing home the groceries," in the words of a local news report.

More wolves were good news for the species, but in the somewhat paradoxical world of wildlife management, it also meant more might soon be killed. I thought of what Mike had told me about wolves in England: that we owed it to the species to make sure they could live safely if we brought them back. Because wolves in Oregon had not been technically "reintroduced," they had just wandered in, the state's ethical responsibility was perhaps different; still, "living and dying with response-ability in unexpected company" was nothing if not the challenge of our time, as Donna Haraway wrote, to summarize the work of anthropologist Anna Tsing. If Oregon's wolf population swelled, the species would be delisted from the state's Endangered Species Act, thus losing the protection that prevented someone from killing one on their property. "The [Rogue] pack might want to keep their distance from their northeastern relatives," wrote the *Oregonian* in an editorial in early 2015, as if wolves could read. I understood the law from a population level, but on the plane of the individual wolf—a viewpoint wildlife biologists tried not to adopt—it sounded like a cruel bargain from a Greek myth. *Go forth, have children, prosper, but at some unknowable point, your children will be hunted by the Gods.* Nine months after the *Oregonian*'s editorial, wolves were delisted from state protection, though those in the western half of the state were still protected federally.

The fall after I left England, the partially decayed carcass of a gun-shot wolf turned up in a national forest in the southern part of the state. The wolf was OR-7's cousin; the forensics lab determined he had been dead since that spring. The summer before, this wolf had been blamed for killing livestock near Ashland, and now at least one headline referred to him as the "killing-spree wolf," as if featured on *America's Most Wanted*. It was harder for me to read about poached wolves after spending so much time around living ones. I thought of how Mosi sometimes stood to greet me at the fence when I entered the Trust in the morning, and I willed myself not to imagine her body through the same lurid, goth filter I sometimes saw my own: dead. Mostly, I thought of the snowy Arctics, playing. It is one thing to imagine the loss of a single wolf, but when you witness pack relationships, you see that one death is not just the loss of a body but the rupture of a vessel. Like human families, each pack is its own ecosystem, with each wolf playing its own part. Every death is a unique tragedy.

A few years earlier, a hunter who allegedly mistook a wolf for a coyote in eastern Oregon was fined $1,000 and had his rifle taken away after he reported the death. Hoping to prevent similar mix-ups, ODFW released an online identification quiz in the months after I returned to the United States. With my newfound familiarity from the Trust, I clicked into it confidently, eager to prove myself to a beige screen framed by a panel of canine faces. At first, I was good. The wolves were darker gray and black, with broader muzzles and rounded ears. The coyotes had more heart-like, foxy faces; ears bigger, paws smaller, legs shorter, coats redder. But then I misidentified a young wolf, a skinny yearling with the blonder coloration of a coyote, and then a few slides later I misidentified a coyote in the snow with a puffed winter coat the color of strong tea, and in the end my score was eighty-five percent, right around average.

Entre chien et loup. From the outside, in retrospect, the call can seem easy to make. It's when you're it that it's harder, with both humans and wolves. To decide *entre chien et loup* is to weigh the cost of fear to yourself against the cost of fear to the creature before you. Learning to listen to my fear was useful, but so too, I was learning, was excavating its roots, tracing its through-lines, and, if need be, dismantling it. The calm I chased on human streets would not come from pepper spray but from metabolizing, and contextualizing, the things that had scared me in the past—from exploring the topography of my own landscape of fear. "In good-enough circumstances, a fearful experience is also an occasion to learn how to be afraid," wrote Jonathan Lear in his biography of Sigmund Freud. In some situations, whether due to the size of danger or temperament of the person, "the experience of fear inhibits the development of the capacity to experience fear." Developing a balanced capacity for fear, then, was like learning to drink strong whiskey. You tip your head back; you grimace at the burn. You learn the feeling doesn't kill you so you do it again.

My summer had started with the man on the train and those weeks alone in the cabin, then bloomed into my skittish walks in Beenham. On a physical level, I had felt near vibratory with vigilance; on the other hand, I had traveled a lot, and traveled alone, and there had been so many moments of calm, and joy, and laughter too. Maybe I was a "coward at heart" like Carter's wolves, but as with a pacemaker under the skin, my fear was manageable in part because it was often indetectable. Alice had trusted me when I told her I would walk each day to the Trust because I felt brave. Feeling like a coward had never stopped me from pushing myself out the door, and what was that but courage after all?

Some six months after I left England, Tsa's phone rang around 7:45 a.m. Her friend was calling to say she had seen a wolf walking alone down a town footpath. It was January. At first Tsa assumed strong winds were to blame for the escape, but when she eventually studied the Trust's enclosures, she saw the front gate of Mosi and Torak's pen had been forced open, padlocks in place but bolts ajar. Though Mosi was inside barking, twelve-year-old Torak was gone. It felt awful to know there had been a stranger in the night. "A lot of people don't particularly believe in having animals in captivity," Tsa later told a *Guardian* reporter.

The next five hours were like something from a spy movie. A helicopter with thermal-imaging tracking, police marksmen, Trust volunteers and staff cruised the countryside. Did older residents of the town think of that other headline-snatching search decades earlier, the one for the "Beast of Beenham," as a true-crime podcast would dub David Burgess? In the days after Jeanette and Jacqueline's murders, the hunt for a weapon had at one point employed more policemen than there were working men in the village. The men cut the grass and burned the undergrowth, turning the gravel pit and surrounding area into a "desolate, stark . . . moonscape," the local paper reported. Swarming officers aside, the two searches had very little in common. One predator terrified the town; the other did not.

Though the primary school was put on lockdown after the wolf escape, anxiety remained low. "We all know the wolves and nobody is worried," a spokesperson said. The Thames Valley Police sent a text urging residents to stay inside, but even that had mixed results. "I had a local surgery appointment this morning as I'm off to Malawi at the end of the month," a local man named Daniel Brownlie told the BBC. "It was a decision between getting malaria tablets or getting eaten by a wolf. I took the risk." Torak traveled eight miles through the West Berkshire countryside, walking through farms and a field of sheep before Tsa eventually coaxed him into a trailer in a neighboring township. A spokesperson from Animal Capture UK said he looked like the "most unaggressive wolf I have ever seen."

The escape made international news, and donations to Torak spiked. The Trust upgraded their CCTV. They donated £5,000 to thank local police cadets. Then, in August 2018, just over a year after I had flown home, the UKWCT made headlines again. "As I approach retirement age and a quieter life, I have made this decision with a heavy heart," Tsa told a local reporter. After twenty-three years, the Trust was closing to the public. The wolves would stay in their enclosures, and the volunteers who knew them would keep taking care of them, but without the zoo license, public visiting days would end.

Mike had been on holiday during Torak's escape, but he'd come back to help with the recapture. When the Trust closed, his job became redundant, and that's when he left for good. Later he would suggest that the health of the wolves had gone downhill since then, the canines not in a shape he ever wanted to see them in. I thought of the wolf watching me through the chain link, and then a deep sadness welled up, and I didn't want to think of the wolves at all. Mike, by then, had moved to live with the researcher with the pink ponytail, the one I had worked beside. They made a cute pair; I suddenly understood they had always been close in age. I had seen the news of their courtship on Facebook, the same place I would later learn of their child. Because I had been at the Trust on her last day there, I replayed their interactions, searching for seeds of their beginnings in the way I later replayed my weeks at the Trust, looking for seeds of its end. An unexpected happening—whether a romance, an assault, a terrorist attack, or an organization closing—can make everything before it both a prelude and a data point, something to plot in the flimsy trajectories of reason our brains treadmill to create. All this for that old punch line: *It has happened. Life goes on.* When I first read that Beenham man's phrase, I thought it sounded passive. Defeatist. Now I held it like a mantra. A reminder to greet those ghosts of history, to honor them, but also to never forget the direction we were sailing: away.

6

Self v. Wolf

The most popular video ever released on YouTube by the Oregon Department of Fish and Wildlife is a short instructional guide for what to expect if you encounter a wolf. The wolf video, with over 15.5 million views, is perhaps popular because people expect the worst and want to imagine it. In this sense, it does not deliver. An ODFW intern who has just had a sighting explains a wolf is most likely to run away. It could bark, or howl, or follow you until you leave its territory, but usually it runs. If it doesn't, it might be because some combination of wind or clothing is concealing you. You should shout, then. Wave an arm. Make yourself, as human, known. In the video, the intern's voice is calm. There is no drama.

In rare cases—maybe the wolf is that statistically more volatile dog-wolf hybrid, or maybe it is guarding its young, or reacting territorially because you are with a dog—the wolf might not turn. It might walk, or run, toward you, hackles raised. This possibility is alluded to on the accompanying ODFW webpage, which recommends that if a wolf poses a threat, you should back away slowly, stand tall, pick up any small children, speak firmly, and, if necessary, make noise. Throw things. Your goal is to prove you are predator, not prey.

I had rehearsed these motions before in bear and mountain lion territory, but seeing them in writing made me realize how similar the choreography was to proving dominance in a human situation. Like the hands-up-in-a-Y power pose my mother taught me to do in the mornings before those dreaded poetry recitations in high school English, these poses made a human bigger. The goal was to convince yourself, but also the viewer, that you were capable of power. Encountering an aggressive animal and an aggressive man are in most ways incomparable, except that in each case, your first defense is perhaps not a well-placed blow but what you telegraph to the creature in front of you: *You do not want to mess with me.* In other words: *I am one of you.*

During that summer of solo travel, I thought often of a scene in *The Point of Vanishing,* Howard Axelrod's memoir about two solitary years spent in a Vermont cabin after losing sight in one of his eyes. One night, the young writer hears a mysterious knock at the door and freezes. A second later, he regains his composure. "If there was a crazy man in the woods, a wild bearded loner liable to do anything, I was him," wrote Axelrod. "I am the crazy man!" The realization comforts him. He knows he can frighten.

Could I? When we are afraid, our own bodies transform. Darwin wrote about how hands turn cold, blood rushes to cheeks, the edges of our vision water. In this state where you feel like prey, your body tries to turn you into predator. Many reactions are involuntary. Skin pales and chills, voice deepens, pupils swell, bodies jerk, hair bristles. This is evolution's way of making creatures "appear terrible to their enemies," wrote Darwin.

Unlike Axelrod, it was once hard for me to imagine myself scaring anyone. To be scary I thought I needed special effects, the way a bad singer turns to auto-tune. Advertisements told me I should carry a noisemaker and a weapon, which would not only protect my body, but give me "peace of mind"—something between a talisman and an immunization against worry. During those weeks alone at the Washington cabin and then in England, I practiced being fierce in front of the bathroom mirror. I narrowed my eyes, brought my voice to a growl, and tried to script what I might have said to the man on the train, or the street, or any of the others. It felt futile. To shout these things—"No!" "Go!"—was to swim upstream in a psyche that had always tried to placate or just get away.

Unlike the friend who bemoaned her "resting bitch face," I suffered from its opposite: my compulsive friendliness disguised a squirming stomach. My smile was a tic, head nodding along unconsciously when someone spoke, the vestiges of being an elementary school teacher's pet. "Has anyone ever told you you were too *nice*?" a drunk acquaintance once asked over the end of her smoldering cigarette. I told myself she was jealous because the man she liked was, for a paltry hour, flirting with me, but I now suspect she just glimpsed in me a kind of woman she had worked to reject in herself, or a kind she had never been allowed to be. She thought I hewed too close to what our culture wanted from a woman. She didn't know me, not at all, but she knew I could be shy in the group dynamic we interacted in, where she took a spotlight, stirring the pot. To the men in our group, I was the lesser threat.

In *Slouching Towards Bethlehem,* Joan Didion wrote that being underestimated was its own survival strategy. "My only advantage as a reporter is that I am so physically small, so temperamentally unobtrusive, and so neurotically inarticulate that people tend to forget that my presence runs counter to their best interests," she wrote. "And it always does." I didn't like her assertion that journalists were always selling somebody out. It vacuumed the complexity from too many interactions, flattening the power dynamic to one of user and used. But as I stared at the woman through her haze of smoke, I thought of how benignity could be as much an act as the fierce faces I practiced in the mirror. That performing innocence could be as big a threat as performing aggression. As big a lie too.

We often think invoking fear in someone means wielding physical advantage over them. Yet this staging of predator-prey, with one body dominant over another like a science textbook diagram, obfuscates subterranean currents of power, especially where two humans are involved. Though some of my armors are obvious—I am tall for a woman, athletic and physically able—others can be too easily overlooked, encoded in the fabric of our world. For example: I am white; I am neurotypical; I am educated; I have a supportive family with a financial safety net; I present primarily as the woman I identify as. The constellation of these privileged identities has meant an assumption of my "goodness" is socially encoded too. Someone like me may not have the upper hand in a fistfight, but unwarranted power can induce terror nonetheless.

"If I knew to be cautious of men, I did not learn early enough to be cautious of white women," wrote sociologist and writer Tressie McMillan Cottom, describing the white teachers who shamed her as a child for a Black body that was "wrong or dangerous or deviant." Her word choice here is critical, suggesting one of the ways white women wield power is by projecting danger onto other bodies, deflecting threat to prop up their own constructed victimhood. The security comes by osmosis and is non-transferrable. As Claudia Rankine writes, it "doesn't inoculate her from illness, loss,

or forfeiture of wealth, but it ensures a level of citizenry, safety, mo-
bility, and belonging."

I could feel afraid but be relatively protected; others would be
both feared and unsafe. In the wake of police officers brutally killing Michael Brown, Eric Garner, Tamir Rice, and so many others
who could have been her son, Minneapolis writer Shannon Gibney wrote, "How do you protect the thing you love most in the
world when it is also the very thing that the world most fears?" She
titled the essay "Fear of a Black Mother." Her words are a critical
reminder that invoking "fear" in someone does not mean you have
power over them. Being viewed as "predator" when you walk into a
room does not mean you are safe.

A few months after I left the UKWCT, a hunter called the Oregon
State Police Fish and Wildlife Division to explain that he had had
an encounter with three animals in eastern Oregon. He killed one,
he said, then discovered it was a wolf. Arriving at the scene with an
ODFW biologist, a police officer described the hunter as "talking
extremely fast" and looking "physically shaken." The man said he
had been walking downhill when three doglike animals—at first
he believed them coyotes—began running toward him. "I definitely
felt like she had targeted me," he explained about the last animal
in line. "I feared for my life. It was unnerving. I didn't have a lot of
time to react and so I shot the third one."

The case made me think of Florida's "Stand Your Ground" statute, which states deadly force is allowable on one's own property
if the owner "reasonably believes that using or threatening to use
such force is necessary to prevent imminent death or great bodily
harm." But what is "reasonably"? As criminal law professor Ekow
Yankah told CBS News in the months after George Zimmerman

shot and killed the unarmed Trayvon Martin: "We have to decide
what counts as 'reasonable' to be afraid of, and nobody should pretend that that isn't socially and culturally loaded." I do not believe
shooting a wolf and shooting a human are—or should be seen—as
equivalent, but I do believe many of the societal narratives that prop
up claims of self-defense in their aftermath are related. Because
of that metaphor of wolves-as-dangerous-men and vice versa, they
are mutually enforcing too. I cannot write here that Zimmerman
"murdered" Martin because though a special prosecutor charged
him with second-degree murder, he claimed self-defense, and a jury
acquitted him of all charges. In the eyes of the law, Zimmerman
remains innocent. His alleged fear was both a shield and its own
form of sword.

The coyote hunter's report of self-defense in the face of the
charging wolf was challenged by photos later released to the media
via public records requests, which showed his bullet entering in the
middle of the wolf's spine and exiting near its shoulder. It was
the flight of a bullet sent through an animal most likely fleeing away
from, not toward, a human. Fifteen environmental groups filed a
request to the governor to reopen the investigation and prosecute,
but she ruled that the verdict of self-defense could stay. "Too many
wolves have been found shot in Oregon where the shooters have
not been identified," wrote the governor in her comment. It made
me think of the logic of "George Washington and the Cherry Tree":
that he who confesses his mistake deserves to walk free. But did
the hunter? Did the hypothetical bravery of his confession forgive the
fear that made him kill?

In those months after I left England, I thought often of the
wheeling helix of predator and prey that exists inside both humans
and animals. About the moments where the balance would flip, and
power could shift. Where "predator" would become "prey," and back,

and forth. And who decided, anyway? With humans, it depended not only on how everyone saw themselves in the equation, but how the world saw them. I hated to admit when I felt like a victim, but denying the reality of that lived fear was like trying to keep ants out of an old house. Furthermore, it felt myopic to tally the moments of my victimization without considering when I had been perpetrator too. When had my actions scared another? When had I ignited real fear, creating a problem, becoming a so-called wolf? In a life of hazy moments, one day is crystal. Like so many monumental days, this one swallowed me. Spit me up as someone new.

When I think of that day in Sicily now, I think of what learning about predator-prey dynamics taught me about eating. That though we all eat to stay alive, eating is also when we are at our most vulnerable. The deer knows it best: when our heads are down, our guards are too.

I was born on October 11, and because of the place and time—just around 8:30 a.m., right in time for the school I later loved so much, my parents would say—my star chart is a cascade of Libras. Libra sun, Libra moon. That balancing scale tattooed across my character if you believe it, which I do. My indecision is as much a part of me as my teeth. Both a bit too big for size. In northern German tradition, my birthday week was marked by the feast of St. Gallus on October 16, which signified the passage between fall and winter. Legend dictated children born during that week would arrive in a state of liminality, as if every child was thrown between two seasons of being. These mid-October baby girls were said to grow into "nightmares." The boys, werewolves.

I have always delighted in werewolf stories. Unlike the morals and eulogies of wolf stories I grew up with, contemporary werewolf stories rarely take themselves too seriously. They are tragedies with a campy, narrative familiarity. Like romantic comedies, the trajectory is foreshadowed, often arriving in three acts.

First there is an encounter. Someone is living their daily life and then there is an intervention. The bite is always a surprise. As if a door has been pried open, something strange has entered the body.

Act two is transformation. If the story follows the point-of-view of the recently infected, as in Jack Nicholson's *Wolf* (1994) or the feminist coming-of-age horror film *Ginger Snaps* (2000), there is some crisis of dread and questioning. How is my body changing? Will it ever go away? What will happen to the people around me? The plot unspools these answers.

Act three is conclusion. Maybe the werewolf is stopped, cured with an antidote or killed with a silver bullet, or maybe they just become full beast, their human clothes tattered as they dash into the woods. Even in that final act, something has been cured. A transformation is complete; the beast is free of human conscience. This is perhaps the werewolf at its most evil and enviable. The creature is untethered from any guilt or shame he once felt about wreaking havoc. He eats what he wants.

I wonder now if I would have gone to Sicily were it not for the professor. The summer before my last year of college, he said my problem was I thought I could be both a normal person and a writer. The professor had seen my hunger on our small campus, and it worried him. The way I wanted to write an honors thesis *and* edit the college newspaper; the fact I had friends *and* a boyfriend, and that I spent afternoons with them both on the quad, walking in packs between the library and our off-campus house. I wanted to tell the professor that these relationships distracted me from the stress that clawed my chest, subsiding otherwise only when I drank it into submission on Friday and Saturday nights. Instead, I opened and closed my mouth, cheeks cardinal red above the notebook where I scrawled his words, as if taking notes in class. It seemed the professor thought I was a glutton for activity, distracting myself from what mattered.

"My advice is get a job in a rural boarding school after graduation." A pause, amusement on his face. "Put yourself in a twenty-first-century convent and then you'll get the writing done." His voice was coolly confident, like a dentist diagnosing a cavity. Because I wanted to believe the nice things he said about my writing, I felt I must believe the hard things he said about my life.

After graduation, as friends signed leases together for apartments along the Atlantic, I took a job working on a documentary in the rural Sicilian countryside. My relationship over; my notebook packed. The Norse term for werewolf is *vargr*, which means restless. Just as I had left the West Coast, now I would leave the East Coast. It seemed a natural trajectory, a continuation of a distancing I had already begun, a flexing of self-sufficiency I had perhaps, in my college camaraderie, let slacken. A part of me wanted to show the professor that I could throw myself into work, and not into relationships. I would be at a villa, not a boarding school, but I would still be surrounded by fields. I would not date, or watch television, or get distracted with family, and when I had free time, I would write. Sure, I would eat literally every meal the island served me, but metaphorically, I would train my hunger. This is what I told myself. I would keep it on track.

I landed in Sicily just as the sun boiled over the clouds, turning the sea around the island to blue glass. From the air, the rippling backside of Monte Pellegrino jutted above Palermo like a child's volcano diorama, lush with a pixilation of prickly pear blooms against brown sugar cliffs. The city barnacled the land beneath it, spilling pink stucco houses toward the bone-white beach. In the distance, a road unzipped tawny hills splotched sage with olive groves.

If I was there to practice solitude, I was also there to eat. I had been hired to help manage a documentary produced by a farm-to-table cooking school on the two-hundred-year-old wine estate of descendants of Frederick II. The estate was in the rural, sleepy inland, an hour-and-forty-five-minute journey from Palermo by two rattling silver trains. I knew no Italian and had never made a film, so in my interviews, I stressed a passion for "storytelling" and waxed on my experience assisting with a documentary a few years before. I wasn't their first-choice candidate, but when she wasn't willing to commit for long enough, they moved on to me. Someone hungry for work, with nothing on the horizon.

Within a month, my boss sent me to Milan to edit early footage with the director. "*In bocca al lupo!*" she said as I walked out the door. *Into the wolf's mouth!* It was a colloquial expression, an idiom with roots in opera. Like "break a leg," it was a paradoxical wish of good luck.

"*Crepi!*" I learned to respond. *Let it die!*

Around this time, an op-ed ran in a Naples newspaper urging Italians to reimagine both the saying and the animal that inspired it. Mother wolves often picked up their young in their mouths, instinctively pulling them away from danger. To be in the wolf's mouth, the writer urged, might not mean facing death but its opposite: to be protected by the guiding, maternal spirit of the wolf.

"*Lunga vita al lupo!*" the op-ed suggested as an alternate response. *Long live the wolf!*

If an American toddler knows anything about a wolf, it is that the wolf is hungry. The hungry wolf prowls through fairy tales, idioms, and that clichéd metaphor of etiquette, as when the parent tells the child, *Stop wolfing down your food.* One reason wolves may be portrayed this way is that they are literally often trying and failing to attain food. "It is rarely possible [for them] to kill," write biologists David Mech and Rolf O. Peterson. Another reason may be how the animal must kill. Wolves' paws do not rotate like cougars' do, which means they are unable to climb trees or hold their prey down. Rather than hide and wait for prey, they follow it, their claws dulled by the miles they traverse to reach it. Whereas large cats will kill with one penetrating bite—I think of my father eating ribs—a wolf must bite repeatedly. Sometimes this means they eat before the animal is dead. This kind of kill is less efficient, so it's a slower way to go. A crueler way to die, we think, as if wolves kill to enact cruelty. They do not. A wolf does not kill to incite fear, he kills to keep himself alive. The harm he causes—not just in his meal, but in the animals who escape with elevated stress levels—is incidental, but registers nonetheless.

A wolf can eat a deer in as little as three hours and leave nothing but stomach contents on the ground. This is the appetite conjured by the verb "wolfing." Yet wolves are also apt to save kills for later, returning to a carcass multiple times to feed, or burying meat a distance away in a cache so it is safe from packmates and other predators. A livestock producer who walks into a field of nearly intact sheep carcasses is apt to feel his animals have been massacred indiscriminately, but for wolves often stymied in their hunts, this sort of "surplus killing" is probably best understood as an unavoidable biological impulse, recognizable to any human who tries to eat one potato chip from the bag. In his 1931 *Turi's Book of Lappland,* Sámi author Johan Turi writes that a "wolf does only what it must," comparing the mechanism that restrains their appetites to "the waves of the sea, how high they are allowed to raise themselves." In the modern Western world, a lack of knowledge about the wolf's feeding habits has contorted into the archetype of wolf as unhinged killer, glutton for blood.

Such assumptions of lupine greed have often been weaponized as ammunition to kill the canines. During extermination campaigns in North America and Europe throughout the twentieth century, hunters not only sprinkled poison over the bodies of bait, but laced meat with razor blades and nails, and staked steel wires with chicken-wrapped fish hooks near den sites. Faced with a new reality of lethal meat, wolves began to learn the risk of returning to a previous night's carcass. What had once been a good meal could now mean convulsions of death. As wolf pups learned to avoid these carcasses, evidence suggests the other species who watched them may have too. Ravens have long been observed guiding wolves to kills before diving in to pick at the scraps; inversely, they have been shown to avoid carcasses when wolves were absent, suggesting that they relied on wolves "like the food tasters monarchs used to employ to sample all their food before it was passed on to them," writes wolf researcher Rick McIntyre. A reminder that we rarely eat alone—our meals depend on a trust, however subliminal, in others.

The werewolf, of course, is hunger without reins. There are examples in late-nineteenth-century Germany of the saying, "He is hungry like a werewolf." Why not just say "hungry like a wolf"? I can only imagine the difference is the unnaturalness of the hunger. We expect a wolf to bite into a deer's still-warm haunch; when a man-wolf does it, the action takes on the giggly horror of the uncanny. I am thinking of when werewolf-Jack-Nicholson, in *Wolf,* tucks into a fawn like it's a fried chicken drumstick, and another when man-Jack-Nicholson realizes, midday by the office urinal, that the bloody stumps of someone's fingers are in the pocket of his suit jacket. In gaining animal, the werewolf loses the logic of man. He has been bitten, and now, like passing a baton, he bites. The werewolf is both victim and perpetrator. He eats the wrong things. His appetite is a function of hunger gone awry.

Within a month of my arrival in Sicily, my boss asked if I would stay longer as her personal assistant. She was a contessa in her early fifties, the self-professed bohemian of the aristocratic family who favored wide red linen pants and cheerily refused to dye her halo of silver curls. I had always been a people-pleaser, compulsively trying to anticipate others' needs before they needed me to assist them, and it seemed natural to professionalize the reflex. Plus, I adored her, in awe of her independence. I said I'd stay all year.

She toured often for work and spent part of her time in a beach house outside Palermo, so when I wasn't eating five-course meals with her and her international guests, I was alone on the estate with whichever English-speakers had talked their way into managing the garden or apprenticing in the kitchen for a few months. Across the courtyard, the Sicilian groundskeeper and cook lived with their teenage children in an apartment where the television was often on and voices were often raised, speaking in a strong regional dialect that only loosely overlapped with the textbook Italian we were trying to learn. Though we were all technically working for the same aristocratic family, they knew we were transient. When guests arrived, our job was to drink rosé with Australian retirees while they blotted grease from fried triangles of chickpea *panelle* in the kitchen. Afterward, we helped with the dishes, and sometimes they invited us to smoke in the garage. When they asked, I joined, trying on a few lines of newly acquired language while I coughed against a table of drying garlic. But the distance was always clear. We consumed what they produced.

At some point, grinning at my propensity for second portions, a cook referred to me as *buona forchetta*. A good fork. I chose to take it as a compliment. By the time I understood the name could have an edge—suggesting I was not selective enough in my tastes, too easily pleased with the pile on my plate—it was too late. The harm had been done. If *buona forchetta* held a warning, my ears were closed. My mouth was open.

Around the time OR-7 and his new mate were raising their first pups, the signals from his satellite collar finally turned erratic. The GPS receivers on collars tend to last about three years, and OR-7's had gone nearly four, broadcasting throughout his approximately 4,000-mile journey. Though the radio portion of a collar will generally last a bit longer, their signals are cumbersome to track, only traceable from the ground with handheld antennas. After years of pinging his location every six hours to government biologists, OR-7's satellite collar was now sending locations every few days, or not at all. OR-7 would go from being a media darling to a creature who slipped unseen between the trees—just another wolf, the thing he had always been. "OR-7 was following the archetypal 'hero's journey,' the pattern outlined by Joseph Campbell," wrote nature writer Brenda Peterson in *Wolf Nation: The Life, Death, and Return of Wild American Wolves*. "Eventually the hero must earn a reward and return to share his knowledge with 'the ordinary world' he once left."

At some point, biologists changed their mind about not wanting to re-collar him. Some fans of the wolf applauded the chance for continued surveillance, others pleaded to let go. "Wolves and other critters don't exist so that we can peer into their lives, whether with joy or horror or love or curiosity or any other human emotion or intent," read an op-ed in the Eugene *Register-Guard*. The traceability of a wolf, though, isn't done for human entertainment. It's a way for officials to give livestock producers a heads-up if a wolf is nearby, so preventive measures can be taken and deaths can, hopefully, be avoided—not only for cows, but for wolves. That fall of 2014, two biologists backpacked into the rugged Rogue River wilderness to try to find OR-7 and his family. It's a place of razor-sharp ridges, cascading chilly water, and dense stands of hardwood. The wolves were traveling miles a day, making them hard to keep up with. Even harder was predicting where they would step. Tramping through the brush, the biologists heard the tease of adult howls, and occasionally high-pitched pup ones. But by the time they left the forest, no wolf from OR-7's pack had stepped into their traps.

The next month, a smattering of GPS signals appeared on a ranch in southern Oregon's Wood River valley. Those days had been dense with fog, the local paper reported, and when the ranch manager said he'd heard wolves, the still-pulsing collar brought confirmation: OR-7 had wandered into open land to scavenge from a 1,100-pound cow carcass just over a mile from the edge of the forest. "The satellite download took me right to a skeleton," ODFW biologist Tom Collom told a journalist. Once the wolf had gone to feed, then twice, then three times. Birds had feasted too, whittling the body down. It is a rancher's responsibility to bury carcasses a few feet beneath the earth, but when large herds of cows range over large areas, life and death can be hard to monitor. No depredations had been traced to OR-7 or his mate since they had made a home in the valley, but that didn't mean the trend would continue. "As long as he doesn't eat the cattle, I couldn't care less," ranch manager Steve Bailey told a reporter. And if he did? The collar would incriminate him—unless its signal had died by then, in which case his appetite would remain a secret.

The villa that housed the cooking school had bright blue windows and stone walls dripping garnet bougainvillea. Chickens wandered among wood barrels of kitchen herbs in the inner courtyard. Beyond the gates, the family's vineyards upholstered the hills like corduroy. I had never seen such an edible world. On my evening jogs I filled my fists with figs and persimmons and almonds and tangerines, then joined the other interns to harvest dinner from the garden. We cut scabby clumps of purple broccoli and glossy bulbs of eggplant and the pale green *cucuzza* squash that hung from the trellises like long, thin arms. We made salads that bloomed with purple borage and yellow oxalis and washed it all down with the same wine locals came to buy outside, filling red plastic tanks as if it were a Nero d'Avola gas station.

I slept in a basement bedroom beneath my boss's living quarters. Linoleum floor, pink satin–covered dresser, a twin bed beside a small window shadowed by a heavy metal grate. Every night, the groundskeeper closed the towering front gate and sealed the villa and courtyard off from the world with an iron bolt against the royal blue doors. In the morning, I woke to the scrape of the gate opening and the toenails of the terrier Aurora launching herself toward the sunny cobblestones beyond. My first few nights I marveled at the multiple intricate locks on each outward-facing window near my bedroom, indulging fantasies about whatever feudal or Mafioso histories had necessitated such relics. But a few days later, when one of the housekeepers noticed I had not triple-bolted the windows before bed, she scolded me. For once, I was not the fearful one. And because I could not understand her fear—I did not read the Italian papers, did not have the vocabulary to ask her, did not even want to ask my boss—I played at their charade of security, normalizing it as much as breakfast with seven kinds of homemade jam.

A few years after returning from the island, I came across an essay by high-wire artist Philippe Petit about mastering anxiety. "I see fear as an absence of knowledge," he said, noting that to conquer a hypothetical fear of spiders, he would only have to study the science, view documentaries, observe spiders in a zoo, and interview experts who worked with them. I agreed with Petit about wolves, but it felt like in other categories, knowledge could metastasize fear. We cannot fear what we do not know exists, and in Sicily, I was ignorant. The compulsive satellites of my ears were forced to slow down. The metal bars felt like an insurance policy against things that had other times kept me up at night. One form of protection, though, can be just another form of distraction. Like the stone villa, I came to feel myself impermeable. In writing off the threat of danger coming from outside, I neglected to imagine the harm I myself could be capable of causing.

Life at the cooking school was how I imagined life on a small ship. We padded around one another like dogs, often affectionate, occasionally snarling.

Paul came in January, during the height of our off-season, when I was still mourning the departure of his predecessor, an English horticulturalist with a love for Cuban dance music. She and I had shared a room, giggling into the evenings as we pressed flowers into notebooks, giddy as young sisters. What Paul liked to do more than giggle was work out and talk about it afterward. He was German, in his midtwenties, older than me, with sinewy limbs and thin glasses. Even after a day bent over in the garden, he preached the gospel of fitness, stretching on a latticed wood bench in the courtyard, arms raised with one of those foam-studded elastic bands. He knew I ran too, but I ran to be alone, away from the constant banter of the estate. Lacking the ability to tell him this directly, I dodged his offers of companionship with excuses, then darted out in the wet dawn.

I knew he was sweet and just wanted friendship, and I appreciated that he killed a slow-dying, window-smacked bird with the bottom of a garden shovel, but he leaned in too close when we talked. *They don't make them like you back home,* he said once, kneading his fingers into my shoulder after lugging his plant classification binders to where I was typing in the library. I didn't know what that meant, and if I did, I didn't believe him. But we were bored. Some days we flirted at dinner, and I suspected I was being insouciant, but it also felt like playing Ping-Pong, and what was the harm in hitting a ball already coming toward me in the air?

Other days I hoped Paul would stay in the garden and give me space. *Some days I could almost throttle him,* I wrote in my journal, the print so small it was like the path of a sneaking mouse. *I know that is wrong.*

Around the time Paul arrived, a jack-of-all-trades photographer, artist, and chef from Toronto came to spearhead a graphic design project. Kiley was also a few years older than me, tiny with spiraling coils of brown hair, quiet on first impression around guests and then quick to call the bullshit later, jabbing her pencil while talking theatrically over a glass of red wine around our "intern kitchen" table. I liked her immediately. Everything she cooked was gold.

Winter in Sicily had looked like spring since December, ever since the dirt between the vines exploded green with clover and favas, their blossoms the silky yellow and white of fresh eggs. In February, when "the marchesa" flew off for a cooking tour in

Australia—loading us with to-do lists and making us promise, with a laugh, *not to get too lonely* for the three weeks she was gone—the three of us stood outside the blue gate and waved until the sound of her silver car faded away and we heard only the leaves of the eucalyptus trees rattling in the breath of an oncoming squall.

For weeks we had been eating piles of tender, thin-leafed wild greens that the gardener harvested from the hills around the school. It was a favorite "relax food" when no guests were around, boiled and drenched in lemon juice with a teacup of warm chicken broth, a respite from the breaded meat and lemon custard puddings we had grown used to. One day the gardener let Kiley and me accompany him foraging, and we wandered the roadside, filling plastic grocery sacks with wild fennel fronds. He taught us to thumb off the chewy outer layers of the stalk so only the bright anise-smelling inner strips remained. The ground beyond the road was pure mud, dark peanut butter on the rubber boots we had borrowed, but everywhere twiggy green shoots stretched upward, transforming hills that had baked all summer then been burned by farmers in the fall, the land tattooed with black streaks of ash.

That night, after Kiley sautéed a handful of chopped fennel greens into spaghetti with sautéed onions and currants, I closed my eyes to chew. There was a thrill in eating something totally undomesticated, a plant that could thrive without our intervention, indifferent to our care. A joy in having intersected its wild journey. Maybe this was why people liked hunting. You respected the animal as you ate it, but in the end, the creature you were most proud of was yourself.

The next day, Kiley and I went out again. Paul was in the garden, working late as usual. Walking the one-lane road beneath the cooking school toward the giant scabby palms that arched above the official entrance to the family's winery, we filled wicker baskets with the curl-edged green leaves that splotched the slopes above the roadside. This time we were after chard. We had often seen locals stop their cars to gather it. "In Sicily chard grows everywhere. It is a great joy for everybody when they appear," wrote my boss's mother, founder of the cooking school, in her 1999 cookbook *Herbs and Wild Greens from the Sicilian Countryside.* "Country people, worried about the state of their digestive systems, think the greens have arrived just in time to cure, in a natural way, all their ailments."

It had rained all day, sky matte as a gray stone, but now a rainbow appeared, spilling pink like someone had taken a knife to the bruised clouds. We recognized a few people—workers, or distant relatives involved with managing the winery—and all of them stopped to wave and ask if we wanted a ride. The Sicilians were often confused by our voluntary strolling and jogging. Now we pointed to our baskets of shaggy green and gave the universal thumbs-up: *We're doing this for fun.* We flashed our little North American smiles and waved them on.

Is there any truth behind that canon of fantastical werewolf stories? I have heard some Victorian ghost encounters can be chalked up to hallucinations stemming from carbon monoxide poisonings. People were indeed hearing voices; they just misidentified why. Inherited stories about werewolves might similarly be held to the light, not only as transmissions of cultural mores but, in some cases, as explanations for otherwise inexplicable real-life encounters. Though most Indigenous tribes in the Pacific Northwest have positive associations with wolves, the Chilcotin of what is now British Columbia have reportedly feared them, believing contact with the animal could lead to nervous illness and possibly death, writes David Moskowitz in his book *Wolves in the Land of Salmon.* Could rabies be one explanation for such a set of symptoms? For as long as humans have been recording history, the virus has thrived beside us, existing on every continent except Antarctica. "Hominids likely would have had a tradition of fearing, avoiding, and killing wolves for that reason alone," wrote Mech. What he overlooks, though— and what Pierotti and Fogg subsequently point out through their lens of Indigenous history and evolutionary biology—is that before the arrival of the first Europeans, the rabies virus was likely present only in bats and skunks, with canine rabies rare or absent in the dog breeds of Native Americans. The specter of the rabid wolf is itself a vector of colonialism.

One might fear the wolf without knowing that fear stemmed from settler invasion, which had sickened not only so many Indigenous people but the animals around them. In *Of Wolves and Men,* Barry Lopez recounts a Blackfoot story where a man bitten by a rabid wolf was bound with ropes and rolled in a green buffalo hide, a fire stoked on and around him until the hide began to burn, an attempt to draw the disease out through his sweat. The Blackfoot refer to their own ancestors as "the wolf people," and the tribe has a long history of existing symbiotically beside wolves, helping to protect them while learning from their behavior, likely taking hunting cues for how to ambush prey and drive bison off cliffs. What did they make of it when rabies first arrived? When an animal so long familiar turned suddenly aggressive, jaw frothing? Though a tracker might be able to identify rabies in the swerve of a wolf's footprints, I can imagine how easy it would be not to distinguish the two at all: you fear rabies, but what you say you fear is wolf.

How many of our stories about the perceived bloodlust of wolves and werewolves are really stories about rabies? Especially those from before 1885, when Louis Pasteur's vaccine de-escalated the disease in much of the developed world from the death sentence it had once been. "Many human victims of rabies are reported to rage in delirium, howl like wolves in their agony, go into violent frenzies and attack and bite those around them," wrote Matthew Beresford in *The White Devil,* citing the disease in his history of European werewolf legends. A rabies-infected animal will likely not see symptoms for a few weeks, or months, or, in rare cases, years. As the wound heals, the body seems to forget. But the virus is a stow-away in the blood, and by the time it reaches the brain, the wound reemerges, "as if by magic, with some odd sensation occurring at the site," write Bill Wasik and Monica Murphy in *Rabid: A Cultural History of the World's Most Diabolical Virus.* At the site of the bite, a tremor, maybe coldness, maybe heat, a stabbing pain. Pupils dilate and fevers rise. Sometimes appetite departs; a fear of water arrives. Saliva streams from the mouth and tears from the eyes. The world can fog with hallucination. Some male patients report perpetual erections, even orgasms. I cannot help thinking of werewolf-Jack-Nicholson, whose wolf bite transforms him from a tired middle-aged man into one with glinting eyes and a new sexual appetite.

In 1833, a group of fur traders and their Indigenous guides were camping in what is now Wyoming, near Yellowstone National Park, when a mad wolf ran into camp and began biting humans. These trappers had heard rumors of "mad" wolves attacking, and that their victims had "gone mad" too. When the wolves bit a bull, he began to bellow, pawing the ground. A bitten trapper became delirious, refusing to cross small streams, holding back the whole party until they abandoned him. Later they found his strewn clothes ripped from his back. "He had run away quite naked, and never was found," read one account. As a victim of the virus, the man had become his own monster.

Some decades later, a U.S. Army officer recorded a similar ac-count of a rabid wolf entering an Arkansas River field hospital, "charg[ing] round most furiously" and biting anything it could reach, "mov[ing] with great rapidity . . . tearing tents, window curtains, bed clothing." It seems plausible such diseased wolves became not only stand-ins for the animal but doppelgängers for the werewolf. During such an attack, noises could be otherworldly due to the paralysis of a rabid animal's laryngeal muscles. Like a werewolf, the rabid wolf is a vicious predator, even though to ferry the infection, it has been a victim of a bite too. Once infected, a rabid wolf loses his normal fear of humans. "Sick wolves fly at you just like birds," wrote eighteenth-century Japanese author Nishimura Hakū. "When they see people they just come at them and bite."

To aid those soldiers bitten by the rabid wolf in the Arkansas fort, the men's wounds were cauterized with silver nitrate, a typical treatment at the time. Reading this, I thought of the urban legend stipulating that a "silver bullet" was needed to kill a werewolf, and I wondered. America's first werewolf film, aptly titled *The Werewolf*, had been released by Universal Studios in 1913. It was a short silent film, with white actors pretending to be on a New Mexico Navajo reservation, and a woman who could turn into a werewolf trying to avenge her tribe against invading white men while training her daughter to do the same. This film, like many at the time, was shot on two reels of highly flammable silver nitrate film; when a fire swept through the Universal studio just a decade later, all negatives instantly burned. Silver may not destroy the beast, but silver nitrate had destroyed *The Werewolf* film.

The idea that a silver bullet will stop a werewolf has roots in the legendary Beast of Gévaudan, that mythical wolflike predator alleged to have killed over a hundred victims in the mountains of southern France in the 1760s. Often the victims were young female shepherds; a local newspaper noted the loss of an eighteen-year-old "celebrated for her rare beauty." The hunt for their killer lasted years, drawing in bounty hunters who chased the 600-livre prize. In the words of one celebrated local wolf-hunter: "Many men with guns have arrived . . . they beat the woods every day with dragoons at their side. This will only cause more trouble, since we have no command over them." It is a familiar song: the invasion of men who think they are saviors becomes a new problem. Finally, in 1767, a local farmer killed a wolf, and the carcass was delivered to Versailles. According to legend, *La Bête* was killed with a silver bullet made from a melted chalice, or the coin of the Virgin Mary. In the centuries since, the silver bullet has become a symbol. Not just a prescription to kill the beast, but a remedy we crave that might not exist at all.

Toward the end of college, my roommate Eliza and I developed a bit where we asked those we sat with at lunch what they were most afraid of. Usually there would be a pause. *You serious?* Eventually the cork would pop. One friend spoke at length about imagining his mother dying; another about being buried alive, answering so swiftly it was as if the fear sat always like a pill beneath his tongue. Always we nodded, supportive and curious, treating the question like something between a conversation prompt and anthropological study.

"Just as the seed of health is in illness, because illness contains information, our fears are a treasure house of self-knowledge if we explore them," wrote New Age author Marilyn Ferguson in 1980. My interest in how others lived with their fears was selfish. I wanted advice on how to live with my own. All the same, I felt our question was impossible to answer truthfully. Not only to rank one's fears on a hierarchy—those internal acrobatics of would-you-rather—but to offer them to an audience. My own fears, so often, were selfish and small. Abstractly I feared earthquakes and nuclear bombs and fascism, but at the end of the day this meant I feared pain; a lack of hope or will to live; my own death. Mostly I feared the space before death. The seconds or hours where I would know everything I would never do. I suspect we talked about fears so readily then, at twenty-one, because most of us felt so insulated from their reality. So many of my college friends had parents who were not only breathing, but, at least then, married. Our own health so boring we didn't even think of it.

I didn't play the fear game in Sicily because I didn't think much about dying, my brain too full of everything else. But that night we cooked the greens Kiley and I harvested, I felt particularly buoyant, giddy with the gift of far-flung independence. We were playing some sort of would-you-rather as we cooked, Marvin Gaye on the tinny laptop speaker behind us, Kiley and I flushed and goofy with wine, while Paul, who had never had a sip—he was *an athlete*, he told us—shook his head at us with a smile. By the time we were at the table, passing around artichokes stewed in wine, oily discs of grilled eggplant, a bowl of leftover lamb stew, and that sautéed pile of our greens, everything seemed so perfect, so how-I-had-imagined-this-year, that I couldn't help swinging the conversation to mortality.

"Okay, a question. Would you rather know in advance the exact day you were going to die, or would you rather just, you know, drop?"

"What a question, Berry," said Paul. "Some nerve." But he was grinning, pouring the lamb broth over the greens and forking a wad of it onto a tear of bread, eyes narrowing with thought.

"Are we talking, like, knowing years in advance, or weeks, or days?" Kiley took a swig of wine, folding her arms over her plate in that let's-get-down-to-business gesture.

"Either way," I said. "For the sake of argument: say you have at least a year's warning."

We circled the question and heaped our plates, the sky blackening as a breeze rolled in, bringing the eucalyptus trees and orange grove right to our noses, the candle in the center of the table spasming with light. We talked; we ate. Somewhere inside our bellies, unknown for another hour or so, the toxins from the first bites of the greens were working their way into our bloodstreams. Doughing our minds, our eyes, our walk. But that comes later. The poison, at first, was nearly pleasant. Like wine on an empty stomach. The room made silky around the edges.

"I'll say it: I'd rather just drop dead," said Kiley eventually, and we all laughed because by that point, it seemed so obvious. Torture was knowing an unwanted change was coming over one's body and being unable to stop it.

Slovakians will "merrily term a drunkard a *vlkodlak*," writes Baring-Gould, because this word for "werewolf" also implies "he who makes a beast of himself." Becoming a beast, then, is not always a passive act. You can do it to yourself. In the Serer religion of Senegal, wolves are known as "seers"—transcendent, intelligent creatures capable of knowing in advance who will die. As with many folk beliefs, the legend likely carries shades of truth. Canines have been known to howl and bark before earthquakes. They have also been trained to smell the COVID-19 virus on a body before a person knows they've been infected.

When I think back to that evening in the little apartment, I think of all the moments an intervention might have occurred. When that little Aurora, who lived across the villa courtyard, ran up to us, tongue out, eyes wide, barking as always, but barking, maybe, differently?

When Kiley and I waved off the Sicilians who stopped to offer us a ride. When Paul, that trained horticulturalist, walked in from the garden and we showed him what we'd harvested, and he ran a hand through the leaves, smiling absentmindedly. *Nice, nice, ladies.* When Kiley mentioned the greens tasted bitter, maybe too metallic bitter, and poisonous plants often had this taste? When Paul got up, then, to examine the uncooked leaves, telling us they weren't all chard, but *Maybe dock? Maybe borage? We're probably fine.* That's when I brought up a conversation I had recently had with our boss about the Italian word *amaro*, bitter, which was a cherished Italian flavor, like umami, one that us fluorescent-supermarket-eaters rarely appreciated and had to get used to. "We're *honing* our *palates*," I said tipsily, brattily. "Plus, we've never even heard of poisonous plants around here."

"The flavor is just too much for me," said Kiley. "One of you can have my serving." Paul raised his eyebrows at me, winking.

"Your call, Berry." I didn't love the taste, but I thought that's probably why the wild greens were a power food. All those antioxidants. Ever the Libra, I considered. I thought of how often I wanted to eat the last bite, the one marooned on the plate by unspoken etiquette when I ate out with friends. I also thought of Paul. Of all the men we could be stuck with in the countryside, he was so kind. Yes, he sometimes talked too much, taking too long to answer an easy question, but he had been a selfless spirit. I felt bad for the days I had flirted and then, an hour later, wished him throttled. I owed him more. I passed the plate.

"You're a doll," he said.

It wasn't until after we had peeled one orange after another, each one tasting rotten, and then tried to drink water and found that tasting rotten too, mouths *dry as moldy stinking cotton,* as Paul said, that the panic seeded.

"I don't feel right," he said. "I feel woozy." I did too, but I was trying to convince myself it was the wine. Paul, it occurred to me, had never been high, never had a drink. At this point, under the table, I googled poisonous plants in Sicily, trying to counter Kiley's mask of terror with a wooden, this-happens-every-day smile on my face. A photo of a plant with purple flowers lit up my screen, a sight I recognized from the hillsides in December. *There's no way we ate that,* I thought. What I said was: "Maybe we should all just try to go vomit for good measure. Just in case."

I had never tried to make myself vomit before. Now I tried, but I couldn't do it. Walking back to the kitchen, I felt sheepish, but also like I was hovering about six inches above the linoleum. Paul and Kiley were waiting when I got back, similarly unsuccessful.

"I feel so tired," said Kiley, leaning into a chair. "I think we did something really bad." I too felt tired. Slow motion, swaddled in something I couldn't see. Paul was silent, starstruck, moving with a sort of robotic stagger in his polyester track pants. We asked how he felt and he just looked at us, blinking. *I take back everything I felt about you being tolerable,* I thought, glaring at him. *You're too dramatic.*

At some point, we walked to the apartment of the Sicilian cook and groundskeeper. TV flickered through the curtains, and for a minute we hesitated. It was their night off, was it worth bothering them? When the door finally opened, we held out the basket of greens. *Mi dispiace, mi dispiace.* We knew enough words to say, *Sorry. We ate. We bad. Poison?* They looked at the leaves, smelled them, shook their heads. *Non mortale,* they said, gesturing to the dark hills. *Nothing deadly out there.*

"I'm really freaked out," said Kiley as we trudged back. Paul was silent. His eyes were popped and unblinking, like he had been possessed. Glancing between them, I boiled some water for tea.

"Let's all take a deep breath," I said. "I think we're getting each other a little wound up."

My sophomore year of high school, I fainted in sex ed. We were in a hot room watching a movie about diaphragm insertion when I suddenly had the sensation of being vacuumed, my head sucked up to the tiled ceiling. I watched myself get up for water, and then my legs disappeared. Collapsing, I knocked my head on a cabinet as I went down. When I came to, the whole class was standing above me. I tried to lift my head then dropped it as the room spun. My gym teacher dialed 911.

The first thing I learned after the experience was that, maybe, something was wrong with my heart. The follow-up stress test had revealed a little knick, something indeterminate but uneven and tachycardia-esque, and my anxious mind read between the doctor's slow words and believed I might drop dead any minute. Sure I had grown nauseous from the movie, but I sensed there was more, something small and mean inside me that had poked its head out, threatening to strike.

The second was that my reputation was cemented as the family's low-grade hypochondriac. Feeling unable to walk for the hour after fainting, I had required an ambulance ride from the school to the hospital next door, something I now know cost about half my graduate student stipend.

"I thought, 'Oh god, Erica, just stand up,'" said my father recently, recounting the trip with an eye roll. We had been lucky to have some insurance, but it hadn't been enough. My family could absorb it, but other things had been sacrificed along the way. My fear, and my willingness to act on it, had cost us all.

Essayist Brian Dillon poses the hypochondriac's essential question as "[h]ow do we know, any of us, when we are sick and when we are well?" The anxious mind will "listen constantly, in a kind of trance, for communications from [her] body," trying to puzzle this answer out. I know the feeling well. Like a seismologist with a streak of fatalism, I wait and wonder about the rumbling signs below; always I wonder if my wondering will be my last.

Will you believe me if I say that spring in Sicily felt different? I was tired of being called out for my nervous mind. I had come to suspect my fear would always be present but never be real. My worry would always ache like a phantom limb. Maturity, I figured, was learning to ignore it.

An hour later we were in the groundskeeper's car and Paul was not making sense. It had taken only a few minutes to swallow any pride about crying wolf and commit to getting a ride to a hospital, pronto. Everything was closed on a late Saturday night; no ambulance would ever come. Interrupting the Sicilians again felt like our only chance of survival. While an operatic Italian singing competition unspooled on the television behind us, we pointed to our throats and heads and pleaded. Soon we were on the road, a drive of nearly an hour to the hospital through the winding black countryside. Rural Sicilian roads are notoriously bad, but this season, after the winter's rains had buckled and gutted the pavement, was the worst. Our only choice was to swerve between the potholes, honking at the tight curves to warn anyone coming. Paul was in the front passenger seat, legs jerking uncontrollably and his mouth a mixtape of animal noises and garbled panic. Kiley's head was against the window. I couldn't tell if she was crying.

"*Rapido,*" I said, leaning toward the driver's seat, unsure if it was even a word. "*Per favore, rapido.*" From the back seat, the cook had called the bilingual cooking school manager, who had gone home to his family across the island, and when she handed the phone to me, her eyes brimmed like teacups. "*Ciao,*" I said, aware the lever of my tongue was not acting quite as I wanted it to. I tried to count the meter of my breath while I spoke, to convince myself I could keep breathing, keep awake. It was nice to hear English through the tiny phone. I told him we were very embarrassed. He said he had already notified the emergency room. We tried to bolster one another with cheery assurance. But speaking felt like walking through a marsh. Every now and then, I slipped in the wet squelch and was pulled into blackness by invisible hands. I would shake back into consciousness when I heard my name being called, over and over, through the phone. "Erica, Erica, Erica, stay with me. *Erickina.*" My nickname. Little Erica.

Then, as the car slowed to inch around a tight bend, Paul grew louder in volume and babbling howl, and at some point—had the car stopped?—he opened the door, vaulted out, and began to stagger up the hillside. Already in some cave of consciousness I felt responsible. Me, who had offered him that last serving, plucking so many leaves from the earth. When I tried to tell my body to go after him, though, I was stone. The word "lunatic" has its root in the word "luna"—that old idea of being driven to madness by the moon. Moonlight is how I remember Paul rambling up the hillside. His body jerking and his voice an animal shriek, like the villain in a community theater performance, shadow lit by a metallic silver glow. Later, reading that nineteenth-century Oregon settler's account of frenzied poisoned wolves throwing themselves against the cabin door then wobbling off into the night, I would think of this night. Of the way the poison in our dinner had transformed Paul.

The groundskeeper flung open the car door to run after him. My eyes blinked shut.

The first academic study of lupine shapeshifters, *The Book of Werewolves*, was written by eccentric English scholar and Anglican priest Sabine Baring-Gould in the 1860s. In his eyes, the leap from man to werewolf was not extraordinarily far. "Under the veil of mythology lies a solid reality, that a floating superstition holds in solution a positive truth," he wrote. At the root of his analysis is an assumption that humans are all first and foremost predators, creatures who "naturally, in common with other carnivora, [are] actuated by an impulse to kill, and by a love of destroying life." All parents know this, wrote Baring-Gould. Children are cruel.

Rather than endorsing werewolves as real-life hybrids roaming the woods and escaping scientific discovery, as some contemporary cryptozoologists do, Baring-Gould tethers the alleged transformations to physical and psychological aberrations. An audience for Scandinavian fables and romances, for example, would hear a werewolf story and know that "a form of madness or possession, under the influence of which men acted as though they were changed into wild and savage beasts," was real, because they had a legacy of sagas and poems about those Berserkers, the Old Norse warriors said to fight in a trancelike state while wearing animal skins.

By the end of the middle ages in Europe, lycanthropy began to be seen primarily as a mental disorder, one often associated with schizophrenia, as it is classified today. No longer did a werewolf signify literal shapeshifting, as pagan belief cast it, nor a pact with the Devil, as Christian doctrine rebutted. During that virtual epidemic of Middle Ages werewolf trials, which unfolded nearly parallel to the witch trials, a single French magistrate sentenced six hundred people to death on accusations of lycanthropy. By the early 1600s, that hysteria had given way to empathy. Maybe the werewolf was just a person struggling with mental illness, a "victi[m], not considered blameworthy," as one Englishman wrote in 1593, someone whom "others merely perceive . . . to be *wolflike*," in the words of historian Beresford. Austrian scholar Bruno Bettelheim argued childhood autism could have been interpreted as werewolfism in the sixteenth and seventeenth centuries, as severely affected children had been known to crawl on all fours, snarl, bite, build dens, and refuse clothing. Baring-Gould, meanwhile, devoted a whole chapter to possible real-life explanations for werewolves. He includes hallucination and madness brought on by rabies, fever, monomania, and—I cried out when I read it—ingesting a poisonous plant.

The nurses met us with wheelchairs. Paul was sent straight to a bed, Kiley and I wheeled to an office with our box of leaves. It was a gift to avoid the waiting room. Time felt precious, like a large fish we had caught, for a second, on a line. How easy it could leave us. And what would happen then? I tried to speak, but words turned to slurry somewhere between mind and lips. Even if I'd had them, I would have struggled to put them in the right language. We weren't able to converse in Sicilian; the country hospital didn't have soap in the bathrooms or blue plastic gloves. Maybe it evened out. We were mutually unprepared to cope with our problem. Later, I realized I had given the doctor my parents' Oregon address as just 2559 California, USA.

Eventually we handed them the plastic box, gingerly, as if a creature was inside.

"We don't know what this is," managed Kiley, in Italian. "We ate for dinner. Two hours ago."

Someone—a doctor finishing his shift, maybe—leaned forward to prod them and give them a smell. Everyone else was in scrubs the color of soft green mints, arguing over possibilities. It was clear nobody knew what we had eaten. The last thing I remember was someone taking out a phone to photograph the leaves, presumably to text to someone who might know more. I had the watery sense this flip-phone photo winging its way across Italy was our best option for making it to morning. I began that dumb atheistic fumble for prayer.

When they wheeled me into a hospital room, the blank plaster of the walls was sterile beneath the fluorescent lights. My eyes wanted nothing more than to shut, but I sensed that to do so would be to give up, throwing in the towel on a life I was still trying to shape. I was amused, soon, to realize I had been wrong: the walls were not empty but talking. Lines of typed poetry danced across their jaundice-colored surface like a politician's ticker tape. In the next room, Paul was wailing, his bed shaking. From the quake of the mattress, I could tell his seizing body had been strapped down. His voice was a tangled yelp; it occurred to me I was the only one in the ward who could translate his cries.

"Help me, please, help me." His voice squeezed with pain and convulsion. Crying for his parents, and to stay alive. A mean squeak inside me felt superior. My whole body rattled like a broken toy, but I wasn't yelling. There were no doctors by my bed. My throat felt like it had been tied into a tight furry knot, and look: every breath was an accomplishment. I wanted a prize.

Every now and then the machine next to me would siren and nurses would run between the folding walls that separated Paul's room from mine. This felt like a relief, but also like a sign something was wrong. Why weren't they pumping our stomachs? Fifty-something, twenty-something: the ding of my blood pressure, the brush of a finger tracing my forehead before peeling up my eyelids. The nurses shook their heads, whispering under their breath. *Mamma mia.* At some point they brought in Kiley, who lay in a bed beside me, practicing Italian with a nurse to cork her own horror. From the gestures of the doctors, I gathered our pupils had oozed far into the irises of our eyes, like oil spilled into a green sea.

"*Hai preso la cocaina?*" one asked, leaning toward me with a clipboard. I winced, somewhere between a laugh and a shudder. I was surprised they were questioning our story about dinner, accusing us of using drugs. I thought of Amanda Knox and wondered if they would arrest us. What would my parents say? What would they say when they learned that I, a neurotic worrier, had accidentally drugged myself? Eaten my way to death at a gourmet cooking school! At some point I stopped mourning the mistakes I had made that evening and began to mourn the mistakes I had made through life. The estranged high school friend I had always meant to apologize to. The ex who I wanted to tell still mattered. Mostly, I felt shame. In all my imaginings of leaving our world, I had never thought I would be taking someone with me. And so the reckoning with my mortality became a reckoning with my own capacity for harm.

Late Saturday bled into early Sunday. At some point it was quiet. The doctors had closed the doors to Paul's room. How clear it suddenly was that he had died, and I had played a part in killing him. As the heart machine sang beside me, I stared at the string of electric poetry somehow still slithering around the walls. I marveled at their bold font, in English. It did not occur to me to question if they were real. I wondered who would break the news to my parents, and if it would be the same person who told Paul's. Then I closed my eyes and prepared myself to join him.

Contemporary Western pop culture predominantly portrays werewolves as vessels of potent masculine power, but ancient tales paint a different picture, where men are transformed into wolves by the influence and actions of women. "You loved a shepherd, a herdsman, who endlessly put up cakes for you, and everyday slaughtered kids for you. You struck him, turned him into a wolf. His own boys drove him away, and his dogs tore his hide to bits," says the protagonist of *The Epic of Gilgamesh* to a goddess as he turns her down in marriage in the Mesopotamian tale, written sometime between 1300 and 1000 BC. Two thousand years later, in 906, Regino of Prüm wrote of women who "go out at night" and "wander off the straight and narrow path" toward evil, making it so, as his contemporary Burchard de Worms put it, "a man can, at will, transform himself into a wolf." A Liberian tale describes a lazy husband ordering his wife to shape-shift into a leopard to capture food so he does not have to hunt. She does transform, but it's toward him she turns her claws, infuriated that it is her responsibility to fill his plate. Each night we were alone, Paul walked into the apartment after work. Did he expect to be fed by Kiley and me, or did we just train ourselves to feed him? In the Liberian legend, the newly animal wife torments her husband until he agrees to hunt again.

Regardless of gender identity, the werewolf was frequently depicted not only as a terrorizer but as a punished person. An Armenian legend warns of the child-snatching *mardagayl,* people condemned to spend seven years in a wolf's body as penance for some mortal sin. Every night the punished person transformed to a wolf, returning to their human form at dawn. From what I can find, the *mardagayl* was very often imagined to be a woman. In their wolf form, the *mardagayl* ate their own children. They then moved on to children of relatives, then of strangers. To be cursed as *mardagayl* was to lose not only your human form but your lineage; to cannibalize your bloodline, labor, body, love. Folktales are vessels for lessons, and in this one, the harm falls not just on the child victim but on the woman who must wake each morning and remember, or discover, what she has done the night before as wolf. The moral is as much for the child to stay away from dark places as it is for the woman to stay away from dark sins.

The guilt of a perpetrator who does not mean to hurt is in no way equivalent to the harm felt by the victim, but it seems to me the best contemporary werewolf stories excavate the emotional reality of each. In that feminist werewolf film *Ginger Snaps,* Ginger gets her period and is mauled by a werewolf on the same night. The equation between menstruation and lycanthropy is clear: both cycles are allegedly tied to the moon. The werewolf attack is not Ginger's fault. She did not ask for it. She was, however, walking in a park at night with her little sister, during a week where neighbors kept waking to find their own dogs gutted and flayed, as parents urged their young to stay inside. Ginger courted risk: she did not get away with it.

At first, she is in denial. Sure, her body is changing—thin hairs sprouting from the claw gashes across her chest—but what are the odds? She knows no one else who has had this experience. When she details her symptoms of blood and body hair to the school nurse, the older woman smiles and nods. "Everyone seems to panic their first time," she says. It is only after Ginger aggressively initiates unprotected sex in the back of a popular guy's car that she accepts her condition is different. Rather than a guy making her pregnant, she makes him werewolf.

If the climax of a werewolf story is learning whether the monster will be stopped or the lead victim will be killed, the terror begins with the slow burn of transformation. The moment where the protagonist realizes they are helpless to intervene in the changes happening to their body. Whether through puberty, aging, illness, or gender dysphoria, many of us know the feeling of looking down and feeling total dislocation; that *how-can-this-be-me*.

The morning after Ginger loses her virginity in the back of the car, her younger sister, Bridget, wakes to find Ginger creeping back into her twin bed and crying softly.

"Ging? What happened?" asks Bridget, her eyes wide. "Did he hurt you? If he hurt you you should tell." Her only frame for female tears is one of victimhood, but when Bridget tracks down her older sister in the bathroom, she finds her mouth stained with blood, her nose twitching. Ginger has just killed the neighbor's dog. Her horror, we soon understand, is not in what has happened to her—it is what she herself has done.

Later I would hear doctors sent the flip-phone photo to a poison center in Parma, where someone identified the leaves as young mandrake, which, for a few weeks of the year, looks almost like wild chard. Some sort of antidote arrived by helicopter, but stormy weather prevented it from landing at the hospital, and a brave driver traveled to pick it up while the doctors stood around Paul's bed and took guesses about how long until the toxins reached his brain. What was that antidote? Did I receive it? Did it help? I have no way of knowing. I only know I survived.

At some point in the night, my fear shifted zones. Wobbled away from what poison was doing to my body and oozed into the hospital room itself. If I had felt sequestered at the villa, the hospital was the opposite. I had no control over my shaking body or the room it was in. At times it seemed the whole countryside had entered to gossip and play sentry at our bedsides. I remember one nurse looked like someone I went on a bad date with once. Tall and tawny with a shelf of cheekbones. Sometimes I woke to see him at my bedside, other times he was chatting with Kiley. His hair was covered under some sort of burgundy do-rag. The lights in the room were dim. At some point he held my hand, then kissed my forehead. Was it normal for nurses to give you a peck? *Vampiric,* I wrote later in my journal. Talking about it with Kiley, she would later say she remembered his attention, but not his lips. Had I hallucinated it? How to know, now, what was real, that night?

Daylight was euphoria. That first sunbeam a whisper in my ear. *You made it.* When I realized I could move my limbs, I tried to unplug my IV, hoping to escape in a rare moment when the room was empty. The doctors wanted to keep me another night and—entrapped by the expectations of American health care—I was terrified what it would cost. I couldn't spend another night tethered and tubed to the bed, pinned and watched like a bug to the page. At the same time, I thought I was back at the villa, where I needed to answer emails for my boss. Because I was not there, though, I never found my basement room with the pink silk dresser. Blood streaked my arm where I yanked out the IV. At the revolving glass door at the front of the hospital, the nurses caught me. Lucidity hit me as their arms wrapped my torso.

"*Mi dispiace,*" I said, because it was embarrassing to have helped kill someone and embarrassing to have lost my mind. "*Molto dispiace.*"

Sicily is located at the tip of Italy's boot, the island like a spur connected to the toe of the mainland by a bridge on the eastern side of the island. It is surrounded by three seas: the Ionian, the Mediterranean, and, the closest sea to us at the cooking school, the Tyrrhenian. If you follow that sea north across blue raspberry Jell-O waters, you reach Corsica, a French island between Florence and Rome.

In her book *The Dream-Hunters of Corsica*, midcentury British writer and Corsican expatriate Dorothy Carrington writes about the island's legendary *mazzeri*, whose traditions she dates to pre-Neolithic inhabitants of the island in 7000 BC. These "dream-hunters" are "mostly women, [who] hunt in packs and tear their prey to death with their teeth, like hounds." The animals they kill are said to represent certain people from their villages, now cursed by the *mazzeri*'s eye. Except none of this violence is literal, it is dreamed, conjured, writes Carrington, by women who "dose themselves with certain hallucinogenic plants that grow in Corsica, such as mandrake." A *mazzeru* did not actually kill, she just dreamed herself a beast, and in that dreamworld, made her neighbors die. I imagine her vision blurring as she lies her body down, snout widening and nails lengthening as she avenges every petty frustration of waking life.

Because I did not know we had eaten mandrake, and I did not know mandrake's history was so intertwined with conversations about witchery and shape-shifting women and their alleged sins, it is up to you whether to believe me when I say that on that night, I felt it. Not just the poison, but the freedom of having been pushed to the brink of the world as I knew it. My life would end, or it would continue with the knowledge that Paul's would not. Even through the slush of hallucination-fogged brain, I understood I was in a new reality. I had once been someone who mostly kept my body in control, who looked out for others, who did not cause a fuss. That self had disappeared. *Poof.*

As the nurses walked my staggering, shaky body back to the room, we paraded through hallways of doctors and patients and their families. My tangled hair was matted to my neck, a jagged creek of blood on my arm. I wanted to prove I was reliable, so I smiled through cracked lips, a chain of incoherent English-Italian greetings leaking from my mouth. The onlookers' eyes met mine, but their looks were new. Not just pity, but nerves.

"Who hasn't ever wondered: am I a monster or is this what it means to be a person?" wrote novelist Clarice Lispector in *The Hour of the Star.* The root for *monstrum,* that Latin word for monster, is *monere*—to warn. As if the scary thing is not the problem but the alert about the problem. It is hard to think back on that night in the hospital and not see it as a divine warning. A reminder that however comfortable or safe I may feel, my guard must never fall that far down again. If I was often too quick to worry about worst-case scenarios, in Sicily I was too good at forgetting danger existed at all.

Bleached by day, the poetry on the walls was gone. I did not yet understand it had never been there. Someone sent a nun, smiling in black cotton, to Kiley's and my beds. Filipino, she was the first English speaker we had encountered all night. She told us Paul was sleeping upstairs.

"Alive?" Kiley asked, shocked. The nun nodded, then began to pray for us. The morning-shift doctors came in, and one demanded we drink two liters of a milky blue laxative, shot by shot from a Dixie cup. It was the worst thing I had ever tasted. He yelled at us to finish and yelled when we said we couldn't. I demandcd we be released to go home. They refused. I imagined the cheek-kissing surveillance of the nurse. We pleaded. Eventually they relented.

At the car, the groundskeeper and chef hugged us close, red-eyed from a night slumped in the waiting room. *Non mangiare verdure,* they said, echoing the doctor. Don't eat vegetables for a while. Pasta from a crisp plastic package—I couldn't imagine wanting anything else. Driving home, I watched the shadow-blur of passing bushes and mused to Kiley about how odd it was to be chased by packs of large black dogs. Just another madwoman, imagining wolves.

From the front seat, the groundskeeper did not understand I was still hallucinating, so he took the words as a sign of vitality. "*Brava!*" he said, clapping me on the knee. Kiley looked ill. I tried to make her feel better by chatting, but the toxins had shredded my short-term memory, and no sooner would I start a sentence than I would forget where it was going.

"Maybe it's better if we don't talk," she said through tight lips. I nodded, lucid enough to wonder if this would be the rest of my life.

Back at the villa we went to our respective rooms to lie down. My pupils were so big I could not read. I knew I should tell my family what had happened, but my phone screen swam in front of me. In the shower, my shampoo grew big eyes and a grotesque red cartoon mouth. I mistook it for an old friend, and we chatted for thirty minutes.

Through the day, my vision, like my memory, returned slowly. Brain like a window defogging after a hot shower. I kept staring at my pupils in the mirror, putting a hand to my still racing heartbeat. I could not believe any of me was still there. By the time we visited Paul in the hospital the next afternoon, I was confident the poison had passed through my body like a storm, leaving me rattled but intact. That's when we learned Paul had been in a coma for fifteen hours, and that at one point, they had given him two minutes to live. How had he lived longer? The guess was because he was so active and healthy, but nobody knew. *CrossFit! No booze!* I thought again and again about how close I had been to taking that last serving. Some shred of obnoxious good-girl martyrdom had, for once, saved me.

In the weeks that followed, after Kiley's internship was up, and after Paul underwent follow-up testing, then came back, healthy and whole, we bonded over the odds of our survival. *Divina Provvidenza,* as the local Italian newspaper article reported. We also bonded over the uncomfortable awareness of our self-induced terror. It was easy to laugh, now, chuckling as we side-eyed the garden salads. We never talked about who was to blame. He knew I had helped pick and prepare the mandrake, but I knew he was a trained horticulturalist. I convinced myself this was a sort of equilibrium: that he saw it the same way.

Each back in our respective countries that summer, Paul recounted his story to a prominent newspaper. Toward the end of the article, Paul noted that he did not harbor hard feelings toward the co-workers who had set him on this path. When I read his description of "the girls" having mild symptoms and being discharged swiftly, my eyes widened, surprised how trivial my night had become on the page. Didn't he remember the part where he had identified the leaves?

The article had over 120 online comments. It was masochism to scroll through many. One commenter said the problem wasn't foraging, but the arrogance of Paul's dumb "friends." Another suggested that though Paul might have had doubts about the food, he had perhaps tried to impress us by eating it, because turning down food offered by "an attractive member of the opposite sex" is hard.

A man had almost died, and women were to blame. Had Kiley and I been arrogant? If so, had our arrogance been cruel? Maybe we had been too comfortable. We had thought we knew the land around our home, thought we knew the limits of our knowledge. But Paul was not our prey, and we were not predators; we were all just people who had been, for a night, too clumsy with our lives. What happened with the mandrake had scared me, deeply, more than anything I had lived through before. But when I traced the tail of my fear, it didn't lead to another human, but to myself: my hands, which had cut the plant, and my head, which had told me it was safe. If I had picked up a new kind of bravery in Sicily—an optimistic, extroverted spontaneity propped up by good wine and the *che serà, serà* attitude of so many kind people I met—I had also let go of the neurotic risk-assessment I hauled through America. I had become more fun, and less worried, and sometimes it felt I had paid my dues.

In Greek mythology, the sorceress Circe lives on a Mediterranean island, unmarried and alone. I picture Sicily, the only such island I know, its white-sand coves flanked by dark crumbs of lava rock and clusters of prickly pears. In Madeline Miller's bestselling novel-ization of the legend, *Circe,* she imagined a world where ships appeared on the goddess's horizon, their sailors begging for food and shelter. In Miller's telling, Circe fed the men, and they thanked her, and then they pushed back their plates, and their expressions changed. Now they were hungry for her. Soon Circe learned to protect herself against their abuses of hospitality. She brewed an herbal potion to spike their wine. By the time the men set down their forks, Circe had only to utter a word and their bodies would morph, bones snapping as they shrank to beast. Her island filled with transformed men. The outcome of Miller's telling is true to earlier legends—in Virgil's *Aeneid,* a passerby hears the noise of Circe's captives radiating off the island, those "Herds of Howling Wolves that stun the Sailors' Ears"—but in dramatizing Circe's role as victim, Miller provides a motive for Circe's poisonings.

Her retelling stays with me because it holds a different sort of man-to-wolf transition. One where the men who drop to four legs become less and not more dangerous. Unlike the men, the wolves are loyal. In one 1889 painting, Circe glows at the top of a marble stairway covered in petals, while tigers, lions, and wolves flank and lounge at her feet. It is easy to imagine she has poisoned the men to protect herself. Rather than dread the turn of man to animal, she initiates it.

The year I left Sicily was the year I arrived in Minneapolis, where, tucked into the trees of a museum's outdoor sculpture park, I found a bronze sculpture of a life-sized woman stepping out of a wolf's belly. The piece was *Rapture,* a 2001 creation by West German–born American artist Kiki Smith. The woman is naked, her hair short or nonexistent, her breasts low and belly curved. The wolf lies on its spine, tongue out and four paws in the air, one of which is grasped by the woman as she emerges, one bare foot at a time. Her expression is flat, as calm as someone stepping from the bath.

I returned to the sculpture often, observing it like a still from a movie and imagining what had happened in the minutes before. At first glance it seemed some iteration of Little Red, a victim freeing herself from the beast who had devoured her. But what if the woman's exit from the wolf was not an escape, but a birth? They were holding hands, after all. What if the wolf wasn't dead; what if the woman had just stepped from its belly? Hadn't I been born by cesarean, my mother sliced open so I wouldn't come out upside down? What if the woman was not separating herself from the wolf, but bringing its essence with her?

My instinct was confirmed when I saw *Born,* a color lithograph Smith created a year after *Rapture,* depicting a red-caped woman and child emerging from the belly of a supine wolf, cherry tongue lolling from the side of its snout. The two humans share a look of tenderness, hands grasping one another even as the wolf's paws grasp their skirts. It is a tangle of limbs; the scene is unequivo-cally a birth. Then there is *Wolf Girl,* an etching tinted with watery blue, which shows a girl beneath a bonnet whose face is spiky with fur, her smile cracked to reveal two rows of sharp teeth, her ex-pression carrying the bashful pride of a school photo. The girl is both woman and wolf, a child born of a pairing, a love affair. Of these works, curator Helaine Posner says, "Instead of presenting [the wolf and woman] in their traditional roles as predator and prey, Smith reimagines these characters as companions, equals in purpose and scale."

I agreed with Posner's read, but I did not want to stop at imag-ining the equality between woman and wolf—I wanted to imagine the fluidity between them too. As if one could continually give birth to the other, or as if one was always just riding inside the other, waiting to crack out. As if the woman was not trapped inside the wolf but was the wolf, and was now just trading skins.

In many Indigenous views, human-animal hybridity is not only nat-ural but expected. A body, like the material world it belongs to, is porous, "the lantern through which the spirit shines," wrote Baring-Gould, invoking Buddhist belief. The Tlingit see themselves as the descendants of two wolves who shed their furs and took to two legs. In a lithograph by Inuit Cape Dorset artist Ningeokuluk Teevee, a woman unzips her human skin to reveal a fox. Describing the work, she said: "I wanted to show how people could change from one thing to another but still be the same person."

Folklorist Teresa Pijoan recounts a story told to her by a Zuni tribal member, about a woman kidnapped in a Navajo raid who escaped into the mesa, starving and thirsty as it started to snow. She woke to find a white wolf staring at her. The wolf shares his kill and pushes the body of his warm prey over the woman's freezing limbs. The next night, after a day of travel, the wolf returns to sleep beside her and keep her warm. On the fifth day, she reaches her village, the wolf by her side. The men watch their approach, calling out that they will kill the beast that follows her. She yells that the wolf has saved her life and they must never touch him, but he has already disappeared. When she returns to her house, she finds her family dead. Years pass, until one day the woman understands it is her turn to die. Too frail to stand, she crawls into the streets of the town. Suddenly, she turns her head to howl. Her limbs tighten, her wrinkled skin bristles to white fur, her eyes glow like ice on a lake. She runs out of the town and into the trees. Some say she still stands at the mouth of a canyon, sometimes wolf and sometimes woman, sometimes in-between. I can almost see her white hair rippling, her legs strong in the wind.

To talk about a werewolf has often been a way to gesture toward otherwise unspeakable fears. Fears of losing control, of oneself or one's loved ones. Of a body that has been legible—a lover that has been kind, or a self that has been orderly—suddenly going off script. A werewolf is often rendered as a performance of violence, but the smoke show of transformation can disguise the fact that any story of change is also a story of loss. For a new body to stand before you, an old body has disappeared. The werewolf does not just stoke fear, then, but also grief.

Though werewolf stories often maintain a pedagogical slant, as with parents teaching children not to roam after nightfall, stories can also become a form of first-person testimony. While the werewolf has been a vessel for fear-based bigotry, as with homophobic allusions to a strange beast "riding" a traveler from behind, as in some Dutch and German legends, it's also been a way to validate the experiences of those whose traumas might otherwise be left invisible. Sexual assaults; pedophilic predation; abortions and miscarriages—all might be telegraphed through the lens of witnessing a werewolf. A study of Flemish-German werewolf legends describes a farmer's story sounding "more like a piece of oral history than as a migratory legend," and notes how many of these legends were stories passed down by grandmothers and mothers, as if through accounts with the creature one could say, *Look what happened, look how you can still survive.* "Werewolf stories allow a speaker to construct and discuss her views without appearing too bold, and while hiding behind the story's traditionality," wrote Russian scholar Elena Boudovskaia.

The trend exists outside Western tradition too. After the 2010 earthquake in Haiti, rumors of werewolves prowling displacement camps led to the real-life lynchings of multiple men. "After the earthquake, the *loup-garou* fled from prison . . . during the night he went into the tents and tried to take someone's child," a camp resident named Michaelle Casseus told ABC News. Residents set up nighttime patrols to scan for the spirit-beasts while, inside the tents, children remained missing. Thousands had been orphaned, separated from their parents, and left vulnerable to child traffickers trying to monopolize on illegal adoptions. "People talk about *loups-garous* to give a name to their fears, but it is child snatchers who snatch children, not evil spirits," said Haiti's secretary of state for finance Sylvain Lafalaisse. The earth had split open, and the state—and wider world—had failed to care for its victims. That, as a tragedy, was unimaginable. The werewolf was easier to see.

Hispaniola scholar Robin Derby believes stories of Haiti's *bacá*, those spirits said to cause animal-human transformations, persist as a form of resistance against the region's colonial, oppressive history. The hunting and illicit trading of wild meat and livestock enabled a contraband economy allowing fugitive enslaved people, European indentured servants, pirates, and creoles to exist at the fringe of the slave trade. In the Dominican Republic, where Derby recorded men telling stories about encountering and fighting off animal demons, she came to see the spirit animals as a foil for their masculinity. "I think that today in the abandoned countryside, where a lot of Dominican men are located on the lowest rung of the socioeconomic totem pole, there is a lot of entertaining bravado in the telling of these tales," she said in an interview with UCLA's Latin American Institute. It is one thing to witness a transforming or transformed creature, but in narrating the experience, one confirms they have survived it. That they too have been transformed.

In her million-copy bestseller, *Women Who Run with the Wolves*, Clarissa Pinkola Estés describes the shared persecution of woman and wolf, both "predat[ed] ... by those who misunderstand them." Each are "endangered species" whose "spiritual lands have ... been plundered or burnt, dens bulldozed, and natural cycles forced into unnatural rhythms to please others." Estés is a self-described "fairy-tale forensic" whose book combines Jungian spirituality and analysis with the intercultural myths she learned from her Mexican and Hungarian grandmothers. "I come to stories as a *cantadora*, keeper of the old stories," she writes. It is a compelling promise: midlife self-help in the costume of childhood folktale. In her introduction, she explains that an excavated fairy tale can guide a woman's psyche "like a play with stage instruction."

At the opening of the book, Estés writes the Chicano story of La Loba, an old woman, "often hairy, always fat . . . a crower and a cackler" who collects bones in her desert cave. Traveling the arroyos and mountains, she gathers bones, especially wolf bones, re-creating a sculpture of the body from the detritus from the land. Once the skeleton is assembled, La Loba raises her arms and sings above it. Slowly bones rise into fur, flesh hardens, the tail curls upward. Like air entering a balloon animal, the wolf breathes and begins to move. As La Loba sings, the wolf runs up the rocky canyons until she is "suddenly transformed into a laughing woman who can run free." Estés calls this story *un cuento milagro*, a miracle story, a promise that we can resuscitate the wild if we only sing the right song. Too many women wait for a man to summon their bones, writes Estés, but it's solitary work. Only a woman can resuscitate her animal essence and bring it back to life.

Though I had found a fat yellow-paged paperback of Estés's work abandoned in a hotel lobby, its prolific reputation intimidated me, as did its size. When I told people I was writing about wolves, it was one of the two books I was most frequently asked about. The other, Barry Lopez's *Of Wolves and Men*, seemed, if only by title, almost comically opposed. The wolves and women versus the wolves and men.

It wasn't until after leaving Sicily that I finally got around to paging through *Women Who Run with the Wolves*. I knew, by that point, that something had opened in me that poisoned night. The mandrake had planted it, or, in picking the mandrake, I had planted it myself. Sometimes, when I felt the transformative head rush of an edible or a cocktail, I mistook it for illness, a swim cap slipping over my skull. Only then did I understand the symptoms of poison and pleasure are blurry, and often in the dosing. When I ate someone's backyard salad, or when a friend shared foraged berries or mushrooms, I smiled and chewed, then excused myself to check my pupils in the bathroom mirror. It was one thing to worry about my body, but these symptoms paled in comparison to what I felt feeding others. I would pass the bowl then watch their eyes, waiting for the seemingly inevitable point in the dinner party where someone would ask, politely, as Paul at first had done, why they felt so strange.

I thought my "problem," after eating the mandrake, was I had become scared of wild foods. I spent hours googling freak foodborne diseases and trying to urge my roommates they shouldn't grow their own sprouts. It all felt ridiculous, but considering what had happened, somewhat understandable, the thing my therapist was thinking when she mentioned PTSD. Now, in Estés's pages, I let myself find a mirror. "Trying to be good, orderly, and compliant in the face of inner or outer peril or in order to hide a critical psychic or real-life situation de-souls a woman," wrote Estés. "It cuts her from her knowing; it cuts her from her ability to act." Maybe it wasn't fear I had to get over, it was shame. Sure, I was afraid of replicating that night's harm, but mostly I could not forgive myself for having caused it. I had to own my mistake.

I thought I needed bravery. More courage to sit with my own discomfort. Estés's words made me wonder if I just needed to learn to better live beside others' discomfort. I had done something dumb, and it had harmed, horribly, but we were lucky. We sailed free. What, then, had really changed? A speck of the internet had ridiculed us; the cooking school now educated guests and interns about the dangers of foraging. The only thing that changed was my awareness of how directly my choices could cause harm. I thought of Paul, pleading for life in the hospital, and could not forget I had helped send him there.

I had to reconcile the corners of myself. The part of me that wanted so fiercely never to hurt someone with the part of me that, inevitably, would. "You are the guiltiest non-Catholic I've ever met," a boyfriend, raised Catholic, would say when he met me half a decade after I'd eaten the mandrake. *I have a reason to be guilty!* I thought, flashing back to Paul's arms strapped to the bed. But what use was guilt? "If it leads to change then it can be useful, since it is then no longer guilt but the beginning of knowledge," wrote Audre Lorde in *Sister Outsider.* "Yet all too often, guilt is just another name for impotence, for defensiveness destructive of communication; it becomes a device to protect ignorance and the continuation of things the way they are, the ultimate protection for changelessness."

In some way I envied werewolf stories that delivered punishment as a time-based sentence. The idea that a devil would deliver me a wolfskin to wear on full moons for two years until my penance was paid. But I had no sentence. There was no finish line, only the gift of more days and more meals to share with people. This reality would have to exist beside the past. Not just my memory of the hospital, but what had come before. Those few words in my journal wishing to throttle Paul—a hyperbolic joke, sure, but one I'd never forget. As if my pen had willed what so nearly came to pass later.

"Violence for me is part of the psyche," writes Jacqueline Rose. To abolish its specter, as modern feminism often tries to do, is to "replicat[e] that part of the mind which cannot tolerate its own complexity." Rose is not advocating violence, but she is suggesting a willingness to search for its shadow—not only in others, but in ourselves. In *Of Wolves and Men,* Lopez ties humanity's fraught relationship with the wolf to theriophobia. "Fear of the beast," he writes by way of definition. "Fear of the beast as an irrational, violent, insatiable creature. Fear of the projected beast in oneself." When we cannot deal with the beast in ourselves, we project it outward, onto other men and wolves. It would seem one solution to this outsourced violence or anxiety is to reckon with its shadow in our own bones. "To have compassion for the wolf, whom man saw as enslaved by the same base drives as himself, [is] to yearn for self-forgiveness," wrote Lopez.

In Shakespeare's *The Merchant of Venice,* Gratiano tells Shylock about "a wolf, who hanged for human slaughter," a line that smacks of metaphor until you see the account from Elizabethan England of rabbit-killing birds of prey being killed and flayed then "h[u]ng on a gallows, as they do wolves." In seventeenth-century Germany too, a wolf that had attacked people was hung wearing clothes, a wig, and a human mask. As if by killing the wolf a town could purge an evil in its own society, its own blood. Because I wanted to untie the wolf from the gallows, I assumed I should shake the animal free from the things we conflated it with. Surely the werewolf was an embodiment of how we projected the animal onto our human drama, unable to accept the monstrosity ourselves. I did not like that a child who feared werewolves may be more likely to fear wolves too.

Only now do I wonder: What if the werewolf is not shackle but solution? Not a silver bullet but a helpful lens for peaceful coexistence, a way to remember what so many prehistoric and Indigenous cultures have long known about the slippage between selves and bodies and worlds? The werewolf is the embodiment of collapsed distance between Self and Other. To imagine its transforming body is to confront what Donna Haraway calls the "absurdity" of distinctions between individuals, but also, I would argue, between our various inner selves. In her queer-trans reading of *Ginger Snaps,* Heather Tapley suggests that the werewolf detonates not only "the binarized identity categories of man/woman, male/female, and human/animal, but also the entire system of identity signs."

In *Dr. Jekyll and Mr. Hyde,* Robert Louis Stevenson wrote, "Man is not truly one, but truly two." But aren't we more than that too? Stevenson's words bring to mind an oft-parodied proverb, popularly attributed to Cherokee legend though likely scripted by evangelical pastor Billy Graham. A grandfather explains to his grandson that there are always two wolves fighting inside him, one good and one bad. "Who will win?" asks the grandson. "The one you feed," says his grandfather. One popular internet meme of this proverb, which I started seeing around 2019, feels even more revelatory. "Each of us are two wolves," reads the block text above two opposing wolf heads in one image. "One has depression. The other has depression." The punch line of the meme is, it seems to me, solid. There are no true compartmentalizations of self. Stevenson was right that we are "not truly one," but neither are we "truly two." We are both infinitely more and less.

When I think back to that year in Sicily, I see myself as a kaleidoscope of selves wheeling through that poppy-studded countryside, the color from one self always tinting the color of another, no barriers between them, only the truth of their murkiness. The truth of feeling like a foreigner and like I belonged. That I was lonely and loved, consuming and producing, helping and harming. When I now think of that self in the hospital, hallucinating as she ran through the halls, I feel tenderness—she who had surrendered to her transformation; she who could not imagine it would pass. At the same time, I feel a tenderness toward the other self, the one who picked the leaves, whistling as she brought them in. She did not know it at the time, but she too was in the throes of transformation, living a life an ocean away from the people she loved, but also a little further from her fear. If, in my American life, fear so often drove the boat, here in Sicily, the engine was pleasure. Maybe eating almost brought me death, but so often at the cooking school, it had also shaken me out of my speculative anxiety and lifted me closer to life.

I can look back now and see I should have been more cautious, but I can also see how good it felt not to think about caution at all. To accept that living in a body meant sometimes losing control over it. Annie Dillard describes animal appetite as "living in the physical sense . . . without bias or motive." Eating is when I am my most wolf. When I eat, I am most grounded in my body and the world. I forget the whine in my head that says the future is too scary, or I am too cowardly to face it. As Ligaya Mishan writes in the *New York Times,* eating forces us to confront "what we do to others, and so fear our own devouring, of becoming food for worms, as the saying goes, upon death." If eating is a confrontation with mortality, it is also a buffer against its shadow. We feed our bones so they can face another day. When I think of a ravenous wolf now, I do not see a specter of horror: I see a body wired with instinct. A body on the brink of joy.

7

Mother v. Wolf

Downstairs in the guest room of the house my grandparents built in the Montana woods sits a pillow painted with a familiar scene. Framed by dark trees and a hunk of granite, a girl and wolf face one another in the dappled sun. The girl wears a red cape, hood pulled over her short dark curls. She carries a brown umbrella like a walking stick and a basket lined in white linen. The wolf stares at her, but looks more like a panting dog than a menace. The girl too looks curious, something like a smile tugging her cheek. If you did not know the story, you would think they could be friends.

How many summer nights did I lie in the hot, insect-clicking quiet of that room, tossing and turning toward and away from the girl and the wolf? If I thought twice about the pillow, I've forgotten it. Only in the last year, on a forty-eight-hour visit back, did I glance at the cushion while lifting it off the bed and feel the snap of connection. I had come through the woods to grandmother's house, and this was the story I found. A story that had always been waiting for me. Like Little Red, I was raised in a family that believed in letting me walk alone through the trees. Looking at the pillow now, I was surprised to feel less like its bumbling, wandering heroine than like the person who nudged her out the door. When I asked Grandma Sally about the pillow, she said she didn't know who had made it, but it had been passed down from my grandfather's mother. *You should have it when I die,* she told me. *Ha ha.*

From the porch, we sometimes heard wolves howling. They had regained stable populations in the Bitterroot Valley after dispersing from Yellowstone in the 1990s. One snowy childhood morning their tracks appeared in circles around the barn. It was just the one mule and a horse in the stable by then, skittish but safe. Mostly wolves were a thing to wish for on their motion-activated wildlife cameras, which so often just picked up deer. Seeing a predator was like finding beach glass on the shore. Eventually I accepted the wolves and bears and I would share the forest at different hours, the way a friend of mine once lived with two flight attendants who came and went sporadically, and often in the night. Just as with the hills of lupine and balsamroot that spread beyond my grandparents' house, and like the family that gathered inside, I eventually took the wolves for granted. Because I could not see how our lives intersected, I told myself they did not.

The most popular narrative of OR-7 follows him solo across thousands of miles of Oregon and California, then watches him "settling down," finding that other disperser—the lanky dark female wolf skeptics thought environmentalists or government agents had planted—and getting out of sight. As a marriage plot for a certain public, his story ended there. Loneliness blossomed into family. Pups appeared. That was the trajectory of OR-7 I knew from the canon of documentaries and children's books. A wolf defined

by the arc of his solo journey, first away from one family, and then
toward a new one. The most interesting stories do not end with a
homecoming, though, they only thicken. Family begets drama.

As OR-7 and his mate staked new territory in southwestern
Oregon, his web of interconnectedness grew. In early 2015, they
received official "pack status," after at least two of his pups were
documented living through the prior year. Now OR-7 was leader
of the Rogue Pack, named for the region they settled at the southern crest of the volcanic Cascades. Of Oregon's nine packs, his was
then the only one established in the western part of the state since
wolves had been slaughtered to extinction over six decades earlier.
Now "the world's most famous wolf," as *Newsweek* referred to him,
was tethered to a particular landscape. A place known for grassy
meadows and bowl-like plateaus surrounded by mountain hemlock
and white pine, huckleberry, and heather; a national hub for migratory waterfowl; a place where the opaline alpine lakes that dotted
the Sky Lakes Wilderness had been found to hold some of the
most chemically pure water on the planet. It was a good place to be
a wolf, but the wolves weren't alone. When the local Klamath Falls
newspaper posted a question on their website asking if the species
should continue receiving protection as "endangered" animals, 6,280
people voted yes, while 361 said no. Under a subsequent heading
that read "We were hacked," editor Gerry O'Brien wrote, "There are
computer programs that can overrun a poll, skewing the vote. We
think the prowolf faction tipped their hand a bit here."

As a magnet for media attention, OR-7 had always been a symbol of that ideological divide over whether wolf populations should
be allowed to reestablish themselves, and how humans should be
able to respond. Within a few months of the poll, state biologists
discovered that both the radio and satellite portions of OR-7's collar had died, rendering his movements effectively untraceable. In

transitioning from transient into local, he was now in regular prox-imity to ranchers and their herds. Tied not only to his own actions, but those of his kin.

I didn't come home to Oregon for any significant chunks of time in the years after I left for college. A few weeks at the start of a summer, maybe, or a month between jobs. I kept belongings boxed in the basements and attics of kind friends along the East Coast, so even when I was back, it felt temporary, a place to dock, not a marina to stay. My sister had similarly traveled cross-country for school, and eventually across the ocean for work. Because it felt too risky to take unpaid internships in big cities, we took poorly paid gigs in little ones. We were lucky: we could toss ourselves toward far-flung places and then land at home, reorienting ourselves before another takeoff.

My dad's beloved younger sister and her family lived in Port-land, but otherwise my extended family was scattered. As we got older, Annika and I tried, and often failed, to get to Montana once a year. If these familial absences created a void—a sparseness in our Berry-pack formation—it filled with other bodies. On our quick trips home, the back door was often swinging open with neigh-bors and family friends coming to catch up over a cup of tea or a potluck pasta dinner. My honorary aunts and uncles and cousins. There were moments I resented the flurry of company. I wanted the cocoon of my childhood room, not trying to remember which of the three Steves in the extended circle I had already talked to about my road trip. Even on the tired nights, though, there would always be a minute when I leaned over the table for someone's funny story and heard a different rush in my ears. Not the urge to vault myself into a new job—to rearticulate myself to a new audience, as I had craved so fervently when leaving for college—but to lean back into the web of people who already supported me. To trust the feeling of safety I felt there. To come home.

I once thought my parents had such strong connections because they had met each other so young. Surely their decades together had let them accrue lots of friends, the way the person who shows up early to the flea market is rewarded with the best tchotchkes. But throughout my twenties, as I moved to Maine, Sicily, Minnesota, Massachusetts, New York, and Michigan—making new friends in one place while struggling to keep up with old ones in another—I learned that community didn't just gather wherever you rolled, accumulating like some triumphant snowball. We inherit our biological families and decide how close to keep them. We have chosen families only if we try.

My mother biked flowers across the river to a co-worker's doorstep for her birthday. My father, on the day after an ice storm caused mass local power outages, transformed their front porch into a recharge-hotspot, laying out a power strip, taping up a sign with a guest WiFi network and password, and emailing the whole neighborhood. The ethos of family they had passed on to me was not about ancestral heirlooms or genetically adjacent smiles, it was about having a pack where members were tight, but borders were fluid. Where you could roam, but you could always come back.

Wolves are territorial, and generally skeptical of outsiders. One study of dispersers in Alaska found only twenty-one percent of those young wanderers were adopted into new, preexisting packs. Still, in an uncanny mirror of human groupings, biologists studying captive wolf packs have observed a diversity of family structures, including those with "immigrant" wolves. OR-7 and his mate would have been classified as a "nuclear family," with two unfamiliar breeders producing a litter. "Extended families" include parents plus at least one of their siblings, while a pack with one or both of the original parents missing is a "disrupted family." One that welcomes an outside breeder is a "stepfamily," or a "foster family" if the outsider doesn't breed. In a chart of findings published in Mech and Boitani's *Wolves: Behavior, Ecology, and Conservation,* the least observed pack formation is labeled a "complex family." In the case of captive wolves, perhaps pups have been hand-raised elsewhere, and adopted in. It is the name for a unit where history is not easily mapped between its members, where community will exist independent of blood. It's not a prototypical wolf pack by any measure, but when I thought about how I wanted to run into the future, it was the image that lingered in my mind.

The summer after my accidental poisoning, Kathryn Schulz published "The Big One" in *The New Yorker,* her Pulitzer-winning piece about the overdue earthquake and "seven-hundred-mile liquid wall" forecast to decimate the Pacific Northwest with "the worst natural disaster in the history of North America." Home for a visit, I sat with my parents and worried what could be done. Should they move? Where would they go? As I raked my ice-cream spoon against the bowl, I pledged not to move back to Portland, at least not until after whatever shook the earth was done. The world felt scary enough; I didn't need that fear too. Reports later revealed that the expected 8- or 9-magnitude earthquake will likely not only cause deadly explosions and fires, but the country's largest-ever oil spill, bigger than the *Deepwater Horizon*'s, on a stretch of the Willamette River just a few miles from my parents' home.

They have lived on a steep street of creaking old houses since

I was in elementary school, in a neighborhood best accessed by a bridge across a forest ravine. All night, trains and barges announce their presence through the river's industrial area below, the steel galvanizer occasionally rattling the windows. To one side are the shady ravines and tottering firs of the only designated "urban wilderness" in America, and to the other are the warehouses of the industries that have transformed Oregon's natural resources. According to the Portland Bureau of Emergency Management, new, global-warming-heightened threats of wildfire danger have turned Forest Park into "one of the highest threats to public safety in [the] city." If a fire were to start there, one article reminded me, resident escape routes would likely bottleneck at that gateway bridge. I began keeping running shoes under my childhood bed.

What was the moment when the instinct inside me swerved? When I no longer wanted to move my body away from the danger, but toward it? The feeling arrived like many of my stomachaches: imperceptible until suddenly unignorable. It came a few years after I had left graduate school in Minneapolis, and it had something to do with getting older—not just me, but the people I loved. That day looking at the Little Red pillow, I realized that though I was rarely around small children, I was now someone perpetually aware of the threats the people around me faced, who chose to fling the door open anyway. Part of it was facing a future on an ever-heating planet. After years of ruminating on the narratives that snagged my own body, this was a story none of us could flee. While some environmental groups still proclaim that animals—like wolves—are threatened because of "humanity," this is a misanthropic lie. Global warming and environmental devastation are spurred inordinately by the rich, industrialized global north, with their effects borne unjustly by those already impacted by colonialism, racism, and sexism in the global south. The spatial and temporal dimensions of the problem defy conceptualization, what scholar Timothy Morton refers to as a "hyperobject."

Though many residents in my home region are by this metric privileged, I still knew Oregonians whose neighborhoods had, for example, burned. Dwarfed by the scale of a threatened and threatening future, I considered what it would mean to redirect my attention back to the people, institutions, and bioregion I knew best. I did not regret my years away, and I knew I would always want to travel, to see places I did not know. But what if the earthquakes and fires and droughts and floods that made the Pacific Northwest feel vulnerable were not reasons to run away, but reasons to roll up my sleeves and come back?

That first year OR-7 and his mate were raising pups, an Oregon conservation group filed a lawsuit against the U.S. Forest Service to try to block an old-growth logging project. Their claim? If the forest was disturbed, OR-7's den could be too. Biologists had not revealed the exact location of the pups, but it was suspected to be in the area. Disturbing the den, not to mention the larger territory OR-7 and his mate hunted and roamed on, seemed possible.

The expanse of forest under question was some 2,000 acres of never-before-logged land, uncut by roads, not far from both Crater Lake and the headwaters of the Rogue River. Beside OR-7's fledgling pack, this forest was home to Roosevelt elk, black bears, eagles, spawning salmon, and the spotted owl made famous by the timber wars of the 1990s, when even President Clinton had flown cross-country to try to broker a mixed-use solution for our old-growth forests. In some people's eyes, the very possibility wolves could be denned in those trees rendered the land more valuable.

"Our remnants of wilderness will yield bigger values to the nation's character and health than they will to its pocketbook, and to destroy them will be to admit that the latter are the only values that interest us," wrote Aldo Leopold in 1925. The pocketbook value of the contested land was 45 million board feet of timber, enough to support approximately 585 local jobs and 2,835 family homes—structures not only for wolf-haters, but, inevitably, for wolf-lovers too.

Field biologist Arthur Middleton told me a story about a neighbor of his near his research site in Wyoming, a rancher who hated wolves and occasionally killed the collared ones Arthur was trying to study. Perhaps surprisingly, that same rancher, Arthur learned, was organizing nearby landowners to buy up plots of land and prevent development, thereby preserving the pastureland. A herd of cows meant one challenge for a wolf, but a subdivision of single-family homes meant something worse. Sure, Arthur told me, you had to protect the predator, but you also had to protect habitat for the predator's prey. Wolf populations could rebound if a few of them were killed, but if their habitat or food sources disappeared? Forget it. "That rancher was doing more to help wolves than almost anyone around," he told me. The guy wasn't trying to help them, but in conserving the rural landscape, he was doing just that.

I remembered Arthur's words when I read about the lawsuit arguing the proposed timber sale and logging would endanger OR-7's den. In defending their need for cutting the forest, the timber companies did not argue against the wolf, or try to classify the logging as a necessary evil. Instead, Ann Forest Burns, vice president of the American Forest Resource Council, said OR-7's family would benefit from the sale. "Those who are defending the wolves ought to be thinking about what the wolves want," Burns told the Associated Press. Thinning trees would reduce the risk of wildfire, she said, and with new growth, the amount of food for deer and elk would eventually increase, supporting a rise in wolf populations. "No wolf chow, no wolves."

A week after her quote was published in newspapers around the country, a motion-sensor wildlife camera captured a grainy image of OR-7's litter. The pups were small and gray, a few months old, about thirty pounds each. "They have these huge feet on little bodies, just like a dog," the biologist who found the photos told a journalist. That was the summer of 2014, the summer I left for Sicily, when hunger drove me to put more and more distance between me and the people I loved.

In the pine-needle duff around a Douglas fir, a cluster of snouts rose and fell, bobbing in the shreds of sunlight that slipped through the roof of branches. The tip of a wolf's nose is a topography of ridges and creases, each nostril moving independently to track the route of certain scents. *What do wolves want?* Even from miles away, the pups would have known OR-7 and his mate were out there. Searching for roadkill, rabbits, beaver. Somewhere under mossy, ancient trees, parents snapped bones and bloodied their snouts, filling their bellies so they could run back to their pups and spit it all out.

A human is literate on the page, sure, but a wolf is literate with the breeze. Pups learn to read the air: who has passed and how long ago, what sex they are and what they've eaten, the status of their health and mood. Knowledge—even when it seems, like this, a secret power— can only go so far. Would bulldozers come for the trees around their den? Even the sharpest breeze could not reveal. The wolves could not advocate for the land, so they waited, but they did not know they were waiting. True, too, for so many moments in our own lives. What can later seem a run-up to calamity is, at first, just another dewy day.

———

Toward the end of Barry Lopez's *Of Wolves and Men,* he catalogs symbolic archetypes of the wolf, including the warrior-hero, the sexualized she-wolf, and the benevolent wolf-mother. This last category, he posits, "simply does not exist," in any robust historic sense, whether in art or literature or folklore. Like me, Lopez called Oregon home, though the environmental ethic of his essays and stories swoops across forests and tundra worldwide. When his book was published in 1978, a National Book Award finalist, it ushered in a new mode of nonfiction, not just about wolves but about the natural world more broadly. It's an astonishing cross-section of research into the animal, with an eye toward scientific research, Indigenous tradition, folklore, and motif. When I told my undergraduate thesis advisor I wanted to write about wolves, he mentioned *Of Wolves and Men,* then told me to avoid it for a while. *It might sway you too much.* And so I skirted the book for years. By the time I finally read it, I understood that part of why I was still drawn to the stories humans told about wolves was that so many were told to younger generations to teach them about fear. When to have it, how to bear it, how to fight it. All questions I was weighing in my own life, that a legacy of stories about the wolf was helping me articulate, if not to neatly solve.

When I read Lopez's line about the "benevolent wolf-mother" canon, something resonated, though I didn't agree that the category did not exist. There are many Indigenous and global narratives where a wolf's strength and respect come not from its status as warrior, but as a protector. In a Confucian telling, for example, wolves are depicted as caretaking shepherds, seen as "beneficial animals" because they protected rice farms from wild boars and deer. Creation narratives featuring the wolf as the seed of humanity are found from Turkey to Chechnya to Senegal, from Great Plains tribes to Pacific Northwest ones like the Haida, Kwakiutl, Tlingit, Makah, and Quileute. As the late Quileute elder Fred Woodruff told writer Brenda Peterson: "We learned from the wolf how to survive and how to be more human. How to honor our elders, to protect and provide for our families—and we learned from wolves the loyalty you need to really belong to a tribe."

Beyond tales of "benevolent" wolf protectors, I had long been drawn to stories where a wolf's protective instincts rendered her an awe-inspiring—albeit sometimes terrifying—arbiter of justice. In the first published compendium of Inuit oral stories, *Tales and Traditions of the Eskimo,* nineteenth-century Danish glaciologist and Greenlandic scholar Hinrich Rink recounts a tale of the giant, wolflike amarok. In his telling, someone grieving the loss of a loved one is hungry for the distraction of chaos and goes searching for an amarok. Finding the pups instead, he slaughters them, then retreats with his companion to seek refuge in a cave. Soon the old amarok comes running, "a whole reindeer between its jaws . . . having looked in vain for its young ones." The amarok does not charge inside the cave, but runs to the lake, where it appears to haul a human body from the water. In the cave, the hunter falls to the ground, helpless and twitching. As punishment for killing its young, the amarok has found the hunter's soul.

In the Inuit story, the amarok is not explicitly gendered, but its role as fierce protector of loved ones spoke to the energy of "mother" I felt Lopez was conjuring—a spirit embodied by mothers of all gender identities and, accessible, I felt, also to those like me who did not have biological children. I liked the idea that this "mother" archetype was worth a closer look, a beacon, perhaps, as we stumbled into the future. "[L]ooking for the wolf-mother is the stage we are at now in history . . . whether out of guilt or because we have reached such a level of civilization as to allow us the thought, we are looking for a new wolf," Lopez wrote over forty years ago.

Unlike appearances of shepherd-gobbling wolves in fairy tales, stories about wolf mothers felt like a rare kind of lupine trope, one where the spirit from the legend could reverberate in witness accounts.

I didn't know yet whether I wanted to pursue having children of my own. As ecology of fear biologist Liana Zanette had told me, animals under the pervasive stress of a possible predator attack will change behavior accordingly, prioritizing their own survival even when that means having fewer offspring or seeing the quality of life for those offspring diminished. Though under no comparative threat of attack, I knew well how such anxiety shaped my choices about the future. I thought of it whenever I read a new Intergovernmental Panel on Climate Change report and imagined having children.

Still, the question of literal motherhood seemed almost irrelevant to why I was drawn to wolf mother stories. I was at a point where my fear had shifted. As if exhausted by years of bending inward with anxiety, it had sprung outward. I was still thinking about what it meant to live with my fear—to face it, judge it, wield it—but instead of asking what harm could fall on my own body, I was wondering: Who am I responsible for?

When I think about what a half-century absence of wolves did to America's wilderness, I think of a night in an old on-campus college apartment. We were playing a game where you poured whiskey into the bottom of a mason jar and put a square of toilet paper over the top, securing it with a rubber band. Someone put a quarter in the middle and then we took turns lowering a lighter until the flame caught. As the hole widened and blackened, a sinkhole of ash flecked the booze. Each player chose how long to let the flame go; the only goal was to blow it out before the quarter fell, then pass the lighter on. Whoever lost had to fish out the quarter and take a drink.

I was thinking about how much risk I would stomach when my shorts buzzed. *Dad Cell.* He knew better than to call late on a weekend night. A few days earlier, my mother had inexplicably come down with a fever, but I assumed it was a flu. Now, as I stepped outside, I wondered.

"Dad?" Outside on the concrete stoop, the Top-40 that radiated from our open windows seemed comically loud, also dumb, its beat like the guy a few doors down who was always soft-punching people's biceps with a wink. "Everything okay?"

"Hi, Erix," he said. Hearing the nickname I'd had since childhood made my eyes slick. I sat down, tugging the threads of my jean shorts. "I wanted to give you an update on Mom." Her fever had gotten worse. Rolling and spiking and dipping all week. He'd taken her to the hospital when it plateaued, at least for a while, at 105. She was delirious, joints sore, head pounding. They hooked her to an IV and started doing tests, but each was coming back clear, ruling one thing after another out even as the mystery deepened. It was the first time my father had taken her to the ER in the three decades they had spent together, the first time she had been a patient at a hospital since Annika was born.

"I'll keep you posted." The emotion in his voice was pruned but present, its fat vines creeping through his words. "She'll be there overnight, at least. They don't want to take any risks."

We both knew that in forty-eight hours I would be out-of-service in northern Maine, leading a multiday canoe trip for incoming first-year students. When I asked if the doctors had any idea of what might be going on, he said a few words I tried to blink away, the worst of which was *cancer,* which he chased with a statement of optimistic ambiguity, that *I'm sure it'll be fine.* Just a few weeks earlier, I'd hiked to a waterfall with my not-yet-fifty-year-old mother in Montana. Compared to the losses my mother had seen by my age, I was lucky, but luck wasn't immunity. Grief was as inevitable a landmark in my future as joy.

I told my dad goodnight, trying not to envision him alone in their dark house. Back inside, the faces crowded around the table seemed to glow with new life, as if each were a twinkling bulb in the strand of lights that hung above our heads. One after another each bulb would blink out. It seemed impossible, just like it seemed impossible to join my friends around the coffee table, bobbing along to Robyn, ignoring it. Years later, reading *In the Eye of the Wild,* a memoir by French anthropologist Nastassja Martin about surviving a bear attack, I would marvel at her description of life in Russia's remote, frigid Kamchatka Peninsula: "In the forest . . . you don't prepare, you go on as if nothing will ever change until suddenly everything topples . . . Because everyone in the forest knows about it, and because we are always expecting it around the next corner, we maintain a tacit agreement not to say it." In contrast, my life had always been comically safe. Was I allowed to ignore death the same way, or did I owe it something else? That night, whenever the lighter reached me, I played well. Again and again, I never drank the ash. For once my nervousness paid off.

What was growing up if not learning to accept that we would encounter the pain of bodies we loved and be unable to stop it? When I thought of whose pain in the world I most wanted to alleviate, my mother was right there. Her love of brightly colored sneakers, the thin blue bottle of rosewater she dabbed on her neck, the way she was apt to cry, laughing, whenever she saw a clip of a dancing flash mob. To love anyone, anything, means accepting the limits of your own control.

Three weeks after giving birth to my mother's younger brother, my biological grandmother Lorna lay down with a headache. What was she thinking that day? She was twenty-three. Several days later, in a Missoula hospital, she died. The hematomas that bloomed within her, eventually flooding her brain with blood, had lurked quietly until her second childbirth. Back at home, smiley under a sandy halo of hair, my mother was only two years old. If their unit had been a wolf pack, they would have become a "disrupted family." When Sally—the woman I call grandmother, and my mother calls Mom—married into their family a few years later, they became, in both wolf and human lingo, "a stepfamily."

Lorna was not my mother, but the eggs that created me developed inside her, blooming in my mother's fetus through those months Lorna's belly swelled. If I was partially formed by Lorna, I was also formed by her loss, which hung around my mother like an aura only visible in certain light. When I was a child, my mother volunteered one night a week at a nonprofit that offered group counseling for grieving children. Annika and I had fun with my dad on those evenings—cooking "skagamagoosh," his everything-in-the-fridge tortilla-speckled stir fry—but I always missed her desperately, more than when she left on other nights. It felt like too much to feel her absence while also being reminded that for some of the children she was with, there would be no loved one coming back. As with so many kinds of grief, the sadness I felt for Lorna metastasized into fear. Sometimes I feared naps, fearing I too might not wake up. Mostly I feared this would happen to my mother.

Seventeenth-century Europeans referred to mysterious bodily lumps, sores, and knobs as "wolves." Those things that appeared where there should be nothing at all, maybe portending something more. Even after the doctors solved the mystery of my mother's fever, they never found a bump. There was no physical trace of what had bitten her and made her sick. No "wolf."

I got word she was doing better via text a few days later, received in a patch of service on a patch of land in the middle of a lake. Only later did I understand the puzzle. That a few weeks earlier, she and my father had visited some friends in their rustic cabin on a river in central Oregon, and at some point, while she was unaware and probably sleeping, a tick bit her. It passed on relapsing fever, a bacterial infection that comes and goes in waves of agony, stabilized eventually by antibiotics. When the code-cracking epidemiologist refined the prescription, he explained relapsing fever was carried by soft ticks, whose hosts were most often squirrels and rodents.

I don't remember who told me, then, that tick-borne infections had increased with the disappearance of predators in the landscape—a parent? a professor? a friend?—but in their discussion of absence, that person mentioned wolves. *The ecosystem is missing a link,* they told me. *The balance is skewed.* Black-legged ticks who feed on white-tailed deer and carry Lyme disease are an obvious case study. When scientists monitored a Connecticut town for thirteen years, they saw resident-reported rates of Lyme greatly decrease after deer hunts. They predicted cases would go down by eighty percent if the deer density was reduced to around five deer per square kilometer. If it was ticks we feared, then the land needed more hunters, human or animal.

It would be another nine months before I began studying America's legacy of wolves for my senior thesis, but thinking about our lack of predators unlocked a door of inquiry. Did I think a wolf would have eaten the mouse that hosted the tick that bit my mother? No—and to consider it felt like a tongue-twisting nursery rhyme. I also didn't think letting wolves repopulate America was the sole answer for halting tick-borne disease. However, I was beginning to see how wolves, and other predators, could be worth learning to live beside not just because it would be thrilling to spot one on a hike, but because they were part of the ecosystem. Literary critic Carla Freccero wrote that we have too often cast the wolf as a "stand in for a nostalgia for the wholeness of the human and the natural," propping them up as evidence that our world is still a wild place. To make the animal a symbol, whether of fury or devotion, is to deflate its presence as an actor.

As vectors of infection, ticks illuminate not only the web between species, but the very fallacy of imagining we have ever been separate. In the words of biologist Scott Gilbert, "We have never been individuals." The fear I felt for my mother's body was connected to the tick, which was connected to its carrier, which was connected to its predator. The dawning of this interdependence sent a static pulse through my palms. I do not mean to oversimplify the science, only to state what once felt too small and selfish to admit: that I began to think about the wolf because I was worried about my mother. You could say the story of Little Red had tipped upside down. My mother had gone into the woods and been bitten by a creature. Her cells had been attacked by a bacteria; she had collapsed into a bed. The mother in Little Red Riding Hood thought of the wolf because she wanted a safe forest for her daughter to walk through. I thought of the wolf because, in some indirect and messy way, I wanted the same thing. The predators were not the problem, but restoring their populations might be part of a solution.

When I think of that fire-fueled drinking game, I think not only of tick and wolf and mother but of how it feels to grow up in the twenty-first century. To occupy a shrinking square. Burning through fossil fuels and water and forests, the extinction of one animal following the extinction of another, while corporations and the politicians they sway assure us we'll just keep going. Watching the flame. Passing the risk. The lesson of the game, though, is that burning resources always leads to collapse. The quarter drops. Somebody always drinks what's left. Our challenge is to learn to better take care of one another—human, animal, and plant—before we reach that point. As Alexis Pauline Gumbs asks in *Undrowned: Black Feminist Lessons from Marine Mammals*: "How can we listen across species, across extinction, across harm?"

Growing up, I imagined life after high school would follow a bell curve, swelling with exploration and new friends only to winnow down when I found a partner, staked a home, settled into an insular family unit. Society had told me the nuclear family, with a husband at the door, was the thing that would keep me safe. Not just from nighttime intruders, but against floods and fires, my own angst. I wasn't opposed to cultivating the domestic—I am a nester, a true bowerbird—but I had become skeptical it would deliver me the security I chased. I didn't want to grow older in a box, I wanted to grow older on a web, one that stretched to friends outside my house, city, state, and country, swaying in the breeze. I thought of one wolf pack recorded at the turn of the millennium, seven years after the species was reintroduced into Yellowstone, the most unusual pack ever recorded, according to Mech and Boitani. Three packs formed, each one with at least twelve dispersers. Individuals moved among the packs sometimes daily. They produced multiple litters in separate dens, and then, in midsummer, many of the wolves merged, staying together through the winter.

What explains such a unique formation? Canadian researchers have found that "intense harvest" of wolves by humans—whether poached, hunted as game, or killed strategically by government officials—may increase the number of unrelated individuals adopted into packs. When biological family bonds are disrupted, or not allowed to flourish, family is forced to sprawl outward. I thought of human families I knew fractured by incarceration, immigration, abuse, death. In both humans and wolves, disruptions create tremendous stress, but in the right circumstances, new strength can emerge. I felt lucky to grow up beside two sets of great-grandparents on my mother's side—both Lorna's parents, and Sally's. Lorna's brother and his wife, whom we called Meme and Papa, were something like surrogate grandparents, but so were David and Tina, the Maine couple Bowdoin College paired me with when I answered a survey saying I had no family on the East Coast, and also Elise, my high school friend's grandmother in Cambridge, Massachusetts, who hosted me on various layovers and flight cancellations until one day I started planning trips to see just her. My list went on, forking in and out of different generations and time zones, until I realized the people I had met while traveling and living away from home had joined my extended family and old friends in becoming, through constellation, home itself. A pack that could weather the winter and the rising tides, a home an earthquake could not shake.

What is gained by expanding this omnivorous kinship even further? Ecofeminist scholar Donna Haraway writes that "relatives" was first defined as "logical relations" in British English, and only after the seventeenth century did it come to mean "family members." In *Staying with the Trouble: Making Kin in the Chtulucene*, Haraway advocates for an omnivorous interspecies view of kinship as we head into our perilous climate-changed future. "By kin I mean those who have an enduring mutual, obligatory, non-optional, you-can't-just-cast-that-away-when-it-gets-inconvenient, enduring relatedness that carries consequences," she said in an interview. "I have a cousin, the cousin has me; I have a dog, a dog has me." To say *have*, in the context of a wolf, feels strange, like claiming ownership of a cloud. But the feedback loop is still there. "To be any kind of animal at all is to be within obligate mutualisms with a whole range of other plants, animals, and microbes," Haraway told the interviewer. I thought of my mother, the tick, the wolf. If we are all family, then my actions affect wolves, and wolves affect me. This interconnectivity forces me to confront the genesis myth of my body, which is that it was created solely by my mother.

One brisk blue day, I joined U.S. Fish and Wildlife (USFW) biologist John Stephenson to try to trap and collar a wolf. April was the heart of denning season, and somewhere nearby there were pups. He didn't want to risk catching the breeding female—a mother was too critical to risk slowing her down if, say, her foot became sore from the ankle trap—so he laid the traps far from suspected den sites, and now we were going to check them. John had been following OR-7 and his pack for years, working with southern Oregon ranchers to try and deter the wolves before more depredations occurred. He was about my father's age, tall and lanky, a Giacometti; I had read a journalist's description of him as "lantern-jawed," and thought it perfectly captured not only the shape of his face but the warmth it exuded. When it came to wolves, it was easy to see how John had befriended people on both sides of the aisle.

I left Portland around six a.m. to meet John at his pickup by eight, which, as I climbed in, reminded me immediately of my relatives' trucks on the sheep farm and in Montana, their dashboards sifted with fine dust from dirt roads and down windows. We had met on the eastern side of Mt. Hood, and now we drove into the Confederated Tribes of Warm Springs Reservation, less than thirty miles from the river where that tick had sickened my mother some eight years earlier.

Was the balance of predator and prey shifting in that landscape?

After nearly six decades of absence, in 2018, a pair of local wolves were confirmed. They were the first to settle in the northern Cascade Range since the species had recovered in Oregon—the closest ones to Portland—and now they had grown into the White River Pack, with three consecutive litters of pups. In 2021, collars revealed they had spent eighty-seven percent of their time on tribal land; it wasn't hard to tell why. Though some tribal members ran cattle on this communal land, there were no official ranches here, and the reservation's interior forest roads were closed to outsiders, which meant there was little human traffic. The tribe had recently masticated stands of pines to protect against wildfire and create an open landscape for habitat, and though still strewn with stumps and fallen limbs, the thinned land now abutted marshy meadows blossoming and golden in the morning haze. If I were a deer, I would want to graze on all the new grass, right here. If I were a wolf, I would want to eat that deer.

My instinct squared with a recent University of British Columbia study, which found greater vertebrate biodiversity on Indigenous-managed lands in Australia, Brazil, and Canada. Though comprising only five percent of the world's people, Indigenous people's land holds approximately eighty percent of global biodiversity, just one argument for returning stolen land to its original owners. Less than a year after that morning's search for the wolf, Secretary of the Interior Deb Haaland—a member of the Laguna Pueblo tribe—would swear in Cayuse and Walla Walla tribal member Charles F. "Chuck" Sams III as director of the National Park Service. Born in Portland, Sams grew up on the Umatilla Reservation in northeastern Oregon. In an interview with a local news outlet, he pledged to create a space where textbook science and the traditional ecological knowledge of tribal members would come together to steward America's parks, bolstering them against climate change. "I think I bring a unique approach because I believe I am from the landscape," Sams told the journalist, reiterating the symbiosis his people felt toward the earth. "My own creation story tells me that my skin is from the hide of elk, my vision is from the eagle, my hearing is from the owl, that the roots and berries provided my nervous system and that's how I was created as a human being." Through this lens, the forest outside my window was less a resource commodity than an extension of my body.

John had laid the traps on Tuesday, but now it was the following Wednesday, and for the last week he'd been monitoring them with Austin Smith Jr., a biologist from the tribe, and still they hadn't caught a wolf. They had evidence in tracks, scat, and video from the camouflage-colored cameras they'd strapped to trees: an ambling brown bear, sure, but also a parade of six wolves over the course of a few hours. John knew these roads were a corridor, and he thought it was just a matter of time.

"So did you bring that good luck?" His voice was a jangly baritone.

"That was what the doughnuts were for," I said, and he laughed, folding a shimmering wedge of crinkly old-fashioned into his mouth, one from a box I had picked up in a ski town an hour earlier.

"Patience has never been my strong suit," John said as we crossed from asphalt to gravel, then onto a narrow, rutted dirt road. Branches whacked the windows as we drove, occasionally poking through and brushing my arm, snagging my hair, pulling me along. Every now and then we saw trees circled in spray-painted rings or tied with blue plastic tape that flapped in the breeze as markings for loggers. We hadn't been driving long when John lowered his voice. "I always like to be quiet, to start looking for signs as we near the trap."

I wasn't sure what to look for, so I ogled the lemon fuzz of lichen that swaddled the tree trunks then traced it downward, looking for a wolf. I expected we would get out and walk to the trap, but suddenly we stopped in the middle of the road, and John leaned over to peek out the window, pointing at a patch of dirt a foot or so away from the tire, barely mussed. There was the trap. Buried, empty.

"Dang," he said. The traps are set to avoid catching non-target animals, hypothetically sensitive enough to catch a coyote but not a little fox. The biologists posted warning signs in areas with dogs, though this area had little traffic, and they weren't too worried.

"We use these roads because the wolves do, and we like to be able to check them without getting out too much with our scent," John said. To catch a wolf, physically, meant you had to convince it mentally too, burying not just the trap but your own presence. When he set the traps, John wore a different pair of gloves and boots than his regular forest shoes. *Wolf boots.* In his truck, he kept traps in tubs filled with branches and leaves from the surrounding area, to try to keep the smell of forest on them.

Now, as we drove deeper into the labyrinth of unmarked dirt roads, John balanced an iPad with a GPS map on his lap. I clutched my thermos as we rattled up a hill, letting it rest against my lap just as we hit a pothole at the bottom. "Wolf? No wolf," John muttered a minute later. A few traps remained. We journeyed on.

In a National Geographic television series set in the looping daylight of high Arctic summer, photographer Ronan Donovan sets up camp near a white wolf pack, planting cameras near carcasses and behind rocks to stealthily observe pack dynamics. You can't document natural behavior if the animal is responding to you, and very often when we "see" animals, we are really just watching them see us, mistaking their reactions for "natural" behavior. Often that reaction is fear. Donovan assures viewers, though, that these wolves are as unafraid of humans as any on earth. Their homeland of Ellesmere is Canada's northernmost island, so remote that the wolves' blood-lines have never been hunted by humans. It takes him weeks to locate a pack to film. More than one den he finds is empty, iced over with the influx of uneven freezes and spring rain, the product of global warming. He finally encounters a pack for whom his smell conjures more curiosity than anxiety. The mother lets him stay.

In the final episode, after watching her lick and nuzzle and tend her young, we see the mother lead a successful hunt against a muskox calf. A pack often has two hierarchies, one for males and one for females. Doug Smith, head of the Yellowstone Wolf Project, defines a "matriarch" as the "one whose personality shapes the whole pack." His definition somehow feels both obvious and, when I think about what it means to "mother" in a looser, associative sense, also revelatory. The wolf matriarch determines where to travel, when to rest, what route to take, where to den, and when to hunt. As with a human matriarch, though, her selfhood leaks out not just in the *where* and *what* but in the *how*. The *how* of her actions defines the behavior and well-being of the whole pack.

Led by the mother, the wolves charge the muskox herd across the brown tundra, pack spraying around her like a synchronized organism, sowing chaos to pick out the slow. A wolf's prey is often five to ten times its own weight, and even this muskox calf, clumsy with terror and youth, dwarfs the wolves who lunge at its legs. But the mother wolf has won the battle. As an older wolf approaches the fallen muskox, she snarls and lunges, making clear her pups get first dibs. They gorge themselves, snowy heads turned copper with blood, and then they stagger off to sleep, as if under a fairy-tale spell. The mother waits until the whole pack is resting before pull-ing her body from the ground. With a barely visible limp, she turns from her family and toward the mountains. Later, Donovan will tell the camera he'd noticed her hanging back a few days earlier, clearly hurt. Maybe injured from a hunt, or from a run-in with another wolf pack, or maybe just old. Somehow, she rallied herself to get her pups one last meal.

It is impossible to tell what time of day it is, or how much time has passed since the kill. The clouds are flat and bright, the rust-colored tundra buzzes. Even in August, the temperature is likely below 45 degrees. Slowly, steadily, the mother walks away. I think of watching that bison pair years ago in Yellowstone, the hesitancy of the mother buffalo as she tugged herself from her fallen young. This is different. Roles are reversed. The wolf mother knows her pups are safe and fed. Not once, as she shrinks toward the horizon, do we see her look back. When one of her older daughters blinks open an eye and sees the mother leaving, she slowly follows, trailing at a distance, as if aware she is not wanted. Watching their bodies fade, I already know what will happen, as if the cookie-cutters of childhood fiction primed me for grief in real life.

A few days later, that older sister returns alone. The others run to her, having spent their days howling at the site of the carcass, in uneasy limbo with the absence of their matriarch. The mother never comes back. Like my friend's old dog who walked herself to the neighbor's flower bed to die, this wolf has removed herself from the pack. Her last days will, it seems, be alone. She has nourished her young; they will be cared for by the rest of the pack. What looks like an act of abandonment can be an act of care. Her love for her family telegraphed by her choice not to slow them down.

Does the pack grieve the loss of this mother? All predators, Carl Safina argues, must understand death on some level. "Death is a wolf's living," he wrote. "A wolf requires a working knowledge of 'alive' and 'dead.'" To hunt is to understand the tipping point where prey stops moving and turns into food. In the words of Yellowstone wolf-watcher and author Rick McIntyre, "It is crucially instructive for youngsters to observe how older, experienced wolves manage life and death." A wolf pup, then, watches its mother not just for instructions on how to live—to track prey, to hunt, to kill, to den—but also for how to die.

A mother is one of the scariest animals a human can encounter outdoors. She's the one who will fight the hardest, because she has the most to lose. That was what my mother's father told us to watch for on those long days we spent backpacking into the Montana back-country. "Don't let the grizz get you!" he would bark, half teasing, whenever Annika and I ducked away to search for huckleberries. "You know who's waiting behind that cub, don't you?"

"Sure, Grandpa," we'd singsong, but we were already gone. What match was a mama bear to four adults, two Australian shepherds, the snorting mule and horse who carried our food and tents? To be a child on those trips was to lean into the insulation of bigger bodies around us. We never encountered any big predators, even though their evidence was everywhere, from the claw-seared bark of the Ponderosas to the hair-and-berry-clotted poop we yelped at in the trail. Around the campfire we smeared marshmallow from our lips and listened to my grandparents tell stories about their and their friends' encounters. The mountain lion who jumped toward its re-flection in a window and landed atop a bed with a sleeping person; the summer Sally worked in Glacier National Park as a teenage waitress and went camping alone one weekend only to arrive back at the lodge and hear all her friends thought she had been killed—but no, those were two other women mauled by grizzlies overnight.

The prospect of death by roving serial killer or bear never kept me up long during those starry nights. Like so many gifts I received as a child, I failed to see my contentedness as special. Whenever someone brought up the fierceness of mother animals, I thought of the story I'd once heard about a human mother who saw a car rolling toward her infant and turned superhuman by a surge of adrenaline, rolling it right back away. I didn't care if it was an urban legend: its potential lingered. I glimpsed it in the German word *mutterweh*, which translates to "mother's pain" and "hysterical affection." My own mother was five foot six, not a short woman except in our immediate family, where she was soon outgrown. Even when we were the same height, she always seemed more delicate, her short hair as fine as a baby's, her wrists narrower than my own, her slim shoulders so often cold. My father the tall, gentle protector. Were my sister and I ever physically threatened, though, I had no doubt my mother could turn electric. I had seen the muscle pulse in her calf. The hard crystal in her eye whenever Annika or I recounted that we'd been the butt of something mean. It was no leap to imagine my mother rolling up the sleeves of her quick-dry hiking shirt, karate-punching the air, the bear, the beast at our feet.

Nearly a thousand years ago, Pliny the Elder extolled the pharmacological benefits a wolf's body held to a woman. "A wolf's fat, applied externally, acts emolliently upon the uterus," he wrote, "and the liver of a wolf is very soothing for pains in that organ." These alleged healing properties were thought to extend to children too. "A wolf's tooth, attached to the body, prevents infants from being startled," he wrote. To make your child brave, he suggested, you had only to kill a wolf.

Whenever I used to tell my mother about being afraid of this or that, she would look worried. Guilty, maybe, that she had passed something toxic down to me. I knew we were both apt to wake at four a.m. and worry about the world, but I never blamed her. I told her my worries not because I felt she should take responsibility, but because I felt she could absorb them. Because I thought her so strong that, with a few minutes of conversation and a hug, she'd kill the beast inside my head.

OR-7 and his mate got lucky: the Forest Service confirmed their den was not located on land under proposal to be logged. Though the timber sale went through, environmental advocates succeeded at paring back the scale of logging. One conservationist I spoke with told me it was unlikely the wolves would have ever been too affected by the logging because as a generalist species, they are adaptable; they roam. In linking Oregon's beloved wolf to this forest, though, environmental groups had succeeded at raising awareness that these trees were not just a source of money but also a home. Was OR-7's habitat more worthy of salvation than that of, say, the uncollared and unknown wolves, or those other local creatures, the ones without easy faces to smile at, like the bull trout facing wetland loss, or the Fender's blue butterfly dependent on the prairie and oak savanna so often flattened into parking lots? Everywhere in Oregon it seemed you could find a stream sucked dry before the June equinox. It was trickier to preserve habitat when the culprit wasn't one logging company but the warming climate itself, the decades of corporate greed and institutional inaction that had gotten us here. For OR-7, though, new litters of pups appeared.

The first year Ted Birdseye began ranching in a valley south of Crater Lake National Park, he glimpsed the famous wolf just beyond the fence line, recognizable because of his yellow collar. "I stopped my tractor and saw his head go up, then he turned and walked away, like 'fuck you,' almost in slow motion," he told a reporter. It was August in his memory, because not long after, a friend came to bow-hunt elk on his property and saw the wolf as well, just walking the road midday. Later he would know a collared wolf was near his property if he got a call from someone—usually John Stephenson, whom he came to consider a friend—updating him that data had come in. Ted was grateful for such messages, but they were gappy. If the wolf didn't have a collar, no update would come. And if the weather was bad, or the wolf had walked back into one of the canyons, even a collared wolf could travel under the radar.

OR-7 was seven by then, a few years older than most wolves could be expected to survive in the wild. "A bit long in the tooth," as one reporter who had been publishing dispatches put it, after a photo of OR-7 was caught on a trail cam in August 2016. "He looks pretty lean," John told the reporter. "The daily grind might be taking its toll on him." For the third consecutive year, OR-7 and his mate had a litter of pups. When one son dispersed to northern California with an unknown female wolf and had pups, one headline after another celebrated OR-7 turning into a grandpa. As the pack grew, the odds a family member would get tangled in a livestock depredation did too.

It was tempting to wander down the path of lupine fan fiction, to believe OR-7 could sense from his long travels that the farther he stayed from people, the better. As if he knew what had happened to his father a few months earlier, when OR-4 was shot from a helicopter by government officials. Along with his new mate and their offspring, OR-4 had been linked to the deaths of a handful of cattle and sheep, and a rancher requested their removal under an eligibility clause in Oregon's wolf plan. They all died that day. I often heard lethal control of this sort described as an emergency lever, a switch whose presence helped producers feel more in control if wolves continually attacked livestock. To biologist Russ Morgan, it was an emotional decision, even if made in the name of species management. *Men's Journal* published a eulogy to OR-7's father alongside a photograph of his asphalt-colored head and amber eyes, ears glinting with the green plastic of identification tags. "I don't have any remorse for killing them," Russ told a journalist, "but I am sad they aren't here."

Biologically, my mother's late mother Lorna is my grandmother, but we have never stitched the word to her. It doesn't fit the smooth skin and dark pixie cut in the black-and-white graduation photograph on my mother's dresser. She had so much more time to be a daughter than a mother. I used to think only a person's body made a shadow, but their absence does too, less a dark spot floating above the ground than a trench dredged beneath it. A place people trip. My mother and her brother, Ladd, grew up in that space, but she, at least, knew two years before it. Her brother, weeks old when his mother died, learned only to walk in its rut. When he died by suicide two decades later, another shadow followed, and my mother, as she had learned to do, wobbled forward. There's a Serbian story that says if a mother's child has died, she should name her next son Vuk, so the witches don't eat him. *Wolf.* As if the name our parents give us can be a protective spell. As if a wolf is too strong to die. By the time Ladd died, Lorna was long gone too. There was no replacing him, only the arrival, a few years later, of me. The baby who should have been his niece.

"I think mothers and daughters are meant to give birth to each other, over and over," wrote Alice Walker in her essay collection *The Same River Twice.* Recalling that cesarean, my mother said, *They cut you out of me, but I felt like I too was born that day.* "In many Indigenous ways of knowing, time is not a river, but a lake in which the past, the present, and the future exist," writes Robin Wall Kimmerer in *Braiding Sweetgrass.* "Creation, then, is an ongoing process and the story is not history alone—it is prophecy." I can almost see the four of our eyes squeezed tight, my mother and me, our faces like wet prunes. Me dressed in her, the nurse wiping us both. Both of us crying.

The college students I sometimes teach are older than my "uncle" or "grandmother" ever lived to be. On days where they rage about homework and parents, I stop myself from tipping toward them. Reaching my hands out to hug and then to shake them, telling them how lucky they are to hold that thin flame of youth. Not because they will age out of it but because of all the ways they might not. Now that I have moved past my early twenties, I see how the shadow of those untimely family deaths hung over my stay there, despite all my mother's efforts to distract us. It always seemed a gift, not a given, to make it to twenty-five.

My own desire to mother has never been tied to an urge to biologically procreate. As oldest child and oldest cousin, my "mothering" has always been indiscriminate. It floats from elementary school acquaintances to the grandmothers of friends to the children of neighbors to the birds who hit the window and flop, stunned, to the grass. My love language, a boyfriend once told me, is *obviously* acts of service.

Mother means martyr, my mother half joked once on a beach picnic, forgoing her own shortbread cookie so teenage Annika and I could split a second. It wasn't until crumbs were on our lips that we understood she was confessing to decades of sacrifice we had trained ourselves not to see. *Mom!* we shrieked, giddy with guilt, promising never again to be so selfish. She laughed, then, smirking, tugged her right eyebrow up so it hung like an upside-down smile above her eye. *Well, it's true,* the eyebrow said. It was a signature expression; one I hadn't inherited the skill for. The cookie was already gone.

Her words stayed with me. First as shame—a realization of just how *shitty* it could be trying to live up to societal expectations for the selfless mother—but then, to my surprise, as something like desire. A martyr, I understood from a high school history reading about Joan of Arc, was someone who endured suffering on behalf of a cause. Sure, the definition could imply performativity, but at their purest, a martyr seemed noble. I didn't care about being a hero, or saving lives, I just wanted to dissolve my fizzing ego in the fight for something bigger. Surely a martyr would not jog mental circles in her bed at night wondering if the pink mole on her forehead was a melanoma. A martyr, I imagined, had bigger things to worry about. She did not have time to live in the anxious future because she had to live in the fighting now. Real bravery felt hollow if visualized for myself, like throwing karate punches to my reflection in the mirror. But bravery on behalf of someone or something else? Easy.

It wasn't just the mother wolf I was interested in, but also the human mother who encountered the wolf. Any guardian, suggests geographer Yi-Fu Tuan, knows what a powerful teacher fear can be. Not just as a force exerted in a person's own life, but as a tool for taming and setting boundaries for those they are tasked to protect. "We forget that fear was and is a common reason for weaving close family ties," wrote Tuan. A guardian both buffers fear and incites it, turning the volume up and down. In this role of shepherd, she is neither predator nor prey. She is both and neither. The body that stands between.

There was a mother wolf in Yellowstone whose den, one spring, ended up not far from a coyote den. Coyotes rarely den together, and they rarely bother wolves, who they are usually afraid of. But these ones, perhaps bold with the same cliquish spirit that animates teenagers with their friends, ignored the rules. Though wolf pups are fed primarily by their mother and father, they are also supported by other members of the pack, with older siblings and even other pack adults sometimes traveling to the den to regurgitate meat for a new litter. Now, whenever an older wolf walked toward the den, the local coyotes would surround the wolf like cartoon highway robbers. The wolves would have little choice but to regurgitate the meat, the equivalent of handing over their purses before dashing away. The coyotes fattened; the wolf pups did not.

One day, the mother wolf had had enough. She was O-6, a legendary wolf, one of the best hunters that wolf-watchers in Yellowstone had ever seen, a wolf who had once kept an elk trapped in the water for three days before being able to kill it. Now she left her own den and walked toward the coyotes' den, flanked by her pack. I imagine them as a row of wildfire burning the distance between, coyotes watching as they kicked their thin red paws into the dirt. Once at the den, the wolf pack hung back; I cannot help projecting the breathless anticipation of the audience before a concert in the park. Ignoring the snarling, toothy attempts at defense by the coyotes, the mother wolf walked forward to the den's tunneled entrance and began digging.

"One by one, she pulled out each of their pups," wrote Carl Safina in his recounting of the incident. "One by one, she shook it dead." In front of the coyotes and in front of her own pack, she ate each coyote pup. It is impossible for me not to imagine the coyote mother—or mothers—who looked on. Did they understand this was the action of a mother killing in defense of her own hungry pups? Or did they see a maniac? Or a wolf being a wolf? According to Rick McIntyre, the wolf researcher and observer who recorded the incident and has watched wolves in the park for decades, this was the only time he ever saw a wolf eat a coyote.

Just as the coyotes broke precedent to bother the wolves, the mother wolf broke precedent to eat her enemies' young. The coyote pups she ate had likely been fed by meat meant for her own pups. To eat them meant she may regurgitate the meat to her own young, effectively restoring the calories to their intended home. It felt like a war of mothers, their fury and protectiveness so strong it had bent the habits of each of their species.

In Victorian poet Robert Browning's "Ivan Ivanovitch," a mother traveling by sled with her family through a snowy night is pursued by a pack of wolves. Despite her husband's attempts to charge the horses forward, the wolves gain traction. At the front of the pack is a creature who, in the mother's distressed recounting, is more like a human than animal predator: "Satan-faced . . . he laughs and lets gleam his white teeth," his paws "on me . . . pry[ing] among the wraps and the rugs!" Though she tries to counsel her young boys, they keep crying. At some point a switch flips. As her frustration mounts, she can think only of all that is faulty about one "puny" and "sulk[ing]" child.

"Foolish boy! Lie still [or] the villain . . . will snatch you from over my head!" Her words are toothless. She is as unable to calm the squirming son upon her lap as she is to fight the wolves at her feet. By this point, in her retelling, she is offering excuses. "Who can hold fast a boy in frenzy of fear?" Her predicament is not just woman versus wolf, it is terror for her own body versus protectiveness for her young. Unlike that mythological mother from hearsay, this one does not push the car away as it rolls. First one boy is "snatched and snapped," and then the "cursed crew" tumble out. Though she does not explicitly confess to tossing out her children, the choreography is between the lines. In saving herself, she has betrayed those she is responsible for in the worst possible way.

"Now gallop, reach home and die . . ." she shouts to her husband. Behind her, the wolves are now occupied, "fighting for a share . . . too busy to pursue." As the horse tugs the sledge into the night, the mother's attention falls to the infant still in her lap. "I'll lie down upon you, tight—tie you with the strings here—of my heart!" The prose is breathless, capped by exclamation point after exclamation point. This surviving baby, she says, will grow into a hunter. A man who will

> *. . . trace and follow and find and catch and crucify*
> *Wolves, wolfkins, all your crew! A thousand deaths*
>   *shall die*
> *The whimperingest cub that ever squeezed the teat!*
> *"Take that!" we'll stab you . . .*

The first time I encountered this poem, the horror of the mother's ride brought acid to my throat. Not because she was so despicable but because I felt, in a choked, whispered way, empathy. I could imagine the scene like I'd seen it on film, but when I imagined her grief-carved face, I saw not malice but fury. Rage that she had to be both defender and aggressor while her husband had sat alone at the front of the sledge, insulated by the simplicity of cracking the whip.

On a reread, I stopped at the lines above. Galled not just by the mother's behavior to her children but by her pledge of murder to the wolves—not to the pack who terrorized them, but to their own helpless young. Her vengeance was eye-for-eye. In fantasizing the death of wolf pups, she fantasized the hurt of a wolf mother. She had thought losing the ones she was supposed to protect would be less painful than losing her own life. She was wrong.

———

When I came across the blog of Candice, that young woman who flew to Alaska to teach and never made it home, I felt an echo. Not only had we both taken jobs in far-off places we had never before seen, we both seemed to juggle our propensities for adventure alongside our fear. We were dispersers, but anxious ones. Thinking of how Candice's year had ended, I couldn't help considering Chris McCandless, the nomadic hiker depicted in Jon Krakauer's *Into the Wild*, who died of starvation in a rusted school bus in the Alaskan bush. Perhaps I had just always sensed part of the mythos of that state was that it could swallow you.

My mother's brother, Ladd, had gone there as a young adult and never came back. Like McCandless, his communication with family while in Alaska had been sparse, and like McCandless, he had died alone—Ladd a few years earlier, in his bedroom with a gun on a Saturday night in January. In photos of them, they echo each other's green-and-black checkered shirts. Though my grandparents organized a well-attended memorial service for Ladd in Montana, his friends arranged a local one in Alaska, too. Who came to say goodbye? Neither my grandparents nor mother ever saw the 2,300-person town of Dillingham, where he worked in construction during the last year and a half of his life. During his final month on earth, the nights outside his window had been nearly nineteen hours long. Weeks after his death, my mother received a bundle of odds and ends from his friends in the mail. Inside were two postcards with her name on them and no dates. "I'm doing very well," he wrote. His handwriting fell across the body of the cards, with no room for an address or stamp.

"Some people feel like they don't deserve love. They walk away quietly into empty spaces, trying to close the gaps of the past," McCandless had written in his journal. He had orphaned himself from his pack, thinking he could survive on self-reliance alone. When humans invoke "lone wolves," as with terrorists or shooters, we often suggest those wolves are, by virtue of their solitude, exceptionally dangerous. In a wolf's life, the opposite is true. Dispersing wolves face increased threats from other packs, as well as the pressure of their own hunger. Biologists now believe wolves form such tight-knit social connections because they must eat. In many ways the strength of a wolf comes not from the size of its jaw but the interdependent choreography of its pack. Growing up, a pup learns not just self-reliance but how to coordinate a hunt, interact with outsiders, and take care of siblings. What is lost when we equate strength—or even bravery—with going off solo, and not the messy task of digging in to stay?

Candice did not travel to Alaska to live alone. She went to teach. That summer I led adventure camps for teenage girls, I almost did the same. The camp promised to place me in Washington, or Montana, or Alaska. No one in my immediate family had ever been to Alaska, and though a part of me wanted an excuse to go, a bigger part cowered. I was nineteen that summer, the age Ladd had been when he left. I didn't want to hear my mother's voice over the phone when I told her I was going. I didn't have to. The camp placed me in Montana, a few hundred miles from my grandparents. Lying awake that first night, I listened to the rustle of sleeping bags and the slow whistles of breath coming from the twelve fifth-grade girls my co-leader and I were shepherding. Outside, a branch snapped. I would have ignored the noise as a child, trusting it was someone else's problem. Now I had made it mine. Only later would I suspect the thing that tugged me toward the woods that summer was perhaps as primal as what had drawn McCandless. I did not want to go outside to practice being alone; I wanted to practice being in a pack. Not a pup, but a protector.

One cold, dry night when the campers were asleep and I was

filling out paperwork in my tent, two blinding eyes sped toward us on the gravel campground road. I vaguely remembered something I had read a few years earlier about two women being killed in their tent by the forward grind of a mad pickup driver. Let him try, I thought, suddenly drunk with conviction. I would wiggle out of the synthetic embrace of my sleeping bag and leap, superwoman style, onto the hood of the oncoming truck. I would save the girls, I would wake the neighbors, I would make the small-town papers. It had never felt so obvious.

A second later, though—did it stop? Turn around?—the night was quiet. If I felt flushed and foolish, I also felt relief. The next morning, the girls emerged from their tents, knocking against one another like wolf pups stumbling from a den. Their hair was wild, cheeks stenciled with the press of whatever clothes they were balling up as pillows, hauling out sleeping pads for morning yoga. Watching them through the dewy sun, a half circle of barefoot flamingos in flannel pajama pants, I felt a flood of both affection and nausea.

I was well acquainted with my own worries in the outdoors— grizzlies, lightning, rattlesnakes, rockfall, creeps, getting lost—but I had not anticipated how new responsibility would affect them. It was the cold eye of a magnifying glass in the yellow sun. My worry blazed. I worried I would string a bear bag in a too-dead tree and a branch would fall and smash them; that I would glance at the radio while driving and our van and gear trailer would drift off the highway and roll into a ditch; that I would use the wrong pan in a white-walled cowboy tent and the mouse shit would make everyone sick. I worried too about the aftermath. Their parents would hate me. The camp would fire me. I would have to move off-grid. I would become an alcoholic.

The irony was the job required me to hide it all. I never looked braver, or more fun. Years later, I told a friend those weeks of responsibility had been the scariest of my life. That I had not known my body could hold so much worry. "Of course you worried," he said, laughing. "That was your job. That's why things went well."

The night after I turned twenty-five, just a few weeks before the 2016 presidential election, ODFW reported that wolves near OR-7's den had killed an eight-hundred-pound calf, and later, that three wolves were eating it. OR-7 and his mate had seven pups that fall, and the wolf was resisting all efforts to have a new collar put on him, dodging the padded metal foothold traps baited with animal stink. By the end of the year, the pack had been blamed for four livestock attacks, which government biologists called "unusual" and "disturbing."

When they finally trapped, tranquilized, and collared another member of the Rogue Pack, it was OR-7's one-and-a-half-year-old daughter. They caught OR-7 too, but only in a nearby trail camera, his body aging, perhaps scraggly, still wearing the necklace of that old defunct collar. Almost immediately, biologists used his daughter's collar to track the pack's movement deeper into the Wood River valley, toward ranches where they had killed livestock before. "You feel helpless when you don't have a means of protecting your animals," one local rancher had told a journalist. He was referring to the reach of the Endangered Species Act in the western two-thirds of Oregon, which said a rancher couldn't shoot a wolf without risking a year in jail and a fine of $5,000.

If the wolf issue was a "war," though, as some proclaimed, who was winning? In the coming year, the body of a wolf would turn up nearby. Though not one of OR-7's offspring, the latest poached wolf had dispersed from OR-7's home pack in eastern Oregon. It seems likely they shared blood. This was the third federally protected and collared wolf killed recently in southeastern Oregon, including a young mother who had just had her first pup. When a breeding female dies, her offspring are often uncounted casualties too. Despite $40,000 in rewards put up by conservation groups and the Fish and Wildlife Service, only one of the three wolves' killers was ever prosecuted.

Meanwhile, by early 2018, Ted Birdseye had lost three calves to the Rogue Pack. Though each had cost him somewhere between $5,000 and $7,000, he'd been compensated by the state for that. "For me, the loss is more about wasted life," Birdseye told me. He loved his cows, and like a parent, he felt responsible. In September, he lost a dog. The prints of a female descendant of OR-7 were found nearby. By 2019 he had lost more animals to wolves than anyone else in the state. "For those couple of years, it really felt like war," Birdseye told me. "Every night we'd all be wondering, 'Are the wolves going to attack tonight?'" If a dog barked in the night, he'd jolt awake, poised to run outside.

Confirmed livestock depredations in Oregon had increased ninety-four percent between 2019 and 2020, and over half of those were attributed to OR-7's Rogue Pack—in 2020, they killed sixteen times. Through late summer and early fall of that year, ODFW agency staff coordinated a night patrol to keep vigil ninety-nine nights in a row, using infrared cameras to track wolf movements and "haze" them out of livestock pastures, attempting to scare them off with noise boxes, cracker shells, bright lights, and loudspeakers. Sometimes they were successful; other times the wolves killed anyway. Why did OR-7's pack keep attacking domestic animals? Did he himself play a role? "As wolves grow old or if they are injured, they are unable to hunt traditional wild prey as they have in the past," ODFW biologist Russ Morgan had told a reporter.

By the time I visited Birdseye's ranch in 2021, he had a three-mile-long, 7,000-volt electric fence around his pasture, purchased through a combination of crowdfunding from a local environmental nonprofit and federal and state funding. Birdseye acknowledged the project on a wooden sign he had built to face the road, shaded by a miniature shingled roof: *Home of OR-7 and the Rogue Wolf Pack*. Like many of the ranchers I met, Birdseye defied stereotype. He was a sixth-generation livestock producer, but he had a copy of *The New Yorker* next to *Ranch* magazine on his kitchen table, and on a chair in the study, the pelt of a wolf he had once got as a pup from a neighbor and raised as a pet ("Otter, because as a pup she looked like one, all small and sleek"). "I suppose it's karma," he'd told me with a chuckle when I reached out to stroke her fur. "First I kept a wolf captive, and now I'm being punished by them." As we spoke about the depredations on livestock and dogs, his fifth-grade son, who stood stork-like at the edge of our conversation in dusty, knee-torn jeans, seemed to remember every death. I'd forget he was there—he'd be bent over, petting one of the many dogs in the yard—then he'd raise his buzzed head, voice steady and eyes unblinking, to correct his father on a detail.

"You're right, son," Birdseye would say, nodding, his shoulder-length gray curls knocking the red bandanna scrunched around his neck, his voice full of solemn, grateful approval. Then he'd look at me, shake his head, crack a smile. "I swear, sometimes kids know best." Kids, I thought, who had learned how to raise something, then, when it died, to let it go.

I visited Birdseye during a week I spent driving between southern Oregon and northern California, visiting a few of the ranches OR-7 or his offspring had walked through. At the time, I was reading Gretel Ehrlich's book *The Solace of Open Spaces*, about working on a Wyoming sheep farm, and it was reminding me how little so many city dwellers understood about the people who raised their meat, their leather, their wool. "In a rancher's world, courage has less to do with facing danger than with acting spontaneously— usually on behalf of an animal or another rider," wrote Ehrlich. She described how, if a cow was born sick, a rancher might take her home and warm her, massaging her legs until daybreak. "Ranchers are midwives, hunters, nurturers, providers, and conservationists all at once."

Thinking about ranchers as both protectors and producers made me think of an art exhibit I had encountered on a research trip to China. Stoned on jet lag and air pollution, I had staggered into a glass-cased modern art museum in Shanghai and stopped in front of a photograph of a woman in a white nightgown submerged in a milky blue pool. Her lips rose just above the waterline, while a small dolphin swam out in a puff of pink blood from between her legs. This was "I WANNA DELIVER A DOLPHIN," a "synthetic biology" project by Japanese designer Ai Hasegawa that included the interior cross-section of a woman's three-dimensional plastic torso. Instead of a fetus inside the curving belly, there was a tiny dolphin, snug as a pea in a shell. "With potential food shortages and a population of nearly seven billion people, would a woman consider incubating and giving birth to an endangered species such as a shark, tuna or dolphin?" writes Hasegawa on her artist website. "This project introduces the argument for giving birth to our food to satisfy our demands for nutrition and childbirth, and discusses some of the technical details of how this might be possible."

My companion on the trip was vegan. He was impressed with the idea of women birthing endangered animals but hated the idea of having to eat them. It seemed crazy, he said, to consume a creature you mothered. Hasegawa suggested it was the most ethical way to eat. I squirmed, but I wondered. When I had grown cherry tomatoes, their red flesh swelling atop a vine's sagging metal cage, I was always proud to eat them. To taste my love and labor with each sour burst of skin. Was this some mix of what livestock producers felt, stewarding their herds through life and into death?

One sunset evening, after a long day driving and hiking around the Hart Ranch near the base of Mt. Shasta, I got up the nerve to ask fifth-generation rancher Blair Hart the question I had heard over and over from friends in the city. Producers seemed genuinely sad when wolves killed their cows, I told him, but if predators didn't eat the livestock, humans would. "I mean, in the end, you're raising these cattle to be killed, right?"

Blair stared at the hiss of the gas fireplace, and for a second, I thought he might be mad. "We ask ourselves the same question every day," he said. His voice was slow. "If I had my way, we wouldn't sell them. I fall in love with each one. I do. Each one is a prize." He leaned back in the leather sofa, hands folded behind his head. "But at the end of the day we're just in the business of raising a protein source to the buying public. Doing the right thing isn't the easy thing." He paused, shaking his head. "I know every one of them." The love from his words hung in the air.

"We just don't have the luxury not to ship these cattle," said his wife, Susan, her feet curled beneath her on the couch beside him. She said it often seemed Blair was a bad fit for ranching. He was such an animal lover, a spider-saver, his heart was always getting broken. Then she leaned forward: "But isn't that the kind of rancher you want? Someone who can barely be in the industry because his heart is so big? At the end of the day, it's just an overwhelming feeling of responsibility. We have put these animals in a situation where they don't have the tools to care for themselves. You feel a real shame if you know you've exposed them to that." Behind them, through the big windows that framed the hill Susan and I had climbed that afternoon, the sun was leaving. The sky blushed.

There was a pause, then Blair added, "Shame shows you have a conscience. We're responsible for every one of these animals." Susan nodded, then rocked forward like a student with a revelation toward me. "His fear of wolves"—she pointed at Blair, who was watching with a bemused expression—"it comes down to the responsibility he feels for the cows. He just loves all animals."

The year earlier, a neighbor had left a cow carcass out on the hill. Blair knew that to a wolf, that carcass was fair game, and he was worried it would draw them. Not just because he worried about his cows, but because he worried about the wolf. If it came for someone's livestock, a rancher was likely to shoot, shovel, and shut up. Blair's neighbors wouldn't move the carcass, so he just did it by himself. Dug the twelve-foot hole and slid the animal into the earth. How quickly it happened: the more time I spent with ranchers like the Harts, the more I cared about not only the herds they were trying to raise, but the legitimate anxiety they expressed about their animals dying, whether by sickness or predator.

I thought of April Martin Chalfant, a rancher I met who lived on Cheyenne homelands, now the Northern Cheyenne Reservation, and who balanced the knowledge that wolves have long been sacred protectors of her people while also trying to keep her cattle alive. One day she came across a heifer that had been hamstrung, hind end stripped from the tail down the back of her leg, where a predator had bitten and grabbed her haunch. The cow was still alive, and when April saw a big track by the creek bed, and later heard that another rancher had glimpsed a small pack of wolves, she knew. By the time she had gone to get her gun and come back, her cow had died; that night, the body was eaten. Her neighbors lost calves too.

"I was like, 'Oh, how am I going to put this together in my head?'" she told me across the table in a Wyoming saloon, a few years after it had happened. "You know what I mean? Because my inclination would be to shoot it. If had I caught the wolf taking down my heifer that day, I would have definitely shot it. But then I thought, can I do that? Because culturally we have this really intertwined bond with that animal." She paused. "It's a hard thing to wrap my head around. Luckily, I didn't have to because the wolf moved on." The species hadn't reestablished themselves in her part of southeastern Montana, but it was likely just a matter of time. "Culturally, wolves definitely have a place. But you know, what does it all look in real life? I don't know." She sounded genuinely heartbroken.

Most livestock producers love their animals even as they lead them to slaughter. That is what many of us city people don't understand. When I caught up with Joe Whittle in Wallowa County, he related it to subsistence hunting. "Whether you birth an animal, raise it, and then take its life, or go out into the forest and hunt it and take its life, you can really truly feel genuine emotion and care," he said. "Ranchers really do care for their animals, and often when speaking about wolves they'll say 'I like them, but . . .' They're in a system that forces them to create commodity!" Capitalism and its demands are a bigger stress than big-game predators, he thought.

In the meantime, what could be done to help make livestock herds more resilient in the face of expanding wolf populations? "Ultimately we have to teach mother cows to behave differently when there are predators around," said Zoë Hanley, a biologist with Defenders of Wildlife, when I spoke with her on the phone from Portland. Early studies showed that mother moose who survived encounters with wolves were beginning to teach their fear to their calves, putting the next generation further along the learning curve. Fear of wolves, in other words, was not manifesting solely as anxiety in prey, it was something useful, teachable. The animals were evolving, and now their handlers were beginning to as well. In the face of stressors, the best way to find safety was to reimagine social bonds.

"Basically," Zoë told me, "we have to rekindle the herd instinct."

The spring COVID-19 arrived, I was more than 2,400 miles from Portland. I had a yearlong fellowship teaching writing at a small-town high school in northern Michigan. Many of my belongings were still stashed in an attic outside Boston, and when the school year ended, I didn't know where I would go. I was, as always, flinging myself at new things. I had recently flown to interview in another state I had never been to before, a place of hot thunderstorms, even farther from Oregon, where I had broken into an inexplicable, itchy full-body rash for the first time in my life. *Are you going through anything particularly stressful?* my doctor asked. *I don't want to move somewhere new all over again,* I thought. *Nothing really,* I told her. She gave me a cream, and I tried not to look at my own body. As a writer, I was used to chasing financial support wherever I could find it. It had rarely seemed possible to follow emotional support instead.

As news of the virus spread, I told the few friends I had made in Michigan that I thought life was about to get pretty bad. Because I read and spoke often about global warming, my anxieties were, to their ears, nothing new. *I'm sure it'll be okay,* they said, perhaps because they thought it was what I wanted to hear.

Humans have conflated wolves with disease for hundreds of years. "[The wolves] had become a plague," said a German forest officer in 1815. At that time—an era of war and illness and, in the words of historian Martin Rheinheimer, just "a deep, existential fear"—wolves were viewed as one of the most harmful creatures on earth. The wolf hunt, so often, was catharsis. You could not hunt the flood or fever, but you could gather your neighbors and trap the predator. You could shoot the scapegoat. Not only were wolf packs referred to symbolically as diseases, they were often imagined as literal carriers. In the aftermath of the Thirty Years' War, farmers' fields went fallow, turning cropland into forest and bringing wolf packs closer to human settlements. After hunger led citizens to eat their cats, mice proliferated and further decimated harvests, leading to laws banning the hunting of predators like foxes. Soon predators began to be seen as pestilence themselves. Reports of wolves eating corpses and living in the cellars of abandoned houses circulated, the species "multiplying and turning rampant" as human populations dwindled.

Stories from colonial America told a similar story. One Swedish seed collector wrote that wolves were eating the corpses of Indigenous people who had died of smallpox and then attacking survivors in their huts. As if by some karmic mark, some affected wolves began losing hair on their sides and bellies. Their disease became a uniform, and their hair did not grow back for years. Some terrified colonists slaughtered their own dogs to try to prevent interbreeding. If smallpox was the invisible villain, the sick wolves were its physical manifestation. As with rabies, the Europeans' illness made the wolves victims, but also worthy of fear. Now, with the onset of a pandemic, when I imagined going into a grocery store full of chatty, chalky northern Michigan faces, I felt the same way. I wanted to step back.

When I told my co-teacher a few East Coast schools were sending students home, she smiled. *Things take longer to reach us up here,* she said. *You'll see.* I spent the next few nights ferrying between

fluorescent stores on icy roads, buying canned food and cold medicine and searching the aisles for isopropyl to make my own hand
sanitizer. On Friday morning, the principal told us it was our last
day of class. My worry gloated, horribly. Like the Trojan priestess
Cassandra, my doomsday fantasies were proving right.

After school I went to the library for its last open hour. Filling a
bag with books, I tried to psych myself up to survive, solo, whatever
was coming to my little house in the snow. Meanwhile, the person
I had recently started dating in Portland was calling, as were my
parents. My dad was already baking bread and coordinating grocery
runs for their elderly neighbors. Because my mother worked in
healthcare communications, she had a peek into what legislators
were thinking before the news did. "I think if you decide to come
home—and I think you should—you should do it as soon as possible." She was moving her office home, packing up her stash of
afternoon chocolate, trying to stay calm.

Lying awake that night I mulled over who I would ask to bring
me food if I had to quarantine in Michigan. Before that year I had
never lived alone, and now there I was, hundreds of miles from
anyone I had preexisting friendships with and facing a global pandemic. A year and a half earlier, I had ended a relationship with
a person I loved, explaining that I had lost the reins on my independence, and needed them back. Wasn't this that? I was facing
a period without work, in a house with a porch by a lake where I
could write alone, uninterrupted. So often I packed a bag to find
adventure and solitude, but now that, like the possibility of virus,
was everywhere. I thought of the college professor who had told
me to go to a nunnery so I could write. He was right to urge me to
consider living alone, but so often, in the years since, I had turned
away from my pack just because it felt like the best way to prove
I was brave. But to whom? "Wolves live in packs, in collectivities,"

wrote Carla Freccero. She suggests "a feminist . . . wolf that refuses masculinist heroic or demonic individualism might offer a line of flight for both women and wolves."

A day later, I flew. The world could be terrifying, and I was done chasing self-reliance. I was ready to kindle the collective. To go home to the people who had always seen me as strong. If I had once felt claustrophobic under the tangle of giant Pacific Northwest firs, I now wanted nothing more than to walk beneath their canopy, peeking for white blooms of trillium at their base.

And so it felt like a fluke, that first phase of my cross-country move. Lugging my suitcases up three flights of narrow, winding stairs to my old childhood room, I sensed I was done running away. I herded the box-elder beetles off the wall, scooting them out the window into the soggy night. *It's my room, now,* I thought, even though it was really a guest room, my old desk housing the sewing machine. I told myself I had come because my family needed help during whatever loomed because I could not yet face the humming engine of my own will: I wanted to be near them. To rely on them, but also to let them rely on me.

That day in the truck with John Stephenson, we stopped not only to look for wolves in the traps, but also on the motion-activated cameras. "It's really gone quiet," he said, loosening and replaying the tape on the third or fourth one. Two weeks earlier, he had watched wolf after wolf walk by; now the camera showed little but a string of shots of John himself, reaching for its plastic case every morning. Without collars on this new pack, it would be nearly impossible for him to track their travels. He could use a thermal vision camera to scan for heat, the red blobs just specific enough to show you if you were looking at a wolf or a cow, but it was cumbersome, and not ideal for warning ranchers. Hardly a substitute for a radio collar.

We drove on. The dirt road, the jostling, the conversation, it all washed over me. That acute suspense of would-we-see-a-wolf. When two deer bounded out of the grass outside my window, I flinched, pointing wordlessly. Though it seemed unlikely many people knew how to get in here, or find their way out, every now and then we passed a fossil of human life: an abandoned medicine cabinet, flattened cans, and once, a motorboat, beached roadside with creeping rust. By the time we got to the last two traps, John let himself feel optimistic.

"If we're going to see one anywhere, this seems likely," he said. It was where they'd caught and collared OR-93 just last June, the wolf that was now moving through the oak-and-vineyard-patched California countryside of San Luis Obispo, traveling farther south than any dispersing wolf had gone in hundreds of years, a journey only trackable because that wolf had walked into a trap left here at the base of Mt. Hood.

Unsure where traps were when we approached them, I watched the road, as if it were a seam that would open and reveal a wolf. But no: John slowed, and sighed, and that was it. His disappointment palpable. Though I too held out hope for the remaining trap, I couldn't deny I felt a tingle just traveling the road and knowing a wolf had recently done the same, not unlike the curiosity I once felt standing beside Emily Dickinson's old desk. What had the wolves been thinking when they walked here? Maybe it had been the mother, heading toward or away from her pups. Had she thought of them when she was away? To assume an animal feels nothing is to negate what Carl Safina classifies as the North-South-East-West of sentient emotional range: "happy," "sad," "fear," and "love." A wolf knows those four feelings; surely a parent knew their combinations.

In the 1980s, scientists found evidence of wolves burying their own dead wolf pups. *Sadlove.*

It felt helpful, even therapeutic, to imagine plotting my own emotions on these poles. Like a color wheel, it seemed important to register not only what I was feeling, but what lay opposite it on the emotional compass. Those times I had felt most overwhelmed by fear: Wasn't that really being overwhelmed by love? I didn't want to die, and I didn't want the people or land or animals around me to either. Rekindling the herd meant reinvesting in connection. A web brought strength, but with a heightening of care and responsibility, it brought fear too. It illuminated all the bonds I did not want to lose.

One morning, after I had been roommates with my parents and the person I was dating about a month, I creaked down the stairs to fumble for caffeine.

"Well?" asked my dad, already vibrating with coffee in his gray flannel bathrobe. "Did you see the news?" Mid-April in Portland was moody, and though I had woken in sun, the window behind him now shook with rain.

"No." There was so much news those days. The pop-up morgues. The lines at the food banks. After waking up to the news of John Prine's death some days earlier, I had come to dread the mornings, if only because they revealed the unmarked baggage of the nights. There was always a new wolf at the door.

"What is it?"

"The famous wolf," Dad said. "OR-7." He passed me an article he'd pulled up on his iPad. "He's dead."

One of the bestselling contemporary novels in China is *Wolf Totem*, a 2004 semi-autobiographical book by retired professor Jiang Tong, about an urban intellectual who adopts a wolf pup after being sent to live with nomadic shepherds on the Inner Mongolia steppe during the Cultural Revolution of the 1960s. A decade earlier, Chairman Mao had launched a campaign to exterminate wolves as part of an effort to bolster large-scale agriculture; in *Wolf Totem*, wolves are as threatened by invaders as the Mongolians are by the encroachment of Chinese farmers. In one scene, a nomad explains his view of the ecological value of wolves. Not only do they keep ground squirrel, rabbit, and marmot populations in check so they don't overgraze and dig up the herdsmen's pasturelands, the flourishing of grass means the landscape is more resilient to erosion and drought, and less likely to be completely buried under snowfall.

"When the grassland is hit by a 100-year or 200-year blizzard, the toll on our livestock is enormous," he continues, describing the numbers of dead cows and sheep who then appear, stinking, from the snowmelt. "If they aren't buried, an epidemic could kill half the people and animals . . . but wolves will dispose of the dead animals in no time. Plagues aren't a problem as long as there are wolves around." At the time I read this, COVID-19 had left China and locked me in my house. Did that pandemic emerge from a lopsided ecosystem too? As with tick-borne viruses, I didn't think wolves would literally save the day; still, they were my window into the complex beauty of interspecies interaction, my reminder of what was at stake in a future of extinctions and dwindling resources.

The only problem, another herder responded in *Wolf Totem*, was that wolf mothers were forced to compete with human mothers. There are only so many ground squirrels on the steppe. Only so many mouths that could be fed. It was an argument I had heard regarding wolves and grazing populations in Oregon, and people and resources on a warming planet. The logic sprang from anxiety, not imagination, though, and I was beginning to understand what could be gained by seeing the world another way. "That scarcity is the lie," author and activist adrienne maree brown said in an interview. "Actually . . . the society we want to structure and move toward is one in which there's abundant justice, abundant attention, abundant liberation, where there is enough for all of us to feel attended to." It is useful to discuss how dog owners and sheep and ranchers can best share today's land with wolves, but it feels more generative—more interesting—to think about how making room for wolves might compel us to visualize and enact a better, different world for ourselves and other species too. What sort of economic and social structures might help humans live beside wolves not as competitors, but as neighbors, even collaborators? What if the story we told was that one creature's thriving did not have to come at the expense of another?

A mother goes through the woods to grandmother's house, a village over. It's 1970, in Azerbaijan. The mother's six-year-old daughter, Elmira Godayatiova, wants to come too. She follows, wordlessly. Imagine her tiny shadow, steps lit by the adrenaline of a secret. It isn't long before the mother spies Elmira behind her. Maybe it was a snapping branch. A trail of song. The mother scolds her daughter and sends her home. When does she learn Elmira didn't make it? Does the possibility hang over her throughout her visit with her own mother, or does she lose herself in conversation, and learn only when she arrives home to find a father at the door? For days they surely assume the worst. A man, a cliff, a wolf. On the twenty-third day of searching, a forest ranger finds Elmira sitting under a tree. She explains she has been living with wolves, playing with "the doggies and puppies," eating berries and grass, drinking water from a stream. What to do but believe her?

Eight years later, it happens again with an Azerbaijani girl. She is only three, her footprints small as an animal's, when she gets lost in the snow. When they find her sixteen hours later, it's in a cave with a wolf and cubs. The girl is warm and free of harm. She describes the wolf licking her face. Like Little Red, these girls have gone into the woods and run into a wolf. Unlike the fairy tale, the wolf does not fracture her family unit, but becomes it. "Wolves and bears, they say, / Casting their savageness aside, have done / Like offices of pity," wrote Shakespeare in *The Winter's Tale*.

Legend said Rome sprung from a similar generosity, with twin babies Romulus and Remus suckled and raised by a mother wolf after being abandoned on the banks of the Tiber. Nursed to adulthood, the boys become founders of the city. Though wolves were never technically worshipped in ancient Rome, citizens regarded them with enough reverence to avoid harming them when they entered city walls. If one appeared, people drove it toward a gate that would let it exit alive. Whereas hyenas, lions, tigers, leopards, cheetahs, and bears were killed in arenas for sport, there are no records of wolves ever being kept in public or private enclosures in Rome. Wolves were not demons but elements of a natural order. Viewed as nurturers, their predatory instincts were not only acknowledged, but accepted.

The story of a child raised by a family of wolves is now a narrative trope, familiar enough for readers to have accepted Misha Defonseca's fictionalized Holocaust memoir. The genre found popularity in 1894 with the publication of Rudyard Kipling's story collection, *The Jungle Book*. Three years earlier, Kipling's father had published *Beast and Man in India*, a nonfiction story collection that included accounts of Indian children allegedly being raised by wolves. "In many of these accounts the human child, unwanted and abandoned by his parents in the jungle, was nursed by a mother wolf and thrived," wrote Brenda Peterson in *Wolf Nation*. This felt like the cruel paradox of many Western stories about mothers and wolves: that if a human mother was to blame, then—only then—could the wolf mother be redeemed.

One evening, right at the cusp of *entre chien et loup,* Urmila Devi took three of her eight children to the edge of the village, where a grassy opening served as their bathroom. It was mid-August 1996, in the village of Banbirpur, about 450 miles southeast of New Delhi, in northeastern India. This was the season the Ganges did not obey its banks. The air would have been hot breath, the walls of the brick homes rain-stained and sweating with monsoons. At night, mothers tried to hunt the breeze, dragging latticed cots out of cramped homes and tucking their infants in to sleep by their sides.

How long was Urmila out there before she saw the wolf? The *New York Times* later described it as "100 pounds of coiled sinew and muscle." It is not clear if Anand was the youngest, or the slowest, or just on the wrong side of the path. The wolf carried him into the thick, tufted brush of corn and elephant grass that sloped toward the river. The Indian wolf, *Canis lupus pallipes,* is a slighter-built subspecies of the gray wolf now found in North America. The report did not say what happened next, but when I read it I wanted to cover my ears. Surely there was screaming. Other noises too. When did the screaming stop? The police search party did not find the boy for three days. By then, he was a half mile away, and all that was left was his head.

In the five months before Anand's death, thirty-two children had been carried off and killed by wolves in that lush, ravine-pocked Ganges River basin. Twenty others had been seriously mauled. Many victims were under eleven years old. If trends from other parts of India held, more than half of them were likely female. As Urmila shepherded her children through the tall grass on their march to privacy—doing the thing they just had to do—she would have known this encounter was a possibility. She would have existed for months under the cramp of *what if*. Since the attacks began, infants had been kept inside, children herded from the fields. Sometimes it helped, but sometimes wolves did not obey the boundary of the home. They seized children as they slept on porches, and could creep through doorways, leaving marks on dirt floors. "Child-lifting," it had come to be called. At night, men stayed watch with bamboo staves and rifles. The rhythm of Urmila's life would have shaped itself around her fear long before it shaped itself around her grief.

There is a story here about the struggles of conservation. Two decades earlier, India had expanded its animal sanctuaries to cover about five percent of the country, adopting a wildlife protection statute that covered both tigers and wolves. Still, tigers were illegally poached, and India's wolves were not. Unlike a tiger, a trophy that could bring its killer glory, India's wolves had been viewed as a nuisance ever since colonial officers began recording their depredations, wrote historian Steven Rodriguez. Now, as India's protected lupine population soared, human life continued to encroach on wild areas, threatening the wolf's habitat and food sources. In the wet hot terror of that summer of 1996, the villagers of the Ganges River basin tried to reclaim control.

"Crime and punishment applies to every living thing, humans and animals," Ram Lakhan Singh, the animal conservationist who spearheaded local efforts to hunt the "man-eating" pack, told the *New York Times*. "The wolves have to learn that they cannot live next to human beings and misbehave. If they do, they must be killed." Armed with twelve-gauge shotguns and bamboo spears, thousands of citizens and police officers began hunting, but by the time Anand was killed, they had gotten only ten wolves, with no way of knowing if those were the "right" ones.

One hundred and eighteen years before the wolf dragged away Anand, British authorities recorded 624 human deaths by wolf in the same region. It seems improbable this number is accurate; it likely also encompasses deaths brought by other predators and wolf hybrids. Still, the scale is staggering, especially given it is only the tally of 1878. When I first read about that spate of late-nineteenth-century predator attacks in India, it was mentioned in isolation. Only after reading Rodriguez did I understand the forces that shaped those predations: not a freak natural occurrence, but the result of colonial interference inciting environmental injustice.

"Nature cannot be described as acting unjustly," writes historian and political ecologist Adam Pérou Hermans. All the same, "environmentally caused (i.e. 'natural') problems are not independent of human influence." Wolves respond to human activity in a landscape. Those who suffer the burden of wildlife unequally are often marginalized or discriminated against by larger institutions of power. Remember Urmila's family was attacked because they had no safe bathroom. Hermans wrote not about India but about the Wakhi shepherds of eastern Tajikistan, whose stories about wolf predations existed outside Western science and thus could not be "authenticated" by scientists or policymakers. Whether or not wolves attacked people in their region depended on the political cocktail of the surrounding countries, increasing after soldiers and border guards reduced game populations amid unrest in Afghanistan, for example, and decreasing after the Soviets stopped providing the Wakhi with guns when the USSR fell in 1991. Western conservationists should be aware, suggested Hermans, that telling a Wakhi shepherd not to fear wolves was likely a moral reflection of the conservationists' own "well-founded, fear of wolf persecution" more than a response to the situation on the ground.

The problem with wolves in India had long been a problem with humans. Attacks first increased with the Raj's emphasis on expanding railways into previously remote regions—wolf habitat, in other words. In 1857, the British disarmed natives after an attempt at rebellion, leading to a spike of attacks on defenseless locals from animals of all sorts. And 1878, that year of 624 wolf depredations? That was the last year of what is now known as India's Great Famine, the two-year period when 10.3 million people starved to death. Some officers reported hungry wolves were devouring human corpses then turning on starving people. British officers blamed villagers for failing to bury their dead and thus inviting the predation. Wolves were a problem before the famine, but to the Raj, they were an economic one, worrying officials that "fear of these wild beasts" might hinder "extending cotton cultivation," as one English writer put it in 1871. A laborer too afraid to work meant one thing for the property owner but another for the family who depended on said labor for food. With the rise of a government-sanctioned wolf extermination program, pigs and deer proliferated, eating crops and worsening the famine. When resident hunters tried to protect their local land, they were driven off by competing bounty-seeking colonial soldiers.

Cruelest of all, perhaps, is how colonial agents blamed attacks on the behavior of the people they subjugated and, implicitly, the caregivers. They claimed "apathy and inaction" were to blame for the deaths of so many children, as well as a superstitious reverence for wolves and, because more girls than boys were killed, infanticide. In *Lambs Among Wolves: Missionaries in India,* a book published in Calcutta in 1928, author Sister Nivedita incisively attacks missionary rhetoric. "Why, to take explicit instances, do we never hear from them of the strength and virtues of Indian women? Why only of their faults and failures?" She laments how swiftly and unquestioningly missionaries circulated a picture of a so-called crocodile luncheon, of babies served up by their mothers along the banks of the Ganges, falsely implying it as a ritual practice.

What happened between the wolf, Urmila, and her children that night in 1996 did not happen in a vacuum, but on a lineage of imperialism and trauma. In the aftermath of the attack, Anand's ten-year-old sister Sita Devi recounted her brother's death to a cluster of villagers around the town well. "It came across the grass on all four paws," she said. "As it grabbed Anand, it rose onto two legs until it was tall as a man. Then it threw him over its shoulder. It was wearing a black coat, and a helmet and goggles." Sita's story was met with anxious murmurs. Later, her grandfather said, "As long as officials pressure us to say it was a wolf, we'll say it was a wolf. But we have seen this thing with our own eyes. It is not a wolf; it is a human being."

I do not know when people turned against one another that summer. Some rumors pinned the killings on Pakistani infiltrators said to have dressed up as wolves. Others blamed them on the werewolves of local folktales. Twenty people were lynched and 150 arrested. Villages became insular, vilifying strangers. In dislocating fear from the illusory wolf and tethering it to the tangible human, the villagers could better avenge their terror.

We inherit histories; we inherit fears. To reconcile Sita's version of her brother's death is to return again and again to her villain—not a wolf, but an intruder in a big black coat, helmet, and goggles. For $44.95 on Amazon, I can buy a replica of the 1895-era butter-colored pith helmets worn by the British colonial military in India. According to user reviews, it is a popular item. "We used two of these for our musical 'The Secret Garden' which takes place in 1910 Colonial India. Really helped create that sense of realism for the show," wrote one reviewer. "Makes me feel like colonizing uninhabited lands!" said another.

I think, again and again, of Urmila. In a study about locals' attitudes toward large carnivores, a team of Indian researchers found that women felt relatively negative toward wild carnivores, while men felt relatively positive. Feminist political ecologist Monica V. Ogra has written about the intersection of gender and wildlife conflicts in a town at the border of India's Rajaji National Park. Not only were victims of attacks more likely to be young women, women also bore the hidden costs of other predations. When elephants crop-raided, for example, men left the village to search for work, while women juggled children while staying behind to repair fences. Repairs, very often, meant new poles, which required a trip into the woods. "In the forest there is also danger of the *two-legged* animal," one respondent told Ogra. "When we go to the forest it is all fear for us, but we have no choice. We have to go," said another.

In the words of Rodriguez: "The solution is to eliminate poverty, not the Indian wolf." I suspect we can go even further and say that when it comes to land management, the solution is to listen to more caretakers, not only of other humans, but stewards of animals and earth. To hear not just how these voices witness fear, but also what will help them bear it.

The year after I moved back to Portland, four wolves escaped from the Wildlife Science Center outside Minneapolis. The center was started in the early 1990s by biologists, and just like the Trust I visited in the UK, it provided all-ages education and exposure to wolves, as well as hosting long-term scientific studies on captive populations. At the time of the escape, 120 wolves lived in captivity there, the largest population in the country.

Because your best chance at convincing a wolf it should listen to you is if you are there when the pup first opens its eyes, to bottle-feed a pup likely means you have stolen it from a den or bred it in captivity then taken it from its mother. Like the rockslide that spills onto a cliff road, you have broken a throughway; wedged yourself between. The staff at the Wildlife Science Center rarely separated pups from their mothers. When, this time, they took one away in preparation to give it to the International Wolf Center in Ely, Minnesota, their pack of ten wolves "lost its mind," according to a local news report. "Overnight we have a six-foot ground apron," the center's animal care coordinator explained, and "they dug down, over the ground apron and up and went looking for their puppy." Heavy rainfall had collapsed the den, easing the escape of the pup's mother, father, and two others from their pack. In a report released on their Facebook page, the center said the separation "was too much for [the mother] to bear."

Because they had grown up around humans and did not know how to hunt for prey, the wolves posed minimal threat, and the center delayed notifying the public about the escape, worried that neighbors would react out of misplaced fear. Their concerns were right. When word eventually came out, a local news station reported that "people in the area are on the hunt for them." Within a few days, wolves began showing up. First one was hit by a car that broke his back, and had to be put to sleep, then the pup's honorary father ("a shy old man," as the center called him) was shot and killed by a local resident. The two remaining wolves were spotted days later, one on a road and one in a nature preserve, both walking alone, where they were safely tranquilized and returned to the center. Tracks and trail camera footage showed the wolves trying to return to the center; according to the care coordinator, the animals were scared and "just want to go home." I believed this, but I also wondered what a human could know about what was going through those wolves' minds.

I find it almost impossible to imagine the wolves digging out of their enclosure without sentimentalizing it. My brain animates their angst, giving them a plucky Pixar voiceover, filling in the squeals of the pup they are trying so fervently to reach. Americans have separated wolf pups from their guardians for centuries, often in incomparably cruel ways, weaponizing the intensity of devotion to their young. In hunter Ben Corbin's *Corbin's Advice or the Wolf Hunter's Guide,* published in 1900, he marvels at their loyalty like a comic-book villain. "Never kill the young one till you play this game to a finish," he wrote. "You may carry the young ones five miles at night, and the old ones will be with you next morning— such is their affection for their young." This approach took various forms. Sometimes government trappers would kill all pups in a den except for one, which they would save and chain to a tree. When her ailing howls summoned the parents and wolf pack back for help, the trappers would kill them all. Corbin writes that other times, he drove beside a den with his dog pulled behind his buggy. "The old wolves think, of course, the dog is after their young, and they rush at the dog, then I shoot."

In one of his most disturbing anecdotes, Corbin recounts revisiting a den where, the year before, he had killed a litter of pups. This time, he shot a breeding female wolf as it ran from the den. In a grotesque echo of Little Red Riding Hood's woodcutter savior, he then cut open the mother. "Performing the caesarian operation, I soon had the cubs, as yet unborn," he wrote. After digging through the den, he found a total of six pups, which he "laid . . . beside their dead mother for their first meals." In recounting the moment, he cited Scripture ("although you may be dead you yet shall live") and cast himself as the Jesus-like shepherd. Loading the pups in his wagon and riding homeward, he bought a "rubber tit" at the store and became their surrogate mother, feeding them sweet milk. Riding around Bismarck in the wagon, he displayed the pups like a living exhibit, lobbying for a petition to restore a wolf bounty. He did not reveal what happened to the pups, but presumably he killed them, cashing them in for bounties of $1 apiece.

It is hard to read these accounts and not feel the sting of a lonely man's spite. Corbin is so smug, outwitting those protectors with their own responsibility, turning their bonds into bait. *Hurt people hurt people,* a friend of mine says. I think: *Who failed to take care of you, Corbin?* "Motherly" love, caretaking love, can make us fierce, but it can also leave us bare. *Sadlove.* A feeling I, in returning to family and friends in Oregon during a year when illness and death rates soared, was suddenly acutely aware of.

When John rounded the bend to the last wolf trap, I held my breath. It was not yet 10:30 a.m., but sun sloshed around us, igniting dust particles that jumped through the air. I could feel my cheeks already rosy through the windshield. The biologists had last checked the traps the day before, so any wolf we now found might have been there for up to twenty-four hours and would be tired out. Though the trap was anchored in the ground, it was also tethered to a log, so the wolf would be able to drag it without hurting her foot too much.

If there was a wolf, we would get out of the truck. John would tranquilize her with Telazol using a six-foot metal syringe pole. After about ten minutes, her body would slacken, and we'd probably lift her onto the tailgate. She could be eighty to a hundred pounds, so it would take work. There was a whole clipboard to turn to then, checklist splotched blue with water from where it lay in the backseat: apply face-covering to protect her eyes, antibiotic ointment where the dart had punctured the skin, monitor vitals at least three times, flush dirt from eyes, remove sticks from mouth.

The language was almost tender, the way you would check the teeth for stains or breaks then estimate the wolf's age based on a worksheet with a drawing of the jaw. Count pulse and respiration for fifteen seconds each. Weigh, measure her. Attach the collar, Goldilocks right. Know that adult wolves were at their lightest when they were ferrying food to pups, so you had to leave the collar loose enough that they could bulk up.

This was what we would have done if we had found a wolf. But the trap was empty. Nothing but a white butterfly surfing the breeze. John muttered something under his breath as he crouched in the dirt, looking for signs of tracks. "I'm just going to go ahead and pull this one out," he said, beckoning me to the window. Taking a stick from the ground, he plunged it into the earth. The dirt leapt and bit the stick, the metal teeth of the trap, lined with rubber, leaping up. The trap would be boiled now, sanitized for a new wolf. Our day was done.

As we drove out, the truck careening over the ruts—a drive so rugged that within a few hours I would, for the first time in my life, be unable to move my neck side to side or up and down for one, two, three days—I had the feeling of being watched. I'd never gone hunting before, but suddenly I thought of those in my family who did, or had, whom I had never really understood. There was something about going to look for an animal, to focus on being smart enough to try and find it, that sharpened the experience of being in the woods, but also just being alive on earth. It all depended, I thought an hour later as I hiked alone up into the trees to eat my lunch, on the local existence of the animal in the first place. My thrill of co-occupation could not happen if the wolf had not come back.

A month later, I tried to explain myself to Mark Kang-O'Higgins. Mark was an Irish painter and art professor who also taught wildlife-tracking classes at the Wilderness Awareness School in Duvall, Washington. We were walking toward the Pacific Ocean when I asked him if he experienced a similar echo of company in the trees: that ghost of the animal that wasn't exactly there. He nodded in the salt breeze, like, *duh*. Tracking was how he had come to feel at home so many thousands of miles from where he was born.

"The land is storied where I come from," he said, gesturing to the Celtic tattoo on his arm. "There's a depth of stories there, the same way it is for Indigenous peoples here." Tracking let him locate himself, to see where the squirrel had eaten or the deer traveled, to feel, in a sense, less alone in the bioregion he inhabited. In painting he could lose himself, and since he'd started tracking, he'd learned to do that here too. To try and see the world as a wolf or owl might meant to momentarily leave the world as himself. I thought of the novels I loved, how I thrilled at the chance to slip into another character's skin, just as I once played dress-up in my mother's old prom dress, trying to conjure how it had felt to grow up her. To follow an animal's trail, Mark said—suddenly distracted by the base of a Douglas fir, where what looked like tiny bark chips were the pinecone-shred of a red squirrel—was to see the world gain a whole new dimension. Like reading a book written by someone who was not human at all.

OR-7 hadn't been with his pack during the state's annual winter wolf count, and given his age—eleven years old, over twice as long as wild wolves were expected to live in the wild—the signs seemed to be clear. Still, a part of me held out hope. There was no body!

Maybe he was still out there, sniffing for pee behind some tree. My optimism soon gave way to acceptance. The incredible thing was not that he had died, but that he had lived so long, in a place where wolves were more likely to be killed by humans than by any other means.

OR-7 left his family in Oregon a year after I left my own, but a decade had gone by, and now we had both slowed our wandering and returned to a pack. If it once felt easy to scoff at his celebrity and the people who obsessed over him, it was harder to admit I had been ensnared. Me, someone who had never uniquely cared about wolves, had let his life live rent-free in my brain. I'd fallen into the rabbit hole—or, rather, the wolf den, like the dusty tunnels I had narrowly avoided tripping over at the back of the wolf enclosure in England. I had been drawn to OR-7 for the spectacle, but I had left caring about him as a real, flesh-and-blood *Canis lupus*—just like any other wolf. Constellating him from geotags and grainy photos, it was easy to feel like a stalker, peering at a creature that did not want to peer back at me. I had always understood I would never know him, never clear the hurdle of what was too interior, too private, too wolf.

So why had I watched him, or watched others watch him? The answer was easy. I wasn't a biologist or livestock producer, I was just a member of the curious public, and this wolf was the easiest to track. As one biologist told me: "OR-7 wasn't that special, he was just in a collar." When I thought about what my fixation on his life and the stories people told about it had taught me, it was less his *who*-ness than the glasses I had to surveil him, to trace how his life collided with everything else. I had thought the story of the wolf would bump into the story of the cow, but it was also the story of drought, heightened wildfire seasons, increased suburban development, ranches going out of business and being turned into ranchettes. Cul-de-sacs of environmentally minded people who had fled into the country during COVID-19 could fracture wolf habitat the same way a sheep ranch could. Following OR-7's life had not just made me care more about wolves, it had made me care about the long-lashed cows and the people who tended them, and especially the ecosystems we all shared. I had seen the slippage between us and them; predator and prey; history and current day. There was no binary between farm and forest: everything was habitat.

A year after OR-7's death, a study from Wisconsin reported the recovery of wolf populations had led to a twenty-four percent decrease in deer–car collisions, saving the lives of dozens of people and the state some $10.9 million annually in losses. "Predators always scare way more prey than they can actually kill," biologist Liana Zanette told journalist Ed Yong. Not only were deer populations smaller with predation, but wolves were also creating a "landscape of fear" on the asphalt, and deer were staying away. The ripples from growing wolf populations extend in other surprising ways too. Researchers in Yellowstone are examining what is known as the "predator cleansing effect," where, say, a wolf would help sustain ungulate populations by feeding on the sickest in their herd. Their focus is on the potential for wolves to prey on deer suffering from chronic wasting disease, a contagious neurological sickness experts fear could jump to humans, but which wolves do not yet seem to get sick from themselves. "Wolves wouldn't be a magic cure everywhere," Ellen Brandell, the doctoral student in wildlife ecology helping lead research into this "predatory cleansing" effect, told the *New York Times*. "But in places where it was just starting and you have an active predator guild, they could keep it at bay and it might never get a foothold."

I am as wary of the wolf-as-savior narrative as I am of the wolf-as-villain one, but if research like this left me giddy, it was less because I saw the wolf on a pedestal than that it illuminated the narrative complexities of a fuller ecosystem. A deer—the wolf's "prey"—could be spared contagion because a wolf—the "predator"—killed a sick member of its herd. In this logic, that old binary of wolf versus deer sags. So often my mind snagged on moments where we were unintentionally scaring or hurting or harming one another, but we could also take care of one another in surprising, sometimes unintentional ways. These studies also illuminated how wolves could make life less scary for humans, however indirectly and unintentionally. I didn't think this was the reason to champion them—wolves deserve to live regardless of how they influence us—but it was a good reminder: we don't exist with wolves in a boxing ring, but on something like a crowded dance floor, our shadows overlapping as we come in and out of contact with other species and one another, touching lives in nearly untraceable ways.

"Attention forms the ground not just for love, but for ethics," wrote Jenny Odell. I had started my research by bringing attention to the wolf, but with enough time and space, attention becomes omnivorous. The shadow wolf led to the real wolf. The love and the ethic spilled outward. Maybe the wolf had dragged me onto the dance floor—really, I'd chased it—but now I was here, surrounded by a texture of life I'd never let myself see, and all I wanted to do was keep trying to imagine a world where we could all stay.

I kept looking for a wolf during those days I traced bits of OR-7's old path through northern California and southern Oregon. It had been just over a year since he died, and my road trip had become something like an homage. I would never see the wolf, but I might see what he had seen. It was also the first solo trip I had taken since moving back to Portland, and I was eager to prove I too could leave my pack for a few days, feel not just the head rush of solitude but also the tingling elasticity of bonds that let me go then welcomed me back. I had an apartment waiting for me in Portland, one where I had unpacked boxes of books that had sat in storage for years. From there, I could walk to my parents' house for dinner, but also into the forest, or up to the porches of friends new and old. Staying put was making me better at recognizing the names of things, not just people on the block, but the daphne and mock orange that scented the air, and the cedar waxwings and swifts that shared the sky. If anxiety had, for years, tried to tell me I was alone, tuning my gaze to these new frequencies of the world had become a form of quiet resistance.

Now, not more than a few days after I left Ted Birdseye's ranch, he called to say he'd heard from ODFW that a radio signal showed a wolf had passed through his property, on the same day as I. One of OR-7's descendants? A day after I left the Harts' ranch, they texted me the same thing. I felt like a wolf was on my tail, which was as silly as thinking I was on his. I was traveling land we shared, the only thing that had changed was that now I knew it.

Toward the end of my trip, I used an app to book a campsite on a small family farm outside Ashland, Oregon. A few encounters with strangers had made my heart flop, but nothing had escalated, and I was learning to respond by reorienting myself to the elements within my control. Instead of re-circling my discomfort, I would cobble together sensory distractions, tearing into lip-staining Sour Patch Kids, turning up Stevie Nicks in the rental car until I couldn't hear myself sing, leaving a voice message for an old friend.

The campsite I now pulled into was a quarter mile or so from an old farmhouse, where a tanned, scruffy guy who smelled like pot and had two dusty, elfin children leaping at his feet opened the cattle gate and pointed me down a dirt road. He padlocked the gate behind me, and it wasn't until I flirted with panic—Was this place horror-movie idyllic? Was he locking me in, or keeping someone out?—I remembered I had just chosen to sleep in a field of animals that should not escape. The campsite was sunny and mowed, with a hammock hanging from an oak tree and a picnic table, a wire fence separating me from a pasture with a few lethargic cows. I liked that the gables of the house were visible in the distance; it made me feel how I had felt as a child, sleeping beside Annika in that musty mushroom tent on Gramps's farm, knowing a glowing kitchen was a short jog away. Those sleepovers had been a sort of inoculation, training us that we could be afraid of the night and run inside, or we could be afraid of the night and stay, then find ourselves rewarded by pink dawn leaking through a leafy sky.

Now, I crawled in early, no rainfly, just a night sweet with spring grass and first stars. It was the first time I had slept alone in a tent in years. I sent a few texts—*Good night*s, *Love you*s, pictures of another dumb perfect sunset—then turned off my phone, even as the residue of words sent by the people I loved seemed to float around me, glowing. I hadn't bothered to bring that old keychain of pepper spray in. If, by some freak percentile, I woke needing protection, I would need other things too, and wasn't I spontaneous, couldn't I trust I would figure it out? I was drifting off when what must have been a bird flapped from a tree, waking me. Jerking upright, I took a deep breath, then told my howling heart to chill. *Go away*, I thought, but tenderly, as if telling a whining dog to lie down. *You mean well, but stop.*

Sleeping outside foiled my instincts to solve night's noises and shadows, and I had forgotten that this was part of the thrill: humbling myself to lie beside the things I could not control. Now, in the distance, cows jostled for clover. A little moo. As my eyes shut, my breath steadied, joining theirs, warm and slow. *Tell me a story about a wolf to help me fall asleep*, said the child inside me. So I did.

Acknowledgments

This book was written primarily on the stolen, unceded land of the Kalapuya and Chinookan peoples, who, with the Willamette Valley Treaty of 1855, were forced to leave their homelands. Wolves were not the only ones driven away by settler-colonialist policies, and part of the project of this book is to begin to understand the ways my own body participates in the exclusion and alienation of others, both human and animal. I want to begin by acknowledging the living legacy of tribal ancestors and descendants who live in the area today. A portion of the proceeds from this book are being donated to the Columbia River Institute for Indigenous Development to support language revitalization, healing initiatives, and cultural preservation in the Pacific Northwest. You can learn more about the foundation's work at www.criid.org.

I owe fierce gratitude to the people whose words and time are in these pages, a few of whom I have been in touch with on and off for a decade: Roblyn Brown; Kent Laudon; John Stephenson; April Martin Chalfant; Joe Whittle; Ted Birdseye; Curt and Kim Jacobs; Susan, Blair, and Alex Hart; Arthur Middleton; Liana Zanette; Zoë Hanley; Mike Collins and others at the UK Wolf Conservation Trust;

and Tabitha Viner. I am also grateful for the countless conversations that do not appear directly in these pages but that have informed my views at one point or another: thank you to all who have spoken to me about wolves over the years. To Anne and Kevin March for hosting me on multiple research trips. To Karin Vardaman for speaking about her nonprofit Working Circle, which works to support both the return of wolves to native lands and the viability of working ranches—you have given me hope for a future of shared lands. To every writer I cite: thank you for giving me so much to think about.

This book would not have happened without the fierce advocacy of my agent Marya Spence, who understood the howl of this project from our first phone call, and who has so often been the light of faith at the end of my tunnel of doubts. It is one thing for an agent to help a writer publish, but through her generous, brilliant inquiries, Marya has so often been the voice who makes me want to sit down and write. Thank you. Second, I am so grateful to my British agent, Emma Leong, whose transatlantic enthusiasm and insights have given this book both life and lift outside the United States. Thank you for championing me as a debut author and for thrifting the best wolf apparel imaginable. So many others at Janklow and Nesbit have provided invaluable editorial and logistical support, in both the United States and the United Kingdom, and a heap of extra gratitude for Natalie Edwards and Mackenzie Williams.

This project began as a Bowdoin College thesis, and I am indebted to my advisor, Anthony Walton, for belief that some version would one day exist as a book. My thesis committee—Connie Chiang and the late, great John Dewitt—were invaluable voices in challenging me to think critically in disciplines outside my own. Thank you to those other Bowdoin professors whose inquiry and encouragement taught me much about rigor and writing, both on the page and in a life—Guy Mark Foster, Russ Ryman, Susan Faludi, Aviva

Briefel, Marilyn Reizbaum, Jill Pearlman, and Matthew Klingle, among many others. To David Hecht, whose trust in me as a researcher set me on the path thinking about the stories we tell about science and ourselves. Before that: to the memory of Ann Fyfield, and to Holly Walsh, Tony Stocks, Art Leo, Peter Shulman, Daniel Bosch, and the other educators who inspired me to write, and keep writing, as a teenager.

My time at the University of Minnesota's MFA program was a huge gift of financial support, intellectual provocation, mentorship, and companionship—exactly what I needed for this project to evolve and bloom. To Kim Todd for bouncing ideas, deadlines and reading recommendations, and sharing wisdom about the mad world of creating a book. You were one of the first people to believe in this book in its current form, and your encouragement was great oxygen to keep going. To Julie Schumacher, for humor and guidance and faith. To V. V. Ganeshananthan, for her generous early read of this work, and for answering so many questions along the way. To Dan Philippon and Charlotte Melin, whose Environmental Humanities Initiative opened my eyes to the possibilities of omnivorously interdisciplinary work. To Patricia Hampl and Charles Baxter, for your writing and teaching and dinners. The book is shaped by years of feedback from my MFA cohort, the one and only cahoot—Kristin, Will, Anessa, Alexis, Liam, Joe, Miriam, Connor, Hannah—thank you for wisdom and whiskey and sharing feedback and your own words, which continue to inspire me. Thanks also to Jonathan, Emily, Carolyn, Kendra, Mihret, Jordan, Anna, Allie, Mike, D, Roy, Amanda, Mae, and Kelsey, who also provided particularly guiding feedback on this project at one time or another.

The evolution of this book included various publications of excerpts and adjacent work, and I'm grateful to those editorial processes for helping me think through these ideas along the way.

Thank you to Tina Chang, Michele Filgate, Matthew Gavin-Frank, Brian Oliu, Matt Donovan, Joni Tevis, and Robin Hemley, who selected portions for various awards and recognition, thus buoying me when I thought about stopping. Thank you to *Literary Hub* and Jess Bergman's sharp edits, for publishing "Why Do We Fear Wolves?," which became the seed for the "Land v. Wolf" chapter, and to the *Southeast Review* for publishing "Cry Wolf," that kernel of an essay that became the whole book. To Stephanie G'Schwind and *The Colorado Review* for publishing "On Worry," bits of which bloomed into parts of this book. To *Creative Nonfiction* and Hattie Fletcher for publishing an earlier werewolf essay, "The Beast of Bray Road," in *True Story*. Much was made possible by the financial support of UMN's College of Liberal Arts Fellowship, Walter H. Judd Fellowship, the O'Rourke Travel and Research Fund, the Gesell Award, the Association of Writers and Writing Programs, the Minnesota State Arts Board, the Udall Foundation, and Bowdoin College's Tom Cassidy Student Support Fund.

Thank you to Jen Monnier, whose fact checking of selective portions of this manuscript were a master class in process and precision. It was an honor to be in conversation and to see the research through your lens.

Thank you to all at Flatiron and Macmillan who championed this book through various stages of metamorphosis. To Meghan Houser, who first saw what it could be, and to Nadxieli Nieto, whose conversations and editorial feedback have indelibly shaped what it has become. Thank you for having such faith in the project's weave and for asking the questions I needed to hear. To Kukuwa Ashun, whose editorial and logistical support have been invaluable in making this process feel legible to a first-time author. To the invaluable others who helped with production and behind the scenes: Megan Lynch, Katherine Turro, Christopher Smith; Emily Walters, Jason

Reigal, Frances Sayers, Sarajane Herman, Rima Weinberg, Susan Groarke, Donna Noetzel, and David Lindroth Inc. I am so thrilled this book found a home at Canongate, who have ushered in *Wolfish* wonderfully from Britain: thank you to Hannah Knowles, whose brilliant editorial eye and unwavering investment in the book made me feel both anchored and inspired. To Helena Gonda, whose ideas for the book helped it find its feet and then to fly. To Caitriona Horne, Aisling Holling, Jenny Fry, and Aa'Ishah Hawton. To the capacious energies of Sarah Russo, Laura Di Giovine, Poppy Hatrick, and Laci Durham at Page One Media.

To Blair Braverman, Michelle Nijhuis, Lyz Lenz, Elizabeth Rush, Rachel Monroe, and Alex Marzano-Leznevich for inspiring me for so long with your mastery of words, and then lending some of your own to early copies of this book.

I've been thinking in some capacity about wolves since 2013, and since then I've lived in more than seven geographic places. In the sense that this book is an archive of my mind during those years, it is also a community effort, one buoyed by conversations and reading recommendations but also by warm meals and meandering strolls. It is impossible to name all who have walked beside me during those years, but you know who you are: your companionship has propped me up. I am grateful to those in my Bread Loaf and Tin House workshops, and to Paisley Rekdahl and Elissa Washuta and Cutter Wood for being my instructors there, for providing provocation and conversation on early drafts. To my fellow BL waiters, especially to Isle for negronis and rants, and to Mary, Morgan, Vince, and Daphne, for answering questions as I waded through the first-book maze. To Liv for organizing the Slack of Champions.

In many ways the writing of this book was made possible by those who gave me places to hole up with my laptop, so I am indebted to the support of the Ucross Foundation, Monson Arts,

Willapa Bay AiR, the Marble House Project, the Kimmel Harding Nelson Center for the Arts, Craigardan, PLAYA, Hypatia-in-the-Woods, and the Alliance for Young Writers and Artists. My head and heart are much fuller for having overlapped with the artists I did there, many of whom are now dear friends. Special gratitude to Masa, for composing "Kohaku" after our conversations. To Emma, Lanse, and Michele, who helped me find home in the Adirondacks, and to Harry and Megan, for making me laugh there. To Fabrizia, Rosie, Henna, Mario, and Haley for so many long, perfect dinners in Sicily and beyond. To Molly, Judy, Deirdre, Teresa, Fleda, and John, for warmth and inspiration in Traverse City. To Elise, and David and Tina, for becoming my New England kin. To those family friends who feel like family-family in Portland.

To Walt, Nora, Toph, Natalie, Abby, Naomi, Leo, Garrett, Peter, Zach, Jordan, Dan, Chelsea, Emma, Maya, Maggie, Charlie, Jonathan, Thea, Josh, Ben, Zoe, Mike, and so many others for years of text threads and hikes and conversations, for knowing when to help me face the work and when to distract me from it. To Nuzha, for pie and that editorial eye, the combination of which made this book feel, finally, real. To Carolyn, Emily, Sophie, Becky, Linda, Eliza—what can I say that is not a cliché about how much I value our friendships?

Lastly, to my parents, for nourishment in the fullest sense of the word. For teaching me to face the fear, but also to spiral toward the light. And to my sibling, Annika, a dream thought partner in facing the world. So many of the ideas I want to write about bloom not on the page but during our phone calls—here's to so many more.

Notes

Introduction

1 **She was two years old:** "OSP Fish & Wildlife Division Is Seeking Public Assistance in Locating the Person(s) Responsible for Shooting a Wolf in the Sled Springs Wildlife Management Unit," Oregon State Police, Jan. 11, 2022, https://flashalert.net/id/OSPOre/151462?alert=1.

2 **"wolf moon":** "Full Moon for January 2020," *Old Farmer's Almanac*, Jan. 23, 2019, https://www.almanac.com/content/full-moon-january.

2 **Hunger, said that old:** Jennifer Speake and J. A. Simpson, *Oxford Dictionary of Proverbs* (Oxford: Oxford University Press, 2015), 153.

2 **"[W]e could extend the image":** Lewis Hyde, *A Primer for Forgetting: Getting Past the Past* (New York: Farrar, Straus and Giroux, 2019), 53.

4 **For information about the Catherine Pack poisoning:** "Oregon State Police Seeking Public Assistance in the Poisoning of Catherine Wolf Pack-Union County," FlashAlert.net, Oregon State Police, Dec. 2, 2021, https://flashalert.net/id/OSPOre/150545.

4 **"in the act of biting":** "Oregon Wolf Conservation and Management Plan," Oregon Department of Fish and Wildlife, June 2019, 48, https://www.dfw.state.or.us/Wolves/docs/2019_Oregon_Wolf_Plan.pdf.

4 **In a state with around 170:** "Oregon Has at Least 173 Wolves, a 9.5 Percent Increase over Last Year," Oregon Department of Fish and Wildlife, 2021, https://dfw.state.or.us/news/2021/04_Apr/042121.asp.

4 **In the last twenty-one years:** "$16,500 Reward Offered for Info on Wolf Killed Illegally in Oregon's Wallowa County," Center for Biological Diversity, Jan. 13, 2022, https://biologicaldiversity.org/w/news/press-releases/16500-reward-offered-for-info-on-wolf-killed-illegally-in-oregons-wallowa-county-2022-01-13/.

4 **In March 2022, the Oregon:** "Oregon DOJ Hires Anti-Poaching Prosecutor," Oregon Department of Fish and Wildlife, Mar. 14, 2022, https://www.dfw.state.or.us/news/2022/03_Mar/031422.asp.

4 **"a level that can make significant":** "Reward Climbs to Nearly $50,000 for Information on Poisoned Wolves," Oregon Department of Fish and Wildlife, Dec. 15, 2021, https://www.dfw.state.or.us/news/2021/12_Dec/121521.asp.

5 **"Humans do not live with biological":** Garry Marvin, "'Man Is a Wolf to Man': Wolf Behavior Becoming Wolfish Nature," in *In the Company of Wolves: Werewolves, Wolves and Wild Children,* eds. Sam George and Bill Hughes (Manchester: Manchester University Press, 2020).

5 **"symbolic wolf":** L. David Mech and Luigi Boitani, eds., *Wolves: Behavior, Ecology, and Conservation* (Chicago: University of Chicago Press, 2003), 290.

5 **"a wolf's day":** David C. Posthumus, *All My Relatives: Exploring Lakota Ontology, Belief, and Ritual* (Lincoln: University of Nebraska Press, 2018), 133.

6 **Perhaps the first bounty:** Mech and Boitani, *Wolves,* 312.

6 **Haida and Tlingit:** Raymond John Pierotti and Brandy R. Fogg, *The First Domestication: How Wolves and Humans Coevolved* (New Haven, CT: Yale University Press, 2018), 156–57.

6 **"Each species recognized a skill set":** Ibid., 5.

6 **"brother, grandfather, relative":** Ibid., 13.

6 **"The wolf is the only animal":** Garry Marvin, *Wolf* (London: Reaktion Books, 2012), 92.

6 **Citations in the Linnell et al. 2021 report:** John D. C. Linnell, Ekaterina Kovtun, and Ive Rouart, *Wolf Attacks on Humans: An Update for 2002–2020,* Norwegian Institute for Nature Research (NINA), 2021, https://brage.nina.no/nina-xmlui/bitstream/handle/11250/2729772/ninarapport1944.pdf?sequence=1&isAllowed=y.

6 **For citations in the Linnell et al. 2002 report:** J. D. C. Linnell, R. Andersen, Z. Andersone, L. Balciauskas, J. C. Blanco, et al., *The Fear of Wolves: A Review of Wolfs Attacks on Humans,* Norwegian Institute for Nature Research (NINA), 2002, https://www.nina.no/archive/nina/pppbasepdf/oppdragsmelding/731.pdf.

7 **In a place where millions:** Linnell et al., *Wolf Attacks on Humans,* 3.

7 **Wolves have historically roamed:** Mech and Boitani, *Wolves,* 246.

7 **Other than humans, wolves were once:** L. David Mech, "Where Can Wolves Live and How Can We Live with Them?," *Biological Conservation* 210 (2017): 310.

7 **The Pacific Northwest's oldest fossilized:** David Moskowitz, *Wolves in the Land of Salmon* (Portland, OR: Timber Press, 2013), 177.

7 **For information on the oldest archaeological evidence of humans:** Ellen Bishop, "Ancient Nez Perce village site yields oldest date of human habitation in North America," *Wallowa County Chieftain,* Sept. 4, 2019, https://www.wallowanezperce.org/news/2019/9/30/ancient-nez-perce-village-site-yields-oldest-date-of-human-habitation-in-north-america.

8 **"symbolic biology":** Noel Carroll, "Nightmare and the Horror Film: The Symbolic Biology of Fantastic Beings," *Film Quarterly* 34, no. 3 (1981): 16–25.

8 **"guilt, vague environmental concern":** Mech and Boitani, *Wolves,* 300.

8 **For more information on a biologist's view of Farley Mowat's** *Never Cry Wolf*: Ibid., 104, 294.

8 **"overtly optimistic":** Linnell et al., *Wolf Attacks on Humans,* 11.

9 **"The wolf situation in Oregon is extraordinary":** Alastair Bland, "Wolves Are Returning to Oregon—but Not All Locals Want Them," *Smithsonian Magazine,* Aug. 31, 2012, https://www.smithsonianmag.com/travel/wolves-are-returning-to-oregonbut-not-all-locals-want-them-23593132/.

10 **"more books may have been written":** Mech and Boitani, *Wolves,* xi.

10 **"When you decide to speak nearby":** Cathy Park Hong, *Minor Feelings: An Asian American Reckoning* (New York: One World, 2021), 103.

10 **Lakota hunters once stepped:** Karen Jones, "Writing the Wolf: Canine Tales and North American Environmental-Literary Tradition," *Environment and History* 17, no. 2 (May 2011): 202.

11 *Jägeristaten*: Roger Bergstrom, Karin Dirke, and Kjell Danell, "The Wolf War in Sweden," in *A Fairytale in Question,* eds. Patrick Masius and Jana Sprenger (Cambridge: White Horse Press, 2015), 58–63.

11 **"jumping together":** Edward O. Wilson, *Consilience: The Unity of Knowledge* (London: Vintage Books, 1999), 8–9.

12 **"Symbols are problems":** Elissa Washuta, *White Magic* (Portland, OR: Tin House Books, 2021), 73.

12 **"What frightens us today":** Charlotte Chandler, *It's Only a Movie: Alfred Hitchcock: A Personal Biography* (New York: Simon and Schuster, 2005), 4.

13 **For Isabel Wilkerson's metaphor about the old house:** Isabel Wilkerson, *Caste: The Origins of Our Discontents* (New York: Random House, 2020), 15–17.

13 **"Who is this 'we'"**: Claudia Rankine, *Just Us* (Minneapolis: Graywolf Press, 2020), 331. See also the anthology *Catastrophism: The Apocalyptic Politics of Collapse and Rebirth*, where Eddie Yuen writes that the "seemingly innocuous 'we'" has had the "pernicious effect of erasing the very meaningful class and geographic differences within humanity." Sasha Lilley, David McNally, Eddie Yuen, and James Davis, *Catastrophism: The Apocalyptic Politics of Collapse and Rebirth* (Oakland: PM Press, 2012), 25.

13 **Contemporary predatory wolf attacks**: Linnell et al., *Wolf Attacks on Humans*, 17, 19.

13 **"'Fear' involves such a complex"**: Rachel H. Pain, "Social Geographies of Women's Fear of Crime," *Transactions of the Institute of British Geographers* 22, no. 2 (1997): 233, http://www.jstor.org/stable/622311.

14 **Wolves that live in colder climates**: Mech and Boitani, *Wolves*, xv.

14 **"outside of the anglophone"**: Amia Srinivasan, *The Right to Sex: Feminism in the Twenty-First Century* (New York: Farrar, Straus and Giroux, 2021), xiv.

15 **"After decades of advocacy"**: Mech and Boitani, *Wolves*, 341.

15 **For predictions of wolf-human interactions in coming decades**: Linnell et al., *Wolf Attacks on Humans*, 29.

15 **A wolf will howl after feeding**: Mech and Boitani, *Wolves*, 98.

1. Adventure v. Wolf

17 **For more information about B-45's crossing**: Jim Yuskavitch, *In Wolf Country: The Power and Politics of Reintroduction* (Guilford, CT: Lyons Press, 2015), 4.

17 **A wolf can swim**: Mech and Boitani, *Wolves*, xv.

18 **For information about the Nimiipuu in Hells Canyon**: Allen Pinkham, Steven Ross Evans, and Frederick E. Hoxie, *Lewis and Clark Among the Nez Perce: Strangers in the Land of the Nimiipuu* (Washburn, ND: Dakota Institute Press of the Lewis and Clark Fort Mandan Foundation, 2013), 2, 3, 10, 29. Tátlo, from the Nez Perce Language Program of the Nez Perce Tribe, provided invaluable linguistic support.

19 **three things any young wolf needed**: Mech and Boitani, *Wolves*, 16.

19 **"seems to me a title ill-suited"**: Jayson Jacoby, "Wolves' First Foray into Oregon Livestock Leads to Troubling Questions," *Baker City Herald* (OR), Apr. 17, 2009.

19 **"She appears to be doing"**: Bill Monroe, "Gray Wolf Enters Oregon from Idaho," *Oregonian*, Feb. 18, 1999.

20 **"Civilization and savagery"**: Dick Mason, "Bringing in 15 Elk from Wyoming in 1912 Wasn't Without Controversy," *Observer* (La Grande, OR), Dec. 12, 2008.

20 **"She presents a somewhat odd"**: Monroe, "Gray Wolf Enters Oregon from Idaho."

21 **"something from the past is missing"**: Brooke Jarvis, "The Insect Apocalypse Is Here," *New York Times Magazine*, Nov. 27, 2018, https://www.nytimes.com/2018/11/27/magazine/insect-apocalypse.html.

21 **"when the dog sleeps"**: Edward Coke, *Institutes of the Laws of England: Containing the Exposition of Many Ancient and Other Statutes . . .* (London: E. and R. Brooke, 1797), 63.

25 **Early twentieth-century anthropologist**: Moskowitz, *Wolves in the Land of Salmon*, 238.

31 **"She had the prettiest"**: Marguerite Holloway, "Wolves at the Door: Can We Learn to Dance with Wild Things Again?," *Discover*, June 1, 2000, https://www.researchgate.net/profile/Marguerite-Holloway /publication/265021915_WOLVES_AT_THE_DOOR_CAN_WE _LEARN_TO_DANCE_WITH_WILD_THINGS_AGAIN/links /555dad7908ae6f4dcc8c42e8/WOLVES-AT-THE-DOOR-CAN-WE -LEARN-TO-DANCE-WITH-WILD-THINGS-AGAIN.pdf.

31 **Research shows that when a wolf**: Mech and Boitani, *Wolves*, 16.

31 **"The little sound of it jingles"**: Elena Passarello, *Animals Strike Curious Poses: Essays* (Louisville: Sarabande Books, 2017), 207.

32 **"functionally extinct"**: Christine Adams-Hosking, "What Happens When an Animal Is Declared 'Functionally Extinct,'?" *Pacific Standard*, May 13, 2019, https://psmag.com/environment/what-happens-when-an -animal-is-declared-functionally-extinct.

32 **In his canonical global environmental**: J. R. McNeill, *Something New Under the Sun: An Environmental History of the Twentieth-Century World* (New York: W. W. Norton, 2001), 3–4.

34 **For more information about the oil spill**: Kale Williams, "New Carissa 21 Years Later: Napalm, a Torpedo and 70,000 Gallons of Spilled Oil on the Oregon Coast," *Oregonian*, Feb. 4, 2020, https://www.oregonlive.com /environment/2020/02/napalm-a-torpedo-and-70000-gallons-of-spilled -oil-an-environmental-disaster-on-the-oregon-coast-21-years-later.html.

34 **ODFW officials were hearing**: Yuskavitch, *In Wolf Country*, 7.

34 **For details of B-45's capture**: Aimee Lyn Eaton, *Collared: Politics and Personalities in Oregon's Wolf Country* (Corvallis: Oregon State University Press, 2013), 11; Yuskavitch, *In Wolf Country*, 9.

35 **One was found shot**: Eaton, *Collared*, 112–13.

35 **According to ODFW Stop Poaching Campaign coordinator**: Monica Samayoa, "Oregon Hires Its First Anti-Poaching Special Prosecutor," Oregon Public Broadcasting, Mar. 16, 2022, https://www.opb.org/article /2022/03/16/oregon-hires-anti-poaching-special-prosecutor/.

35 Sixteen hundred oral comments: Eaton, *Collared*, 21.

36 "Being against wolves brought": Carter Niemeyer, *Wolfer: A Memoir* (Boise, ID: Bottlefly Press, 2012), 322.

36 "I understand the issue with wolves": Eaton, *Collared*, 25.

36 "never seen anything like it": Ibid., 38.

36 For more information about the committee: Ibid., 22, 38–39.

37 "Man Spots Wolf—or Not": Associated Press, "Man Spots Wolf—or Not—in Oregon," *Spokesman Review*, Feb. 22, 2009, https://www.spokesman.com/stories/2009/feb/22/man-spots-wolf-or-not-in-oregon/.

38 For more information about the first sounds of pups: Eaton, *Collared*, 41–43.

38 "a proverbial mother": Jay Simpson, "The Story of Wolf B-300," *Wolf OR-7 Expedition*, Nov. 19, 2014, https://or7expedition.org/the-story-of-wolf-b-300-mother-of-wolf-or-7-oregons-first-wolf-resident/.

39 "They don't want us using": Chris Collins, "Wolf Suspected in Sheep Killings," *Baker City Herald*, Apr. 14, 2009, https://www.bakercityherald.com/archive/wolf-suspected-in-sheep-killings/article_0bfaeada-d66e-5817-8a81-edb7c537621d.html.

39 The nonprofit Defenders of Wildlife: Richard Cockle, "Agency Links Wolves to Livestock Attack," *Oregonian*, Apr. 16, 2009.

39 while data suggests that wolf kills: "Wolves and Livestock," May 2020, Center for Human-Carnivore Existence, https://extension.colostate.edu/topic-areas/people-predators/wolves-and-livestock-8-010/.

40 "I guess I'm not really happy": Cockle, "Agency Links Wolves to Livestock Attack."

42 "Wolf Point got its name": "History of Wolf Point," City of Wolf Point, Montana, https://ci.wolf-point.mt.us/community/page/history-wolf-point.

42 "If you don't punish people": Maggie Nelson, *On Freedom: Four Songs of Care and Constraint* (Minneapolis: Graywolf Press, 2022), 50.

43 When a wolf chews a kill: Mech and Boitani, *Wolves*, 48.

43 For details about dens and pups: Ibid., 45–46, 78, 100, 184.

44 Pup mortality: Vadim Sidorovich, Annik Schnitzler, Christophe Schnitzler, and Irina Rotenko, "Wolf Denning Behaviour in Response to External Disturbances and Implications for Pup Survival," *Mammalian Biology* 87 (Nov. 2017): 89–92, https://www.sciencedirect.com/science/article/abs/pii/S1616504716301902.

46 "not a reenactment of such a trauma": Melissa Febos, *Girlhood* (New York: Bloomsbury, 2021), 212.

47 "I walk to work in bright": Lyudmila Savitskaya and Robert Coalson, "Christmas Lights and Pitchforks: Terrified Russian Villagers Try to Keep

Encroaching Wolves at Bay," RadioFreeEurope/RadioLiberty, Nov. 10, 2018, https://www.rferl.org/a/christmas-lights-and-pitchforks-terrified -russian-villagers-try-to-keep-encroaching-wolves-at-bay/29593185 .html.

2. Girl v. Wolf

49 **For details from Berner's life in Alaska:** Candice Berner, *Adventures of an Alaskan Bush Teacher,* https://cberner.blogspot.com.

49 **After graduating college:** Courtney Anderson, "Local Woman Dies in Alaska; Adventure Was Hallmark of Her Life, Father Says," *Allied News,* Mar. 18, 2010, https://www.alliednews.com/news/local_news/local -woman-dies-in-alaska-adventure-was-hallmark-of-her-life-father-says /article_1976afec-934a-5454-a16e-8e2be9f5b3f5.html.

52 **For a report on the day of the Berner attack:** Lem Butler, Bruce Dale, Kimberlee Beckmen, and Sean Farley, "Findings Related to the March 2010 Fatal Wolf Attack Near Chignik Lake, Alaska," Alaska Department of Fish and Game, 2011, https://www.adfg.alaska.gov/static/home/news /pdfs/wolfattackfatality.pdf.

53 **"All stories are about wolves":** Margaret Atwood, *The Blind Assassin* (New York: Anchor Books, 2001), 344.

54 **"her first menstruation":** Michelle Orange, *Pure Flame: A Legacy* (New York: Farrar, Straus and Giroux, 2021), 93.

55 **"[E]ven dressed almost mannishly":** Min Jin Lee, "Opinion: Asian Americans Have Always Lived with Fear," *New York Times,* Mar. 18, 2022, https://www.nytimes.com/2022/03/18/opinion/asian-american-violence -fear.html.

55 **"You cannot separate what it means":** Tressie McMillan Cottom, *Thick: And Other Essays* (New York: The New Press, 2019), 61–62.

56 **"We're all stuck in our bodies":** Olivia Laing, *Everybody: A Book About Freedom* (New York: W. W. Norton, 2021), 179.

59 **For information about *koryos* wolf rituals:** Eric A. Powell, "Wolf Rites of Winter," *Archaeology* 66, no. 5 (2013): 33–36, http://www.jstor.org/stable /24363683; Michael P. Speidel, "Berserks: A History of Indo-European 'Mad Warriors,'" *Journal of World History* 13, no. 2 (2002): 253–90, http:// www.jstor.org/stable/20078974; and Bruce Lincoln, *Death, War, and Sacrifice: Studies in Ideology and Practice* (Chicago: University of Chicago Press, 1991), 134.

59 **Scholars speculate the men:** Birgit Anette Olsen, Thomas Olander, and Kristian Kristiansen, eds., *Tracing the Indo-Europeans: New Evidence from Archaeology and Historical Linguistics* (Oxford: Oxbow Books, 2019), 97.

60 **Bands of young men pillaged:** David Wyatt, *Slaves and Warriors in Medieval Britain and Ireland, 800–1200* (Leiden, Netherlands: Brill, 2009), 95.

60 **"To put on mask-clothing":** Eduardo Batalha Viveiros de Castro, "Cosmological Perspectivism in Amazonia and Elsewhere," *HAU Journal of Ethnographic Theory,* 2012, https://haubooks.org/viewbook/masterclass1/cosmological_perspectivism.pdf.

60 **Sometimes relatives from the men's:** David W. Anthony and Don Ringe, "The Indo-European Homeland from Linguistic and Archaeological Perspectives," *Annual Review of Linguistics* 1, no. 1 (2015): 213–14, doi:10.1146/annurev-linguist-030514–124812.

61 **For Navajo relationship with wolf:** Steve Pavlik, *Navajo and the Animal People: Native American Traditional Ecological Knowledge and Ethnozoology* (Wheat Ridge, CO: Fulcrum Publishing, 2014).

61 **Contrast this:** Aleksandar Loma, "Problems of Chronological and Social Stratification in Historical Anthroponomastics: The Case of 'Lupine' and 'Equine' Proper Names Among the Indo-European Peoples," *Onoma* 55 (2020): 15–34, https://www2.helsinki.fi/sites/default/files/atoms/files/wolf_and_horse_handout.pdf.

61 **"We have manhandled":** Yu Xiuhua, *Moonlight Rests on My Left Palm: Poems and Essays* (New York: Astra Publishing House, 2021), 125.

61 **"There was no talking":** Jennifer Wolch and Jody Emel, *Animal Geographies: Place, Politics, and Identity in the Nature-Culture Borderlands* (London: Verso, 1998), 107.

62 **"The first subject matter for painting":** John Berger, *About Looking* (New York: Pantheon Books, 1980), 5.

62 **For Perrault's version of the story:** See https://sites.pitt.edu/~dash/perrault02.html, citing Andrew Lang, *The Blue Fairy Book* (London, ca. 1889), 51–53; Lang's source: Charles Perrault, *Histoires ou contes du temps passé, avec des moralités: Contes de ma mère l'Oye* (Paris, 1697).

64 **For information about "The Tiger and the Children":** Alan Dundes, *Little Red Riding Hood: A Casebook* (Madison: University of Wisconsin Press, 1989), 59, and Jack Zipes, ed., *The Trials and Tribulations of Little Red Riding Hood* (New York: Routledge, 1993).

64 **"region of death":** Zipes, *The Trials and Tribulations,* 1–2.

64 **There was no huntsman:** Faye R. Johnson and Carole M. Carroll, "'Little Red Riding Hood' Then and Now," *Studies in Popular Culture* 14, no. 2 (1992): 71, http://www.jstor.org/stable/45018122.

65 **For information on rendezvous sites:** L. David Mech and Luigi Boitani, eds., *Wolves: Behavior, Ecology, and Conservation* (Chicago: University of Chicago Press, 2003), 31, 46.

65 **The better hunters:** Barry Lopez, *Of Wolves and Men* (New York: Scribner, 1978), 32.

65 **Dispersing is risky:** Ibid., 35–37, 65–67; Moskowitz, *Wolves in the Land of Salmon,* 76; and Mech and Boitani, *Wolves,* 12.

67 **The Russian language:** Joanna Pocock, *Surrender* (London: Fitzcarraldo Editions, 2019), 190.

68 **For information on that 2011 winter:** Eaton, *Collared,* 52–59.

69 **Later, when reporters asked:** Beckie Elgin, *Journey: The Amazing Story of OR-7, the Oregon Wolf That Made History* (Portland, OR: Inkwater Press, 2016), 17–19. For other details about collaring, see Rachael Pecore-Valdez, "It All Began with a Collar," Wild Peace Alliance, May 29, 2014, http://or7expedition.org/it-all-began-with-a-collar/.

70 **A few days later, just five:** Russ Morgan, "Oregon Wolf Conservation and Management Plan: 2011 Annual Report," Oregon Department of Fish and Wildlife, 6, https://www.dfw.state.or.us/wolves/docs/oregon_wolf_program/2011_Wolf_Conservation_Management_Plan_Annual_Report.pdf.

72 **"afraid of being beautiful":** Katherine Dykstra, "Siena," *The Common* 10, Nov. 1, 2015, https://www.thecommononline.org/siena/.

75 **For information about catching prey:** Moskowitz, *Wolves in the Land of Salmon,* 114, 220.

75 **Russ and Roblyn were monitoring:** Morgan, "Oregon Wolf Conservation," 6.

75 **When they checked the computer:** Elgin, *Journey,* 24–25.

76 **"We are what we can imagine":** Robert Hass, "Winged and Acid Dark," in *Time and Materials: Poems 1997–2005* (New York: Ecco Press, 2007) p. 11.

77 **For text of Brothers Grimm version:** Brothers Grimm, "Little Red-Cap (Little Red Riding Hood)," *Grimm's Fairy Tales* (Florida Center for Instructional Technology: Lit2Go ETC, 2019), https://etc.usf.edu/lit2go/175/grimms-fairy-tales/3083/little-red-cap-little-red-riding-hood.

77 **"male governance":** Zipes, *The Trials and Tribulations,* 57.

78 **"Wolves are trapped in folkloric":** Jessica Tiffin, *Marvelous Geometry: Narrative and Metafiction in Modern Fairy Tale* (Detroit: Wayne State University Press, 2009), 93.

79 **"It felt good, in a bad way":** Rachel Monroe, *Savage Appetites: True Stories of Women, Crime, and Obsession* (New York: Scribner, 2020), 74.

79 **"missing white woman syndrome":** "Gwen Ifill Coins the Term 'Missing White Woman Syndrome,'" C-SPAN, Aug. 5, 2004, https://www.c-span.org/video/?c4666788/user-clip-gwen-ifill-coins-term-missing-white-woman-syndrome.

82 **In her book *Complaint!*:** Sara Ahmed, *Complaint!* (Durham, NC: Duke University Press, 2021), 13.

83 **"etymology [that] suggests consequences"**: Melissa Febos, *Girlhood* (New York: Bloomsbury, 2021), 227.

84 **"The limits of my language"**: Ludwig Wittgenstein, *Tractatus Logico-Philosophicus* (New York: Cosimo, 2007).

84 **"polluted and inescapable"**: Wilkerson, *Caste*, 69.

84 **"Looking on the bright side"**: Audre Lorde, *The Cancer Journals* (New York: Penguin, 2020), 66.

85 **Years later, in graduate school**: "Little Red Riding Hood," *Father Tuck's Fairy Tales* (New York: Raphael Tuck and Sons, n.d.).

86 **"The power of the damsel"**: Ruby Hamad, *White Tears/Brown Scars: How White Feminism Betrays Women of Color* (New York: Catapult, 2020), 60–61.

86 **"White men used their ownership"**: Ibid., 51.

86 **"the alignment of childhood with innocence"**: Hong, *Minor Feelings*, 74.

86 **Australian philosopher Joanne Faulkner**: Maria Tumarkin, *Axiomatic* (Oakland, CA: Transit Books, 2019), 199.

87 **"Eventually, we'll forget the thing"**: Matthew Gavin Frank, *Preparing the Ghost: An Essay Concerning the Giant Squid and Its First Photographer* (New York: Liveright, 2015), 263.

87 **For more on Nazis and Little Red**: Alan Hall, "Nazi Fairy Tales Paint Hitler as Little Red Riding Hood's Savior," *The Telegraph*, Apr. 15, 2010.

87 **This bears out in the contemporary**: Wilkerson, *Caste*, 241.

87 **"Blackness . . . is"**: Jacqueline Rose, *On Violence and On Violence Against Women* (New York: Farrar, Straus and Giroux, 2021), p. 241.

87 **"I was never taught"**: Morgan Jerkins, *This Will Be My Undoing: Living at the Intersection of Black, Female, and Feminist in (White) America* (New York: HarperCollins, 2018), 131.

88 **"all those who travel under the sign"**: Sara Ahmed, *Living a Feminist Life* (Durham, NC: Duke University Press, 2017), 14.

88 **"Violence hovers around the deviant"**: Sara Ahmed, "Notes on Feminist Survival," FeministKilljoys.com, Mar. 27, 2018, https://feministkilljoys.com/2018/03/27/notes-on-feminist-survival/.

89 **"For a significant part of the female"**: Mithu Sanyal, *Rape: From Lucretia to #MeToo* (London: Verso Books, 2019), 34.

91 **The animal most deadly**: Emma Marris, *Wild Souls: Freedom and Flourishing in the Non-Human World* (New York: Bloomsbury, 2021), 10.

91 **The second most deadly animal**: Moskowitz, *Wolves in the Land of Salmon*, 73.

91 **"in myth, men who commit"**: D. Steiner, "'Wolf's Justice': The Iliadic Doloneia and the Semiotics of Wolves," *Classical Antiquity* 34, no. 2 (2015): 335–69, https://www.jstor.org/stable/26362659.

91 **Its murder rate is around double**: "2019 Crime in the United States,"

Federal Bureau of Investigation, https://ucr.fbi.gov/crime-in-the-u.s/2019
/crime-in-the-u.s.-2019/topic-pages/tables/table-4.

91 **the sexual assault rate:** Zachariah Hughes, "Alaska's Rate of Sexual Assault Is Four Times National Average, According to Latest FBI
Numbers," Alaska Public Media, Nov. 12, 2019, https://www.alaskapublic
.org/2019/11/12/alaskas-rate-of-sexual-assault-is-four-times-national
-average-according-to-latest-fbi-numbers/.

91 **These percentages skew higher:** Avery Lill, "Western Alaska Still Has
State's Highest Rate of Reported Felony Sex Crimes," KDLG Public Radio, Sept. 6, 2018, https://www.kdlg.org/crime/2018-09-06/western-alaska
-still-has-states-highest-rate-of-reported-felony-sex-crimes#stream/0.

91 **On paper, Alaska:** Matt Leseman, "Alaska Has Fourth Highest Rates
of Murdered and Missing Indigenous Women," Alaska's News Source,
Oct. 2, 2019, https://www.alaskasnewssource.com/content/news/Alaska
-has-fourth-highest-rates-of-murdered-and-missing-indigenous-women
-562035771.html.

91 **More than two-thirds:** "Figure 1: Estimates of Lifetime Interracial
and Intraracial Violence," National Institute of Justice, 2014, https://nij.ojp
.gov/media/image/19456.

92 **around half of the cases were declined:** "U.S. Department of Justice
Declinations of Indian Country Criminal Matters," U.S. Government
Accountability Office, Dec. 13, 2010, https://www.gao.gov/products/gao
-11-167r.

92 **In November 2018:** Urban Indian Health Institute, "Missing and
Murdered Indigenous Women and Girls," Nov. 14, 2018, https://www.uihi
.org/resources/missing-and-murdered-indigenous-women-girls/.

92 **"The removal of evidence":** Sara Ahmed, "Evidence," FeministKilljoys
.com, July 12, 2016, https://feministkilljoys.com/2016/07/12/evidence/.

92 **"orders of magnitude":** Pierotti and Fogg, *The First Domestication*
p. 156–57.

92 **For official report of Berner attack:** Lem Butler, Bruce Dale, Kimber-
lee Beckmen, and Sean Farley, "Findings Related to the March 2010 Fatal
Wolf Attack Near Chignik Lake, Alaska," Alaska Department of Fish and
Game, 2011, 5.

93 **News coverage of Berner:** Reuters, "Teacher Mauled to Death by
Wild Wolves While Jogging in Alaska, Police Say," New York *Daily News,*
Mar. 12, 2010, https://www.nydailynews.com/news/national/teacher
-mauled-death-wild-wolves-jogging-alaska-police-article-1.177004

93 **"This case represents":** Linnell et al., *Wolf Attacks on Humans,* 28.

94 **"I do not consider the suffering":** Jeffrey Moussaieff Masson, *Beasts:
What Animals Can Teach Us About the Origins of Good and Evil* (New York:
Bloomsbury, 2015), p. 30.

95 **"[F]eminism has nothing to gain"**: Jacqueline Rose, *On Violence and On Violence Against Women,* 171.

95 **"Why does the chicken cross"**: Lily Hoang, "On Chickens," *Gulf Coast Magazine* 30, no. 1 (Winter/Spring 2018).

95 **"small and mighty"**: James Halpin, "Wolves May Have Killed Village Teacher," *Anchorage Daily News,* Mar. 9, 2010, https://www.adn.com/alaska-news/article/wolves-may-have-killed-village-teacher/2010/03/09/.

95 **"doing what wolves do"**: Jacqui Goddard, "Wolf Attack Jogger: Hunt Planned by Plane and on Foot for Deadly Pack," *The Telegraph,* Mar. 10, 2010, https://www.telegraph.co.uk/news/worldnews/northamerica/usa/7436354/Wolf-attack-jogger-hunt-planned-by-plane-and-on-foot-for-deadly-pack.html.

96 **For more details of the Liz Parrish sighting:** Elgin, *Journey,* 29–30.

96 **"I was stunned"**: Jeff Barnard, "Wandering Wolf Inspires Hope and Dread," Associated Press, Nov. 28, 2011, https://komonews.com/news/local/wandering-wolf-inspires-hope-and-dread.

96 **"whether women were somehow"**: Maggie Nelson, *The Red Parts: Autobiography of a Trial* (Minneapolis: Graywolf Press, 2016), 112.

97 **"There was no adjustment"**: Rebecca Solnit, *Recollections of My Nonexistence: A Memoir* (New York: Penguin, 2020), 47.

97 **"global pandemic"**: "Gender-Based Violence (Violence Against Women and Girls)," World Bank, Sept. 25, 2019, https://www.worldbank.org/en/topic/socialsustainability/brief/violence-against-women-and-girls.

97 **"the entire female gender"**: Anne Carson, *Glass, Irony, and God* (New York: New Directions, 1995), 134.

97 **"the heroine [became] responsible"**: Maria Tatar, ed., *The Classic Fairy Tales* (New York: W. W. Norton, 1999), 3.

97 **"Oh Grandmother, I need to go"**: Paul Delarue, "The Story of Grandmother," in *Little Red Riding Hood: A Casebook,* ed. Alan Dundes (Madison: University of Wisconsin Press, 1989), 59.

98 **"All fairy tales are about survival"**: Kate Bernheimer, "Power Imagined: Fairy Tales as Survival Strategies," University of Arizona, the 2020 SBS Downtown Lecture series, https://www.youtube.com/watch?v=C28-paZlJtA.

98 **For more information on Perrault:** Zipes, *The Trials and Tribulations,* 24–31.

98 **"Inner and outer nature"**: Ibid., 78.

99 **"I felt that if I could have married"**: Alberto Manguel, "Little Red Riding Hood" (New Haven, CT: Yale University Press, Jan. 19, 2021), http://blog.yalebooks.com/2021/01/19/little-red-riding-hood/.

100 **"Every person with a body"**: Anne Boyer, *The Undying: Pain, Vulnera-*

bility, Mortality, Medicine, Art, Time, Dreams, Data, Exhaustion, Cancer, and Care (New York: Farrar, Straus and Giroux, 2019), 132.

101 **first known time on film:** "Southern Oregon Hunter Captures First Photo of Elusive OR-7 on Trail Camera," *Oregonian*, Jan. 4, 2012, https://www.oregonlive.com/pacific-northwest news/2012/01/southern_oregon_hunter_capture.html.

102 **the detail about this new wolf:** Jeff Barnard, "Group Retracing Trek of Wandering Oregon Wolf OR-7," Associated Press, Mar. 19, 2014, *Yahoo! News*, https://news.yahoo.com/group-retracing-trek-wandering-oregon-wolf-7-072442801.html?fr=sycsrp_catchall.

3. Town v. Wolf

107 **"a local patch":** Helen Macdonald, *H Is for Hawk* (New York: Grove Atlantic, 2015), 241.

107 **"as remarkable for what it pretends":** James Baldwin, "On Being 'White' . . . and Other Lies," in *Black on White: Black Writers on What It Means to Be White,* ed. David Roediger (New York: Knopf Doubleday, 2010), 177.

108 **For a more comprehensive overview of pre-Columbus "wilderness" myth:** Emma Marris, *Wild Souls: Freedom and Flourishing in the Non-Human World* (New York: Bloomsbury, 2021), 63.

108 **"almost a pre-agricultural society":** Oscar Johnson, "The Kalapuya of Clackamas County," *Smoke Signals*, Grand Ronde Tribe (Spring 1999), http://www.usgennet.org/usa/or/county/clackamas/kalapuyas.html.

108 **"[T]he 'end times' arrived":** Lilley et al., eds., *Catastrophism*, 24.

108 **Throughout the Americas, 90 percent:** Marris, *Wild Souls*, 63.

108 **Kalapuya population is estimated:** David L. Doctor, "LCC Research Guides: Kalapuya: Native Americans of the Willamette Valley, Oregon," Lane Community College, https://libraryguides.lanecc.edu/kalapuya.

109 **One estimate is that only ten percent:** Blaine Harden, *Murder at the Mission: A Frontier Killing, Its Legacy of Lies, and the Taking of the American West* (New York: Penguin, 2021), 35.

109 **"In many places":** Marris, *Wild Souls*, 63.

109 **"To not remember is perhaps":** Claudia Rankine, *Just Us* (Minneapolis: Graywolf Press, 2020), 55.

109 **"recognition as nations with full rights":** Manuel Iron Cloud, "Sungmanitu Tanka Oyate: Wolf Nation," in *War Against the Wolf: America's Campaign to Exterminate the Wolf,* ed. Rick McIntyre (Stillwater, MN: Voyageur Press, 1995), 261.

109 **To the Cherokee:** Teresa Pijoan, *White Wolf Woman: Native American Transformation Myths* (Atlanta: August House Publishers, 1992), 51–52.

110 **"In our astronomy"**: Linda Hogan, "The Fallen," *The Book of Medicine* (Minneapolis: Coffee House Press, 1993). Reprinted in McIntyre, *War Against the Wolf,* 279.

110 **For information about Linnaeus's naming**: James Serpell, *The Domestic Dog: Its Evolution, Behaviour and Interactions with People* (Cambridge: Cambridge University Press, 1995), 8.

110 **"mountain dogs"**: Brett L. Walker, *The Lost Wolves of Japan* (Seattle: University of Washington Press, 2009), 32.

111 **"O lord wolf"**: Ibid., 79.

111 **"If the definition of a dog"**: Raymond Pierotti and Brandy Raelene Fogg, "Neocolonial Thinking and Respect for Nature," *Ethnobiology Letters* 11, no. 1 (2020): 49, 54.

111 **"father of Hokkaido agriculture"**: Walker, *The Lost Wolves of Japan,* 131.

111 **For the story of wolves at Ingram's door**: Oregon Pioneer Association, "A Wolf Story," in *Transactions of the Annual Reunion of the Oregon Pioneer Association,* Volumes 34–40 (Portland, OR: Peaslee Bros. and Chausse, 1907), 613, https://www.google.com/books/edition/Transactions_of_the _Annual_Reunion_of_th/lwgXAQAAMAAJ?hl=en&gbpv=1.

112 **For Lewis and Clark's wolf encounters**: Kenneth C. Walcheck, "Of Wolves and Prairie Wolves," *We Proceeded On* 30, no. 2 (May 2004), Lewis and Clark Trail Heritage Foundation, lewisandclark.org/wpo/pdf /vol30no2.pdf#page=21.

113 **"I redoubled my cries"**: Michael Jenkinson, *Beasts Beyond the Fire* (New York: Dutton, 1980), 215.

113 **"very numerous in this country"**: Richard Cockle, "Oregon Gets Taste of Living with Wolves," *Oregonian,* June 17, 2010, http://www.oregonlive .com/news/index.ssf/2010/06/oregon_gets_taste_of_living_wi.html.

113 **"as helpless as most duchesses"**: R. B. Townshend, "A Tenderfoot in Colorado," *A Tenderfoot in Colorado* (Boulder: University Press of Colorado, 2008). Reprinted in McIntyre, *War Against the Wolf,* 76–78.

113 **splintered in the face of factionalism**: Dane Bevan, "Public Meeting at Champoeg, 1843," Oregon History Project, Oregon Historical Society, 2004, https://www.oregonhistoryproject.org/articles/historical-records /public-meeting-at-champoeg-1843/#.YkZrUy-B2Am.

113 **For agenda and results of "wolf meetings"**: T. T. Geer, "Incidents in the Organization of the Provisional Government," *Quarterly of the Oregon Historical Society* 2, no. 4 (1901): 366–80, http://www.jstor.org/stable /20609512.

113 **For mural**: Gary Halvorson, "State Capitol Mural," 2010, photograph, Oregon State Archives, https://sos.oregon.gov/archives/records/county /Pages/scenic-images-new.aspx?topic=mural.

114 **Hegel wrote that a threat:** Claudia Rankine, *Don't Let Me Be Lonely: An American Lyric* (Minneapolis: Graywolf Press, 2004), 84.

114 **"The situation was wholly unlike":** Geer, "Incidents in the Organization . . . ," 366.

115 **"Killing wolves, of course":** William G. Robbins, *Landscapes of Promise: The Oregon Story, 1800–1940* (Seattle: University of Washington Press, 1999), 77.

115 **"some last-ditch effort":** Walker, *The Last Wolves of Japan,* 70.

116 **For Esther Stutzman's story:** Esther Stutzman, "Indigenous Storytelling: Kalapuya Creation Story," recorded Aug. 30, 2001, Archaeology Channel, https://www.archaeologychannel.org/audio-guide/indigenous-storytelling-kalapuya-creation-story.

116 **Until the 1978 passage:** Lee Irwin, "Freedom, Law, and Prophecy: A Brief History of Native American Religious Resistance," *American Indian Quarterly* 21, no. 1 (1997): 35–55, https://doi.org/10.2307/1185587.

116 **"They are intrinsic":** Joy Harjo, *An American Sunrise: Poems* (New York: W. W. Norton, 2019), 29.

117 **made to cede the entire:** Confederated Tribes of Grand Ronde, "Our Story," Confederated Tribes of Grand Ronde, 2018, https://www.grandronde.org/history-culture/history/our-story/.

117 **"This country is not good now":** Johnson, "The Kalapuya of Clackamas County."

117 **"Binary oppositions, oversimplified":** Hamad, *White Tears/Brown Scars,* 42–43.

117 **One piece of seventeenth-century:** Barry Lopez, *Of Wolves and Men* (New York: Scribner, 1978), 170.

118 **"truly fearful":** Harden, *Murder at the Mission,* 35.

119 **wild men:** Isabelle Charmantier, "Linnaeus and Race," Linnean Society of London, Sept. 3, 2020, https://www.linnean.org/learning/who-was-linnaeus/linnaeus-and-race.

119 **"without shame":** Katherine Angel, *Tomorrow Sex Will Be Good Again: Women and Desire in the Age of Consent* (London: Verso Books, 2021), 13.

119 **"belief that races exist":** Nell Irvin Painter, *The History of White People* (New York: W. W. Norton, 2011), xii.

119 **Townsend, meanwhile:** Asher Elbein, "The Bird World Is Grappling with Its Own Confederate Relic: McCown's Longspur," *Audubon Magazine,* July 20, 2020, https://www.audubon.org/news/-bird-world-grappling-its-own-confederate-relic-mccowns-longspur.

120 **In researching perceptions of wolves in Albanian:** Garry Marvin, "Wolves in Sheep's and Other Clothing," *Beastly Natures: Animals, Humans,*

and the Study of History, ed. Dorothee Brantz (Charlottesville: University of Virginia Press, 2010), 70.

121 **"at least temporarily, a California":** "Oregon Wolf OR7 Enters California," *Heppner Gazette-Times,* Jan. 4, 2012, https://oregonnews.uoregon.edu/lccn/sn97071042/2012–01–04/ed-1/seq-1/#words=wolf.

121 **For CDFW updates on OR-7:** "Gray Wolf Updates," California Department of Fish and Wildlife, https://wildlife.ca.gov/Conservation/Mammals/Gray-Wolf/Updates/ArticlePage/51.

123 **For Gubbio wolf altarpiece:** *The Wolf of Gubbio,* painted by Sassetta, 1437–44, egg tempera on poplar. National Gallery, London, https://www.nationalgallery.org.uk/paintings/sassetta-the-wolf-of-gubbio.

123 **"We did not domesticate dogs":** Brian Handwerk, "How Accurate Is Alpha's Theory of Dog Domestication?," *Smithsonian,* Aug. 15, 2018, https://www.smithsonianmag.com/science-nature/how-wolves-really-became-dogs-180970014/. For more on the debate: Brian Hare and Vanessa Woods, "Opinion: We Didn't Domesticate Dogs. They Domesticated Us," *National Geographic* online, Mar. 3, 2013, https://www.nationalgeographic.com/animals/article/130302-dog-domestic-evolution-science-wolf-wolves-human; and L. David Mech and Luc A. A. Janssens, "An Assessment of Current Wolf *Canis Lupus* Domestication Hypotheses Based on Wolf Ecology and Behaviour," *Mammal Review* 52, no. 2 (2022): 304–14.

124 **"A wolf does not bark":** David Hunt, "The Face of the Wolf Is Blessed, or Is It? Diverging Perceptions of the Wolf," *Folklore* 119, no. 3 (2008): 321–22, http://www.jstor.org/stable/40646471.

124 **For wolf vs. dog brains:** Carl Safina, *Beyond Words: What Animals Think and Feel* (New York: Henry Holt, 2015), 223–25.

124 **"Man took the (free) wolf":** Donna Haraway, *The Companion Species Manifesto: Dogs, People, and Significant Otherness,* Vol. 1 (Chicago: Prickly Paradigm Press, 2003), 28.

124 **"trash pile theory":** Riley Black, "What Good Were Dogs in the Ice Age?," *Slate,* Feb. 17, 2021, https://slate.com/technology/2021/02/why-humans-domesticated-dogs-research.html.

125 **"The great majority of . . . new":** "Slavery: A National and Oregon Summary," 2019, Oregon Secretary of State, Oregon.gov, https://sos.oregon.gov/archives/exhibits/black-history/Pages/context/slavery.aspx.

126 **For more on the Lash Law:** Nina Strochlic, "Oregon Once Legally Banned Black People. Has the State Reconciled Its Racist Past?," *National Geographic,* Mar. 8, 2021, https://www.nationalgeographic.com/history/article/oregon-once-legally-barred-black-people-has-the-state-reconciled-its-racist-past.

126 **First, they rejected slavery:** William Robbins, *Oregon: This Storied Land* (Portland: Oregon Historical Society Press, 2005), 48.

126 **"In arriving at this conclusion"**: Cheryl A. Brooks, "Race, Politics, and Denial: Why Oregon Forgot to Ratify the Fourteenth Amendment," *Oregon Law Review* 83 (2004): 731.

126 **For more on the Black exclusion clause**: Ibid., 738–39.

126 **"by what it ha[s] been walled against"**: Rose, *On Violence and On Violence Against Women,* 239.

127 **"wooly headed, [and] animal jawed"**: Brooks, "Race, Politics, and Denial," 744.

127 **In 1850, the U.S. Congress**: Strochlic, "Oregon Once Legally Banned Black People."

128 **"When we try to pick out anything"**: Michelle Nijhuis, *Beloved Beasts: Fighting for Life in an Age of Extinction* (New York: W. W. Norton, 2021), 90. For more on Muir's view of Indigenous influence on landscape: Marris, *Wild Souls,* 64.

129 **"confine the Indians to smaller areas"**: Nijhuis, *Beloved Beasts,* 32.

129 **one warden patrolled its trails**: Karen Jones, "From Big Bad Wolf to Ecological Hero: *Canis Lupus* and the Culture(s) of Nature in the American–Canadian West," *American Review of Canadian Studies* 40, no. 3 (2010): 341.

129 **"The Indians losing their stock"**: Joseph Henry Taylor, "1865: Twenty Years on the Trap Line," in McIntyre, *War Against the Wolf,* 57–58.

130 **For information on colonial laws**: Ibid., 30–35.

130 **"our efforts to destroy these animals"**: Jones, "From Big Bad Wolf to Ecological Hero," 342.

131 **"animals . . . drift in from Mexico"**: Jennifer Wolch and Jody Emel, *Animal Geographies: Place, Politics, and Identity in the Nature–Culture Borderlands* (London: Verso, 1998), 101.

131 **"The fact that Canada had something"**: Ibid., 346.

132 **welfare scroungers**: Jones, "From Big Bad Wolf to Ecological Hero," 345.

132 **"black-hearted criminals"**: Ibid., 341.

132 **The police would treat the area**: David Sykes, "Ranchers, Sheriff Relate Experiences Living with Wolves in Wallowa County," *Heppner Gazette-Times,* Mar. 14, 2012, https://oregonnews.uoregon.edu/lccn/sn97071042/2012-03-14/ed-1/seq-1.pdf.

132 **"Wolves are a public concern"**: Eaton, *Collared,* 2.

132 **"a very efficient, four-legged"**: Cockle, "Oregon Gets Taste of Living with Wolves," https://www.oregonlive.com/news/2010/06/oregon_gets_taste_of_living_wi.html.

134 **"holds a cigarette paper"**: Bill Stockton, *Today I Baled Some Hay to Feed the Sheep the Coyotes Eat* (Kalispell: Montana Institute of the Arts Foundation, 1982), 41–42.

139 **"almost cultlike status"**: Malia Wollan, "Lone Wolf Commands a Following," *New York Times,* Jan. 28, 2012, https://www.nytimes.com/2012

/01/28/us/wildlife-activists-follow-lone-wolfs-trek-into-california.html
?src=tp&smid=fb-share.

139 **There was even a bumper sticker:** Winston Ross, "OR-7 Wolf: Can
the Legendary Border Crosser Save His Endangered Species?," *Newsweek*,
July 4, 2018, https://www.newsweek.com/or-7-wolves-wolf-endangered
-species-list-border-crossing-conservation-1007634.

139 **"Claiming and being identified with a love":** Michelle Orange, *Pure
Flame: A Legacy* (New York: Farrar, Straus and Giroux, 2021), 176.

141 **Cows outnumber people:** Richard Cockle, "Some Welcome Wolf Return, Others Concerned Two Permanent Packs Have Made Their Homes
in Northeast Oregon," *Ashland Daily Tidings* (OR), June 19, 2010, https://
infoweb-newsbank-com.proxy.multcolib.org/apps/news/document-view?p
=AMNEWS&docref=news/151198A8F6107828.

141 **"Wolves are about as welcome":** "Letter: Wolf Protection 'Slap in the
Face,'" *Wallowa County Chieftain* (Enterprise), Dec. 10, 2009, infoweb
.newsbank.com/apps/news/document-view?p=AMNEWS&docref=news
/14FD395777C85D70.

146 **more than 83,000 automated messages:** "Oregon Wolf Conservation
and Management 2013 Annual Report," Oregon Department of Fish and
Wildlife, 2014, https://www.dfw.state.or.us/Wolves/docs/oregon_wolf
_program/Oregon_Wolf_Annual_Report_2013.pdf.

148 **"an outlaw":** Anne Carson, *Glass, Irony, and God* (New York: New
Directions, 1995), 124.

149 **"traveller's tales":** Linda Tuhiwai Smith, *Decolonizing Methodologies:
Research and Indigenous Peoples* (London: Bloomsbury Academic, 1999), 8.

149 **"A radio-collared wolf's":** Mark Freeman, "OR-7 May Be Looking for
Love in Wrong Places," *Mail Tribune* (Medford), Jan. 15, 2012.

149 **"His mind right now is on love":** Ibid.

149 **"He's baaaaack":** Mark Freeman, "OR-7 Comes Back to Jackson
County," *Mail Tribune* (Medford), Mar. 3, 2012.

150 **"Crossing the border":** "Sister of OR-7 Died in Foothold Trap," Center for Biological Diversity, Apr. 30, 2013, https://www.biologicaldiversity
.org/news/press_releases/2013/wolf-04–30–2013.html.

150 **"He'll go until he finds a female":** Freeman, "OR-7 May Be Looking
for Love in Wrong Places."

151 **"If science suggests Nez Perces migrated":** Pinkham et al., *Lewis and
Clark Among the Nez Perce*, 2, 3, 10, 29.

151 **For details of Chief Joseph's march:** Mark Herbert Brown, *The Flight
of the Nez Perce* (New York: Putnam, 1967), 407.

152 **"Their summer range, transitional range":** Paige Blankenbuehler,
"Why Have Gray Wolves Failed to Gain a Foothold in Colorado?," *High*

Country News, Sept. 1, 2021, https://www.hcn.org/issues/53.9/south
-wolves-perilous-path-to-colorado-wolf-restoration.

152 **"That concept [of eradication] is foreign to us"**: Todd Wilkinson,
"The New West: Remembering the Role Nez Perce Played in Bringing
Back Wolves," *Buckrail-Jackson Hole News*, Apr. 23, 2019, https://buckrail
.com/the-new-west-remembering-the-role-nez-perce-played-in-bringing
-back-wolves/.

153 **"remembering is never a quiet act"**: Rankine, *Just Us*, 131.

154 **The Greek word for "not forgetting"**: Hyde, *A Primer for Forgetting*, 63.

154 **"The European newcomer"**: Joseph M. Marshall III, "The Wolf: A
Native American Symbol," in McIntyre, *War Against the Wolf*, 286.

154 **For Nez Perce land reclamation**: Associated Press, "Nez Perce Still
Tied to Wallowa County," *Indian Country Today*, Sept. 12, 2018, https://
indiancountrytoday.com/archive/nez-perce-still-tied-to-wallowa-county.

154 **"The Nimiipuu—the people"**: Bill Bradshaw, "Coming Home:
Tribe Gets More Homeland Back," *Wallowa County Chieftain*, May 5,
2021, https://www.wallowa.com/news/coming-home-tribe-gets-more
-homeland-back/article_5b91684a-ac2b-11eb-99c8-5f67d48a8c70.html.

155 **"Conservation is a Western construct"**: Jessica Hernandez, *Fresh
Banana Leaves: Healing Indigenous Landscapes Through Indigenous Science*
(Berkeley: North Atlantic Books, 2022), 72.

155 **The traumatic expulsions of humans and animals**: Carla Freccero, "A
Race of Wolves," *Yale French Studies*, no. 127 (2015): 123, http://www.jstor
.org/stable/44512264.

4. Truth v. Wolf

157 **In French the word** *loup*: Barry Lopez, *Of Wolves and Men* (New York:
Scribner, 1978), 220.

159 **"When someone says you can't attribute"**: Safina, *Beyond Words*, 29.

161 **"There is no peace for prey"**: Ibid., 172.

162 **"I spun the stories golden"**: Catherine Pierce, *The Tornado Is the World*
(Ardmore, PA: Saturnalia Books, 2016), 70.

163 **"very public and historic trek"**: Mark Freeman, "OR-7's Signal
About to Fade," *Mail Tribune* (Medford), Mar. 27, 2014, https://search
-ebscohost-com.proxy.multcolib.org/login.aspx?direct=true&db=nfh&AN
=2W61812716017&site=ehost-live.

163 **"like Voyager, he'll leave"**: Robert Galvin, "Another Life in the
Woods," *Mail Tribune* (Medford), Sept. 15, 2013, https://search
-ebscohost-com.proxy.multcolib.org/login.aspx?direct=true&db=nfh&AN
=2W61890731389&site=ehost-live.

164 **roots in Aesop's Fables:** Lopez, *Of Wolves and Men,* 253.

164 **Wolves appear in at least twenty-five:** D. L. Ashliman, "Wolves in Aesop's Fables," University of Pittsburgh, Mar. 22, 2003, https://sites.pitt .edu/~dash/aesopwolf.html.

164 **Aesop's version of the fable:** *Aesop's Fables* (New York: Race Point, 2015), 37.

164 **In later versions:** William Ellery Leonard, *Aesop and Hyssop: Being Fables Adapted and Original with the Morals Carefully Formulated* (Chicago: Open Court Publishing, 1912), 80; John Hookham Frere, William Edward Frere, and Bartle Sir Frere, *The Works of John Hookham Frere in Verse and Prose* (London: B. M. Pickering, 1872), 265.

169 **A time stamp reads:** Oregon Department of Fish and Wildlife, 2009, Baker_depredation_April_2009_odfw, https://www.flickr.com/photos /odfw/17086810757/in/album-72157623481759903/.

169 **"caught red-handed":** Robert Hendrickson, *Encyclopedia of Word and Phrase Origins* (New York: Facts on File, 1997), 135–38.

170 **first confirmed wolf kill of livestock:** Ed Merriman, "Photos Confirm Wolves Killed Keating Lambs," *Baker City Herald,* Apr. 15, 2009, infoweb .newsbank.com/apps/news/document-view?p=AMNEWS&docref=news /13551E3D628C5C40.

170 **For more on depredation investigations:** Niemeyer, *Wolfer,* 174, 177–79, 209.

171 **For more on Arendt and truth:** Rebecca Panovka, "Men in Dark Times: How Hannah Arendt's Fans Misread the Post-Truth Presidency," *Harper's Magazine,* July 14, 2021, https://harpers.org/archive/2021/08 /men-in-dark-times-hannah-arendt-post-truth/.

171 **"Evidence has to be spoken of":** Sara Ahmed, "Evidence," FeministKilljoys .com, July 12, 2016, https://feministkilljoys.com/2016/07/12/evidence/.

171 **"What if your skin is too dark":** Tressie McMillan Cottom, *Thick: And Other Essays* (New York: New Press, 2019), 6.

171 **"A lie is not a lie":** Maggie Smith, "Parachute," *Good Bones* (North Adams, MA: Tupelo Press, 2017), 54.

171 **Nineteenth-century Swedes:** Karin Dirke, "Where Is the Big Bad Wolf? Notes and Narratives on Wolves in Swedish Newspapers During the Eighteenth and Nineteenth Centuries," in *A Fairytale in Question: Historical Interactions Between Humans and Wolves,* eds. Patrick Masius and Jana Sprenger (Cambridge: White Horse Press, 2015), 114.

172 **"Every threat that issued forth":** Martin Rheinheimer, "The Belief in Werewolves and the Extermination of Real Wolves in Schleswig-Holstein," *Scandinavian Journal of History* 20, no. 4 (1995): 284.

172 **"Calling something a lie":** Cyrus Dunham, *A Year Without a Name: A Memoir* (Boston: Little, Brown, 2019), 54.

172 *inter canem et lupum*: Lopez, *Of Wolves and Men,* 209.

173 **temperatures in Arizona:** Marguerite Holloway, "As Phoenix Heats

Up, the Night Comes Alive," *New York Times*, Aug. 13, 2019, https://www
.nytimes.com/interactive/2019/climate/phoenix-heat.html.

174 **Rebecca Rose Anderson:** "Obituary: Rebecca Rose Anderson," *Red Lake Nation News*, Nov. 30, 2015, https://www.redlakenationnews.com /story/2015/11/30/obituaries/rebecca-rose-anderson/41582.html.

174 **According to the Centers for Disease:** Urban Indian Health Institute, "Missing and Murdered Indigenous Women and Girls," Nov. 14, 2018, https://www.uihi.org/resources/missing-and-murdered-indigenous -women-girls/

175 **"mean world syndrome":** George Gerbner, "Cultivation Analysis: An Overview," *Mass Communication and Society* 1, no. 3–4 (1998): 175–94.

179 **For more on Grossman:** Radley Balko, "Opinion: A Day with 'Killology' Police Trainer Dave Grossman," *Washington Post*, Feb. 14, 2017, https://www.washingtonpost.com/news/the-watch/wp/2017/02/14/a-day -with-killology-police-trainer-dave-grossman/.

179 **"Some people may be destined":** Loren W. Christensen and Dave Grossman, *On Combat: The Psychology and Physiology of Deadly Conflict in War and Peace* (Columbia, IL: PPCT Research Publications, 2007), 187.

180 **"Where is the moral":** Anne Sexton, "Red Riding Hood," *Transformations* (Boston: Houghton Mifflin, 1971), 74.

181 **"Fearfulness obscures the distinction":** Marilynne Robinson, "Fear," *New York Review of Books*, Sept. 24, 2015, https://www.nybooks.com /articles/2015/09/24/marilynne-robinson-fear/.

183 **"What is the value of proof?":** Carmen Maria Machado, *In the Dream House: A Memoir* (Minneapolis: Graywolf Press, 2019), 226.

184 **For details of attack and news coverage:** Sarah Burns, *The Central Park Five: The Untold Story Behind One of New York City's Most Infamous Crimes* (New York: Vintage Books, 2012), 26–31, 69–71.

184 **"relishing the solitude":** Trisha Meili, *I Am the Central Park Jogger: A Story of Hope and Possibility* (New York: Scribner, 2004), 32.

184 **"more than a dozen young":** Don Singleton and Don Gentle, "Wolf Pack's Prey," *Daily News* (New York), Apr. 21, 1989, https://www.nydailynews .com/services/female-jogger-death-savage-attack-roving-gang-article-1 .1304506.

185 **For details on forced confessions:** Jim Dwyer and Kevin Flynn, "New Light on Jogger's Rape Calls Evidence into Question," *New York Times*, Dec. 1, 2002, https://www.nytimes.com/2002/12/01/nyregion/new-light -on-jogger-s-rape-calls-evidence-into-question.html.

185 **"Whose boys get to be":** Claudia Rankine, *Just Us* (Minneapolis: Graywolf Press, 2020), 265.

185 **For text of the Trump ad:** Mike Hayes, "Donald Trump Insists the Exonerated Central Park Five Are Guilty in Rape Case," *BuzzFeed News*,

Oct. 7, 2015, https://www.buzzfeednews.com/article/mikehayes/donald
-trump-insists-the-exonerated-central-park-five-are-gu.

185 **"stark, staring"**: Ronald Reagan, "Remarks in New Orleans, Louisiana, at the Annual Meeting of the International Association of Chiefs of Police, Sept. 28, 1981," American Presidency Project, University of California, Santa Barbara, https://www.presidency.ucsb.edu/node/247693.

185 **"radical ideological shift"**: Rachel Monroe, *Savage Appetites: True Stories of Women, Crime, and Obsession* (New York: Scribner, 2020), 100.

186 **For more on the real attacker**: Burns, *The Central Park Five,* 205.

187 **"The Women Who Cried Wolf"**: Shenequa Golding, "The Women Who Cried Wolf in 2016," VIBE.com, Dec. 23, 2016, https://www.vibe
.com/2016/12/women-who-lied-on-black-men-in-2016/screen-shot
-2016-12-21-at-4-41-11-pm/.

187 **"Much of social programming"**: Alice Bolin, *Dead Girls: Essays on Surviving an American Obsession* (New York: HarperCollins, 2018), 191.

187 **"Black Peril"**: Ruby Hamad, *White Tears/Brown Scars: How White Feminism Betrays Women of Color* (New York: Catapult, 2020), 46–47.

187 **"The claim of innocence is a double-edged"**: Gloria Wekker, *White Innocence: Paradoxes of Colonialism and Race* (Durham, NC: Duke University Press, 2016), 17.

188 **"Lying is related to intelligence"**: Po Bronson and Ashley Merryman, *NurtureShock: New Thinking About Children* (New York: Grand Central, 2009), 82.

188 **"Glad am I, George"**: Mason Locke Weems, *The Life of Washington: A New Edition with Primary Documents and Introduction by Peter S. Onuf* (Armonk, NY: M. E. Sharpe, 1996), 10.

189 **Researchers in Portugal**: Sofia Lino, Neftalí Sillero, João Couto Torres, Xavier Santos, and Francisco Álvares, "The Role of Fire on Wolf Distribution and Breeding-Site Selection: Insights from a Generalist Carnivore Occurring in a Fire-Prone Landscape," *Landscape and Urban Planning* 183 (2019): 111–21.

189 **For information on OR-7 and the Chips Fire**: Mark Freeman, "OR-7 Still Prowling Northern California," *Mail Tribune* (Medford), Aug. 28, 2012.

190 **"I was like the wolves"**: Blake Eskin, "The Girl Who Cried Wolf: A Holocaust Fairy Tale," *Boston Magazine,* Aug. 18, 2008, https://www
.bostonmagazine.com/2008/08/18/the-girl-who-cried-wolf-a-holocaust
-fairy-tale/.

190 **"Transformed by injustice"**: Misha Defonseca, *Misha: A Mémoire of the Holocaust Years* (Boston: Mt. Ivy Press, 1997), 107.

191 **For more detail on the Defonseca case**: Eskin, "The Girl Who Cried Wolf."

192 **"aren't acting out of boredom"**: Neil Parmar, "Crying Wolf: Fabricated Crimes," *Psychology Today*, July 1, 2004, https://www.psychologytoday.com /articles/200407/crying-wolf-fabricated-crimes.

192 **"a shameless liar"**: Marbod Rennes, excerpt from *Woman Defamed and Woman Defended: An Anthology of Medieval Texts* (Oxford: Oxford University Press, 2002). Reprinted in *Lapham's Quarterly: Fear* (New York: American Agora Foundation, 2017), 73.

193 **For Rich on lying**: Adrienne Rich, *Women and Honor: Some Notes on Lying* (Pittsburgh: Motheroot, 1977), 415–18.

194 **"Yes, my name is Monique"**: Eskin, "The Girl Who Cried Wolf."

194 **"a stone I drop"**: Defonseca, *Misha*, 247.

194 **dream they were Black or Jewish**: Rankine, *Just Us*, 200.

195 **"Oregon's Wandering Wolf"**: "Oregon's Wandering Wolf Finds a Mate," *The Observer* (La Grande), May 12, 2014, https://search -ebscohost-com.proxy.multcolib.org/login.aspx?direct=true&db=nfh&AN =2W6814186645&site=ehost-live.

195 **"Love Finds a Way"**: Mark Freeman, "Love Finds a Way for OR-7," *Mail Tribune* (Medford), May 13, 2014, https://search-ebscohost-com.proxy .multcolib.org/login.aspx?direct=true&db=nfh&AN=2W62097298123 &site=ehost-live.

195 **"If that is correct"**: Lynn Terry, "OR-7 No Longer a Lone Wolf," *Oregonian*, May 13, 2014, infoweb.newsbank.com/apps/news/document-view ?p=AMNEWS&docref=news/14DCCC77330DAFD8.

195 **"I'm very surprised"**: Freeman, "Love Finds a Way."

196 **"The cute story of OR-7"**: "Letters to the Editor," *Oregonian*, Aug. 29, 2014.

5. Country v. Wolf

200 **"It is, I promise, worse"**: David Wallace-Wells, "When Will the Planet Be Too Hot for Humans? Much, Much Sooner than You Imagine," *New York Magazine*, July 9, 2017, https://nymag.com/intelligencer/2017/07/climate -change-earth-too-hot-for-humans.html.

200 **"often preceded by astonishment"**: Charles Darwin, excerpt from *The Expression of the Emotions in Man and Animals* (New York: D. Appleton and Co., 1886). Reprinted in *Lapham's Quarterly: Fear*, 49–50.

201 **"fac[ing her] fear of death"**: Eve Ensler, *Insecure at Last: Losing It in Our Security-Obsessed World* (New York: Villard, 2008), 18.

202 **For overview of Yolande**: "David Burgess Jailed for 27 Years for 1966 Murder of Yolande Waddington," *The Telegraph*, July 23, 2012, http://www .telegraph.co.uk/news/uknews/crime/9420865/David-Burgess-jailed-for -27-years-for-1966-murder-of-Yolande-Waddington.html.

202 **"having a body in the world"**: Boyer, *The Undying,* 262.

202 **"courting couples"**: Steven Morris, "National: DNA Traps Nanny's Murderer 46 Years On: Tests Pin Death of Yolande, 17, on Double Killer in Jail: Police to Check If He Has Links to Unsolved Cases," *The Guardian,* July 24, 2012, https://www.proquest.com/newspapers/national-dna-traps -nannys-murderer-46-years-on/docview/1027570182/se-2?accountid =37296.

203 **For overview of responses to "lone wolf"**: "The Times Taken to Task over Their 'Lone Wolf' Presentation of the Finsbury Park Attack," June 20, 2017, https://www.sott.net/article/354239-The-Times -taken-to-task-over-their-lone-wolf-presentation-of-the-Finsbury -Park-attack.

205 **"howled a little"**: Angela Carter, *The Bloody Chamber: And Other Stories: 75th Anniversary Edition* (New York: Penguin, 2015), 159.

205 **"just as he had been, years ago"**: Zipes, *The Trials & Tribulations,* 285.

205 **"wolves are less grave"**: "The Werewolf," in "Angela Carter Papers: 'The Bloody Chamber and Other Short Stories' 2," British Library, MS 88899/1/34 : [1975–1979].

206 **"Worry, like attention"**: Elisa Gabbert, *The Unreality of Memory: And Other Essays* (New York: Farrar, Straus and Giroux, 2020), 53.

206 **For historical details about London environment**: J. R. McNeill, *Something New Under the Sun: An Environmental History of the Twentieth-Century World* (New York: W. W. Norton, 2001), 66, 106.

207 **"canines that are uniquely social"**: Austin D. Hoffman, "Lupine Sensibilities: Dynamically Embodied Intersubjectivity Between Humans and Refugee Wolves," *Refract: An Open Access Visual Studies Journal* 2, no. 1 (2019): 141.

209 **"The forest closed upon her"**: Carter, *The Bloody Chamber,* 146.

212 **"live a life fitted"**: Hoffman, "Lupine Sensibilities," 151.

212 **"to risk falling into the related"**: Amitav Ghosh, "Brutes," *Orion Magazine,* Sept. 1, 2021, https://orionmagazine.org/article/brutes/.

215 **In some Japanese and Inuit**: Ralph Häussler, "Wolf and Mythology," 2016, https://ralphhaussler.weebly.com/wolf-mythology-italy-greek-celtic -norse.html.

216 **"have noted [that] nonhumans"**: Hoffman, "Lupine Sensibilities," 151.

216 **"Perhaps we have to dwell"**: Angel, *Tomorrow Sex Will Be Good Again,* 95.

216 **"Can a Village Ever Get Over"**: Adam Lusher, "Can a Village Ever Get Over a Trauma Like This?," *Sunday Telegraph,* Aug. 25, 2002, 16, https:// www.proquest.com/newspapers/can-village-ever-get-over-trauma-like -this-on/docview/309434219/se-2?accountid=37296.

217 **For details on Palmer's life:** "Obituary of Roger Palmer, Sportsman Who Established Two Packs of Hounds and Bred European Wolves at His Farm Near Reading," *Daily Telegraph*, Apr. 5, 2004, https://www.proquest .com/newspapers/obituary-roger-palmer-sportsman-who-established /docview/317845575/se-2?accountid=37296.

217 **"timeless rural bastion":** "About the House," Dorney Court, http: //dorneycourt.co.uk/about/the-house/.

217 **adopted a pup:** "History," The UKWCT, https://ukwct.org.uk/index .php?page=history.

218 **"He's mad that trusts":** William Shakespeare, *King Lear,* ed. Horace Howard Furness (New York: Signet Classics, 1963), 206.

219 **"You become responsible, forever":** Antoine de Saint-Exupéry, *The Little Prince* (Ware, UK: Wordsworth, 1995), 82.

221 **For more on wolf extermination in the UK:** James Edmund Harting, *A Short History of the Wolf in Britain* (Redditch, UK: Read Books Limited, 2009), 27, 90.

221 **"vagrants and vagabonds":** Yi-Fu Tuan, *Landscapes of Fear* (Minneapolis: University of Minnesota Press, 1979), 134.

222 **"Woe to this bank":** Harting, *A Short History of the Wolf in Britain,* 40–41.

222 **"people are wont always":** Ibid., 9.

222 **"a blow on the skull":** Ibid., 60–61.

223 **"warlike":** McNeill, *Something New Under the Sun,* 329.

223 **"honest about the fact":** Emma Marris, *Wild Souls: Freedom and Flourishing in the Non-Human World* (New York: Bloomsbury, 2021), 135.

223 **For a study on changing attitudes to wolves:** Christopher K. Williams, Göran Ericsson, and Thomas A. Heberlein, "A Quantitative Summary of Attitudes Toward Wolves and Their Reintroduction (1972–2000)," *Wildlife Society Bulletin* (1973–2006) 30, no. 2 (2002): 575, http://www.jstor.org /stable/3784518.

224 **in a study from 2009:** A. J. Bath, "Working with People to Achieve Wolf Conservation in Europe and North America," in *A New Era for Wolves and People, Wolf Recovery, Human Attitudes, and Policy,* ed. Marco Musiani, Luigi Boitani, and Paul C. Paquet (Calgary, BC: University of Calgary Press, 2009), 190–91.

226 **"They're terribly shy":** Channel Seven, Melbourne, "Danger: Wolves on Set—The Making of the Company of Wolves (HSV 7, 1985)," Internet Archive, https://archive.org/details/DangerWolvesOnSetTheMakingOf TheCompanyOfWolvesHSV71985.

227 **"the same two as the late Christopher":** Colin Thorne, "20 Years at the Trust," *Wolf Print,* no. 55 (Summer 2015): 16.

227 **"with a huge wolf who when tired"**: Linda Malliff, "Kenai, the Houdini of Wolves," in ibid., 17.

229 **For details of murder and Burgess**: Lusher, "Can a Village Ever Get Over a Trauma Like This?"

229 **"The man with the staring eyes"**: Burt May, "Seven Months of Terror," *Reading Evening Post*, Sept. 26, 1985.

230 **"The 'Average' Boy"**: Lee Wilson, "The 'Average' Boy Convicted of Savage," *Reading Evening Post*, July 21, 1967.

230 **"Because I felt like it"**: Linda Fort, "Yolande Waddington Trial Told of Jail 'Confessions,'" *BerkshireLive*, June 28, 2012, https://www.getreading.co .uk/news/local-news/yolande-waddington-trial-told-jail-4200090; Morris, "National: DNA Traps Nanny's Murderer 46 Years On."

232 **"slow lope, tails high"**: Cristina Eisenberg, *The Wolf's Tooth: Keystone Predators, Trophic Cascades, and Biodiversity* (Washington, DC: Island Press, 2013), 37.

232 **"Where wolves go around"**: Ibid.

232 **For contention over "keystone species"**: Emma Marris, "Rethinking Predators: Legend of the Wolf," *Nature* 507, no. 7491 (2014): 158–60.

232 **"psychological topography"**: Ed Yong, "Scared to Death: How Predators Really Kill," *New Scientist* 218, no. 2919 (2013): 36–39.

232 **more berries for grizzly**: William J. Ripple, Robert L. Beschta, Jennifer K. Fortin, and Charles T. Robbins, "Trophic Cascades from Wolves to Grizzly Bears in Yellowstone," *Journal of Animal Ecology* 83, no. 1 (2014): 223–33.

233 **"reciprocal myth making"**: Arthur Middleton, "Opinion: Is the Wolf a Real American Hero?," *New York Times*, Mar. 9, 2014, https://www.nytimes.com /2014/03/10/opinion/is-the-wolf-a-real-american-hero.html.

235 **"Fear makes for a redeemed"**: Adam Nicolson, "Chasing Wolves in the American West," *Granta*, Aug. 7, 2014, https://granta.com/chasing -wolves-in-the-american-west/.

235 **"I call this exchange"**: Barry Lopez, *Of Wolves and Men* (New York: Scribner, 1978), 62.

235 **"decide to fill our entire existence"**: Spencer Quong, "Survival as a Creative Force: An Interview with Ocean Vuong," *Paris Review*, June 5, 2019, https://www.theparisreview.org/blog/2019/06/05/survival-as-a -creative-force-an-interview-with-ocean-vuong/.

236 **both a wolf and its prey may hesitate**: L. David Mech, *The Wolf: The Ecology and Behavior of an Endangered Species* (Minneapolis: University of Minnesota Press, 1981), 245.

236 **"Eventually, to behold"**: Jenny Odell, *How to Do Nothing: Resisting the Attention Economy* (Brooklyn, NY: Melville House, 2019), 145.

236 **For Tuan on fear and curiosity**: Tuan, *Landscapes of Fear*, 10.

237 **For Berger on staring at animals in wild vs. zoos:** John Berger, *About Looking* (London: Knopf Doubleday, 2011), 4–5, 28.

237 **"most persuasively describes England":** Robert Winder, *The Last Wolf: The Hidden Springs of Englishness* (London: Little, Brown, 2018).

238 **"I wish that we would not fight":** Helen Macdonald, *H Is for Hawk* (New York: Grove Atlantic, 2015), 265.

238 **"The farmstead is a haven":** Tuan, *Landscapes of Fear,* 6.

238 **"Reading about murder":** Ibid., 131.

239 **"dissolved into the landscape":** Ibid., 144.

239 **"Behind it lay numerous":** Ibid., 141.

239 **"sense of temporal entanglement":** Claudia Rankine, *Just Us* (Minneapolis: Graywolf Press, 2020), 145.

240 **For details on aftermath of murders:** Lusher, "Can a Village Ever Get Over a Trauma Like This?"

240 **For details on BBC filming:** Tsa Palmer, "Director's Letter," *Wolf Print,* no. 56 (Autumn/Winter 2015): 7, https://ukwct.org.uk/wp/issue56.pdf.

241 **For details on earlier attack:** "Yolande Waddington Trial Told of Earlier Attack," BerkshireLive, July 3, 2012, https://www.getreading.co.uk/news/local-news/yolande-waddington-trial-told-earlier-4198733.

242 **"We . . . have been nothing more":** "Since You Asked: OR-7's Mate Likely Walked Similar Path," *Mail Tribune* (Medford), May 3, 2015, https://www.mailtribune.com/since-you-asked/2015/05/02/or-7s-mate-likely-followed-similar-path/.

242 **"bringing home the groceries":** "Oregon Wolf OR-7 Is Alive, Well and Still Bringing Home the Groceries," *Capital Press* (Salem), May 26, 2017, https://www.capitalpress.com/state/oregon/oregon-wolf-or-7-is-alive-well-and-still-bringing-home-the-groceries/article_3bf39755-2c38-5f6f-817a-b1d2899991b8.html.

243 **"The [Rogue] pack might want to keep":** Editorial, "Peaks: OR-7 Leads a Pack; Plus, a Tix Redux," *Oregonian,* Jan. 10, 2015, NewsBank: America's News—Historical and Current.

243 **"killing-spree wolf":** Mark Freeman, "Ashland Livestock Predation: Killing-Spree Wolf Shot Dead," *Mail Tribune* (Medford), Oct. 12, 2017, https://www.mailtribune.com/archive/2017/10/11/wolf-blamed-for-killing-ashland-goats-shot-dead/.

244 **"In good-enough circumstances":** Jonathan Lear, *Freud* (Oxfordshire: Taylor & Francis, 2015), 41.

245 **For details about escape:** Matthew Weaver and Caroline Davies, "Escaped Wolf Was Deliberately Set Free, Sanctuary Claims," *The Guardian,* Jan. 18, 2018, https://www.theguardian.com/world/2018/jan/18/wolf-recaptured-after-five-hours-freedom-when-fence-blew-down.

246 **"desolate, stark":** Lee, "The 'Average Boy' Convicted of Savage," 6.

246 **"As I approach retirement"**: John Herring, "Wolf Trust Will Close Its Doors to the Public at End of August," *Newbury Today*, May 9, 2018, https://www.newburytoday.co.uk/news/wolf-trust-will-close-its-doors-to-the-public-at-end-of-august-9183675/.

6. Self v. Wolf

249 **"If there was a crazy man"**: Howard Axelrod, *The Point of Vanishing: A Memoir of Two Years in Solitude* (Boston: Beacon Press, 2015), 4.

250 **"appear terrible to their enemies"**: Charles Darwin, excerpt from *The Expression of the Emotions in Man and Animals* (New York: D. Appleton and Co., 1886). Reprinted in *Lapham's Quarterly: Fear*, 49–50.

251 **"If I knew to be cautious of men"**: Tressie McMillan Cottom, *Thick: And Other Essays* (New York: The New Press, 2019).

251 **"doesn't inoculate her from illness"**: Claudia Rankine, *Just Us* (Minneapolis: Graywolf Press, 2020), 189.

252 **"How do you protect the thing"**: Shannon Gibney, "Fear of a Black Mother," in *A Good Time for the Truth: Race in Minnesota*, ed. Sun Yung Shin (St. Paul: Minnesota Historical Society Press, 2016).

252 **Police report of wolf shooting**: Marcus McDowell, Oregon State Police: Union County, Incident: SP17393843, Oct. 27, 2017.

253 **"We have to decide what counts"**: Julia Dahl, "The Trayvon Martin Case Exposes the Realities of a New Generation of Self-Defense Laws," CBS News, July 12, 2013, https://www.cbsnews.com/news/the-trayvon-martin-case-exposes-the-realities-of-a-new-generation-of-self-defense-laws/.

253 **"Too many wolves have been found"**: "Oregon Governor Confident with Wolf-Killing Investigation," Associated Press State Wire: Oregon, Jan. 3, 2018.

256 **Norse term for werewolf**: Matthew Beresford, *The White Devil: The Werewolf in European Culture* (London: Reaktion Books, 2013), 11.

258 **For more on wolf killing and eating**: L. David Mech and Luigi Boitani, eds., *Wolves: Behavior, Ecology, and Conservation* (Chicago: University of Chicago Press, 2003), 112, 145; David Moskowitz, *Wolves in the Land of Salmon* (Portland, OR: Timber Press, 2013), 116; Douglas Smith and Gary Ferguson, *Decade of the Wolf: Returning the Wild to Yellowstone* (Guilford, CT: Lyons Press, 2012), 71.

258 **"wolf does only what it must"**: Johan Olafsson Turi, edited and translated into Danish by Emilie Demant Hatt and English by Elizabeth Gee Nash, *Turi's Book of Lappland* (London: Jonathan Cape, 1931), 112.

259 **laced meat with razor blades**: Smith and Ferguson, *Decade of the Wolf*, 37.

259 **On wolves learning risk of eating**: Ibid; see also Safina, *Beyond Words*, 192.

259 **For more on ravens and wolves, see:** Rick McIntyre, *The Reign of Wolf 21: The Saga of Yellowstone's Legendary Druid Pack* (Vancouver, Canada: Greystone Books, 2020), 133–34.

259 **"He is hungry like a werewolf":** Willem de Blécourt, "'I Would Have Eaten You Too': Werewolf Legends in the Flemish, Dutch and German Area," *Folklore* 118, no. 1 (2007): 33, http://www.jstor.org/stable /30035395.

261 **"OR-7 was following the archetypal":** Brenda Peterson, *Wolf Nation: The Life, Death, and Return of Wild American Wolves* (New York: Hachette, 2017), 184.

261 **"Wolves and other critters don't exist":** Paul Neville, "Let Wandering Wolf Go off the Grid: OR-7's Trek Captivated People, but with His Radio Signal Fading, Authorities Should Not Recollar Him," *Register-Guard* (Eugene), Nov. 30, 2014.

262 **two biologists backpacked:** Lynne Terry, "Biologists Unsuccessful in Attempt to Collar Oregon's Wolf OR-7," Oregonlive, *Oregonian,* Oct. 30, 2014, https://www.oregonlive.com/pacific-northwest-news/2014/10 /biologists_unsuccessful_in_att.html.

262 **"The satellite download":** Lacey Jarrell, "OR-7's Movements Tracked to Fort Klamath: Wolf May Have Dined on Cattle Remains," *Herald and News* (Klamath Falls), Nov. 27, 2014, https://www.heraldandnews .com/email_blast/or-7-s-movements-tracked-to-fort-klamath/article _5fdc29c0-75ce-11e4-ae68-4fe372f5c8c7.html.

264 **"I see fear as an absence":** Philippe Petit, "In Search of Fear," *Lapham's Quarterly: Fear* (Summer 2017), p. 214.

267 **On the Chilcotin:** Moskowitz, *Wolves in the Land of Salmon,* 236.

268 **"Hominids likely would have":** L. David Mech, "Do Indigenous American Peoples' Stories Inform the Study of Dog Domestication?," *Ethnobiology Letters* 10, no. 1 (2019): 69–75, https://www.jstor.org/stable /26910058. **See Fogg and Pierotti rebuttal:** Raymond Pierotti and Brandy Raelene Fogg, "Neocolonial Thinking and Respect for Nature: Do Indigenous People Have Different Relationships with Wildlife than Europeans?," *Ethnobiology Letters* 11, no. 1 (2020): 48–57, https://www.jstor.org/stable /26965301. **History of canine rabies:** Andres Velasco-Villa, Matthew R. Mauldin, Mang Shi, Luis E. Escobar, et al., "The History of Rabies in the Western Hemisphere," *Antiviral Research* 146 (2017): 221–32.

268 **Blackfoot story:** Barry Lopez, *Of Wolves and Men* (New York: Scribner, 1978), 123.

268 **"the wolf people":** Russel Lawrence Barsh and Chantelle Marlor, "Driving Bison and Blackfoot Science," *Human Ecology* 31, no. 4 (2003): 581–83, 586, http://www.jstor.org/stable/4603493.

268 **"Many human victims":** Beresford, *The White Devil,* 171.

269 Symptoms of rabies: Monica Murphy and Bill Wasik, *Rabid: A Cultural History of the World's Most Diabolical Virus* (New York: Penguin, 2013), 7–8.

269 He had run away quite naked": Charles Larpenteur, *Forty Years a Fur Trader on the Upper Missouri: The Personal Narrative of Charles Larpenteur, 1833–1872* (New York: F. P. Harper, 1898), 41.

270 For more on rabies and werewolves: Beresford, *The White Devil*, 171.

270 "Sick wolves fly": Brett L. Walker, *The Lost Wolves of Japan* (Seattle: University of Washington Press, 2009), 114.

270 For details on the Beast of Gévaudan: Jay M. Smith, *Monsters of the Gévaudan: The Making of a Beast* (Cambridge, MA: Harvard University Press, 2011).

271 "Just as the seed of health": Marilyn Ferguson, excerpt from *The Aquarian Conspiracy: Personal and Social Transformation in the 1980s* (Minneapolis: University of Minnesota Press, 1987) reprinted in *Lapham's Quarterly: Fear* (Summer 2017), 85.

273 *vlkodlak*: Sabine Baring-Gould, *The Book of Were wolves*, Ebook #5324 (Urbana, IL: Project Gutenberg, July 1, 2002), https://www.gutenberg.org/ebooks/5324.

273 Serer religion: Ralph Häussler, "Wolf and Mythology," 2016, https://ralphhaussler.weebly.com/wolf-mythologie-americas.html.

277 Dillon on hypochondria: Brian Dillon, *The Hypochondriacs: Nine Tormented Lives* (New York: Farrar, Straus and Giroux, 2010), 5, 9.

279 For study of lupine shapeshifters: Sabine Baring-Gould, *The Book of Werewolves: Being an Account of a Terrible Superstition* (London: Smith, Elder, 1865), https://www.gutenberg.org/ebooks/5324.

279 Contemporary views of lycanthropy: Paul E. Keck, Harrison G. Pope, James I. Hudson, Susan L. McElroy, and Aaron R. Kulick, "Lycanthropy: Alive and Well in the Twentieth Century," *Psychological Medicine* 18, no. 1 (1988): 113–20.

280 "not considered blameworthy": Beresford, *The White Devil*, 152.

280 "others merely perceive . . . to be *wolflike*": Ibid., 10.

280 Bettelheim argued: Bruno Bettelheim, "Feral Children and Autistic Children," *American Journal of Sociology* 64, no. 5 (1959): 455–67, http://www.jstor.org/stable/2773433.

283 "You loved a shepherd": Beresford, *The White Devil*, 52

283 "go out at night": Ibid., 91.

283 not only as a terrorizer: Blécourt, "I Would Have Eaten You Too," 29.

283 Armenian legend: Baring-Gould, *The Book of Werewolves*. See also Armenian culture blog: https://www.peopleofar.com/2013/01/31/armenian-werewolves-mardagayl.

287 For *mazzeri*: Beresford, *The White Devil*, 123–24; see also Dorothy Carrington, *The Dream-Hunters of Corsica* (London: Phoenix, 1996).

288 **"Who hasn't ever wondered"**: Clarice Lispector, *The Hour of the Star,* 2nd ed. (New York: New Directions, 2011), 7.

291 **Madeline Miller's bestselling**: Madeline Miller, *Circe* (Boston: Little, Brown, 2018).

292 **Virgil on Circe**: *Virgil's Aeneid* (New York: Penguin, 1997), 183.

292 **one 1889 painting**: Wright Barker, *Circe,* oil on canvas, 1889. Bradford Museums and Galleries, West Yorkshire, UK, https://artuk.org/discover /artworks/circe-23017.

293 **"Instead of presenting"**: Christopher Lyon, "Free Fall: Kiki Smith on Her Art," in *Kiki Smith,* ed. Helaine Posner (New York: Monacelli Press, 2005), 37.

294 **The Tlingit see**: Karen Jones, "Writing the Wolf: Canine Tales and North American Environmental-Literary Tradition," *Environment and History* 17, no. 2 (May 2011): 202.

294 **"I wanted to show how people"**: Keavy Martin, *Stories in a New Skin: Approaches to Inuit Literature* (Winnipeg: University of Manitoba Press, 2012).

294 **Folklorist Teresa**: Teresa Pijoan, *White Wolf Woman: Native American Transformation Myths* (Atlanta: August House Publishers, 1992), 54–59.

295 **The werewolf story as testimony**: Blécourt, "I Would Have Eaten You Too," 35–39.

295 **"Werewolf stories allow a speaker"**: Elena Boudovskaia, "Agency and Patriarchy in Carpatho-Rusyn Werewolf Stories," *Western Folklore* 78, no. 2/3 (2019): 182, https://www.jstor.org/stable/26864150.

295 **"After the earthquake"**: "Haiti Quake Raises Fears of Child-Eating Spirits," Reuters, Jan. 27, 2010, https://www.reuters.com/article /idUSN27182777. **For more context on vodou**: Lauren Derby, "Imperial Idols: French and United States Revenants in Haitian Vodou," *History of Religions* 54, no. 4 (2015): 394–422, https://doi.org/10.1086/680175.

296 **"I think that today in the abandoned"**: Peggy McInerney, "Shape-Shifting and Storytelling in Hispaniola," UCLA International Institute, May 6, 2019, https://www.international.ucla.edu/lai/article/202890.

296 **Estés quotes**: Clarissa Pinkola Estés, *Women Who Run with the Wolves* (New York: Ballantine, 1995), 1, 2, 13, 17, 23, 24, 262.

299 **"If it leads to change then it can be useful"**: Audre Lorde, *Sister Outsider: Essays and Speeches* (New York: Penguin, 2020), 121.

299 **"Violence for me is part of the psyche"**: Jacqueline Rose, *On Violence and On Violence Against Women* (New York: Farrar, Straus and Giroux, 2021), 175.

300 **"Fear of the beast"**: Lopez, *Of Wolves and Men,* 140.

300 **"To have compassion"**: Ibid., 213.

300 **"h[u]ng on a gallows"**: Horace Howard Furness, *Book News: A Monthly Survey of General Literature,* "VII: September 1888–August 1889" (Philadelphia: J. Wanamaker, 1889), 19.

300 **hung wearing clothes:** Martin Rheinheimer, "The Belief in Were-wolves and the Extermination of Real Wolves in Schleswig-Holstein," *Scandinavian Journal of History* 20, no. 4 (1995): 20.

301 **"the binarized identity":** Heather Tapley, "Edgy Un/Intelligibilities: Feminist/Monster Theory Meets Ginger Snaps," *Atlantis: Critical Studies in Gender, Culture and Social Justice* 37, no. 2 (2016): 129.

301 **For a critical look at the "two wolves" quote:** âpihtawikosisân, "Check the Tag on That 'Indian' Story," Feb. 21, 2012, https://apihtawikosisan.com /2012/02/check-the-tag-on-that-indian-story/.

302 **"living in the physical sense":** Annie Dillard, *Teaching a Stone to Talk: Expeditions and Encounters* (New York: HarperCollins, 2009), 68.

302 **"what we do to others, and so fear":** Ligaya Mishan, "In a Starving World, Is Eating Well Unethical?," *T: The New York Times Style Magazine*, Mar. 18, 2022, https://www.nytimes.com/2022/03/18/t-magazine /indulgence-starvation-food-inequality.html.

7. Mother v. Wolf

305 **"the world's most famous wolf":** Winston Ross, "OR-7 Wolf: Can the Legendary Border Crosser Save His Endangered Species?," *Newsweek*, July 4, 2018.

305 **"We were hacked":** Gerry O'Brien, "Wolf Debate Grows Hairy: Contentious Issue Draws Technological Low Blows," *Herald and News* (Klamath Falls), Feb. 7, 2015.

307 **One study of dispersers in Alaska:** L. David Mech and Luigi Boitani, eds., *Wolves: Behavior, Ecology, and Conservation* (Chicago: University of Chicago Press, 2003), 2.

308 **For chart on pack structure:** Ibid., 40.

308 **oil spill:** "CEI Hub Seismic Risk Analysis," Multnomah County, June 24, 2021, https://www.multco.us/sustainability/cei-hub-seismic-risk-analysis.

309 **"one of the highest threats to public safety":** Sophie Peel, "Portland Officials Fear the Largest Urban Forest in America Is a Wildfire Waiting to Happen," *Willamette Week*, July 28, 2021, https://www.wweek.com /news/city/2021/07/28/portland-officials-fear-the-largest-urban-forest-in -america-is-a-wildfire-waiting-to-happen/.

310 **"hyperobject":** Timothy Morton, *Hyperobjects: Philosophy and Ecology After the End of the World* (Minneapolis: University of Minnesota Press, 2013).

310 **For details and quotes about lawsuit mentioning OR-7:** Jeff Barnard, Associated Press, "Lawsuit Seeks to Protect Wolf OR-7, Pups from Timber Sale That May Be Too Close to Den," *Oregonian*, June 19, 2014, https://www.oregonlive.com/pacific-northwest-news/2014/06/lawsuit _challenges_timber_sale.html.

311 **"Our remnants of wilderness"**: Aldo Leopold, "A Plea for Wilderness Hunting Grounds," *Outdoor Life*, Nov. 1925, reproduced in *Aldo Leopold's Southwest*, eds. David E. Brown and Neil B. Carmony (Albuquerque: University of New Mexico Press, 1990), 160–61.

312 **"They have these huge feet"**: Lynne Terry, "More OR-7 Pups Get Their Picture Taken," *Oregonian*, July 25, 2014.

313 **"simply does not exist"**: Lopez, *Of Wolves and Men*, 249.

313 **"beneficial animals"**: Brett L. Walker, *The Lost Wolves of Japan* (Seattle: University of Washington Press, 2009), 127.

314 **"We learned from the wolf"**: Peterson, *Wolf Nation*, 14.

314 **"a whole reindeer between"**: Henrich Rink, *Tales and Traditions of the Eskimo: With a Sketch of Their Habits, Religion, Language and Other Peculiarities* (Edinburgh and London: W. Blackwood and Sons, 1875), 464–65.

317 **"In the forest . . . you don't prepare"**: Nastassja Martin, *In the Eye of the Wild* (New York: New York Review Books, 2021).

318 mysterious bodily lumps: Lopez, *Of Wolves and Men*, 216.

320 **"stand in for a nostalgia"**: Carla Freccero, "A Race of Wolves," *Yale French Studies*, no. 127 (2015): 112.

320 **"We have never been individuals"**: Scott Gilbert, "Holobiont by Birth," in *Arts of Living on a Damaged Planet: Ghosts and Monsters of the Anthropocene*, eds. Anna Tsing, Heather Swanson, Elaine Gan, and Nils Bubandt (Minneapolis: University of Minnesota Press, 2017).

321 **"How can we listen across species"**: Alexis Pauline Gumbs, *Undrowned: Black Feminist Lessons from Marine Mammals* (Oakland, CA: AK Press, 2020), 15.

321 unusual wolf pack: Mech and Boitani, *Wolves*, 1.

321 **"intense harvest"**: Linda Y. Rutledge, Brent R. Patterson, Kenneth J. Mills, Karen M. Loveless, Dennis L. Murray, and Bradley N. White, "Protection from Harvesting Restores the Natural Social Structure of Eastern Wolf Packs," *Biological Conservation* 143, no. 2 (2010): 332–39.

322 For Haraway on history of "relatives": Donna J. Haraway, *Staying with the Trouble: Making Kin in the Chthulucene* (Durham, NC: Duke University Press, 2016), 103.

322 **"By kin I mean those"**: Steve Paulson, "Making Kin: An Interview with Donna Haraway," *Los Angeles Review of Books*, Dec. 6, 2019, https://lareviewofbooks.org/article/making-kin-an-interview-with-donna-haraway/.

324 For information on White River Pack: "Specific Wolves and Wolf Packs in Oregon—White River Pack," Oregon Department of Fish and Wildlife, 2020, https://www.dfw.state.or.us/Wolves/Packs/White_River.asp.

324 For study on vertebrate biodiversity: Richard Schuster, Ryan R. Germain, Joseph R. Bennett, Nicholas J. Reo, and Peter Arcese, "Vertebrate

Biodiversity on Indigenous-Managed Lands in Australia, Brazil, and Canada Equals That in Protected Areas," *Environmental Science and Policy* 101 (2019): 1–6.

324 **For biodiversity on Indigenous lands:** Sherri Mitchell, "Indigenous Prophecy and Mother Earth," in *All We Can Save: Truth, Courage, and Solutions for the Climate Crisis,* eds. Ayana Elizabeth Johnson and Katherine K. Wilkinson (New York: Random House, 2020), 19.

324 **"I think I bring a unique approach":** Pat Dooris, "Chuck Sams, Oregonian and First Native American to Lead the National Park Service, Highlights Project at Fort Vancouver," Kgw.com, Mar. 17, 2022, https://www.kgw.com/article/news/local/the-story/national-parks-director-chuck-sams-fort-vancouver/283-9c503184-97ae-448c-bd8a-3e0c3390aaf5.

327 **For National Geographic episode:** Ronan Donovan, "The Last Hunt," *Kingdom of the White Wolf,* National Geographic Channel, Aug. 25, 2019.

327 **"one whose personality shapes":** Safina, *Beyond Words,* 157.

328 **"Death is a wolf's living":** Ibid., 186.

329 **"It is crucially instructive":** Ibid., 155.

330 **"A wolf's fat":** "The Natural History of Pliny," Pliny the Elder, *A Natural History* (London: G. Bell and Sons, 1856), 361.

331 **"I stopped my tractor":** Ross, "OR-7 Wolf: Can the Legendary Border Crosser Save His Endangered Species?"

332 **"He looks pretty lean":** Mark Freeman, "Wildlife Wolf Pack Grows as OR-7 Slows Down," *Ashland Daily Tidings,* Aug. 2, 2016.

332 **eulogy to OR-7's father:** Melissa Gaskill, "The Life and Legacy of OR4, Oregon's Most Celebrated Wild Wolf," *Men's Journal,* Apr. 13, 2016, https://www.mensjournal.com/adventure/life-and-legacy-of-or4-oregons-most-celebrated-wild-wolf-w202529/.

333 **"I don't have any remorse":** Emma Marris, "OR4 (Wolf)," Oregon Historical Society, Apr. 24, 2019, https://www.oregonencyclopedia.org/articles/or4-wolf/#.YkjY6S-B2Al.

333 **There's a Serbian story:** Aleksandar Loma, "Problems of Chronological and Social Stratification in the Historical Anthroponomastics: The Case of 'Lupine' and 'Equine' Proper Names Among the Indo-European Peoples," Personal Names and Cultural Reconstruction Conference, University of Helsinki, Aug. 21–23, 2019, https://www2.helsinki.fi/sites/default/files/atoms/files/wolf_and_horse_handout.pdf.

333 **"I think mothers and daughters":** Alice Walker, *The Same River Twice* (New York: Washington Square Press, 1997), 172.

333 **"In many Indigenous ways of knowing":** Robin Wall Kimmerer, *Braiding Sweetgrass: Indigenous Wisdom, Scientific Knowledge and the Teachings of Plants* (Minneapolis: Milkweed Editions, 2013), 343.

NOTES   415

335 **"We forget that fear":** Tuan, *Landscapes of Fear,* 31.

335 **For story of mother wolf and coyotes:** Safina, *Beyond Words,* 162–64.

337 **"Satan-faced":** Robert Browning, "Ivan Ivanovitch," in *The Poetic and Dramatic Works of Robert Browning . . .* (Boston: Houghton, Mifflin, 1887), 136–41.

342 **"unusual" and "disturbing":** Lee Juillerat, "Biologists Ramp Up Efforts to Avert Kills," *Mail Tribune* (Medford), Oct. 23, 2016.

342 **When they finally trapped:** "Wildlife Managers Track Daughter of Famed OR-7," *Bulletin* (Bend), Oct. 16, 2017, https://infoweb-newsbank -com.proxy.multcolib.org/apps/news/document-view?p=AMNEWS &docref=news/16792C47FB56B450.

342 **"You feel helpless":** Lee Juillerat, "Managing Wolves 'Death by a Thousand Bites'—Confirmed Wolf Kills Make Ranchers Feel Helpless," *Mail Tribune* (Medford), Oct. 23, 2016.

342 **the body of a wolf would turn:** Zach Urness, "Third 'Endangered' Wolf Killed in Southern Oregon, $40,000 in Rewards Offered for Information," *Statesman Journal,* Nov. 6, 2017, https://www.statesmanjournal.com/story /news/2017/11/06/oregon-wolf-killed-california-klamath-falls-reward-or -25/837697001/.

343 **depredations in Oregon had increased:** Michelle Dennehy, "Oregon Has at Least 173 Wolves, a 9.5 Percent Increase over Last Year," Oregon Department of Fish and Wildlife, Apr. 21, 2021, https://www.dfw.state.or .us/news/2021/04_Apr/042121.asp.

343 **"As wolves grow old":** Steven Dubois, "Oregon Kills Four Wolves That Attacked Livestock," Associated Press, Mar. 31, 2016, https://www.columbian .com/news/2016/mar/31/oregon-kills-4-wolves-that-killed-livestock.

343 **Birdseye's fence:** Jes Burns, "Southern Oregon Rancher Builds Fences and Bridges to Keep the Wolves at Bay," Oregon Public Broadcasting, Nov. 19, 2019, https://www.opb.org/news/article/wolf-wolves-fencing-rancher -cooperation-southern-oregon.

345 **"In a rancher's world":** Gretel Ehrlich, *The Solace of Open Spaces* (New York: Penguin, 1986), 50–51.

345 **"I WANNA DELIVER":** Ai Hasegawa, "I Wanna Deliver a Dolphin . . . ," n.d., https://aihasegawa.info/i-wanna-deliver-a-dolphin.

350 **"a deep, existential fear":** Martin Rheinheimer, "The Belief in Werewolves and the Extermination of Real Wolves in Schleswig-Holstein," *Scandinavian Journal of History* 20, no. 4 (1995): 47.

350 **In the aftermath of the Thirty Years' War:** Alexander Kling, "War-Time, Wolf-Time. Material-Semiotic Knots in the Chronicles of the Thirty Years' War," in *A Fairytale in Question: Historical Interactions Between Humans and Wolves,* eds. Patrick Masius and Jana Sprenger (Cambridge: White Horse Press, 2015), 25, 28.

350 **For details on wolves and smallpox:** Denise Casey and Tim W. Clark, *Tales of the Wolf: Fifty-One Stories of Wolf Encounters in the Wild* (Moose, WY: Homestead Press, 1992), 52, 63.

351 **"Wolves live in packs, in collectivities":** Freccero, "A Race of Wolves," 122.

353 **For the life of OR-93:** Susan Orlean, "The Wolf That Roamed to Southern California," *New Yorker,* Dec. 14, 2021, https://www.newyorker.com/news/afterword/the-wolf-that-roamed-to-southern-california.

353 **North-South-East-West:** Safina, *Beyond Words,* 55.

354 **wolves burying their own dead:** Jones, "Writing the Wolf," 208.

355 **"When the grassland is hit":** Jiang Rong, *Wolf Totem: A Novel* (New York: Penguin, 2008), 254.

356 **"That scarcity is the lie":** Zenobia Jeffries Warfield, "The World Is a Miraculous Mess, and It's Going to Be All Right," *YES! Magazine,* Mar. 27, 2018, https://www.yesmagazine.org/social-justice/2018/03/27/the-world-is-a-miraculous-mess-and-its-going-to-be-alright.

356 **Azerbaijani cases:** Beresford, *The White Devil,* 214–15.

357 **Wolves in Rome:** Mika Rissanen, "Was There a Taboo on Killing Wolves in Rome?," *Quaderni Urbinati di Cultura Classica, Nuova serie* 107, no. 2 (2014): 139, 144, http://www.jstor.org/stable/24645268.

357 **"In many of these accounts":** Peterson, *Wolf Nation,* 152.

358 **1996 wolf attack in India:** John F. Burns, "In India, Attacks by Wolves Spark Old Fears and Hatreds," *New York Times,* Sept. 1, 1996, https://www.nytimes.com/1996/09/01/world/in-india-attacks-by-wolves-spark-old-fears-and-hatreds.html.

358 **For more on "child-lifting":** Kishan Singh Rajpurohit, "Child Lifting: Wolves in Hazaribagh, India," *Ambio* 28, no. 2 (1999): 165, http://www.jstor.org/stable/4314869.

359 **For research on land and animals in colonial India:** Steven Rodriguez, "British Programmes for the Extermination of the Indian Wolf, c. 1870–1915," in Masius and Sprenger, *A Fairytale in Question,* 165–72.

360 **"Nature cannot be described":** Adam Pérou Hermans, "If You Wander in Winter, They Will Eat You: Local Knowledge, Wolves, and Justice in Central Asia," in ibid., 259–79.

361 **missionary rhetoric:** Sister Nivedita, *Lambs Among Wolves: Missionaries in India* (Calcutta: Udbodhan Office, 1928).

363 **locals' attitudes toward large carnivores:** Kulbhushansingh R. Suryawanshi et al., "Multiscale Factors Affecting Human Attitudes Toward Snow Leopards and Wolves," *Conservation Biology* 28, no. 6 (2014): 1665.

363 **"In the forest there is also danger":** Monica V. Ogra, "Human–Wildlife Conflict and Gender in Protected Area Borderlands: A Case Study of

Costs, Perceptions, and Vulnerabilities from Uttarakhand (Uttaranchal), India," *Geoforum* 39, no. 3 (2008): 1408–22.

363 **"The solution is to eliminate poverty"**: Rodriguez, "British Programmes for the Extermination of the Indian Wolf," 172.

364 **"people in the area are on the hunt"**: Babs Santos, "Wolves Escape Wildlife Center in Anoka County," FOX 9, May 31, 2021, https://www.fox9.com/news/wolves-escape-wildlife-center-in-anoka-county.

365 **"Never kill the young one"**: Ben Corbin, "1900: Corbin's Advice or the Wolf Hunter's Guide," in *War Against the Wolf*, ed. Rick McIntyre (London: Voyageur Press, 1995), 124–26.

365 **When her ailing howls**: Peterson, *Wolf Nation*, 6.

370 **"Predators always scare way more prey"**: Ed Yong, "An Unorthodox Strategy to Stop Cars from Hitting Deer," *The Atlantic*, May 24, 2021, https://www.theatlantic.com/science/archive/2021/05/wolves-reduce-deer-vehicle-collisions/618978/.

370 **"Wolves wouldn't be a magic cure everywhere"**: Jim Robbins, "Using Wolves as First Responders Against a Deadly Brain Disease," *New York Times*, Nov. 12, 2020, https://www.nytimes.com/2020/11/12/science/wolves-chronic-wasting-disease.html.

371 **"Attention forms the ground"**: Jenny Odell, *How to Do Nothing: Resisting the Attention Economy* (Brooklyn: Melville House, 2019), 154.